CAPTAIN AMERICA

SHARON CARTER

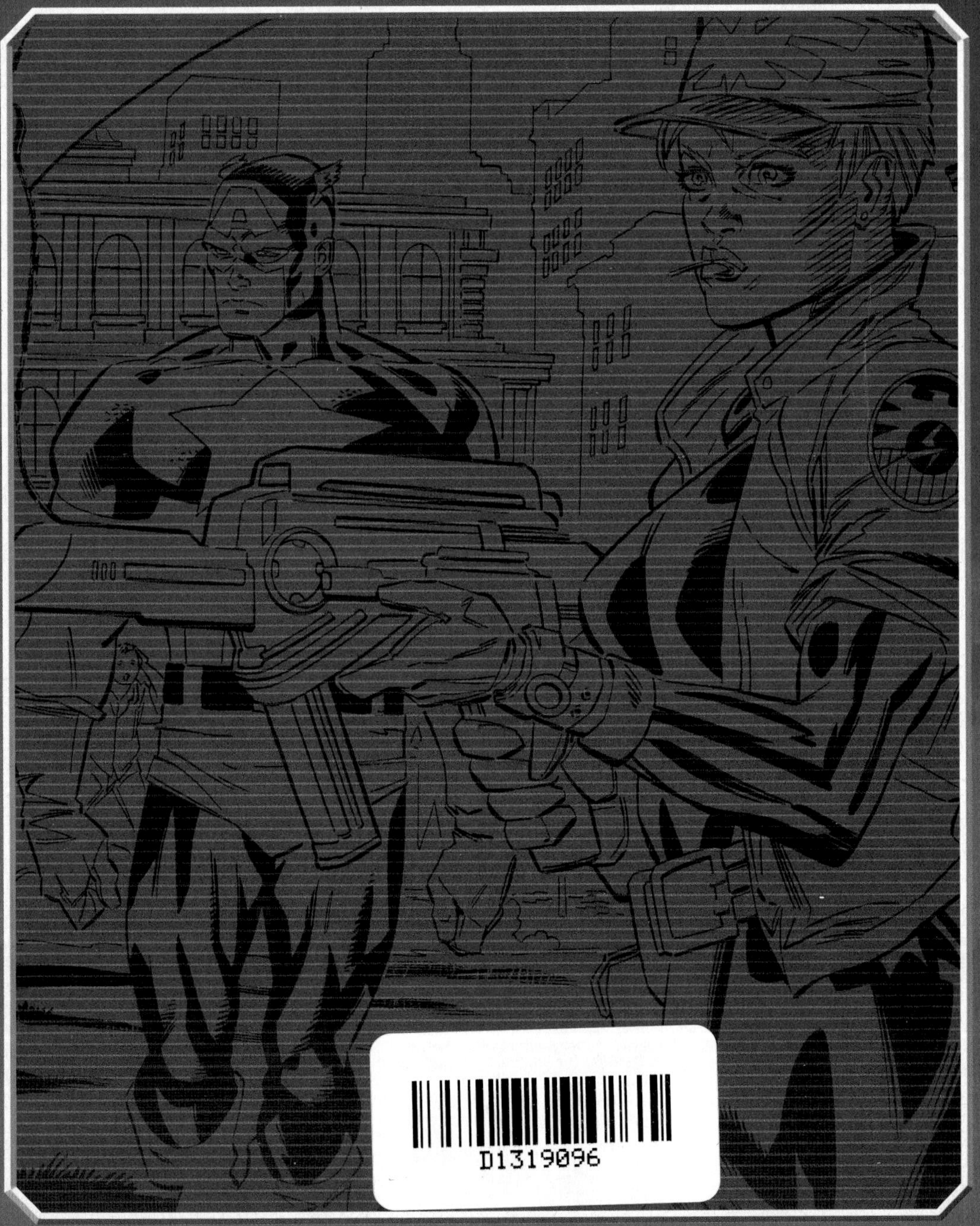

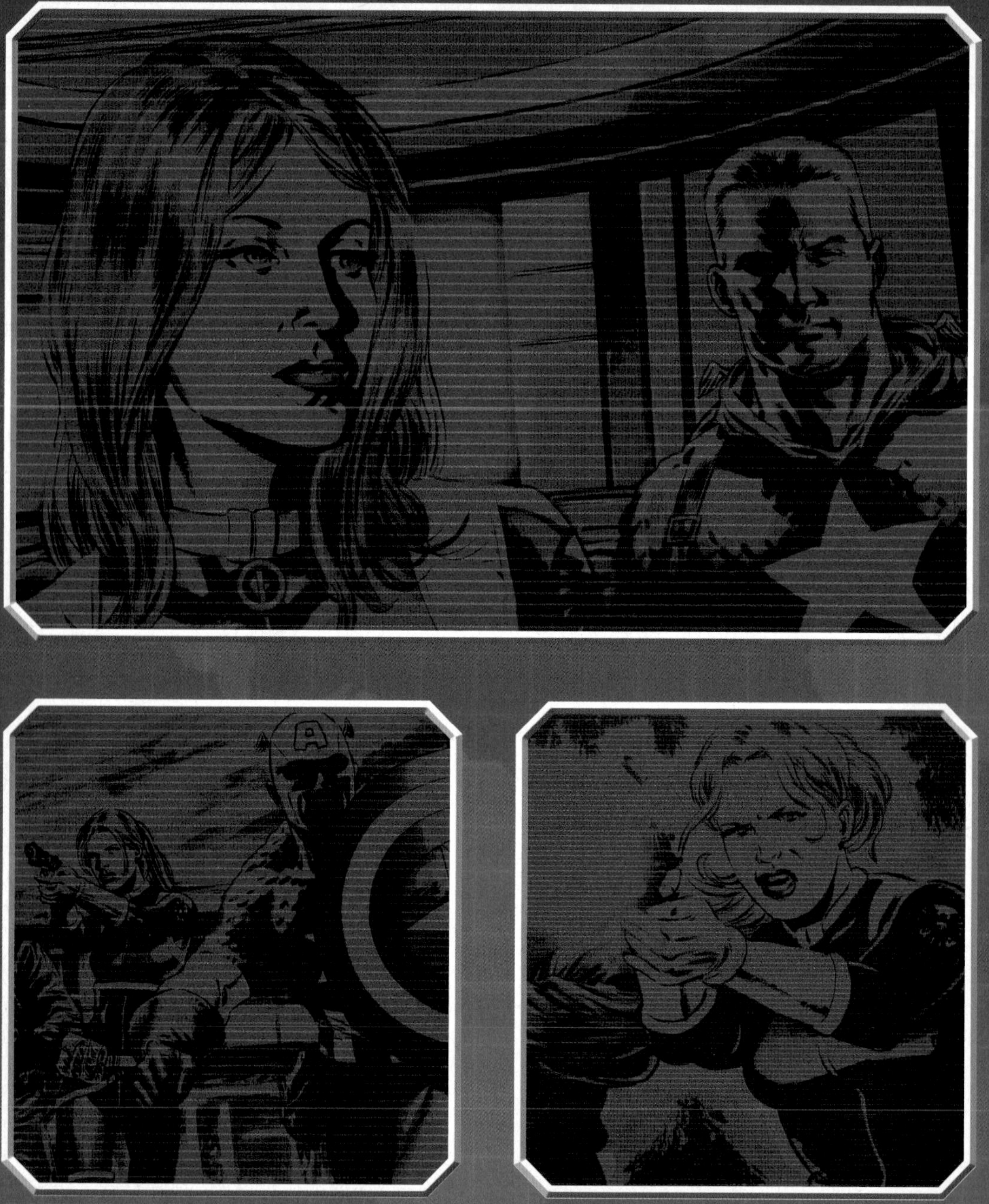

CAPTAIN AMERICA: SHARON CARTER. Contains material originally published in magazine form as CAPTAIN AMERICA: SENTINEL OF LIBERTY (1998) #1, CAPTAIN AMERICA (2004) #16-17, CAPTAIN AMERICA AND THE SECRET AVENGERS (2011) #1, TALES OF SUSPENSE (1959) #75-76 and #85, and AGE OF HEROES (2010) #3. First printing 2020. ISBN 978-1-302-92732-5. Published by MARVEL WORLDWIDE, INC., a subsidiary of MARVEL ENTERTAINMENT, LLC. OFFICE OF PUBLICATION: 1290 Avenue of the Americas, New York, NY 10104. **Printed in the U.S.A.** KEVIN FEIGE, Chief Creative Officer; DAN BUCKLEY, President, Marvel Entertainment; JOHN NEE, Publisher; JOE QUESADA, EVP & Creative Director; TOM BREVOORT, SVP of Publishing; DAVID BOGART, Associate Publisher & SVP of Talent Affairs; Publishing & Partnership; DAVID GABRIEL, VP of Print & Digital Publishing; JEFF YOUNGQUIST, VP of Production & Special Projects; DAN CARR, Executive Director of Publishing Technology; ALEX MORALES, Director of Publishing Operations; DAN EDINGTON, Managing Editor; RICKEY PURDIN, Director of Talent Relations; SUSAN CRESPI, Production Manager; STAN LEE, Chairman Emeritus. For information regarding advertising in Marvel Comics or on Marvel.com, please contact Vit DeBellis, Custom Solutions & Integrated Advertising Manager, at vdebellis@marvel.com. For Marvel subscription inquiries, please call 888-511-5480. **Manufactured between 10/2/2020 and 11/3/2020 by FRY COMMUNICATIONS, MECHANICSBURG, PA, USA.**

10 9 8 7 6 5 4 3 2 1

CAPTAIN AMERICA

SHARON CARTER

TALES OF SUSPENSE #75

WRITER & EDITOR: **STAN LEE**
PENCILERS: **JACK KIRBY & DICK AYERS**
INKER: **JOHN TARTAGLIONE**
LETTERER: **ARTIE SIMEK**
COVER ART: **GENE COLAN**

TALES OF SUSPENSE #76

WRITER & EDITOR: **STAN LEE**
ARTIST: **JOHN ROMITA SR.**
LETTERER: **ARTIE SIMEK**
COVER ART: **JACK KIRBY**

TALES OF SUSPENSE #85

WRITER & EDITOR: **STAN LEE**
PENCILER: **JACK KIRBY**
INKER: **FRANK GIACOIA**
LETTERER: **SAM ROSEN**
COVER ART: **GENE COLAN**

CAPTAIN AMERICA: SENTINEL OF LIBERTY #1

CO-PLOTTER & SCRIPTER: **MARK WAID**
CO-PLOTTER & PENCILER: **RON GARNEY**
INKER: **DAN PANOSIAN**
COLORIST: **JOE ROSAS**
LETTERER: **JOHN COSTANZA**
COVER ART: **RON GARNEY, KLAUS JANSON & CHRIS SOTOMAYOR**
ASSISTANT EDITOR: **PAUL TUTRONE**
EDITOR: **MATT IDELSON**

CAPTAIN AMERICA #16-17

WRITER: **ED BRUBAKER**
ARTIST: **MIKE PERKINS**
COLORIST: **FRANK D'ARMATA**
LETTERER: **VC's JOE CARAMAGNA**
COVER ART: **STEVE EPTING & FRANK D'ARMATA**
ASSISTANT EDITORS: **MOLLY LAZER & AUBREY SITTERSON**
ASSOCIATE EDITOR: **ANDY SCHMIDT**
EDITOR: **TOM BREVOORT**

AGE OF HEROES #3

WRITER: **KELLY SUE DeCONNICK**
PENCILER: **BRAD WALKER**
INKER: **WALDEN WONG**
COLORIST: **JAY DAVID RAMOS**
LETTERER: **DAVE LANPHEAR**
COVER ART: **YANICK PAQUETTE, MICHEL LACOMBE & NATHAN FAIRBAIRN**
EDITOR: **LAUREN SANKOVITCH**
EXECUTIVE EDITOR: **TOM BREVOORT**

CAPTAIN AMERICA AND THE SECRET AVENGERS #1

WRITER: **KELLY SUE DeCONNICK**
ARTIST: **GREG TOCCHINI**
COLORIST: **PAUL MOUNTS**
LETTERER: **DAVE LANPHEAR**
COVER ART: **GREG TOCCHINI**
EDITOR: **LAUREN SANKOVITCH**
EXECUTIVE EDITOR: **TOM BREVOORT**

FRONT COVER ARTISTS: **STEVE EPTING & FRANK D'ARMATA**
BACK COVER ARTISTS: **MIKE PERKINS & FRANK D'ARMATA**

CAPTAIN AMERICA CREATED BY **JOE SIMON** & **JACK KIRBY**

COLLECTION EDITOR: **JENNIFER GRÜNWALD**
ASSISTANT MANAGING EDITOR: **MAIA LOY**
ASSISTANT MANAGING EDITOR: **LISA MONTALBANO**
ASSOCIATE MANAGER, DIGITAL ASSETS: **JOE HOCHSTEIN**
MASTERWORKS EDITOR: **CORY SEDLMEIER**
EDITOR, SPECIAL PROJECTS: **MARK D. BEAZLEY**

VP PRODUCTION & SPECIAL PROJECTS: **JEFF YOUNGQUIST**
RESEARCH & LAYOUT: **JEPH YORK**
PRODUCTION: **MICHAEL KELLEHER & KELLUSTRATION AND RYAN DEVALL**
BOOK DESIGNER: **STACIE ZUCKER**
SVP PRINT, SALES & MARKETING: **DAVID GABRIEL**
EDITOR IN CHIEF: **C.B. CEBULSKI**

INTRODUCTION BY RALPH MACCHIO

The spy who loved me—sometimes. What a woman! That little paraphrase of the James Bond novel title is, of course, referring to the fabulous femme who shares the pulsating pages of this titanic trade paperback with our red-white-and-blue Avenger—Captain America! This fine volume is a rollicking romp through various stages of the relationship between the two stalwarts. When we first encounter her in *Tales of Suspense #75* from the halcyon days of 1966, Sharon Carter is a loyal agent of S.H.I.E.L.D., the world's premier spy agency. And we only learn that in the last few panels of the story, which continues in the following issue. Steve Rogers first notices her on the street and senses some strange connection to her. He doesn't even learn her real name in the segments from *Tales of Suspense #75, 76* and *85*. Fascinating.

When Stan Lee decided to bring back the Living Legend of World War II in *Avengers #4*, the revived hero became quite a hit, and so it was decided to give him his own ten-page feature, starting in *Tales of Suspense #59* in 1964, sharing the billing with the Golden Avenger, Iron Man. Because he'd only recently been thawed out from the iceberg that kept him in suspended animation for decades, this Steve Rogers was a haunted individual, very much a man out of his time. The dead past hangs heavily on Rogers' muscular shoulders during his melancholy musings in these *Tales of Suspense* issues. And so the out-of-nowhere appearance of this blond-haired beauty awakens something in Steve's heart, some strange sense of the past being reborn. In *Tales of Suspense #85*, the evildoers at Hydra have kidnapped this mysterious woman to lure Cap into saving her. Even some nine issues after he first encountered her, Cap still doesn't learn her name or suspect what a prominent role she'll someday play in his life. In addition to all the fantastic fight scenes with the then-new villain Batroc the Leaper and the danger of Inferno 42, it's Cap's almost mystical attachment to Agent 13 that draws us deeply into the events of all three *Tales of Suspense* stories. Lee was just whetting fans'

appetite here. There was much more to come between these two star-crossed characters.

In *Captain America #233*, Sharon Carter supposedly met her end. Mischievous Mark Waid explained away that death and returned her in issue #444. Writer Waid always had a liking for Sharon because he saw her and Steve as such opposites that they played beautifully off each other, as opposites often do. You'll see that strong dichotomy on full display in *Captain America: Sentinel of Liberty*'s first issue from 1998, which is an exceptional tale as written by Mark Waid and penciled by Ron Garney. Over the years, Agent Carter has become increasingly hardened as a woman. Her great-aunt Peggy's wartime exploits inspired her to become part of S.H.I.E.L.D. During her time as Agent 13, she faked her death at the hands of the white supremacist group National Force so she could go on a secret mission for S.H.I.E.L.D. She spent several years on the mission as a mercenary under rugged conditions until she encountered the Kubekult, whose goal was to return Hitler to life. Cap becomes involved and is shocked to find Sharon alive. With her mission completed, Carter returns to S.H.I.E.L.D., though she doesn't renew her romance with Rogers. In *Sentinel of Liberty*, Cap is dealing with a terrorist organization called Millennium Dawn. Sharon shows up, causing Rogers to reminisce about another mission they had been on together years earlier, also in Philadelphia. The professional differences between them came to the fore in that mission, especially Cap's complete unwillingness to kill in cold blood. Sharon is a trained secret agent and will kill an enemy should circumstances dictate it. But she has great respect for this special man who always does the job clean—no killing. When Sharon sees that this mission would ask Cap to compromise and choose between duty and conscience, she decides to spare him that burden. Waid so effectively adds layers of complexity to the volatile relationship between these two without a hint of romantic entanglement intruding. I guarantee you'll be quite moved by the pitch-perfect narrative.

In the mid-2000s, Ed Brubaker was on quite a roll chronicling Cap's adventures. In *Captain America #16–17*, he was ably assisted by the stunning visuals of Mike Perkins. I had the privilege of working with Perkins on our superb adaptation of Stephen King's *The Stand*, which garnered much praise for its top-notch penciling. Perkins drew a truly powerful version of ol' Winghead, right up there with the aforementioned Ron Garney. On the writing front, Brubaker explores the Rogers/Carter dynamic with aplomb. Although the two are not in a romance, there's a good deal of playful back-and-forth that leaves the door open for this on-again, off-again pair to become a couple once more. At this point, S.H.I.E.L.D. director Nicholas Fury has gone missing, and a new person is in charge of the spy agency, Maria Hill. There's a good deal of friction between Cap—who's formed the New Avengers—and the S.H.I.E.L.D. top brass, but not enough to stop this vital mission to, of all places, Pilsburg, Iowa, from taking place. It should be noted that Sharon Carter had risen high enough in the S.H.I.E.L.D. ranks to become executive director for a brief period before the highly analytical Maria Hill replaced her. Cap's old partner, Bucky Barnes, appears in a flashback as the Winter Soldier. And two baddies from the shield slinger's rogues gallery, Crossbones and Sin—the Red Skull's devious daughter— are on hand for the fun. But the real menace is one Aleksander Lukin, CEO of the Kronas Corporation, who our gal Sharon winds up killing in a later issue. Brubaker masterfully unravels the threads in successive stories that are a real treat. His long run on the good Captain's comic is not to be missed. Seek those comics out if you haven't savored them yet.

The final two issues in this tumultuous trade paperback really focus on Carter's amazing espionage abilities. In *Age of Heroes #3*, written by Kelly Sue DeConnick, Sharon has become the Avengers coordinator. This woman certainly gets around. She, Maria Hill and Victoria Hand must take on the super-powered menace of Crusher Creel, the Absorbing Man. The ever-aggressive Carter is the one who suggests they take Creel down without contacting the Avengers. Now, that's what you call guts, especially considering the awesome extent of Creel's absorbing powers and his rather nasty disposition. And let's remember that none of these lethal ladies has a single super-power. Sharon's initial confrontation with the Absorbing Man is a bit of tactical brilliance. *Captain America and the Secret Avengers #1*, also scripted by the talented Kelly Sue, teams Carter up with perhaps the greatest espionage agent in the world—the Black Widow. Agent 13 is able to hold her own, even in this elite company, as the twosome pursue an underage assassin and prevent her from taking her revenge on a killer headmistress. You'll emerge from the tale with an even greater appreciation of Sharon's formidable talents. It's a heck of a read, Marvelite.

Sharon Carter sure has come a long way since her days as a mystery woman intersecting strangely with Steve Rogers' life. Her place in Captain America's pantheon of strong supporting players is secure.

They say behind every great man, there's a great woman. The only difference in the Steve/Sharon dynamic is that our redoubtable Carter isn't simply behind our Living Legend of World War II—she's standing right there beside him!

Enjoy,
Ralph Macchio

Ralph Macchio

Ralph Macchio spent over 35 years at Marvel, starting as an assistant editor and later writing Avengers, Thor *and many others. As editor, he oversaw books across the Marvel line, including shepherding the Ultimate line into existence and editing all of Stephen King's Marvel adaptations.*

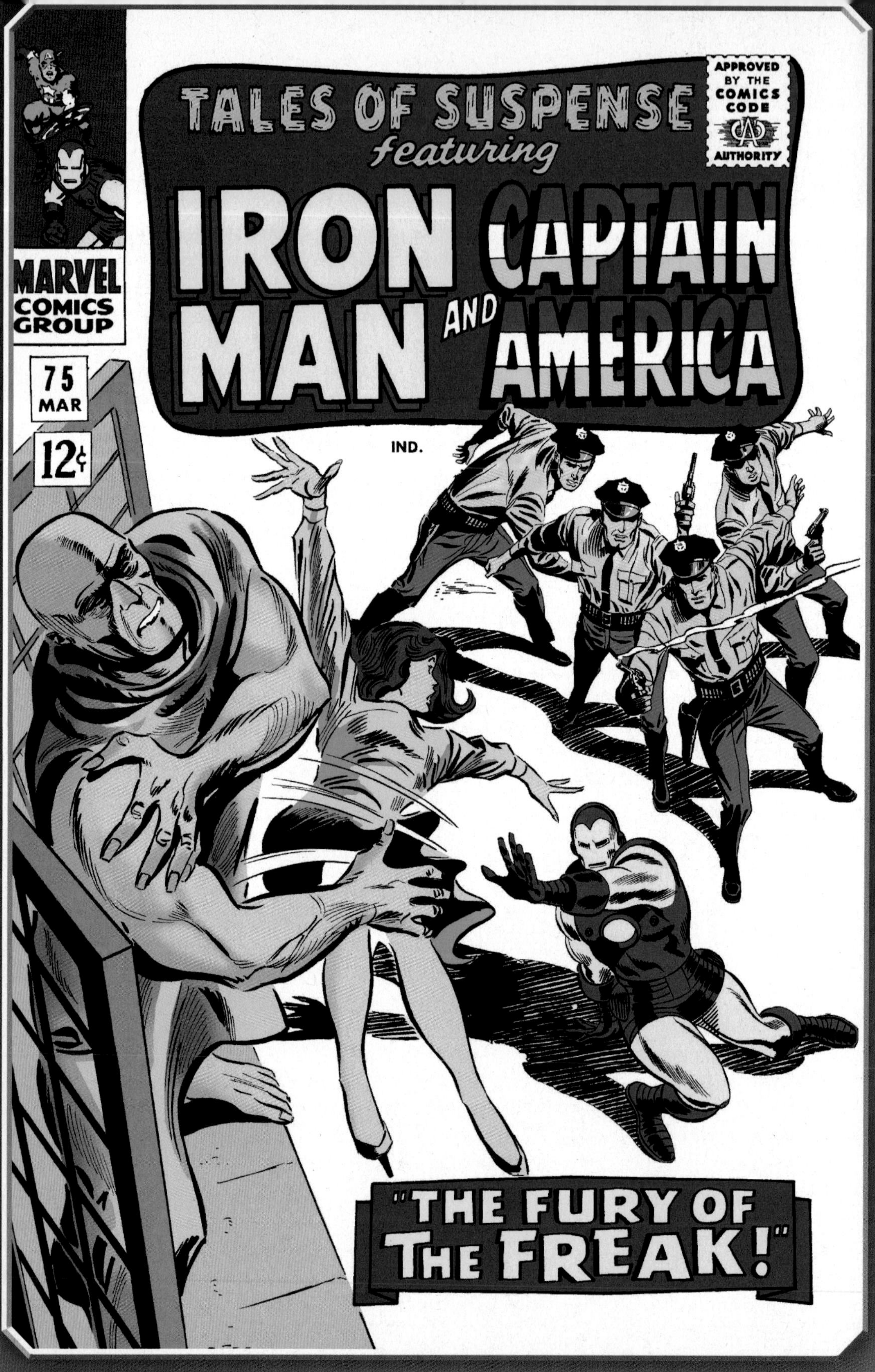

TALES OF SUSPENSE
featuring
IRON MAN AND CAPTAIN AMERICA
APPROVED BY THE COMICS CODE AUTHORITY
MARVEL COMICS GROUP
75 MAR
12¢
IND.
"THE FURY OF THE FREAK!"

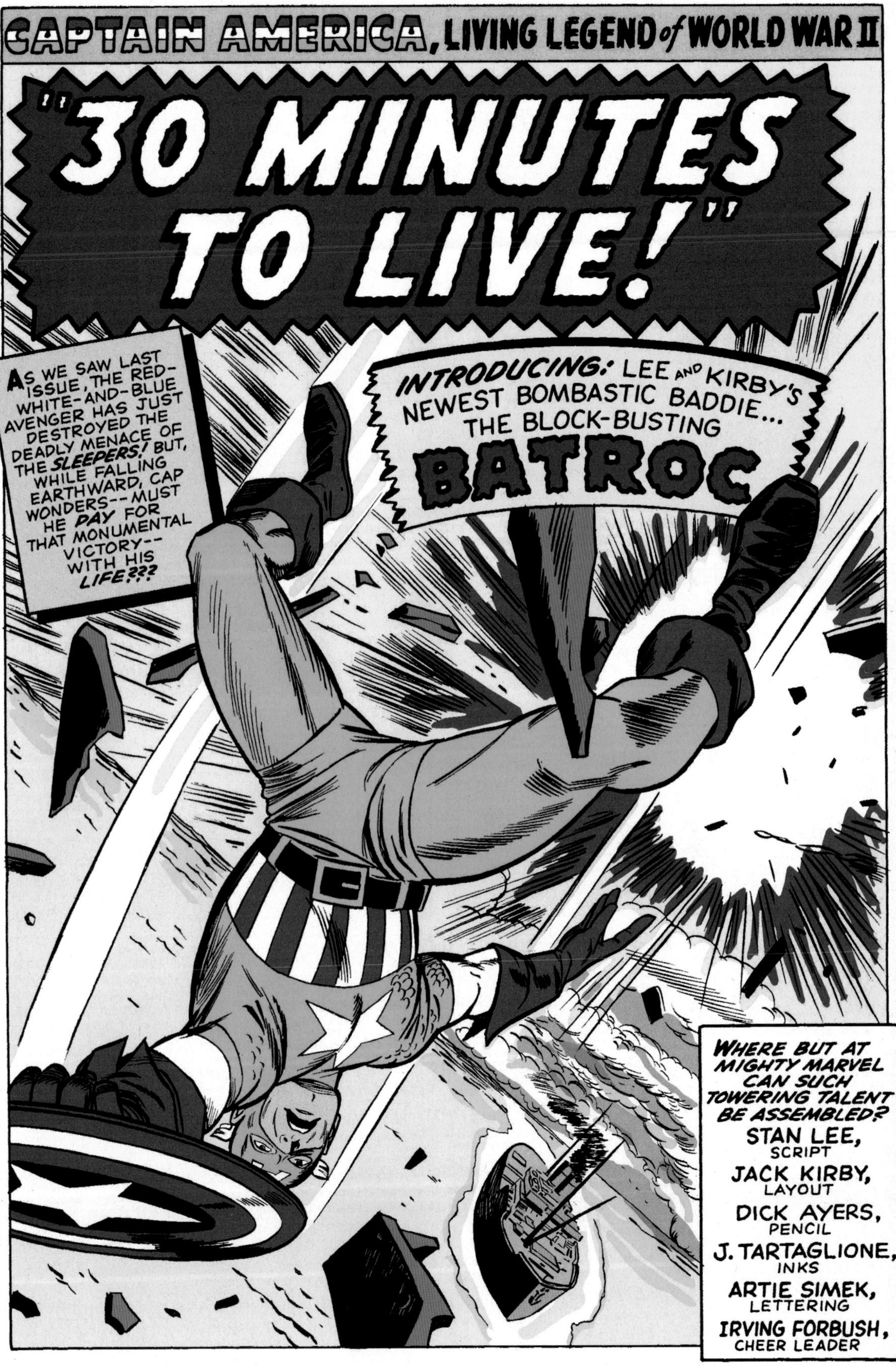
CAPTAIN AMERICA, LIVING LEGEND of WORLD WAR II
"30 MINUTES TO LIVE!"
AS WE SAW LAST ISSUE, THE RED-WHITE-AND-BLUE AVENGER HAS JUST DESTROYED THE DEADLY MENACE OF THE SLEEPERS! BUT, WHILE FALLING EARTHWARD, CAP WONDERS--MUST HE PAY FOR THAT MONUMENTAL VICTORY--WITH HIS LIFE???
INTRODUCING: LEE AND KIRBY'S NEWEST BOMBASTIC BADDIE... THE BLOCK-BUSTING BATROC
WHERE BUT AT MIGHTY MARVEL CAN SUCH TOWERING TALENT BE ASSEMBLED?
STAN LEE, SCRIPT
JACK KIRBY, LAYOUT
DICK AYERS, PENCIL
J. TARTAGLIONE, INKS
ARTIE SIMEK, LETTERING
IRVING FORBUSH, CHEER LEADER

EVEN WHILE CAPTAIN AMERICA HURTLES SEAWARD, DANGER IS A-BORNING IN A HIDDEN SANCTUARY DEEP IN THE HEART OF NEW YORK! AND NOW, WE PAID OUR DOUGH--LET'S WATCH THE SHOW--!

OBSERVE, GENTLEMEN--A SCALE MODEL OF THIS CITY--THE WAY IT LOOKS NOW-- BEFORE ITS MOMENT OF DESTRUCTION!

ENOUGH TALK! BEGIN THE DEMONSTRATION!

IT HAS ALREADY BEGUN! KEEP WATCHING THE CEILING--!

THERE! THAT MINIATURE MODEL PARACHUTE IS CARRYING A MICROSCOPIC AMOUNT OF INFERNO 42-- THE MOST DESTRUCTIVE ELEMENT OF ALL TIME!

INFERNO 42 WAS EXTRACTED CHEMICALLY FROM A METEOR DISCOVERED BY ONE OF OUR AGENTS! UNFORTUNATELY, HE MET WITH A FATAL "ACCIDENT" ONCE HE HAD SERVED HIS PURPOSE TO US!

LOOK! THE ENTIRE MODEL CITY WITHIN THE GLASS TANK IS BEGIN- NING TO SHIMMER AND GLOW--!

NATURALLY! THAT OMINOUS GLOWING IS THE FIRST STAGE BEFORE THE ULTIMATE ACT OF ANNIHILATION! WATCH--!

I CAN SEE NOTHING! THE CITY IS ENVELOPED IN AN AURA OF LIGHT-- LIKE SOME GIGANTIC, BILLOWING, ICY-COLD FLAME....!

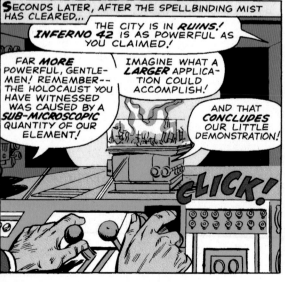

SECONDS LATER, AFTER THE SPELLBINDING MIST HAS CLEARED...

THE CITY IS IN RUINS! INFERNO 42 IS AS POWERFUL AS YOU CLAIMED!

FAR MORE POWERFUL, GENTLE- MEN! REMEMBER-- THE HOLOCAUST YOU HAVE WITNESSED WAS CAUSED BY A SUB-MICROSCOPIC QUANTITY OF OUR ELEMENT!

IMAGINE WHAT A LARGER APPLICA- TION COULD ACCOMPLISH!

AND THAT CONCLUDES OUR LITTLE DEMONSTRATION!

CLICK!

WHY DO WE STILL DELAY? WHY DO WE NOT BEGIN OUR SECRET PLAN FOR WORLD DOMINATION IMMEDIATELY??

BECAUSE THE MASTER CYLINDER OF INFERNO 42 WAS STOLEN FROM US BY AN AGENT OF SHIELD!* WE CANNOT PROCEED UNTIL WE HAVE REGAINED IT! AND, REGAIN IT WE SHALL!

BUT HOW? NO ONE IS POWERFUL ENOUGH TO GET THE BETTER OF SHIELD!

NO ONE EXCEPT-- BATROC!

*SHIELD: SUPREME HEADQUARTERS INTERNATIONAL ESPIONAGE LAW-ENFORCE- MENT DIVISION!--AS EVERY RABID READER OF STRANGE TALES KNOWS! (ANOTHER MIGHTY MARVEL UNABASHED PLUG--STAN!)

2

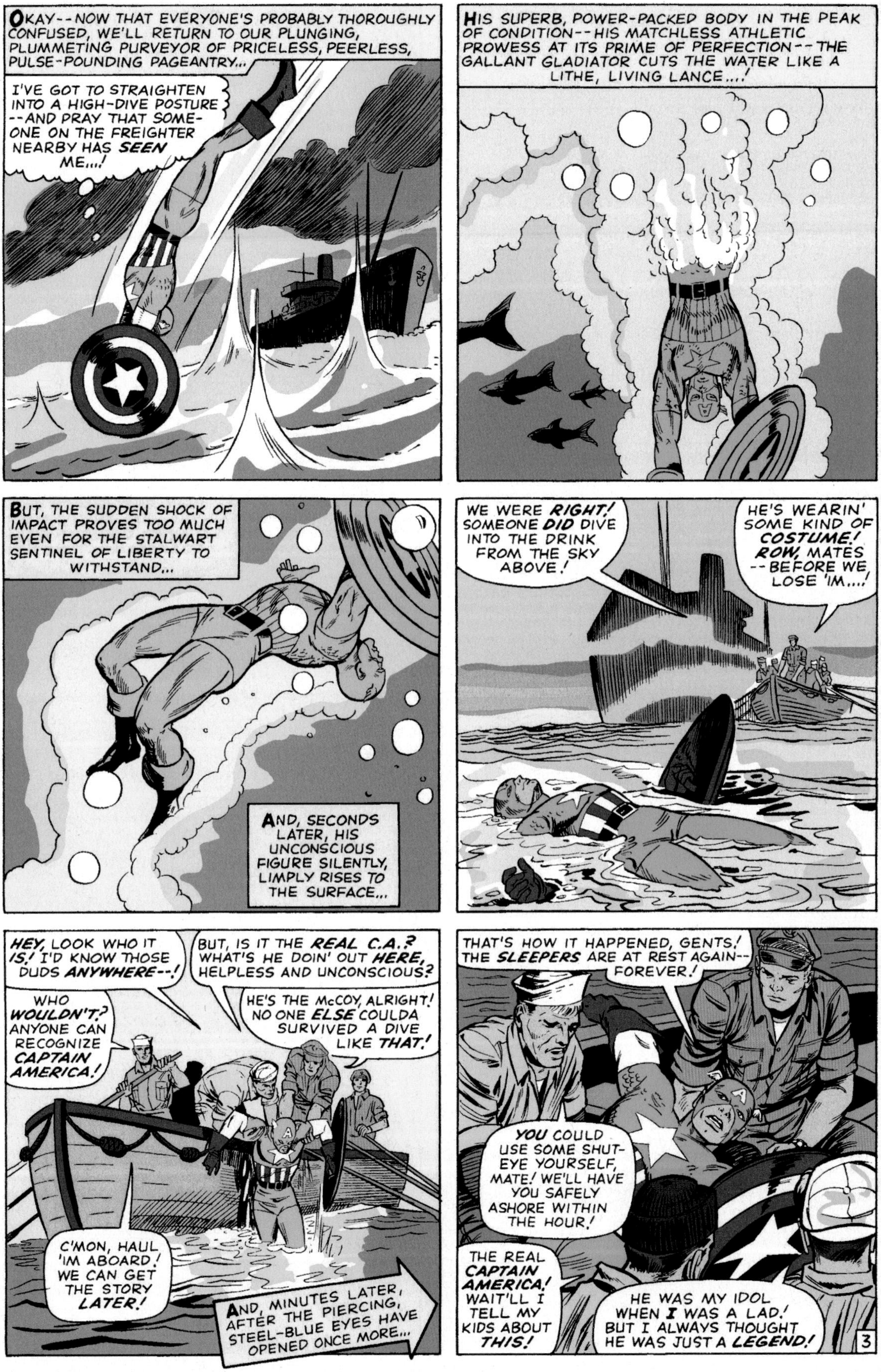

OKAY--NOW THAT EVERYONE'S PROBABLY THOROUGHLY CONFUSED, WE'LL RETURN TO OUR PLUNGING, PLUMMETING PURVEYOR OF PRICELESS, PEERLESS, PULSE-POUNDING PAGEANTRY...
I'VE GOT TO STRAIGHTEN INTO A HIGH-DIVE POSTURE --AND PRAY THAT SOME-ONE ON THE FREIGHTER NEARBY HAS SEEN ME...!
HIS SUPERB, POWER-PACKED BODY IN THE PEAK OF CONDITION--HIS MATCHLESS ATHLETIC PROWESS AT ITS PRIME OF PERFECTION--THE GALLANT GLADIATOR CUTS THE WATER LIKE A LITHE, LIVING LANCE....!
BUT, THE SUDDEN SHOCK OF IMPACT PROVES TOO MUCH EVEN FOR THE STALWART SENTINEL OF LIBERTY TO WITHSTAND...
AND, SECONDS LATER, HIS UNCONSCIOUS FIGURE SILENTLY, LIMPLY RISES TO THE SURFACE...
WE WERE RIGHT! SOMEONE DID DIVE INTO THE DRINK FROM THE SKY ABOVE!
HE'S WEARIN' SOME KIND OF COSTUME! ROW, MATES --BEFORE WE LOSE 'IM....!
HEY, LOOK WHO IT IS! I'D KNOW THOSE DUDS ANYWHERE--!
BUT, IS IT THE REAL C.A.? WHAT'S HE DOIN' OUT HERE, HELPLESS AND UNCONSCIOUS?
WHO WOULDN'T? ANYONE CAN RECOGNIZE CAPTAIN AMERICA!
HE'S THE McCOY, ALRIGHT! NO ONE ELSE COULDA SURVIVED A DIVE LIKE THAT!
C'MON, HAUL 'IM ABOARD! WE CAN GET THE STORY LATER!
AND, MINUTES LATER, AFTER THE PIERCING, STEEL-BLUE EYES HAVE OPENED ONCE MORE...
THAT'S HOW IT HAPPENED, GENTS! THE SLEEPERS ARE AT REST AGAIN--FOREVER!
YOU COULD USE SOME SHUT-EYE YOURSELF, MATE! WE'LL HAVE YOU SAFELY ASHORE WITHIN THE HOUR!
THE REAL CAPTAIN AMERICA! WAIT'LL I TELL MY KIDS ABOUT THIS!
HE WAS MY IDOL WHEN I WAS A LAD! BUT I ALWAYS THOUGHT HE WAS JUST A LEGEND!
3

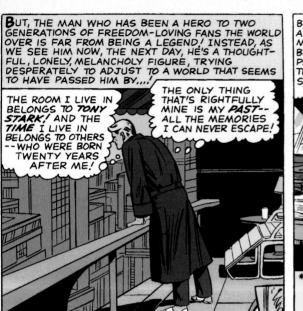

BUT, THE MAN WHO HAS BEEN A HERO TO TWO GENERATIONS OF FREEDOM-LOVING FANS THE WORLD OVER IS FAR FROM BEING A LEGEND! INSTEAD, AS WE SEE HIM NOW, THE NEXT DAY, HE'S A THOUGHTFUL, LONELY, MELANCHOLY FIGURE, TRYING DESPERATELY TO ADJUST TO A WORLD THAT SEEMS TO HAVE PASSED HIM BY....!

THE ROOM I LIVE IN BELONGS TO TONY STARK! AND THE TIME I LIVE IN BELONGS TO OTHERS --WHO WERE BORN TWENTY YEARS AFTER ME!

THE ONLY THING THAT'S RIGHTFULLY MINE IS MY PAST-- ALL THE MEMORIES I CAN NEVER ESCAPE!

BUT, MEMORY IS SUCH AN ELUSIVE THING! SO MANY IMAGES HAVE BEEN BLURRED BY THE PASSAGE OF TIME-- THE TWO DECADES I SPENT IN SUSPENDED ANIMATION! *

YET, SOME MEMORIES CAN NEVER DIE! THEY WILL LIVE FOREVER IN MY BRAIN-- NO MATTER HOW MANY YEARS PASS BY-- THEY'LL REMAIN-- TO HAUNT ME--!

*AS EXQUISITELY EXPLAINED IN AVENGERS #4, THE REASON STEVE ROGERS HAS MAINTAINED HIS YOUTH IS THAT HE WAS FROZEN ALIVE FOR YEARS AFTER WORLD WAR II-- STAN.

CAN I EVER FORGET BUCKY BARNES, THE TEEN-AGER WHO WAS LIKE A BROTHER TO ME? HE SHARED MY BATTLES, MY DANGERS, MY TRIUMPHS!

BUT, THOUGH WE SAVED COUNTLESS LIVES IN THE PAST, HIS OWN WAS SACRIFICED IN THE NAME OF FREEDOM!

AND, WHAT HAS BECOME OF SGT. DUFFY, THE WONDERFUL, WILD NONCOM WHO SWORE THAT STEVE ROGERS WAS THE MOST FOULED-UP G.I. OF ALL TIME!

IF ONLY I COULD HAVE SEEN HIS FACE WHEN HE LEARNED-- IF EVER HE DID-- THAT ROGERS AND CAPTAIN AMERICA WERE ONE AND THE SAME!

BUT, THERE WAS ONE OTHER! OUR LIVES TOUCHED FOR ONLY A SHORT TIME-- BUT I'VE NEVER FORGOTTEN HER! I CAN STILL REMEMBER OUR FINAL DATE--WHEN SHE WHISPERED TO ME, THRU TREMBLING LIPS...

I'LL WAIT TILL YOU RETURN, STEVE! NO MATTER HOW LONG-- NO MATTER WHAT HAPPENS-- I'LL WAIT FOR YOU, MY DARLING,...!

BUT, THAT WAS AN ETERNITY AGO-- IN THE DEAD PAST-- THE FORGOTTEN PAST-- THE PAST WHICH WILL LIVE WITH ME FOREVER!

TODAY, IT'S ALL BEHIND ME! THIS IS A NEW WORLD --A NEW AGE! AN AGE OF ATOMIC POWER, SPACE EXPLORATION, SOCIAL UPHEAVAL--YET, AN AGE OVER WHICH THE THREAT OF WAR HANGS HEAVY ONCE AGAIN!

AND, SO LONG AS DANGER BECKONS, THERE IS STILL A NEED FOR AN OLD RELIC LIKE CAPTAIN AMERICA! A NEED THAT MUST BE MET!

4

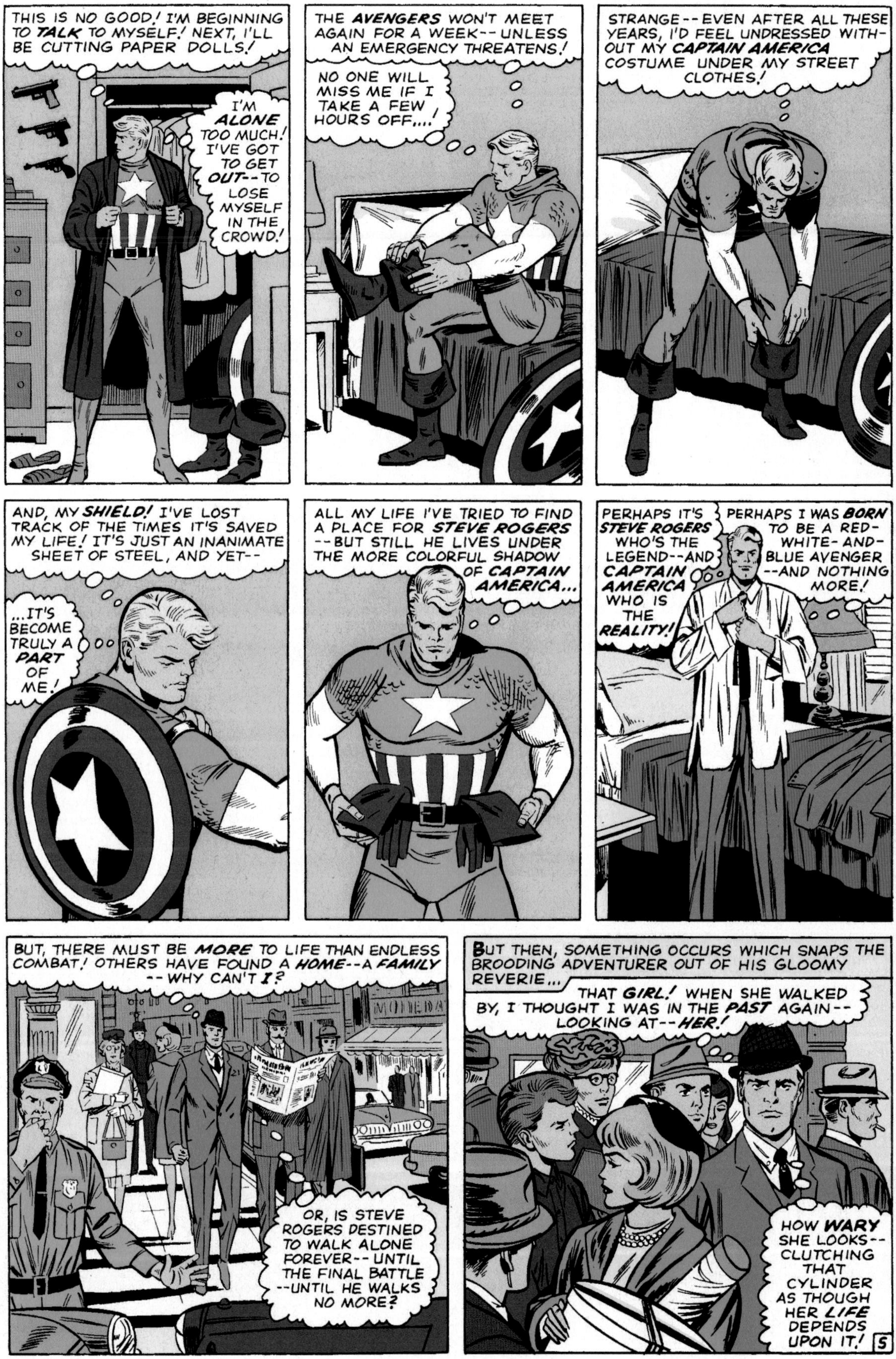
THIS IS NO GOOD! I'M BEGINNING TO TALK TO MYSELF! NEXT, I'LL BE CUTTING PAPER DOLLS!
I'M ALONE TOO MUCH! I'VE GOT TO GET OUT--TO LOSE MYSELF IN THE CROWD!
THE AVENGERS WON'T MEET AGAIN FOR A WEEK--UNLESS AN EMERGENCY THREATENS!
NO ONE WILL MISS ME IF I TAKE A FEW HOURS OFF....!
STRANGE--EVEN AFTER ALL THESE YEARS, I'D FEEL UNDRESSED WITHOUT MY CAPTAIN AMERICA COSTUME UNDER MY STREET CLOTHES!
AND, MY SHIELD! I'VE LOST TRACK OF THE TIMES IT'S SAVED MY LIFE! IT'S JUST AN INANIMATE SHEET OF STEEL, AND YET--
...IT'S BECOME TRULY A PART OF ME!
ALL MY LIFE I'VE TRIED TO FIND A PLACE FOR STEVE ROGERS--BUT STILL HE LIVES UNDER THE MORE COLORFUL SHADOW OF CAPTAIN AMERICA...
PERHAPS IT'S STEVE ROGERS WHO'S THE LEGEND--AND CAPTAIN AMERICA WHO IS THE REALITY!
PERHAPS I WAS BORN TO BE A RED-WHITE-AND-BLUE AVENGER--AND NOTHING MORE!
BUT, THERE MUST BE MORE TO LIFE THAN ENDLESS COMBAT! OTHERS HAVE FOUND A HOME--A FAMILY--WHY CAN'T I?
OR, IS STEVE ROGERS DESTINED TO WALK ALONE FOREVER--UNTIL THE FINAL BATTLE--UNTIL HE WALKS NO MORE?
BUT THEN, SOMETHING OCCURS WHICH SNAPS THE BROODING ADVENTURER OUT OF HIS GLOOMY REVERIE...
THAT GIRL! WHEN SHE WALKED BY, I THOUGHT I WAS IN THE PAST AGAIN--LOOKING AT--HER!
HOW WARY SHE LOOKS--CLUTCHING THAT CYLINDER AS THOUGH HER LIFE DEPENDS UPON IT!

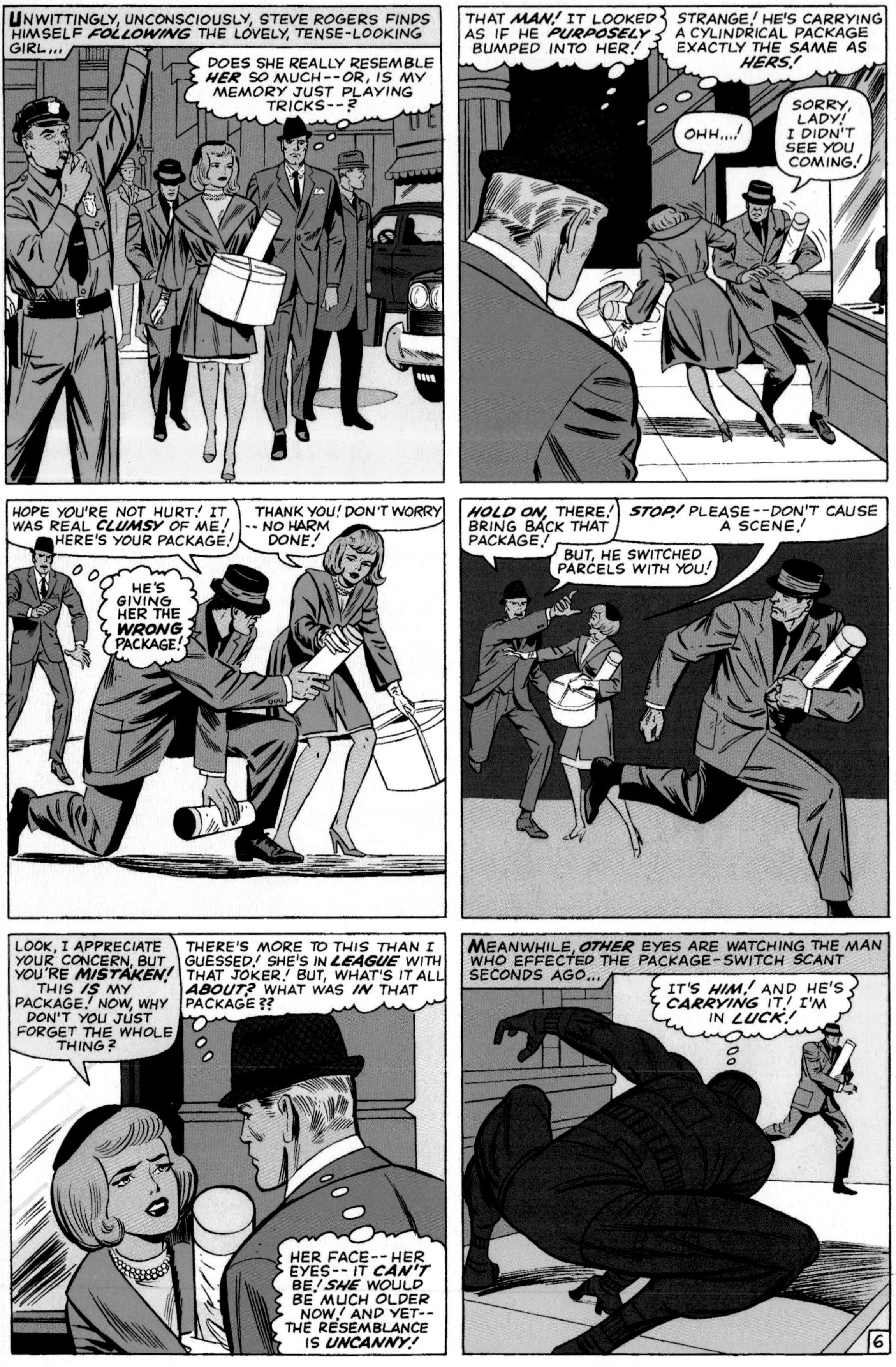
UNWITTINGLY, UNCONSCIOUSLY, STEVE ROGERS FINDS HIMSELF FOLLOWING THE LOVELY, TENSE-LOOKING GIRL...
DOES SHE REALLY RESEMBLE HER SO MUCH--OR, IS MY MEMORY JUST PLAYING TRICKS--?
THAT MAN! IT LOOKED AS IF HE PURPOSELY BUMPED INTO HER!
STRANGE! HE'S CARRYING A CYLINDRICAL PACKAGE EXACTLY THE SAME AS HERS!
OHH...!
SORRY, LADY! I DIDN'T SEE YOU COMING!
HOPE YOU'RE NOT HURT! IT WAS REAL CLUMSY OF ME! HERE'S YOUR PACKAGE!
THANK YOU! DON'T WORRY -- NO HARM DONE!
HE'S GIVING HER THE WRONG PACKAGE!
HOLD ON, THERE! BRING BACK THAT PACKAGE!
STOP! PLEASE--DON'T CAUSE A SCENE!
BUT, HE SWITCHED PARCELS WITH YOU!
LOOK, I APPRECIATE YOUR CONCERN, BUT YOU'RE MISTAKEN! THIS IS MY PACKAGE! NOW, WHY DON'T YOU JUST FORGET THE WHOLE THING?
THERE'S MORE TO THIS THAN I GUESSED! SHE'S IN LEAGUE WITH THAT JOKER! BUT, WHAT'S IT ALL ABOUT? WHAT WAS IN THAT PACKAGE??
HER FACE--HER EYES-- IT CAN'T BE! SHE WOULD BE MUCH OLDER NOW! AND YET-- THE RESEMBLANCE IS UNCANNY!
MEANWHILE, OTHER EYES ARE WATCHING THE MAN WHO EFFECTED THE PACKAGE-SWITCH SCANT SECONDS AGO...
IT'S HIM! AND HE'S CARRYING IT! I'M IN LUCK!
6

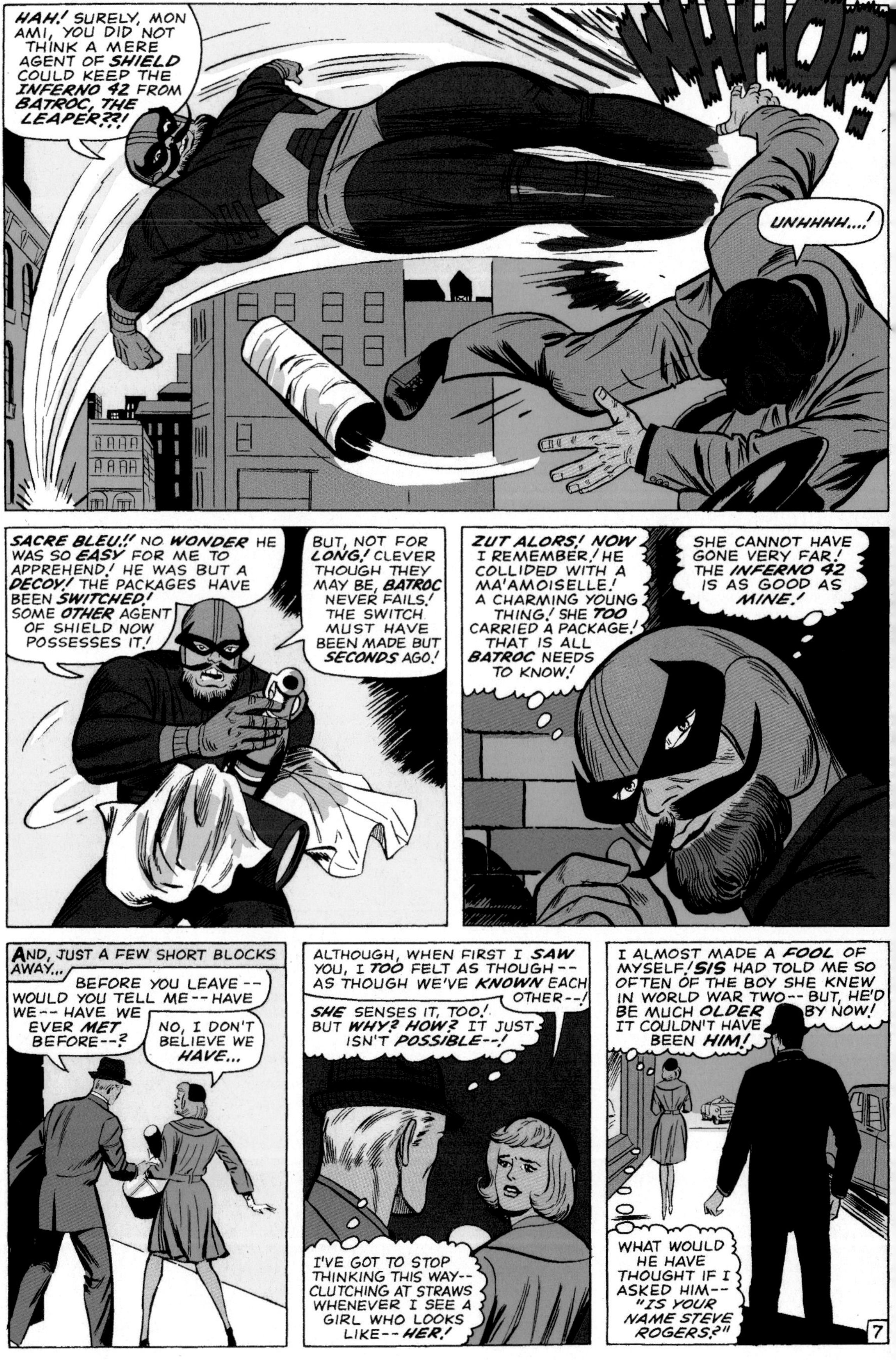
HAH! SURELY, MON AMI, YOU DID NOT THINK A MERE AGENT OF SHIELD COULD KEEP THE INFERNO 42 FROM BATROC, THE LEAPER??!
WHHOP!
UNHHHH...!
SACRE BLEU!! NO WONDER HE WAS SO EASY FOR ME TO APPREHEND! HE WAS BUT A DECOY! THE PACKAGES HAVE BEEN SWITCHED! SOME OTHER AGENT OF SHIELD NOW POSSESSES IT!
BUT, NOT FOR LONG! CLEVER THOUGH THEY MAY BE, BATROC NEVER FAILS! THE SWITCH MUST HAVE BEEN MADE BUT SECONDS AGO!
ZUT ALORS! NOW I REMEMBER! HE COLLIDED WITH A MA'AMOISELLE! A CHARMING YOUNG THING! SHE TOO CARRIED A PACKAGE! THAT IS ALL BATROC NEEDS TO KNOW!
SHE CANNOT HAVE GONE VERY FAR! THE INFERNO 42 IS AS GOOD AS MINE!
AND, JUST A FEW SHORT BLOCKS AWAY...
BEFORE YOU LEAVE -- WOULD YOU TELL ME -- HAVE WE -- HAVE WE EVER MET BEFORE--?
NO, I DON'T BELIEVE WE HAVE...
ALTHOUGH, WHEN FIRST I SAW YOU, I TOO FELT AS THOUGH -- AS THOUGH WE'VE KNOWN EACH OTHER--!
SHE SENSES IT, TOO! BUT WHY? HOW? IT JUST ISN'T POSSIBLE--!
I'VE GOT TO STOP THINKING THIS WAY-- CLUTCHING AT STRAWS WHENEVER I SEE A GIRL WHO LOOKS LIKE-- HER!
I ALMOST MADE A FOOL OF MYSELF! SIS HAD TOLD ME SO OFTEN OF THE BOY SHE KNEW IN WORLD WAR TWO-- BUT, HE'D BE MUCH OLDER BY NOW! IT COULDN'T HAVE BEEN HIM!
WHAT WOULD HE HAVE THOUGHT IF I ASKED HIM-- "IS YOUR NAME STEVE ROGERS?"

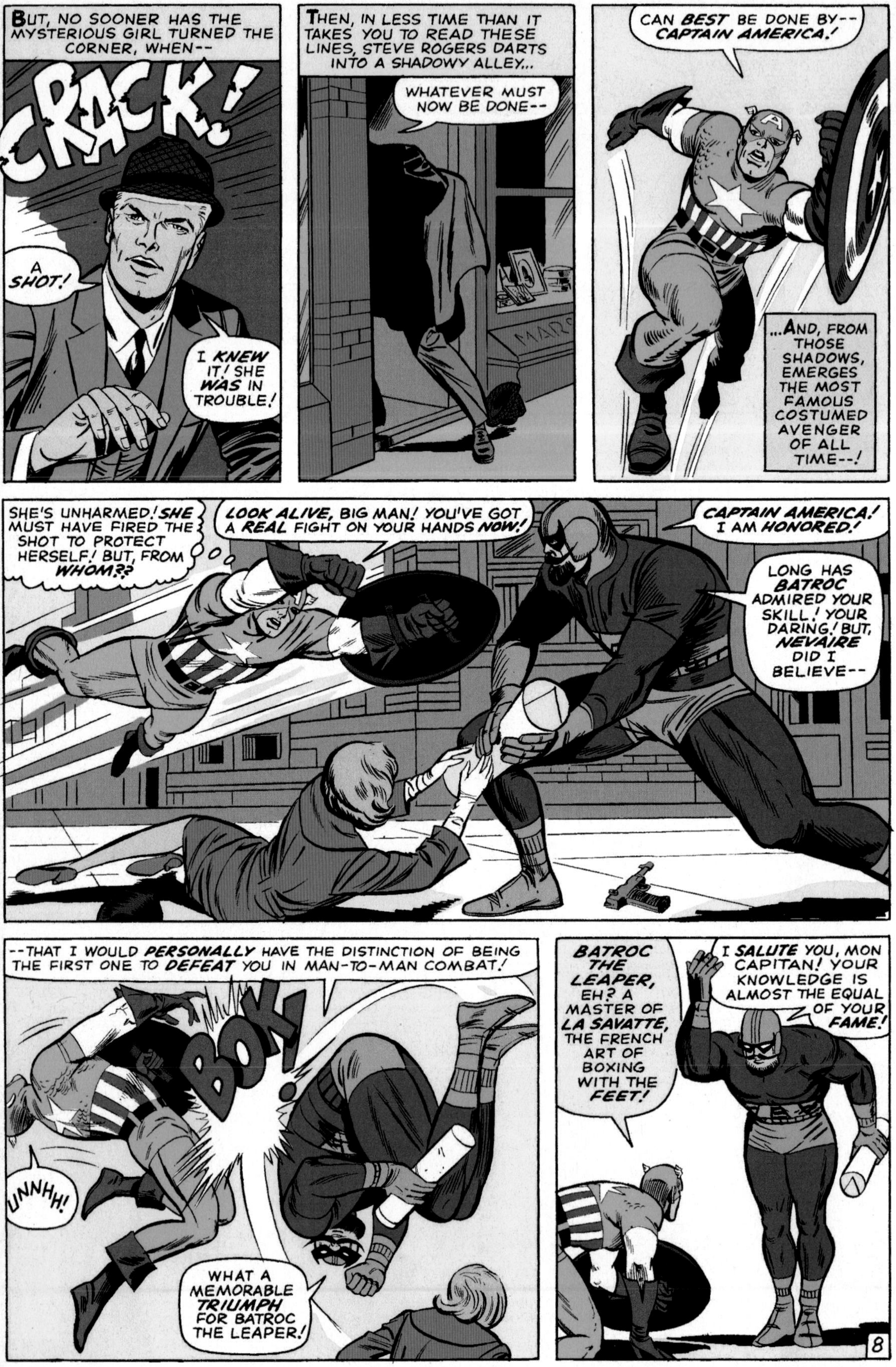

BUT, NO SOONER HAS THE MYSTERIOUS GIRL TURNED THE CORNER, WHEN--
CRACK!
A SHOT!
I KNEW IT! SHE WAS IN TROUBLE!
THEN, IN LESS TIME THAN IT TAKES YOU TO READ THESE LINES, STEVE ROGERS DARTS INTO A SHADOWY ALLEY...
WHATEVER MUST NOW BE DONE--
CAN BEST BE DONE BY-- CAPTAIN AMERICA!
...AND, FROM THOSE SHADOWS, EMERGES THE MOST FAMOUS COSTUMED AVENGER OF ALL TIME--!
SHE'S UNHARMED! SHE MUST HAVE FIRED THE SHOT TO PROTECT HERSELF! BUT, FROM WHOM??
LOOK ALIVE, BIG MAN! YOU'VE GOT A REAL FIGHT ON YOUR HANDS NOW!
CAPTAIN AMERICA! I AM HONORED!
LONG HAS BATROC ADMIRED YOUR SKILL! YOUR DARING! BUT, NEVAIRE DID I BELIEVE--
--THAT I WOULD PERSONALLY HAVE THE DISTINCTION OF BEING THE FIRST ONE TO DEFEAT YOU IN MAN-TO-MAN COMBAT!
BOK!
UNNHH!
WHAT A MEMORABLE TRIUMPH FOR BATROC THE LEAPER!
BATROC THE LEAPER, EH? A MASTER OF LA SAVATTE, THE FRENCH ART OF BOXING WITH THE FEET!
I SALUTE YOU, MON CAPITAN! YOUR KNOWLEDGE IS ALMOST THE EQUAL OF YOUR FAME!
8

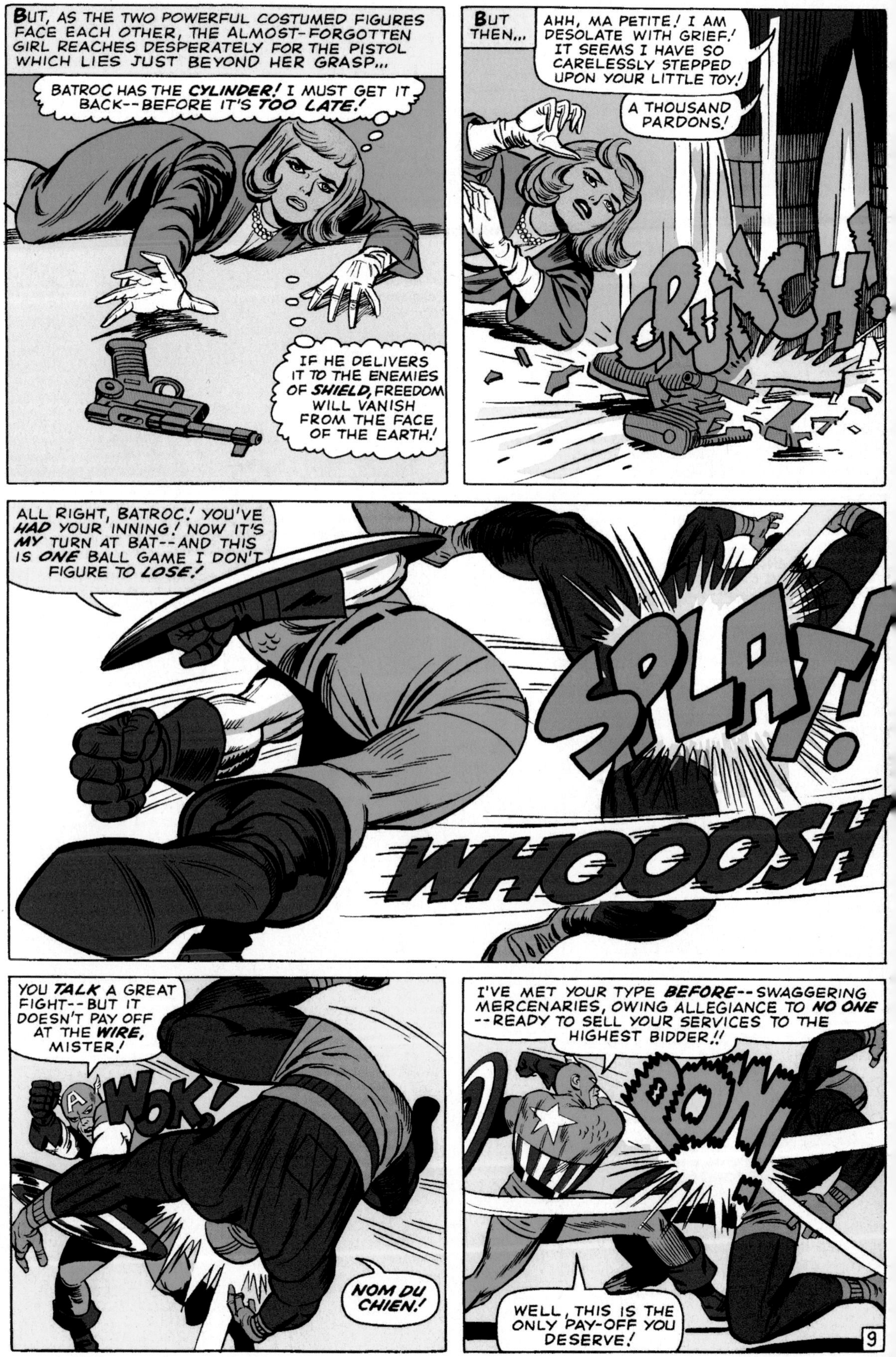

BUT, AS THE TWO POWERFUL COSTUMED FIGURES FACE EACH OTHER, THE ALMOST-FORGOTTEN GIRL REACHES DESPERATELY FOR THE PISTOL WHICH LIES JUST BEYOND HER GRASP...
BATROC HAS THE CYLINDER! I MUST GET IT BACK--BEFORE IT'S TOO LATE!
IF HE DELIVERS IT TO THE ENEMIES OF SHIELD, FREEDOM WILL VANISH FROM THE FACE OF THE EARTH!
BUT THEN...
AHH, MA PETITE! I AM DESOLATE WITH GRIEF! IT SEEMS I HAVE SO CARELESSLY STEPPED UPON YOUR LITTLE TOY!
A THOUSAND PARDONS!
CRUNCH!
ALL RIGHT, BATROC! YOU'VE HAD YOUR INNING! NOW IT'S MY TURN AT BAT--AND THIS IS ONE BALL GAME I DON'T FIGURE TO LOSE!
SPLAT!
WHOOOSH
YOU TALK A GREAT FIGHT--BUT IT DOESN'T PAY OFF AT THE WIRE, MISTER!
WOK!
NOM DU CHIEN!
I'VE MET YOUR TYPE BEFORE--SWAGGERING MERCENARIES, OWING ALLEGIANCE TO NO ONE--READY TO SELL YOUR SERVICES TO THE HIGHEST BIDDER!!
POW
WELL, THIS IS THE ONLY PAY-OFF YOU DESERVE!
9

LUCKY I DOWNED HIM! HE'S STRONG AS AN OX! ALMOST BROKE MY HANDS!

NOW *TALK!* WHAT'S THIS ALL *ABOUT?* WHAT'S IN THAT *CYLINDER?*

I SAID *TALK!* WHY DID *YOU* WANT THAT PACKAGE? IS THE GIRL IN *DANGER?*

BUT *OF COURSE!* WE ARE *ALL* IN DANGER! THE CYLINDER CONTAINS ENOUGH *INFERNO 42* TO BLOW UP THIS ENTIRE *CITY!* RELEASE ME! I WILL *HELP* YOU!

WHY?? WHY WOULD *YOU* WANT TO HELP ME?

BECAUSE ALL OUR *LIVES* ARE AT STAKE-- *MINE* AS WELL!

THE *CYLINDER! SACRE BLEU!* SHE HAS *TAKEN* IT! IT IS *GONE!*

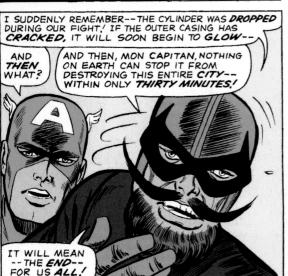

I SUDDENLY REMEMBER--THE CYLINDER WAS *DROPPED* DURING OUR FIGHT! IF THE OUTER CASING HAS *CRACKED,* IT WILL SOON BEGIN TO *GLOW*--

AND *THEN?*

AND THEN, MON CAPITAN, NOTHING ON EARTH CAN STOP IT FROM DESTROYING THIS ENTIRE *CITY*-- WITHIN ONLY *THIRTY MINUTES!*

IT WILL MEAN --THE *END*-- FOR US *ALL!*

LOOK! JUST AS I *FEARED!* IT IS GLOWING-- EVEN *NOW!*

WE MUST CATCH THE GIRL--EVEN *SHE* DOES NOT REALIZE THE DANGER! WE MUST FIND A WAY TO *RESEAL* THE CYLINDER!

IT SHOULDN'T BE TOO DIFFICULT TO OVERTAKE ONE LONE GIRL....!

AHH, BUT *THIS* ONE -- SHE IS *DIFFERENT!*

SHE IS NO *ORDINARY* FEMALE-- SHE IS AN *AGENT OF SHIELD!*

NOW, STAND ASIDE, WHILE *BATROC* PREPARES TO MAKE HIS GREATEST LEAPS!

AN AGENT OF *SHIELD!* I NEVER *DREAMT!* I'VE GOT TO *REACH* HER--!

BUT, STILL NOT SUSPECTING THE IMMINENT DANGER-- DANGER WHICH SHE AND THE ENTIRE CITY FACE-- THE FLEEING GIRL IS DETERMINED *NOT* TO BE STOPPED,...!

THEY'RE *BOTH* FOLLOWING ME NOW! BUT THEY WON'T FIND ME *AGAIN!*

THERE ARE TOO MANY *SHIELD* HIDING PLACES I CAN TAKE REFUGE IN UNTIL THEY'VE GONE....!

THIS WAS ONLY THE *BEGINNING!* THE SUSPENSE MOUNTS--THE MENACE GROWS-- THE FANTASY AMAZES --THE SURPRISES MULTIPLY-- IN THE NEXT INCREDIBLE ISSUE OF *SUSPENSE!* IF YOU MISS IT, BATROC WILL NEVER FORGIVE YOU!

10

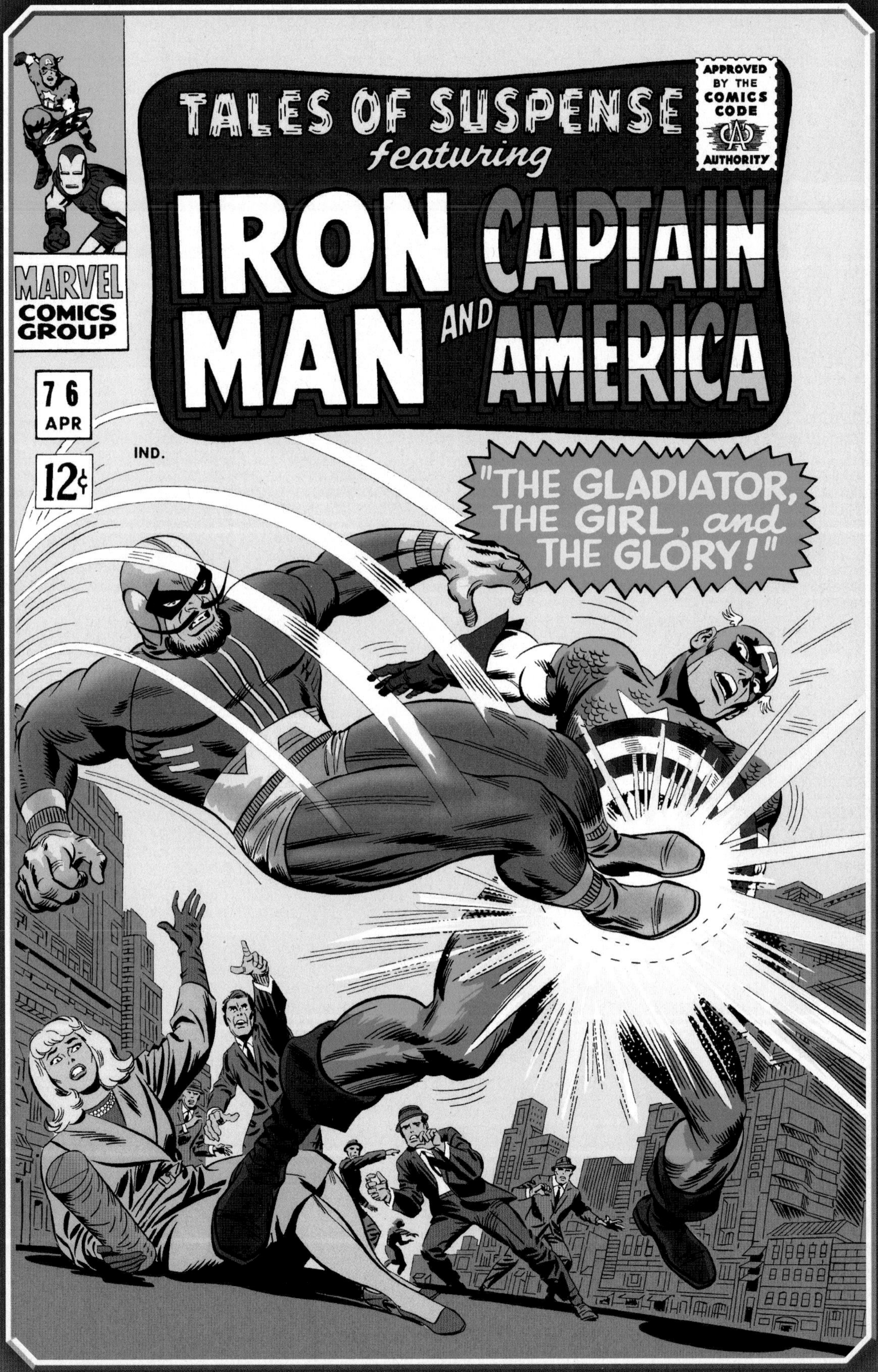
TALES OF SUSPENSE
featuring
IRON MAN AND CAPTAIN AMERICA
APPROVED BY THE COMICS CODE AUTHORITY
MARVEL COMICS GROUP
76 APR
IND.
12¢
"THE GLADIATOR, THE GIRL, and THE GLORY!"

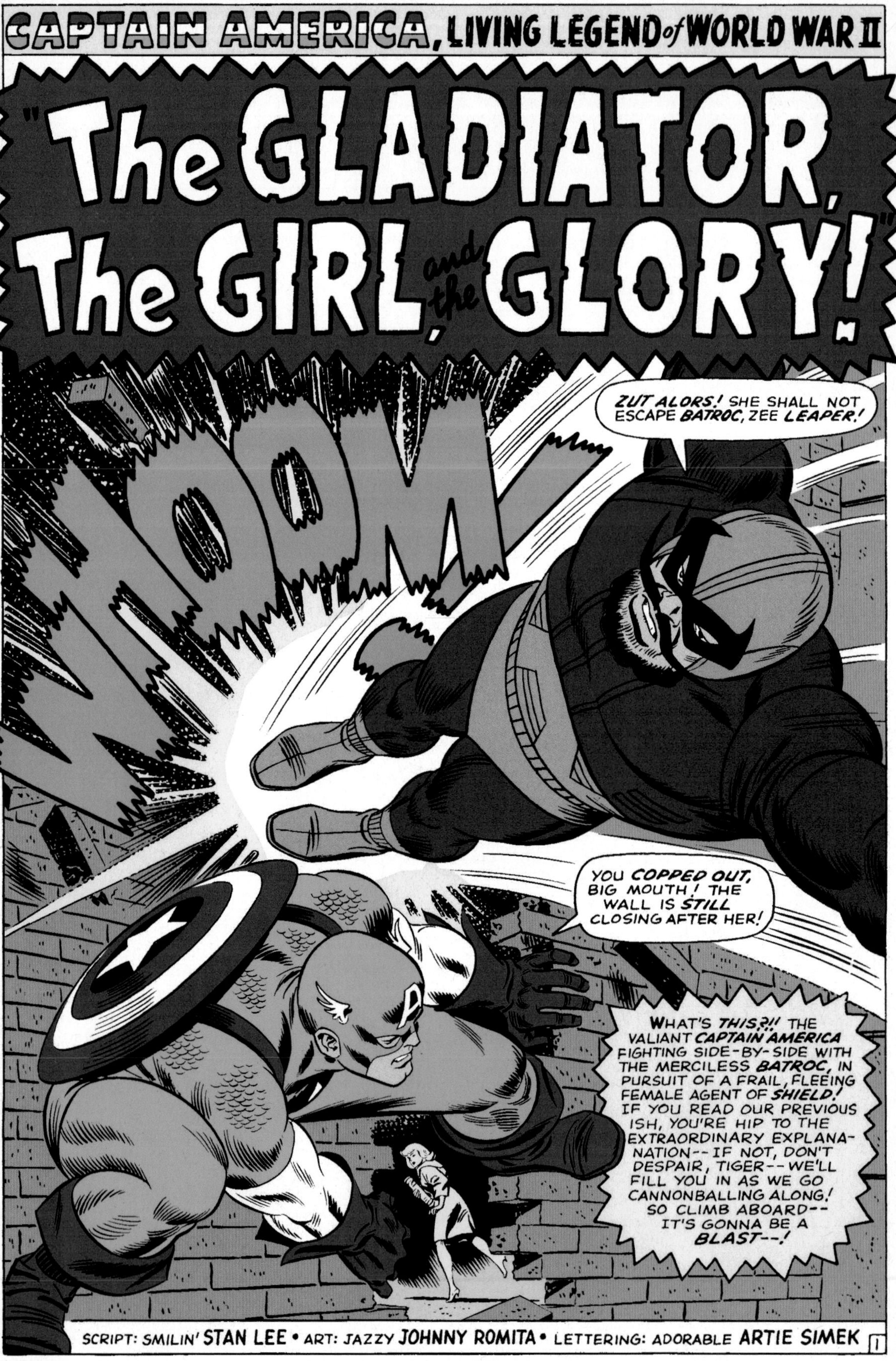
CAPTAIN AMERICA, LIVING LEGEND of WORLD WAR II
"The GLADIATOR, The GIRL, and the GLORY!"
WHOOM
ZUT ALORS! SHE SHALL NOT ESCAPE BATROC, ZEE LEAPER!
YOU COPPED OUT, BIG MOUTH! THE WALL IS STILL CLOSING AFTER HER!
WHAT'S THIS?!! THE VALIANT CAPTAIN AMERICA FIGHTING SIDE-BY-SIDE WITH THE MERCILESS BATROC, IN PURSUIT OF A FRAIL, FLEEING FEMALE AGENT OF SHIELD! IF YOU READ OUR PREVIOUS ISH, YOU'RE HIP TO THE EXTRAORDINARY EXPLANA-NATION-- IF NOT, DON'T DESPAIR, TIGER--WE'LL FILL YOU IN AS WE GO CANNONBALLING ALONG! SO CLIMB ABOARD-- IT'S GONNA BE A BLAST--!
SCRIPT: SMILIN' STAN LEE • ART: JAZZY JOHNNY ROMITA • LETTERING: ADORABLE ARTIE SIMEK
1

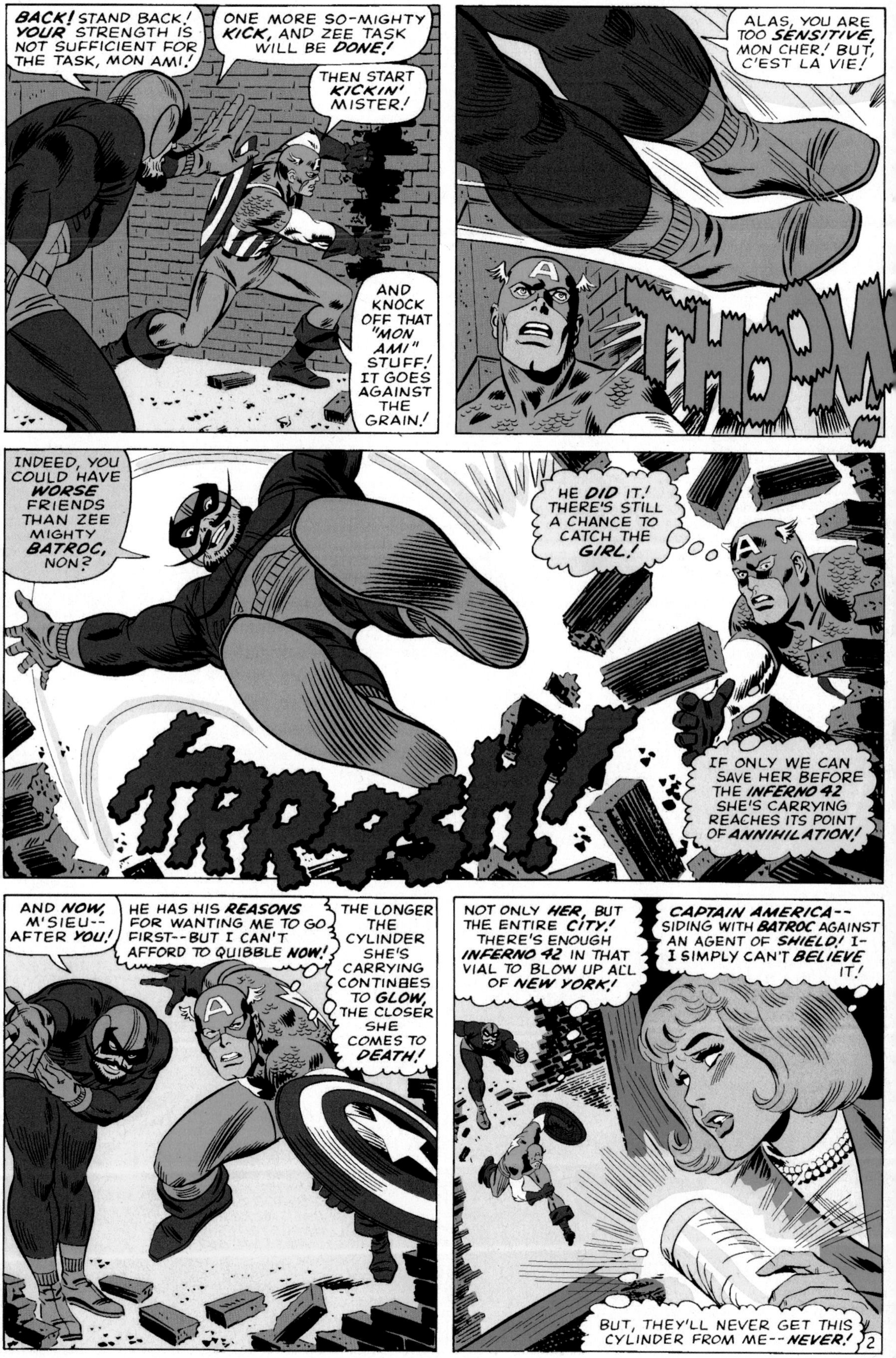
BACK! STAND BACK! YOUR STRENGTH IS NOT SUFFICIENT FOR THE TASK, MON AMI!
ONE MORE SO-MIGHTY KICK, AND ZEE TASK WILL BE DONE!
THEN START KICKIN' MISTER!
AND KNOCK OFF THAT "MON AMI" STUFF! IT GOES AGAINST THE GRAIN!
ALAS, YOU ARE TOO SENSITIVE, MON CHER! BUT, C'EST LA VIE!
THOOM!
INDEED, YOU COULD HAVE WORSE FRIENDS THAN ZEE MIGHTY BATROC, NON?
HE DID IT! THERE'S STILL A CHANCE TO CATCH THE GIRL!
TRRASH!
IF ONLY WE CAN SAVE HER BEFORE THE INFERNO 42 SHE'S CARRYING REACHES ITS POINT OF ANNIHILATION!
AND NOW, M'SIEU-- AFTER YOU!
HE HAS HIS REASONS FOR WANTING ME TO GO FIRST--BUT I CAN'T AFFORD TO QUIBBLE NOW!
THE LONGER THE CYLINDER SHE'S CARRYING CONTINUES TO GLOW, THE CLOSER SHE COMES TO DEATH!
NOT ONLY HER, BUT THE ENTIRE CITY! THERE'S ENOUGH INFERNO 42 IN THAT VIAL TO BLOW UP ALL OF NEW YORK!
CAPTAIN AMERICA-- SIDING WITH BATROC AGAINST AN AGENT OF SHIELD! I-I SIMPLY CAN'T BELIEVE IT!
BUT, THEY'LL NEVER GET THIS CYLINDER FROM ME--NEVER!
2

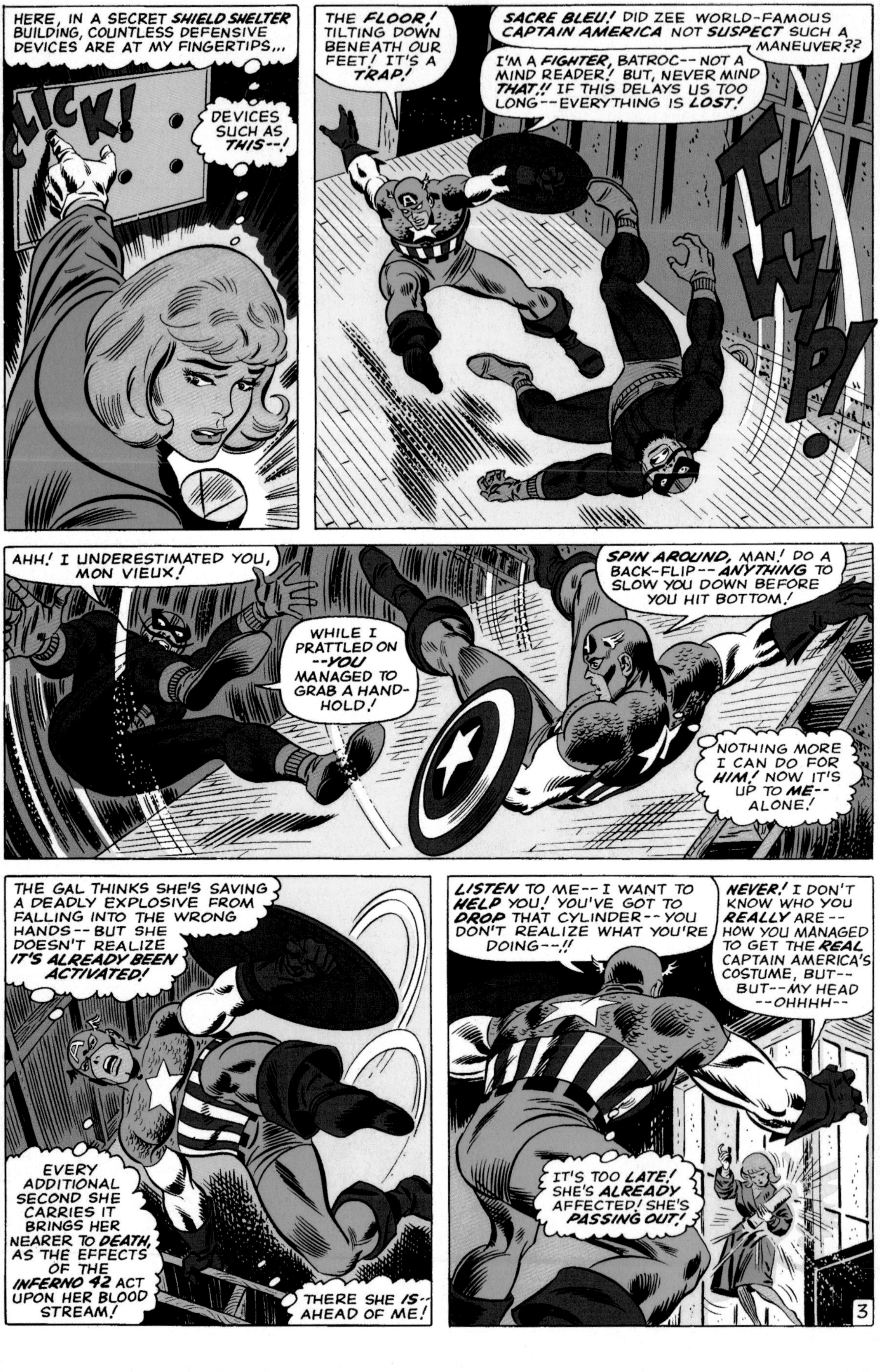
HERE, IN A SECRET SHIELD SHELTER BUILDING, COUNTLESS DEFENSIVE DEVICES ARE AT MY FINGERTIPS...
CLICK!
DEVICES SUCH AS THIS--!
THE FLOOR! TILTING DOWN BENEATH OUR FEET! IT'S A TRAP!
SACRE BLEU! DID ZEE WORLD-FAMOUS CAPTAIN AMERICA NOT SUSPECT SUCH A MANEUVER??
I'M A FIGHTER, BATROC-- NOT A MIND READER! BUT, NEVER MIND THAT!! IF THIS DELAYS US TOO LONG--EVERYTHING IS LOST!
THWIP!
AHH! I UNDERESTIMATED YOU, MON VIEUX!
WHILE I PRATTLED ON --YOU MANAGED TO GRAB A HAND-HOLD!
SPIN AROUND, MAN! DO A BACK-FLIP--ANYTHING TO SLOW YOU DOWN BEFORE YOU HIT BOTTOM!
NOTHING MORE I CAN DO FOR HIM! NOW IT'S UP TO ME-- ALONE!
THE GAL THINKS SHE'S SAVING A DEADLY EXPLOSIVE FROM FALLING INTO THE WRONG HANDS--BUT SHE DOESN'T REALIZE IT'S ALREADY BEEN ACTIVATED!
EVERY ADDITIONAL SECOND SHE CARRIES IT BRINGS HER NEARER TO DEATH, AS THE EFFECTS OF THE INFERNO 42 ACT UPON HER BLOOD STREAM!
THERE SHE IS-- AHEAD OF ME!
LISTEN TO ME--I WANT TO HELP YOU! YOU'VE GOT TO DROP THAT CYLINDER--YOU DON'T REALIZE WHAT YOU'RE DOING--!!
NEVER! I DON'T KNOW WHO YOU REALLY ARE--HOW YOU MANAGED TO GET THE REAL CAPTAIN AMERICA'S COSTUME, BUT-- BUT--MY HEAD --OHHHH--
IT'S TOO LATE! SHE'S ALREADY AFFECTED! SHE'S PASSING OUT!

I-I DIDN'T REACH HER IN TIME! SHE'S BEEN OVERCOME BY THE INFERNO 42!

IT'S UNCANNY! AS SHE LIES THERE-- SO STILL--SO SILENT-- SHE LOOKS MORE THAN EVER LIKE--LIKE THE PAST REBORN! LIKE THE ONLY OTHER GIRL I EVER--LOVED!

IF ONLY I COULD KNOW--WHO SHE REALLY IS--!

AT THAT MOMENT, IN A HIDDEN SANCTUARY IN ANOTHER PART OF THE CITY...

BATROC IS OVERDUE! THE INFERNO 42 SHOULD HAVE BEEN DELIVERED TO US BY NOW! CAN HE HAVE FAILED?

IMPOSSIBLE! BATROC DOES NOT FAIL! WE MUST NOT LOSE HOPE!

BUT--WHAT IF THE CYLINDER HAS BEEN ACCIDENTALLY ACTIVATED??

EVEN IF THE ENTIRE CITY IS LEVELLED, WE'LL BE SAFE HERE, IN THIS ARMORED, SHIELDED, FORTRESS-LIKE CHAMBER! NO MATTER WHAT HAPPENS, WE CANNOT LOSE!

HAVE YOU THOUGHT OF THE POSSIBILITY OF HIS BRINGING THE ACTIVATED EXPLOSIVE IN HERE?

OF COURSE! WE WOULD IMMEDIATELY PLACE IT WITHIN THIS RECEPTACLE--WHICH WOULD HALT THE DETONATION PROCESS!

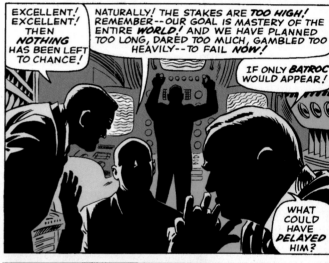

EXCELLENT! EXCELLENT! THEN NOTHING HAS BEEN LEFT TO CHANCE!

NATURALLY! THE STAKES ARE TOO HIGH! REMEMBER--OUR GOAL IS MASTERY OF THE ENTIRE WORLD! AND WE HAVE PLANNED TOO LONG, DARED TOO MUCH, GAMBLED TOO HEAVILY--TO FAIL NOW!

IF ONLY BATROC WOULD APPEAR!

WHAT COULD HAVE DELAYED HIM?

FOR THE ANSWER TO THAT BURNING QUESTION, WE TURN ONCE AGAIN TO THE FREE WORLD'S GREATEST SENTINEL OF LIBERTY--AS HE HEARS--!

I REALIZE NOW-- THE CYLINDER WAS ACTIVATED! YOU WERE TRYING TO SAVE ME! BUT--IT-- IT'S TOO LATE FOR ME! THE ENTIRE CITY IS IN DANGER--!

LEAVE ME! YOU'VE ONLY MINUTES TO FIND A WAY TO KEEP THE INFERNO 42 FROM--FROM DETONATING!!!

LEAVE YOU--AS I WAS FORCED TO LEAVE HER--SO MANY YEARS AGO??

BATROC!

MAIS OUI, M'SIEU! IT IS TIME TO END ZIS INCIDENT, NON?

4

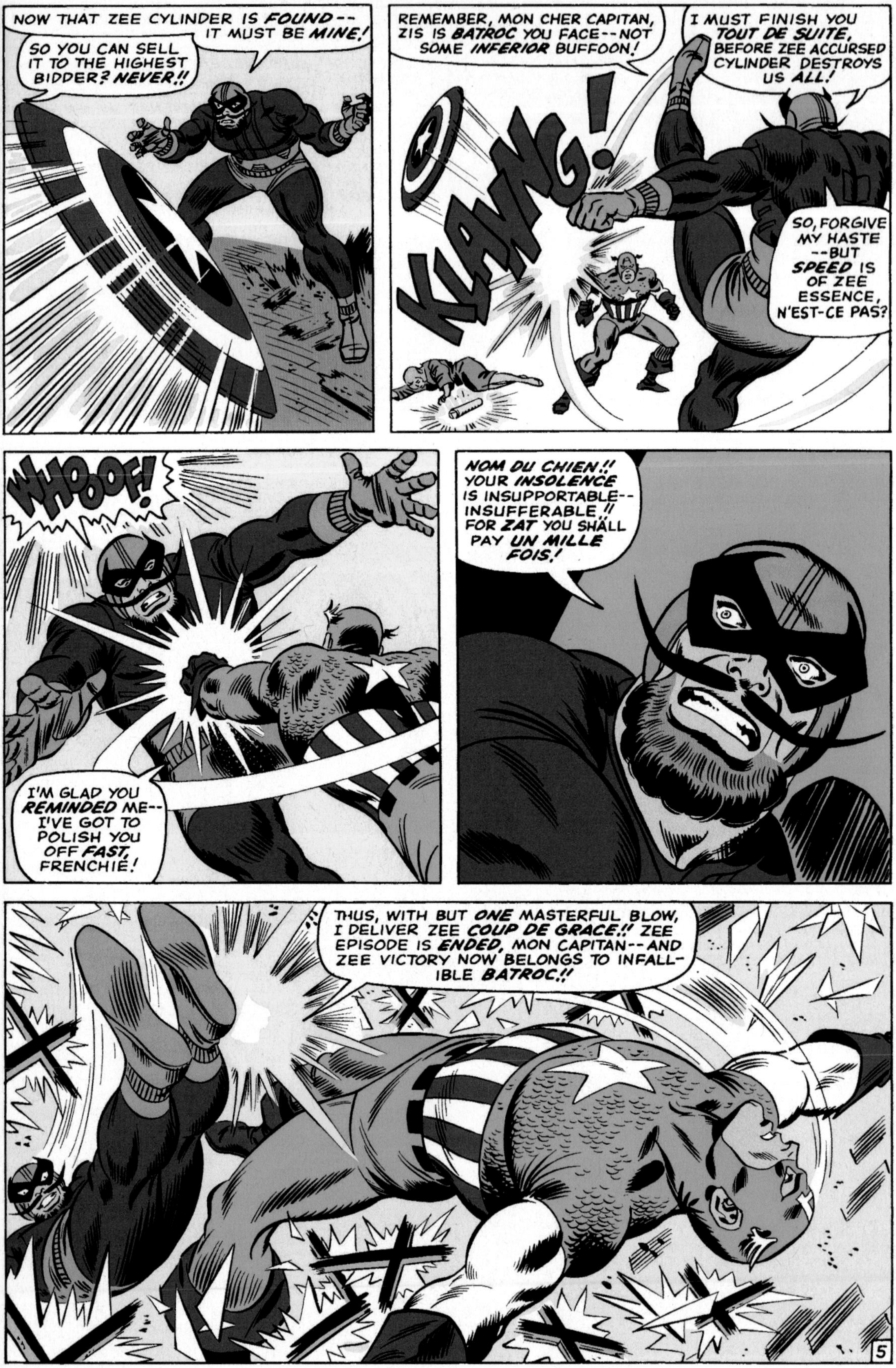
NOW THAT ZEE CYLINDER IS FOUND-- IT MUST BE MINE!
SO YOU CAN SELL IT TO THE HIGHEST BIDDER? NEVER!!
REMEMBER, MON CHER CAPITAN, ZIS IS BATROC YOU FACE--NOT SOME INFERIOR BUFFOON!
I MUST FINISH YOU TOUT DE SUITE, BEFORE ZEE ACCURSED CYLINDER DESTROYS US ALL!
KLANG!
SO, FORGIVE MY HASTE --BUT SPEED IS OF ZEE ESSENCE, N'EST-CE PAS?
WHOOOF!
I'M GLAD YOU REMINDED ME-- I'VE GOT TO POLISH YOU OFF FAST, FRENCHIE!
NOM DU CHIEN!! YOUR INSOLENCE IS INSUPPORTABLE-- INSUFFERABLE!! FOR ZAT YOU SHALL PAY UN MILLE FOIS!
THUS, WITH BUT ONE MASTERFUL BLOW, I DELIVER ZEE COUP DE GRACE!! ZEE EPISODE IS ENDED, MON CAPITAN--AND ZEE VICTORY NOW BELONGS TO INFALLIBLE BATROC!!
5

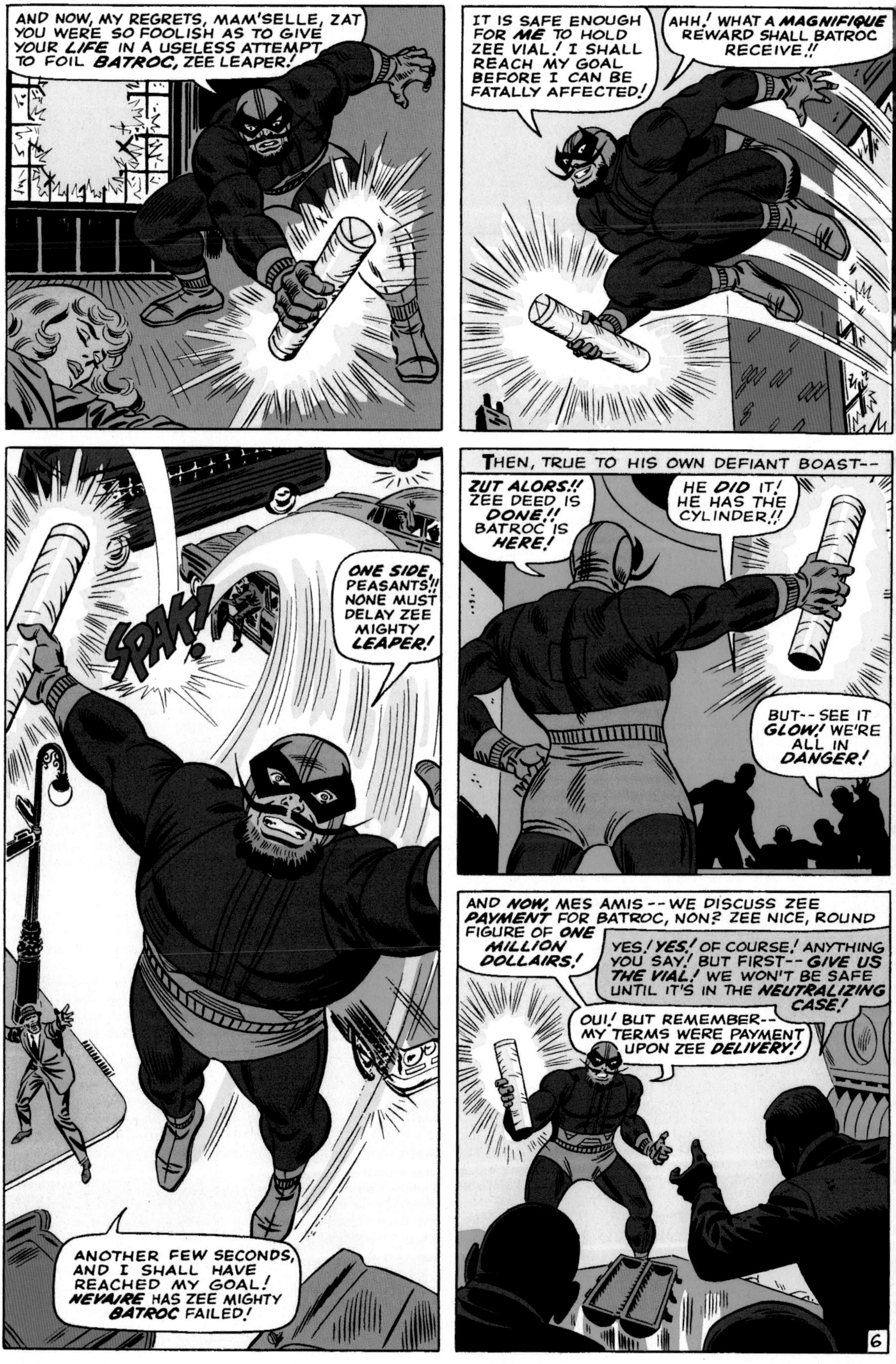
AND NOW, MY REGRETS, MAM'SELLE, ZAT YOU WERE SO FOOLISH AS TO GIVE YOUR LIFE IN A USELESS ATTEMPT TO FOIL BATROC, ZEE LEAPER!
IT IS SAFE ENOUGH FOR ME TO HOLD ZEE VIAL! I SHALL REACH MY GOAL BEFORE I CAN BE FATALLY AFFECTED!
AHH! WHAT A MAGNIFIQUE REWARD SHALL BATROC RECEIVE!!
SPAK!
ONE SIDE, PEASANTS!! NONE MUST DELAY ZEE MIGHTY LEAPER!
ANOTHER FEW SECONDS, AND I SHALL HAVE REACHED MY GOAL! NEVAIRE HAS ZEE MIGHTY BATROC FAILED!
THEN, TRUE TO HIS OWN DEFIANT BOAST--
ZUT ALORS!! ZEE DEED IS DONE!! BATROC IS HERE!
HE DID IT! HE HAS THE CYLINDER!!
BUT--SEE IT GLOW! WE'RE ALL IN DANGER!
AND NOW, MES AMIS--WE DISCUSS ZEE PAYMENT FOR BATROC, NON? ZEE NICE, ROUND FIGURE OF ONE MILLION DOLLAIRS!
YES! YES! OF COURSE! ANYTHING YOU SAY! BUT FIRST--GIVE US THE VIAL! WE WON'T BE SAFE UNTIL IT'S IN THE NEUTRALIZING CASE!
OUI! BUT REMEMBER--MY TERMS WERE PAYMENT UPON ZEE DELIVERY!
6

THEN, IN A MATTER OF SECONDS, THE MISSION REACHES ITS FIENDISH FRUITION--!

YOU HAVE SERVED US *WELL*, BATROC! WITH *INFERNO 42* IN OUR POSSESSION, NOTHING CAN STOP US FROM GAINING MASTERY OF ALL *MANKIND!*

AND, WE SHALL NOT FORGET YOU IN OUR HOUR OF *TRIUMPH!*

I CARE NOT FOR YOUR REMEMBRANCE --NOR FOR YOUR FLOWERY PHRASES, MES AMIS!

BATROC NOW CLAIMS HIS *PAYMENT*--AND ZEE *PATIENCE* OF ZEE MIGHTY LEAPER GROWS *SHORTER* WITH EACH PASSING MOMENT!

THOK!

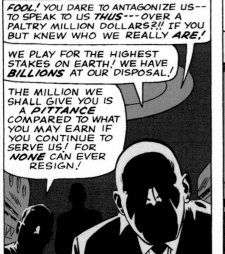

FOOL! YOU DARE TO ANTAGONIZE US-- TO SPEAK TO US *THUS*---OVER A PALTRY MILLION DOLLARS?!! IF YOU BUT KNEW WHO WE REALLY *ARE!*

WE PLAY FOR THE HIGHEST STAKES ON EARTH! WE HAVE *BILLIONS* AT OUR DISPOSAL!

THE MILLION WE SHALL GIVE YOU IS A *PITTANCE* COMPARED TO WHAT YOU MAY EARN IF YOU CONTINUE TO SERVE US! FOR *NONE* CAN EVER RESIGN!

DON'T BOTHER *ANSWERING*, BATROC! IT'S AN *ACADEMIC* POINT, ANYWAY! YOU'RE NOT GONNA BE ABLE TO *SPEND* ANY OF THAT PAYMENT, NO MATTER WHAT! *I'LL* SEE TO THAT!

AND NOW, GENTLEMEN-- I'LL TAKE THAT CYLINDER, IF YOU PLEASE! OR, EVEN IF YOU *DON'T!*

CAPTAIN AMERICA!! BUT-- IT IS *IMPOSSIBLE!!* I CRUSHED HIM LIKE A *BUG!*

BATROC! YOU BLUNDERING *FOOL!* AND YOU CALL YOURSELF *INFALLIBLE!*

DON'T BE TOO HARD ON THE LEAPER! HE DESERVES AN "A" FOR EFFORT! HE DIDN'T GUESS THAT I WAS PLAYING POSSUM, SO HE'D LEAD ME BACK TO *YOU!*

DON'T JUST *STAND* THERE, YOU FRENCH FEATHERBRAIN!! IF YOU WANT THAT MILLION, THIS IS WHERE YOU'LL *EARN* IT! *CAPTAIN AMERICA MUST DIE!*

MAIS CERTAINMENT!! HE HAS BECOME TOO MUCH ZEE *NUISANCE*, ZAT ONE! NO ONE MAKES ZEE FOOL OF *BATROC*, AND LIVES TO BOAST OF IT!

7

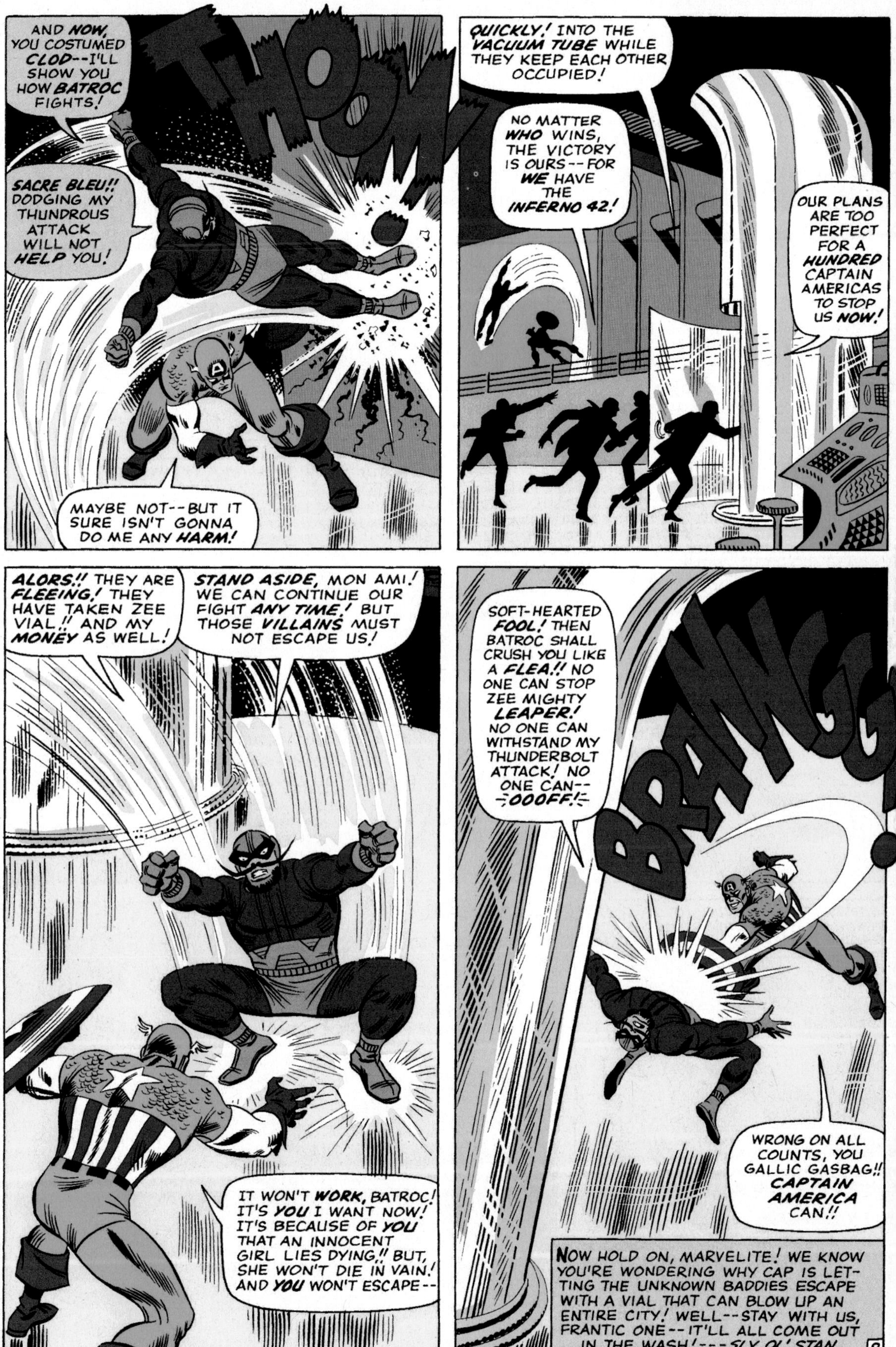
AND NOW, YOU COSTUMED CLOD--I'LL SHOW YOU HOW BATROC FIGHTS!
THOOM
SACRE BLEU!! DODGING MY THUNDROUS ATTACK WILL NOT HELP YOU!
MAYBE NOT--BUT IT SURE ISN'T GONNA DO ME ANY HARM!
QUICKLY! INTO THE VACUUM TUBE WHILE THEY KEEP EACH OTHER OCCUPIED!
NO MATTER WHO WINS, THE VICTORY IS OURS--FOR WE HAVE THE INFERNO 42!
OUR PLANS ARE TOO PERFECT FOR A HUNDRED CAPTAIN AMERICAS TO STOP US NOW!
ALORS!! THEY ARE FLEEING! THEY HAVE TAKEN ZEE VIAL!! AND MY MONEY AS WELL!
STAND ASIDE, MON AMI! WE CAN CONTINUE OUR FIGHT ANY TIME! BUT THOSE VILLAINS MUST NOT ESCAPE US!
IT WON'T WORK, BATROC! IT'S YOU I WANT NOW! IT'S BECAUSE OF YOU THAT AN INNOCENT GIRL LIES DYING!! BUT, SHE WON'T DIE IN VAIN! AND YOU WON'T ESCAPE--
SOFT-HEARTED FOOL! THEN BATROC SHALL CRUSH YOU LIKE A FLEA!! NO ONE CAN STOP ZEE MIGHTY LEAPER! NO ONE CAN WITHSTAND MY THUNDERBOLT ATTACK! NO ONE CAN-- OOOFF!
BRANGG!
WRONG ON ALL COUNTS, YOU GALLIC GASBAG!! CAPTAIN AMERICA CAN!!
NOW HOLD ON, MARVELITE! WE KNOW YOU'RE WONDERING WHY CAP IS LETTING THE UNKNOWN BADDIES ESCAPE WITH A VIAL THAT CAN BLOW UP AN ENTIRE CITY! WELL--STAY WITH US, FRANTIC ONE--IT'LL ALL COME OUT IN THE WASH!---SLY OL' STAN.
8

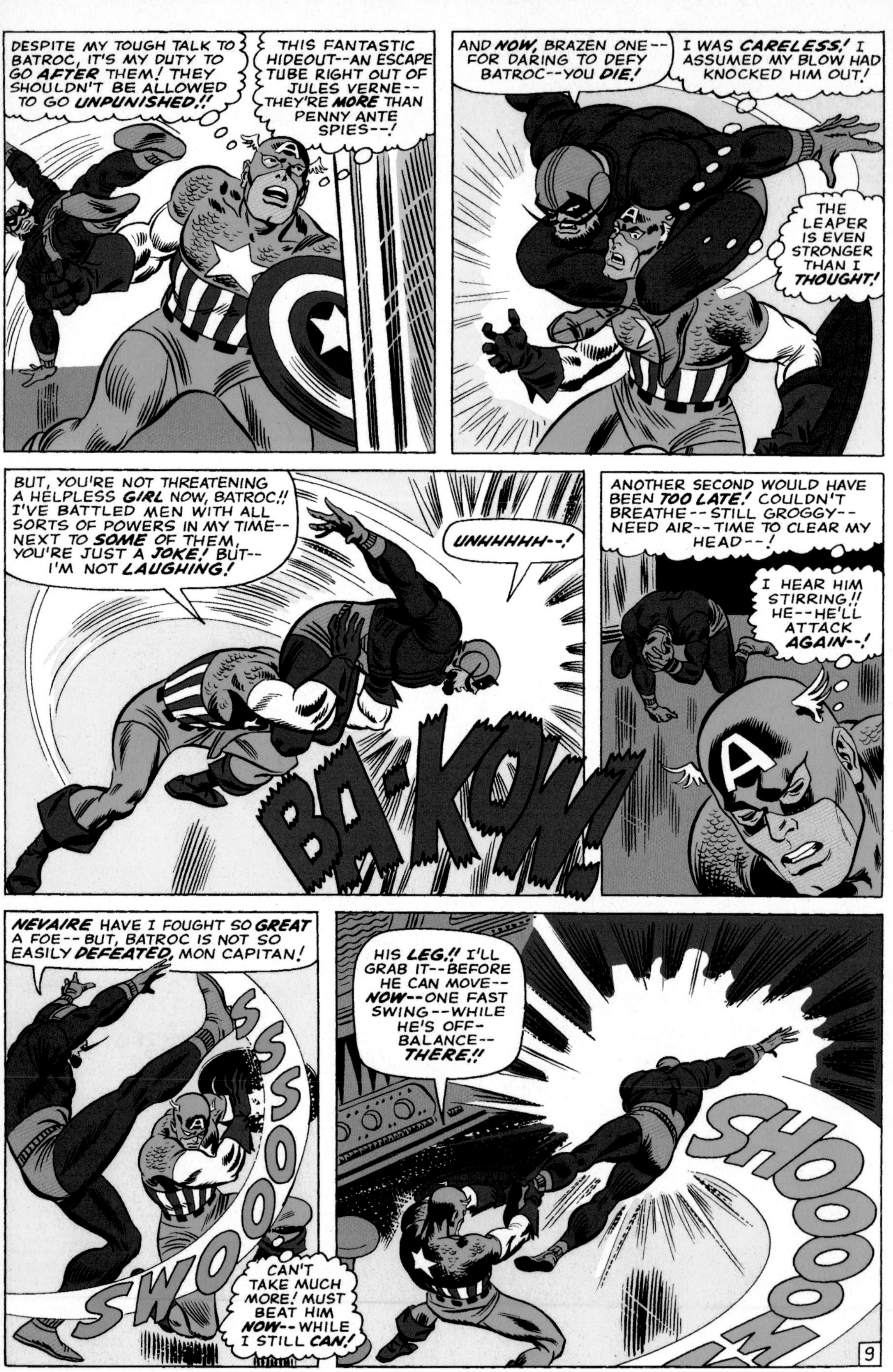
DESPITE MY TOUGH TALK TO BATROC, IT'S MY DUTY TO GO AFTER THEM! THEY SHOULDN'T BE ALLOWED TO GO UNPUNISHED!!
THIS FANTASTIC HIDEOUT--AN ESCAPE TUBE RIGHT OUT OF JULES VERNE--THEY'RE MORE THAN PENNY ANTE SPIES--!
AND NOW, BRAZEN ONE--FOR DARING TO DEFY BATROC--YOU DIE!
I WAS CARELESS! I ASSUMED MY BLOW HAD KNOCKED HIM OUT!
THE LEAPER IS EVEN STRONGER THAN I THOUGHT!
BUT, YOU'RE NOT THREATENING A HELPLESS GIRL NOW, BATROC!! I'VE BATTLED MEN WITH ALL SORTS OF POWERS IN MY TIME--NEXT TO SOME OF THEM, YOU'RE JUST A JOKE! BUT--I'M NOT LAUGHING!
UNHHHHH--!
BA-KOW
ANOTHER SECOND WOULD HAVE BEEN TOO LATE! COULDN'T BREATHE--STILL GROGGY--NEED AIR--TIME TO CLEAR MY HEAD--!
I HEAR HIM STIRRING!! HE--HE'LL ATTACK AGAIN--!
NEVAIRE HAVE I FOUGHT SO GREAT A FOE--BUT, BATROC IS NOT SO EASILY DEFEATED, MON CAPITAN!
SWOOOSSS
CAN'T TAKE MUCH MORE! MUST BEAT HIM NOW--WHILE I STILL CAN!
HIS LEG!! I'LL GRAB IT--BEFORE HE CAN MOVE--NOW--ONE FAST SWING--WHILE HE'S OFF-BALANCE--THERE!!
SHOOOOOM

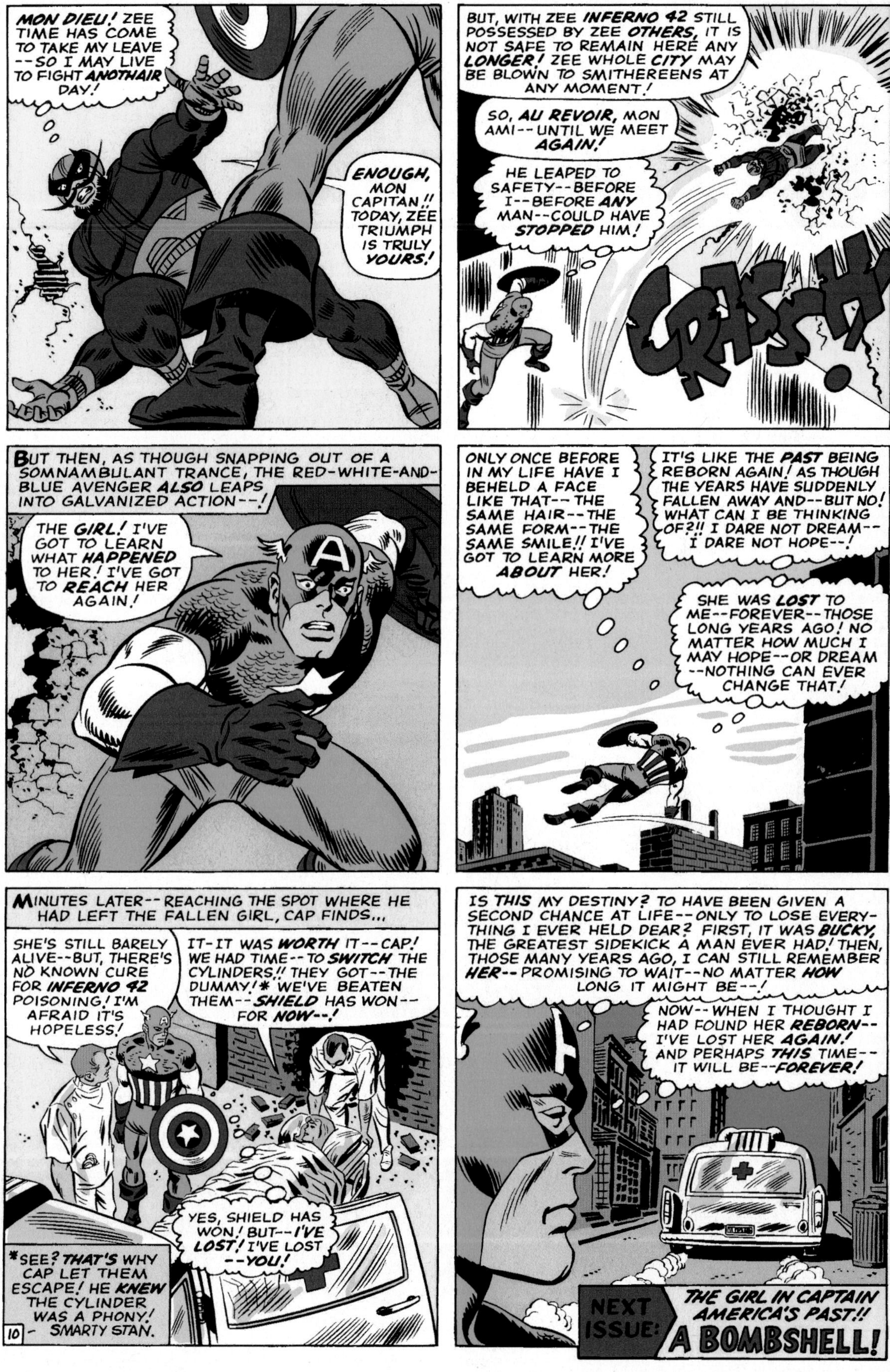

MON DIEU! ZEE TIME HAS COME TO TAKE MY LEAVE --SO I MAY LIVE TO FIGHT ANOTHAIR DAY!
ENOUGH, MON CAPITAN!! TODAY, ZEE TRIUMPH IS TRULY YOURS!
BUT, WITH ZEE INFERNO 42 STILL POSSESSED BY ZEE OTHERS, IT IS NOT SAFE TO REMAIN HERE ANY LONGER! ZEE WHOLE CITY MAY BE BLOWN TO SMITHEREENS AT ANY MOMENT!
SO, AU REVOIR, MON AMI--UNTIL WE MEET AGAIN!
HE LEAPED TO SAFETY--BEFORE I--BEFORE ANY MAN--COULD HAVE STOPPED HIM!
CRASSH!
BUT THEN, AS THOUGH SNAPPING OUT OF A SOMNAMBULANT TRANCE, THE RED-WHITE-AND-BLUE AVENGER ALSO LEAPS INTO GALVANIZED ACTION--!
THE GIRL! I'VE GOT TO LEARN WHAT HAPPENED TO HER! I'VE GOT TO REACH HER AGAIN!
ONLY ONCE BEFORE IN MY LIFE HAVE I BEHELD A FACE LIKE THAT--THE SAME HAIR--THE SAME FORM--THE SAME SMILE!! I'VE GOT TO LEARN MORE ABOUT HER!
IT'S LIKE THE PAST BEING REBORN AGAIN! AS THOUGH THE YEARS HAVE SUDDENLY FALLEN AWAY AND--BUT NO! WHAT CAN I BE THINKING OF?!! I DARE NOT DREAM--I DARE NOT HOPE--!
SHE WAS LOST TO ME--FOREVER--THOSE LONG YEARS AGO! NO MATTER HOW MUCH I MAY HOPE--OR DREAM--NOTHING CAN EVER CHANGE THAT!
MINUTES LATER--REACHING THE SPOT WHERE HE HAD LEFT THE FALLEN GIRL, CAP FINDS...
SHE'S STILL BARELY ALIVE--BUT, THERE'S NO KNOWN CURE FOR INFERNO 42 POISONING! I'M AFRAID IT'S HOPELESS!
IT-IT WAS WORTH IT--CAP! WE HAD TIME--TO SWITCH THE CYLINDERS!! THEY GOT--THE DUMMY!* WE'VE BEATEN THEM--SHIELD HAS WON--FOR NOW--!
YES, SHIELD HAS WON! BUT--I'VE LOST! I'VE LOST--YOU!
*SEE? THAT'S WHY CAP LET THEM ESCAPE! HE KNEW THE CYLINDER WAS A PHONY! - SMARTY STAN.
10
IS THIS MY DESTINY? TO HAVE BEEN GIVEN A SECOND CHANCE AT LIFE--ONLY TO LOSE EVERYTHING I EVER HELD DEAR? FIRST, IT WAS BUCKY, THE GREATEST SIDEKICK A MAN EVER HAD! THEN, THOSE MANY YEARS AGO, I CAN STILL REMEMBER HER--PROMISING TO WAIT--NO MATTER HOW LONG IT MIGHT BE--!
NOW--WHEN I THOUGHT I HAD FOUND HER REBORN--I'VE LOST HER AGAIN! AND PERHAPS THIS TIME--IT WILL BE--FOREVER!
NEXT ISSUE: THE GIRL IN CAPTAIN AMERICA'S PAST!! A BOMBSHELL!

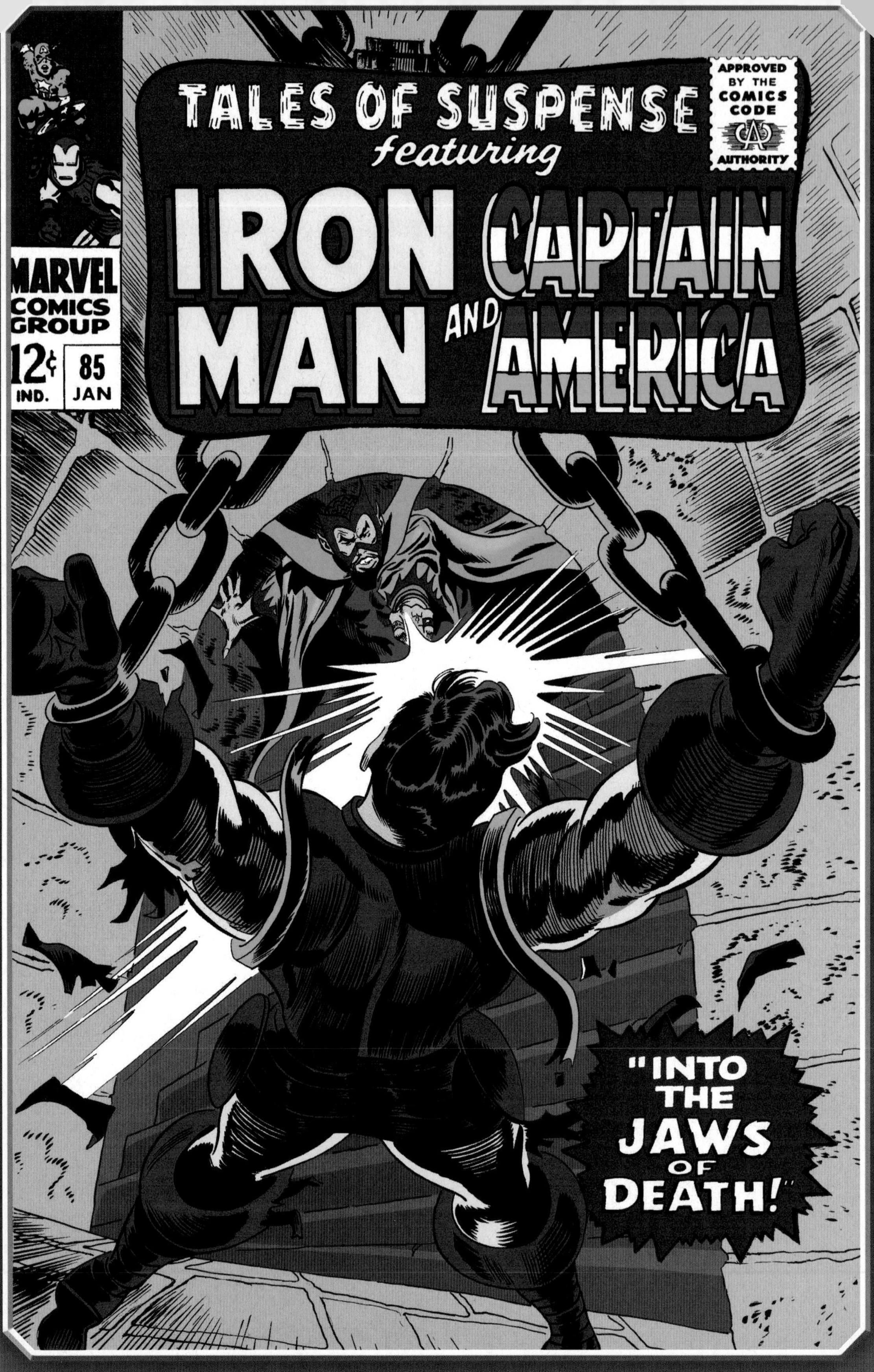
TALES OF SUSPENSE
featuring
IRON MAN AND CAPTAIN AMERICA
APPROVED BY THE COMICS CODE AUTHORITY
MARVEL COMICS GROUP
12¢ IND.
85 JAN
"INTO THE JAWS OF DEATH!"

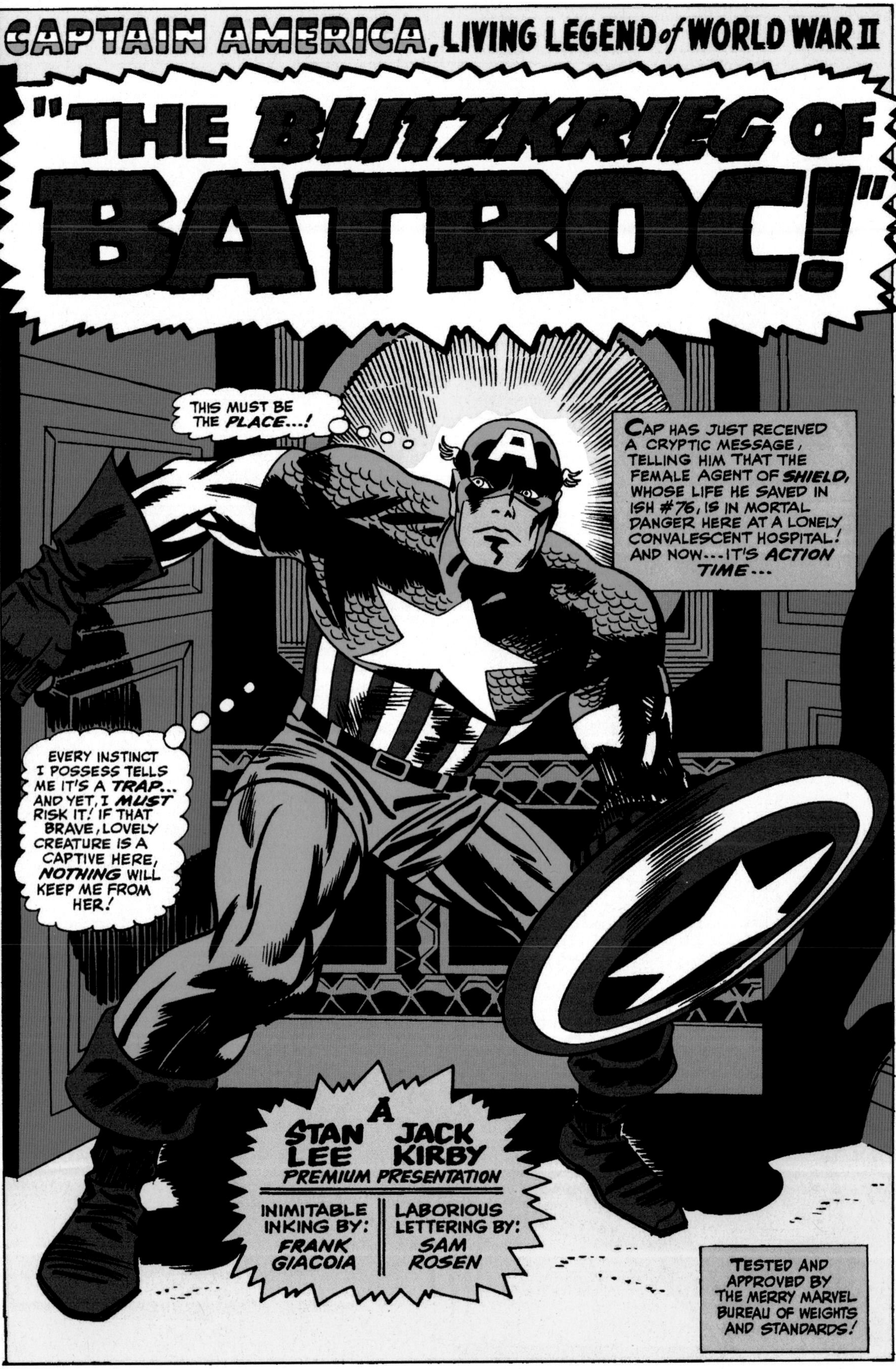
CAPTAIN AMERICA, LIVING LEGEND of WORLD WAR II
"THE BLITZKRIEG OF BATROC!"
THIS MUST BE THE PLACE...!
CAP HAS JUST RECEIVED A CRYPTIC MESSAGE, TELLING HIM THAT THE FEMALE AGENT OF SHIELD, WHOSE LIFE HE SAVED IN ISH #76, IS IN MORTAL DANGER HERE AT A LONELY CONVALESCENT HOSPITAL! AND NOW... IT'S ACTION TIME...
EVERY INSTINCT I POSSESS TELLS ME IT'S A TRAP... AND YET, I MUST RISK IT! IF THAT BRAVE, LOVELY CREATURE IS A CAPTIVE HERE, NOTHING WILL KEEP ME FROM HER!
A STAN LEE JACK KIRBY PREMIUM PRESENTATION
INIMITABLE INKING BY: FRANK GIACOIA
LABORIOUS LETTERING BY: SAM ROSEN
TESTED AND APPROVED BY THE MERRY MARVEL BUREAU OF WEIGHTS AND STANDARDS!

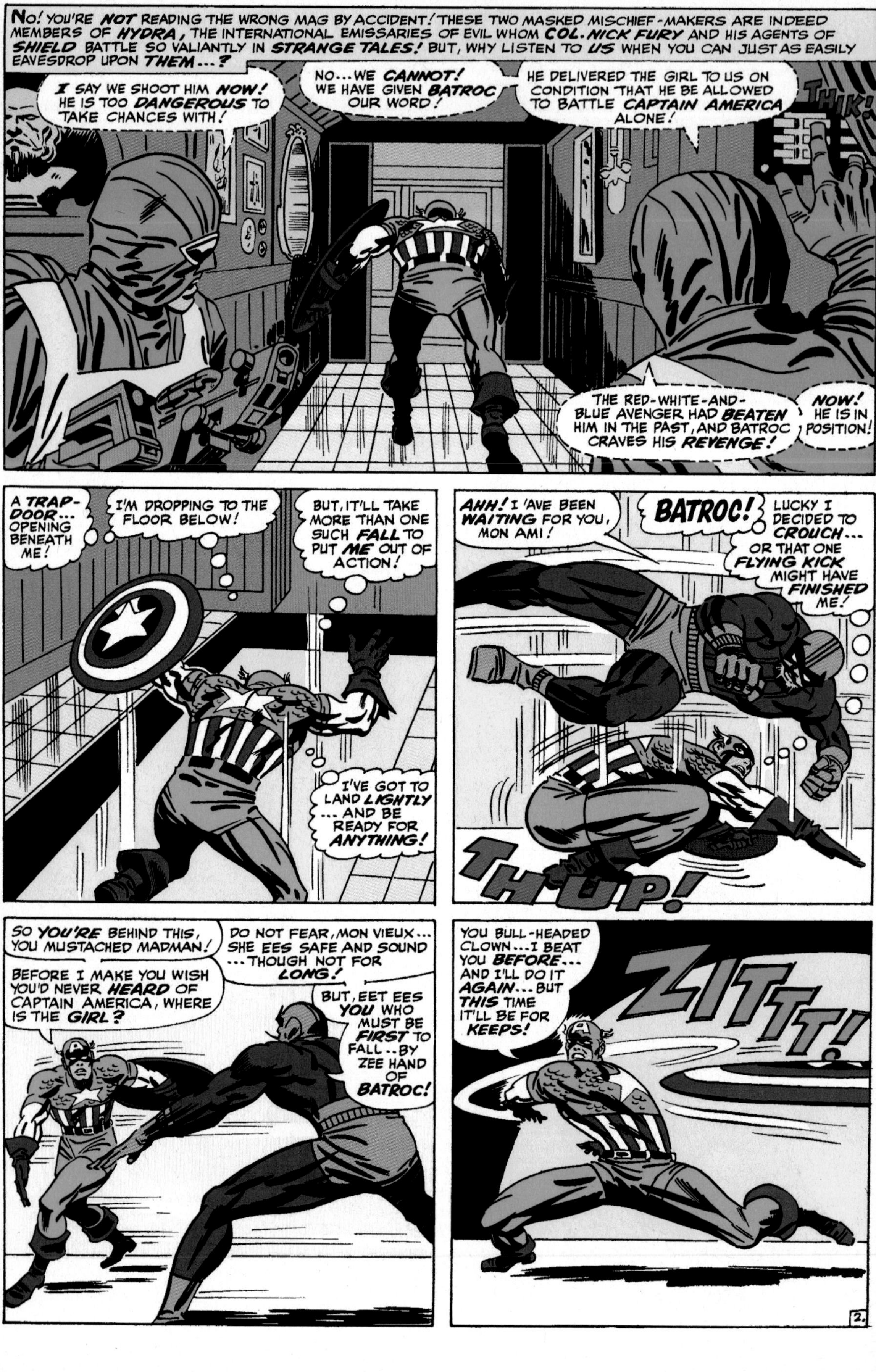
No! YOU'RE NOT READING THE WRONG MAG BY ACCIDENT! THESE TWO MASKED MISCHIEF-MAKERS ARE INDEED MEMBERS OF HYDRA, THE INTERNATIONAL EMISSARIES OF EVIL WHOM COL. NICK FURY AND HIS AGENTS OF SHIELD BATTLE SO VALIANTLY IN STRANGE TALES! BUT, WHY LISTEN TO US WHEN YOU CAN JUST AS EASILY EAVESDROP UPON THEM...?
I SAY WE SHOOT HIM NOW! HE IS TOO DANGEROUS TO TAKE CHANCES WITH!
NO...WE CANNOT! WE HAVE GIVEN BATROC OUR WORD!
HE DELIVERED THE GIRL TO US ON CONDITION THAT HE BE ALLOWED TO BATTLE CAPTAIN AMERICA ALONE!
THIK!
THE RED-WHITE-AND-BLUE AVENGER HAD BEATEN HIM IN THE PAST, AND BATROC CRAVES HIS REVENGE!
NOW! HE IS IN POSITION!
A TRAP-DOOR... OPENING BENEATH ME!
I'M DROPPING TO THE FLOOR BELOW!
BUT, IT'LL TAKE MORE THAN ONE SUCH FALL TO PUT ME OUT OF ACTION!
I'VE GOT TO LAND LIGHTLY ...AND BE READY FOR ANYTHING!
AHH! I 'AVE BEEN WAITING FOR YOU, MON AMI!
BATROC!
LUCKY I DECIDED TO CROUCH... OR THAT ONE FLYING KICK MIGHT HAVE FINISHED ME!
THUP!
SO YOU'RE BEHIND THIS, YOU MUSTACHED MADMAN!
BEFORE I MAKE YOU WISH YOU'D NEVER HEARD OF CAPTAIN AMERICA, WHERE IS THE GIRL?
DO NOT FEAR, MON VIEUX... SHE EES SAFE AND SOUND ...THOUGH NOT FOR LONG!
BUT, EET EES YOU WHO MUST BE FIRST TO FALL..BY ZEE HAND OF BATROC!
YOU BULL-HEADED CLOWN...I BEAT YOU BEFORE... AND I'LL DO IT AGAIN...BUT THIS TIME IT'LL BE FOR KEEPS!
ZITTTT!
2.

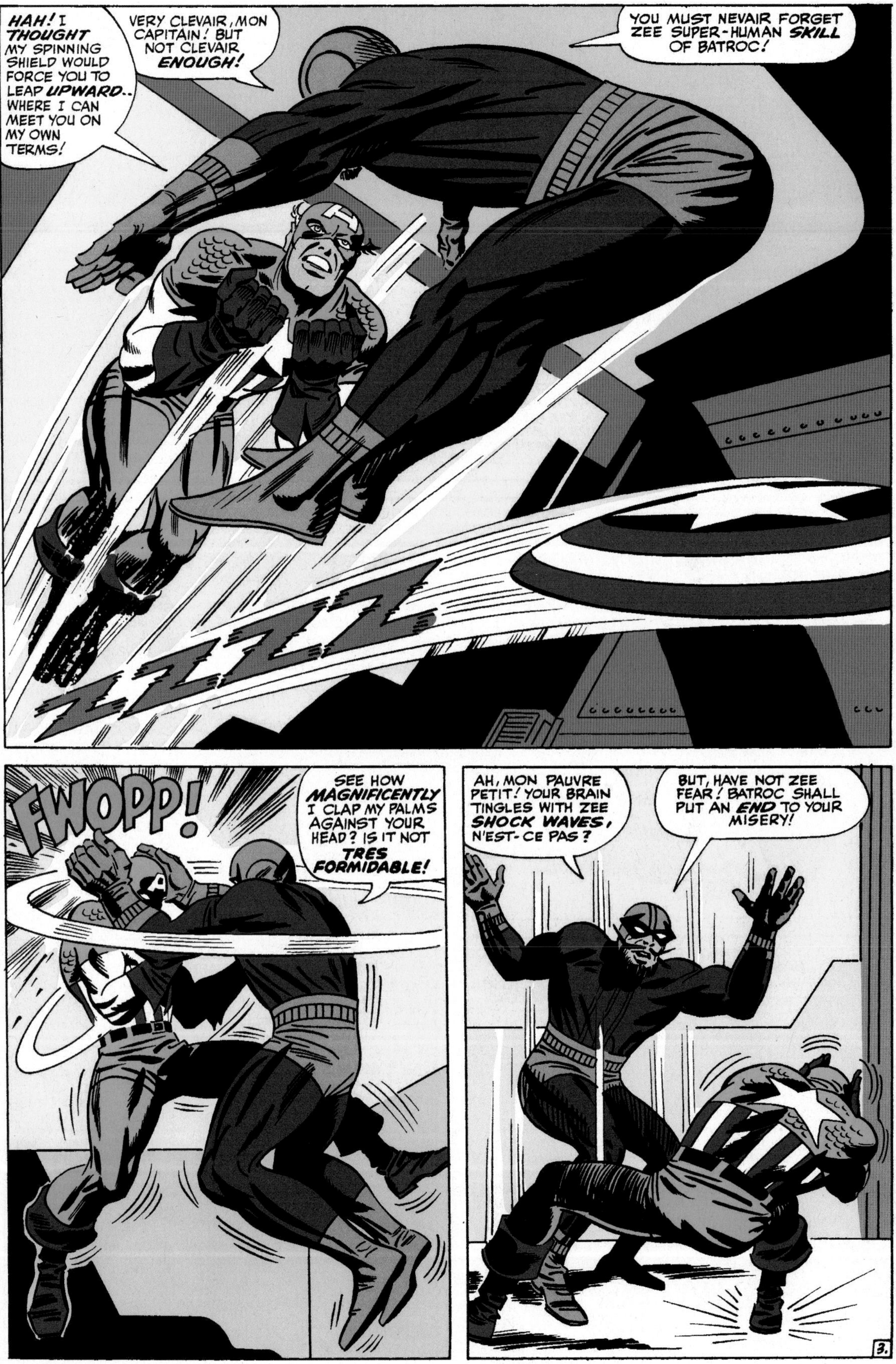
HAH! I THOUGHT MY SPINNING SHIELD WOULD FORCE YOU TO LEAP UPWARD.. WHERE I CAN MEET YOU ON MY OWN TERMS!
VERY CLEVAIR, MON CAPITAIN! BUT NOT CLEVAIR ENOUGH!
YOU MUST NEVAIR FORGET ZEE SUPER-HUMAN SKILL OF BATROC!
ZZZZ
FWOPP!
SEE HOW MAGNIFICENTLY I CLAP MY PALMS AGAINST YOUR HEAD? IS IT NOT TRES FORMIDABLE!
AH, MON PAUVRE PETIT! YOUR BRAIN TINGLES WITH ZEE SHOCK WAVES, N'EST-CE PAS?
BUT, HAVE NOT ZEE FEAR! BATROC SHALL PUT AN END TO YOUR MISERY!
3.

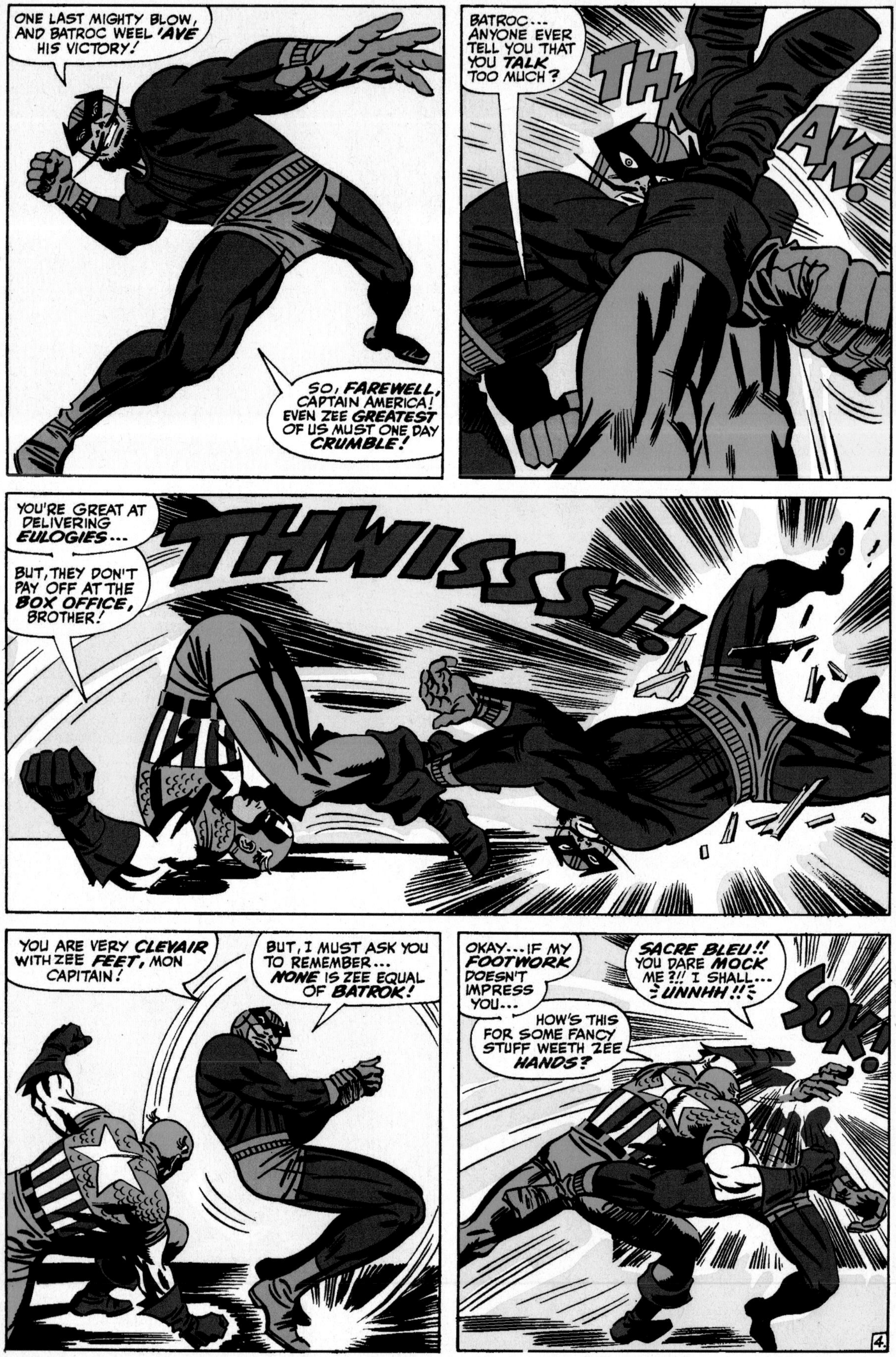
ONE LAST MIGHTY BLOW, AND BATROC WEEL 'AVE HIS VICTORY!
SO, FAREWELL, CAPTAIN AMERICA! EVEN ZEE GREATEST OF US MUST ONE DAY CRUMBLE!
BATROC... ANYONE EVER TELL YOU THAT YOU TALK TOO MUCH?
THWAK!
YOU'RE GREAT AT DELIVERING EULOGIES...
BUT, THEY DON'T PAY OFF AT THE BOX OFFICE, BROTHER!
THWISSST!
YOU ARE VERY CLEVAIR WITH ZEE FEET, MON CAPITAIN!
BUT, I MUST ASK YOU TO REMEMBER... NONE IS ZEE EQUAL OF BATROK!
OKAY... IF MY FOOTWORK DOESN'T IMPRESS YOU...
HOW'S THIS FOR SOME FANCY STUFF WEETH ZEE HANDS?
SACRE BLEU!! YOU DARE MOCK ME?!! I SHALL... UNNHH!!
SOK!
4.

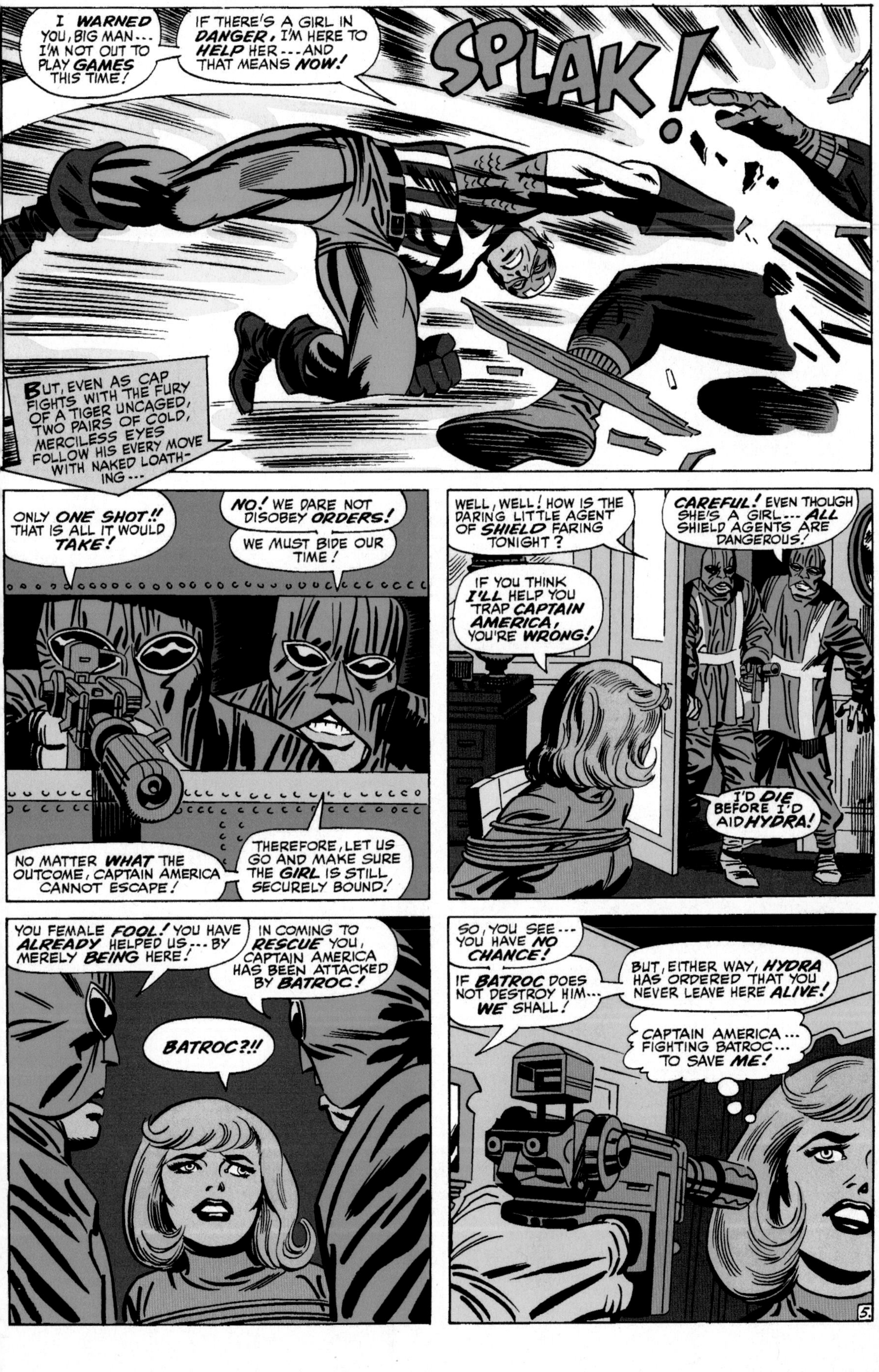
I WARNED YOU, BIG MAN... I'M NOT OUT TO PLAY GAMES THIS TIME!
IF THERE'S A GIRL IN DANGER, I'M HERE TO HELP HER---AND THAT MEANS NOW!
SPLAK!
BUT, EVEN AS CAP FIGHTS WITH THE FURY OF A TIGER UNCAGED, TWO PAIRS OF COLD, MERCILESS EYES FOLLOW HIS EVERY MOVE WITH NAKED LOATHING...
ONLY ONE SHOT!! THAT IS ALL IT WOULD TAKE!
NO! WE DARE NOT DISOBEY ORDERS!
WE MUST BIDE OUR TIME!
NO MATTER WHAT THE OUTCOME, CAPTAIN AMERICA CANNOT ESCAPE!
THEREFORE, LET US GO AND MAKE SURE THE GIRL IS STILL SECURELY BOUND!
WELL, WELL! HOW IS THE DARING LITTLE AGENT OF SHIELD FARING TONIGHT?
CAREFUL! EVEN THOUGH SHE'S A GIRL... ALL SHIELD AGENTS ARE DANGEROUS!
IF YOU THINK I'LL HELP YOU TRAP CAPTAIN AMERICA, YOU'RE WRONG!
I'D DIE BEFORE I'D AID HYDRA!
YOU FEMALE FOOL! YOU HAVE ALREADY HELPED US... BY MERELY BEING HERE!
IN COMING TO RESCUE YOU, CAPTAIN AMERICA HAS BEEN ATTACKED BY BATROC!
BATROC?!!
SO, YOU SEE... YOU HAVE NO CHANCE!
IF BATROC DOES NOT DESTROY HIM... WE SHALL!
BUT, EITHER WAY, HYDRA HAS ORDERED THAT YOU NEVER LEAVE HERE ALIVE!
CAPTAIN AMERICA... FIGHTING BATROC... TO SAVE ME!
5.

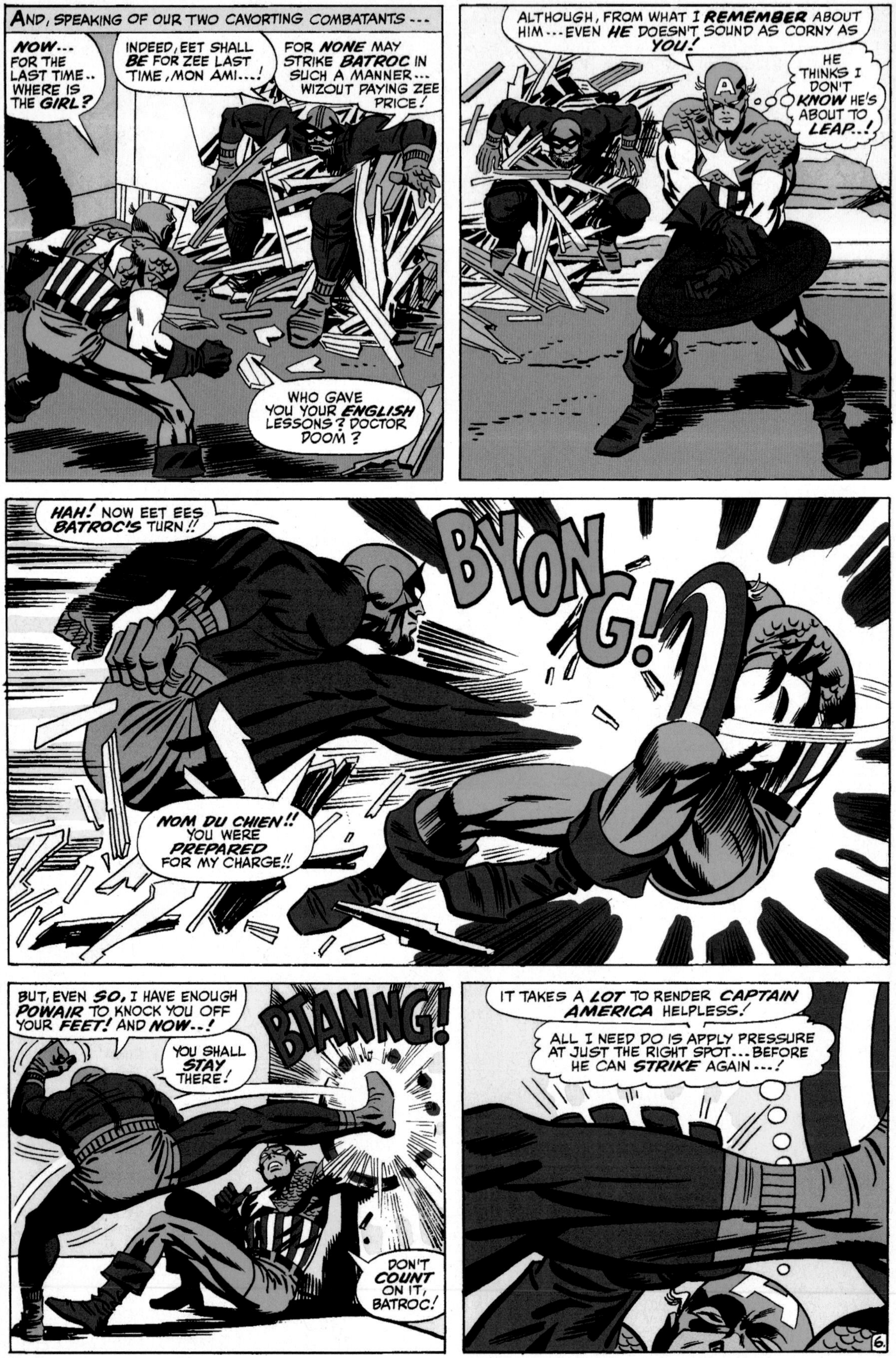
AND, SPEAKING OF OUR TWO CAVORTING COMBATANTS ---
NOW... FOR THE LAST TIME.. WHERE IS THE GIRL?
INDEED, EET SHALL BE FOR ZEE LAST TIME, MON AMI...!
FOR NONE MAY STRIKE BATROC IN SUCH A MANNER... WIZOUT PAYING ZEE PRICE!
WHO GAVE YOU YOUR ENGLISH LESSONS? DOCTOR DOOM?
ALTHOUGH, FROM WHAT I REMEMBER ABOUT HIM --- EVEN HE DOESN'T SOUND AS CORNY AS YOU!
HE THINKS I DON'T KNOW HE'S ABOUT TO LEAP..!
HAH! NOW EET EES BATROC'S TURN!!
BYONG!
NOM DU CHIEN!! YOU WERE PREPARED FOR MY CHARGE!!
BUT, EVEN SO, I HAVE ENOUGH POWAIR TO KNOCK YOU OFF YOUR FEET! AND NOW..!
BTANNG!
YOU SHALL STAY THERE!
DON'T COUNT ON IT, BATROC!
IT TAKES A LOT TO RENDER CAPTAIN AMERICA HELPLESS!
ALL I NEED DO IS APPLY PRESSURE AT JUST THE RIGHT SPOT... BEFORE HE CAN STRIKE AGAIN ---!
6.

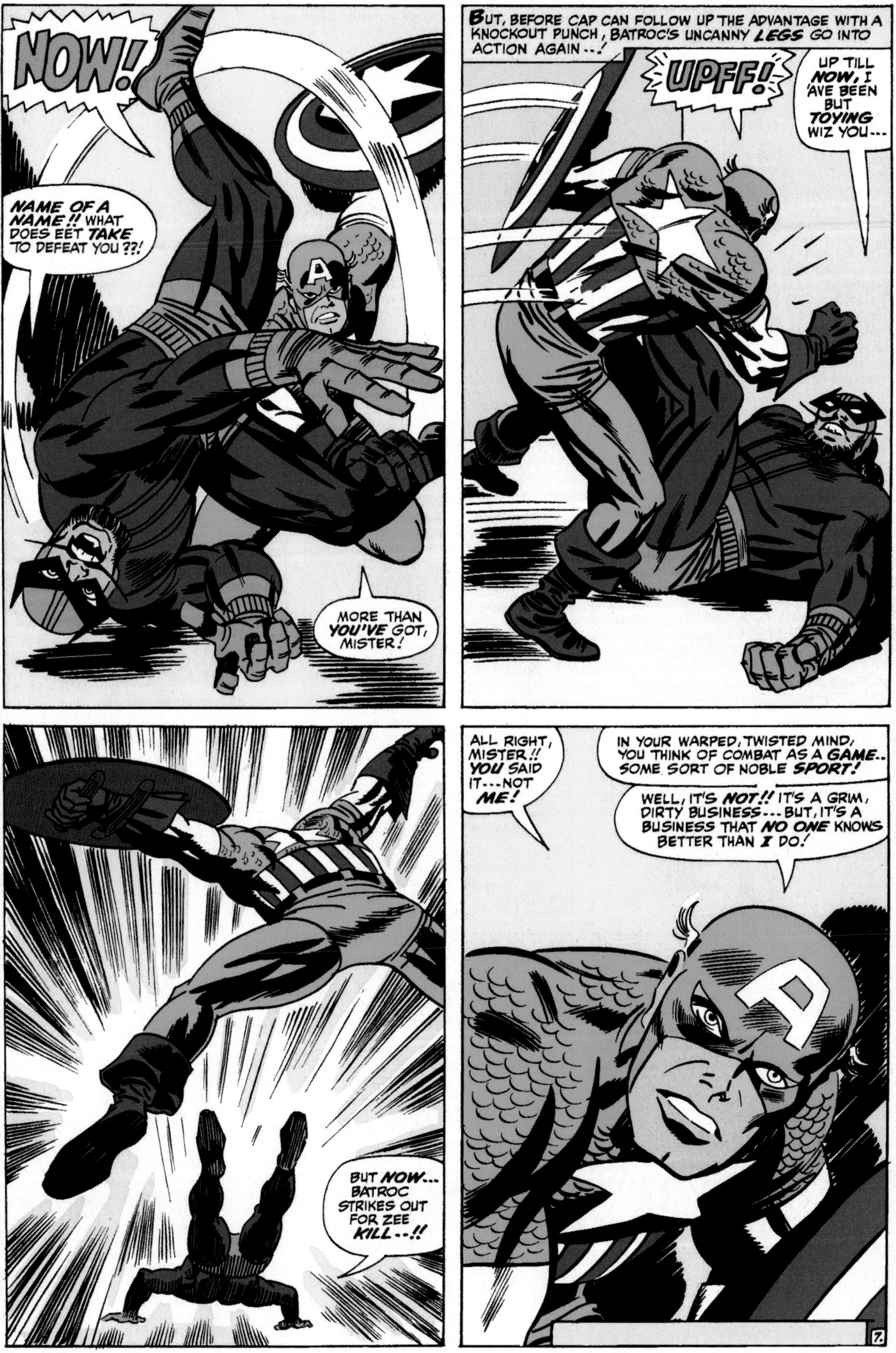
NOW!
NAME OF A NAME!! WHAT DOES EET TAKE TO DEFEAT YOU??!
MORE THAN YOU'VE GOT, MISTER!
BUT, BEFORE CAP CAN FOLLOW UP THE ADVANTAGE WITH A KNOCKOUT PUNCH, BATROC'S UNCANNY LEGS GO INTO ACTION AGAIN--!
UPFF!
UP TILL NOW, I 'AVE BEEN BUT TOYING WIZ YOU---
BUT NOW... BATROC STRIKES OUT FOR ZEE KILL--!!
ALL RIGHT, MISTER!! YOU SAID IT---NOT ME!
IN YOUR WARPED, TWISTED MIND, YOU THINK OF COMBAT AS A GAME.. SOME SORT OF NOBLE SPORT!
WELL, IT'S NOT!! IT'S A GRIM, DIRTY BUSINESS---BUT, IT'S A BUSINESS THAT NO ONE KNOWS BETTER THAN I DO!
7.

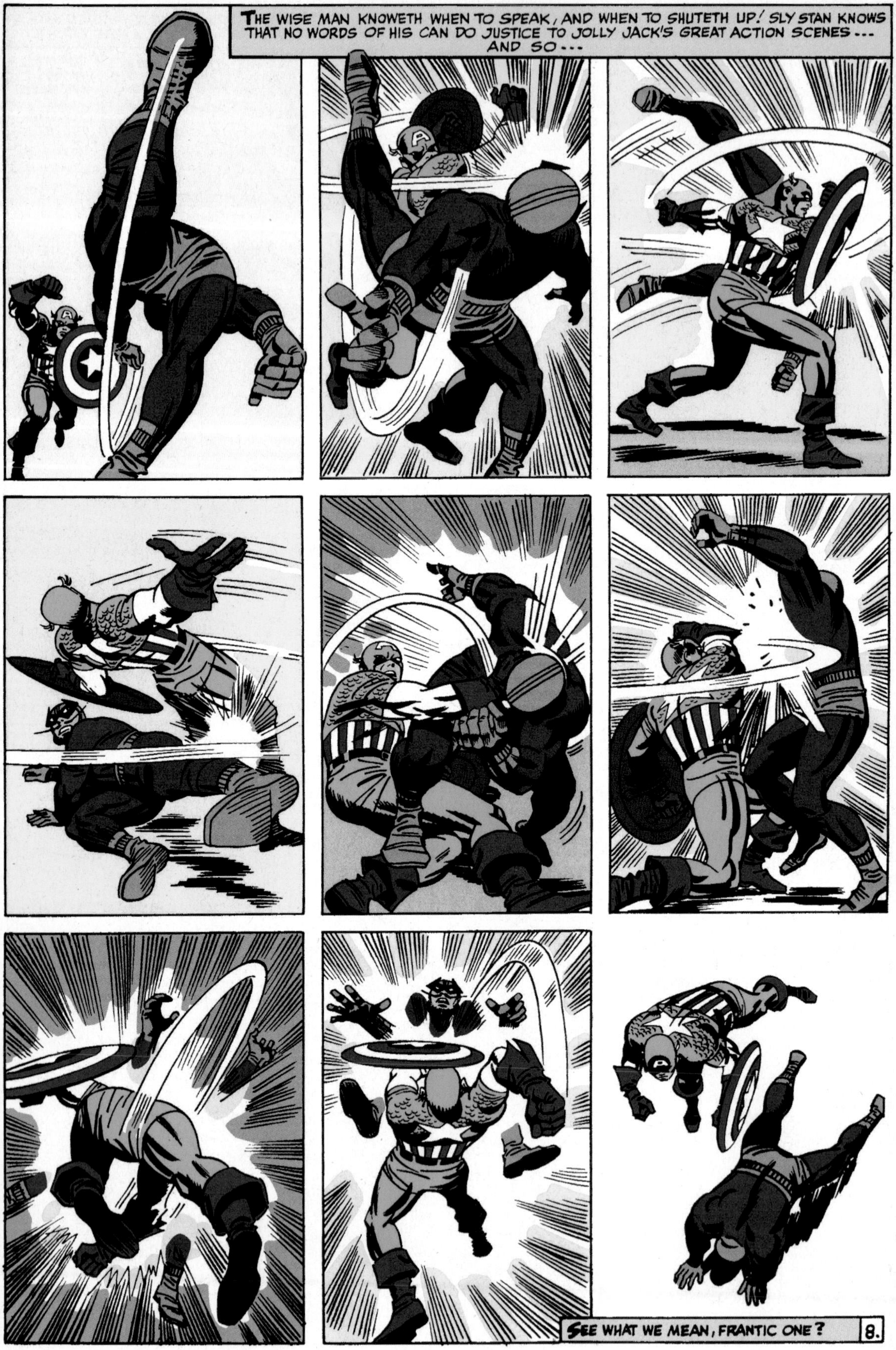
THE WISE MAN KNOWETH WHEN TO SPEAK, AND WHEN TO SHUTETH UP! SLY STAN KNOWS THAT NO WORDS OF HIS CAN DO JUSTICE TO JOLLY JACK'S GREAT ACTION SCENES --- AND SO ---
SEE WHAT WE MEAN, FRANTIC ONE?
8.

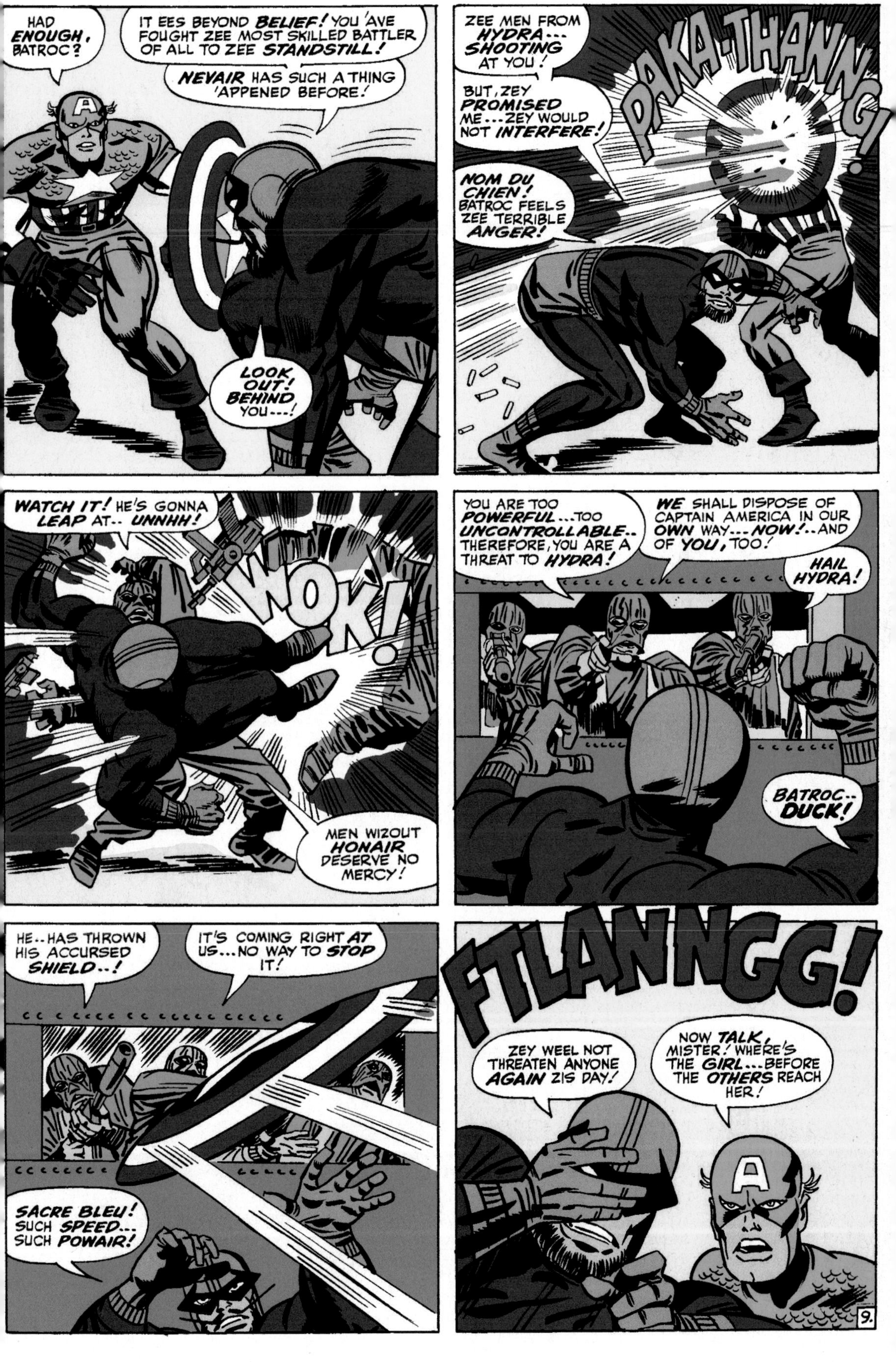

HAD ENOUGH, BATROC?
IT EES BEYOND BELIEF! YOU 'AVE FOUGHT ZEE MOST SKILLED BATTLER OF ALL TO ZEE STANDSTILL!
NEVAIR HAS SUCH A THING 'APPENED BEFORE!
LOOK OUT! BEHIND YOU---!
ZEE MEN FROM HYDRA--- SHOOTING AT YOU!
BUT, ZEY PROMISED ME---ZEY WOULD NOT INTERFERE!
PAKA-THANNG!
NOM DU CHIEN! BATROC FEELS ZEE TERRIBLE ANGER!
WATCH IT! HE'S GONNA LEAP AT-- UNNHH!
WOK!
MEN WIZOUT HONAIR DESERVE NO MERCY!
YOU ARE TOO POWERFUL...TOO UNCONTROLLABLE.. THEREFORE, YOU ARE A THREAT TO HYDRA!
WE SHALL DISPOSE OF CAPTAIN AMERICA IN OUR OWN WAY---NOW!..AND OF YOU, TOO!
HAIL HYDRA!
BATROC.. DUCK!
HE--HAS THROWN HIS ACCURSED SHIELD--!
IT'S COMING RIGHT AT US...NO WAY TO STOP IT!
SACRE BLEU! SUCH SPEED... SUCH POWAIR!
FTLANNGG!
ZEY WEEL NOT THREATEN ANYONE AGAIN ZIS DAY!
NOW TALK, MISTER! WHERE'S THE GIRL...BEFORE THE OTHERS REACH HER!

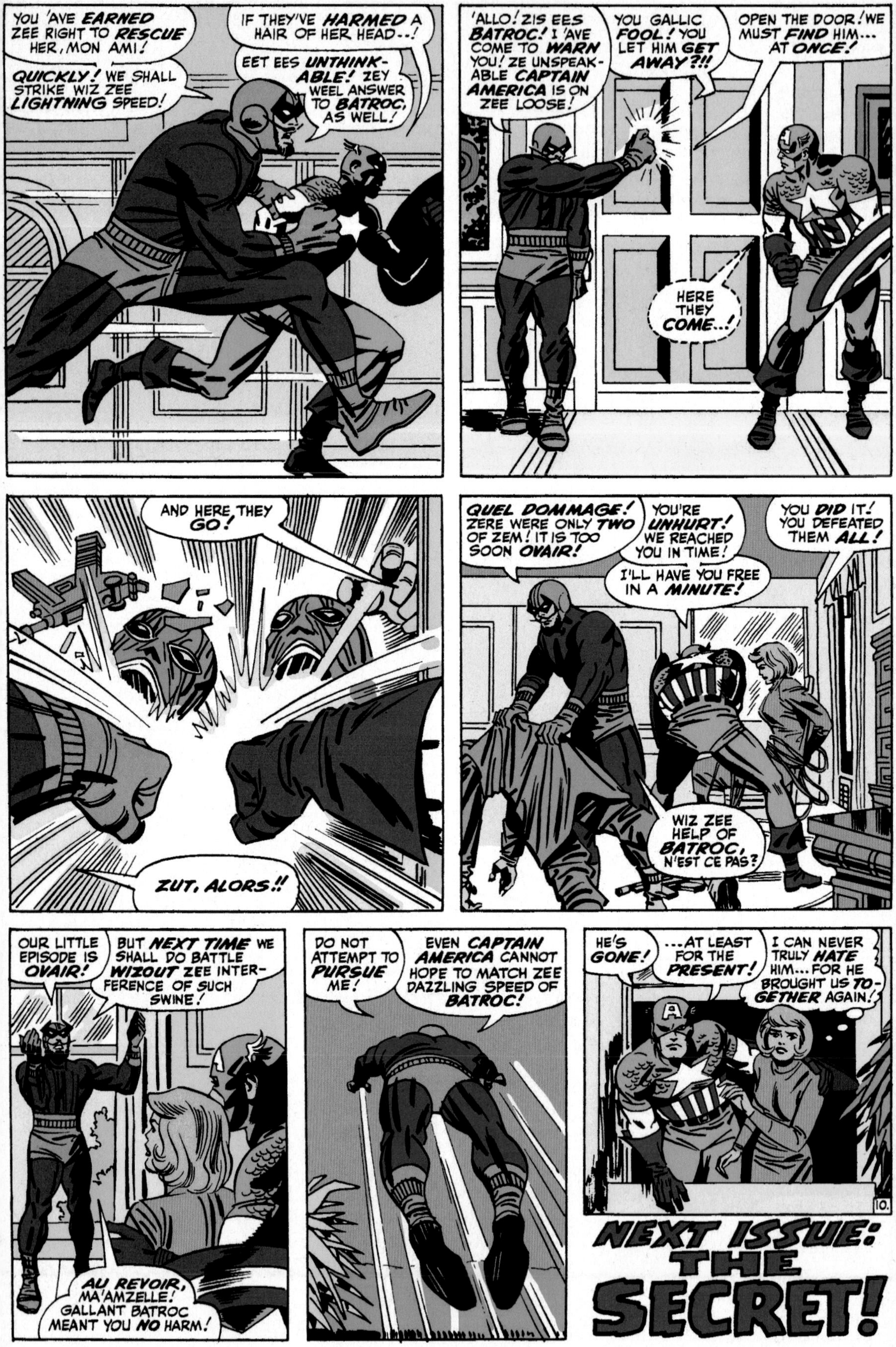
YOU 'AVE EARNED ZEE RIGHT TO RESCUE HER, MON AMI!
QUICKLY! WE SHALL STRIKE WIZ ZEE LIGHTNING SPEED!
IF THEY'VE HARMED A HAIR OF HER HEAD--!
EET EES UNTHINKABLE! ZEY WEEL ANSWER TO BATROC, AS WELL!
'ALLO! ZIS EES BATROC! I 'AVE COME TO WARN YOU! ZE UNSPEAKABLE CAPTAIN AMERICA IS ON ZEE LOOSE!
YOU GALLIC FOOL! YOU LET HIM GET AWAY?!!
OPEN THE DOOR! WE MUST FIND HIM... AT ONCE!
HERE THEY COME..!
AND HERE THEY GO!
ZUT, ALORS!!
QUEL DOMMAGE! ZERE WERE ONLY TWO OF ZEM! IT IS TOO SOON OVAIR!
YOU'RE UNHURT! WE REACHED YOU IN TIME!
I'LL HAVE YOU FREE IN A MINUTE!
YOU DID IT! YOU DEFEATED THEM ALL!
WIZ ZEE HELP OF BATROC, N'EST CE PAS?
OUR LITTLE EPISODE IS OVAIR!
BUT NEXT TIME WE SHALL DO BATTLE WIZOUT ZEE INTERFERENCE OF SUCH SWINE!
AU REVOIR, MA'AMZELLE! GALLANT BATROC MEANT YOU NO HARM!
DO NOT ATTEMPT TO PURSUE ME!
EVEN CAPTAIN AMERICA CANNOT HOPE TO MATCH ZEE DAZZLING SPEED OF BATROC!
HE'S GONE!
...AT LEAST FOR THE PRESENT!
I CAN NEVER TRULY HATE HIM... FOR HE BROUGHT US TOGETHER AGAIN!
10.
NEXT ISSUE: THE SECRET!

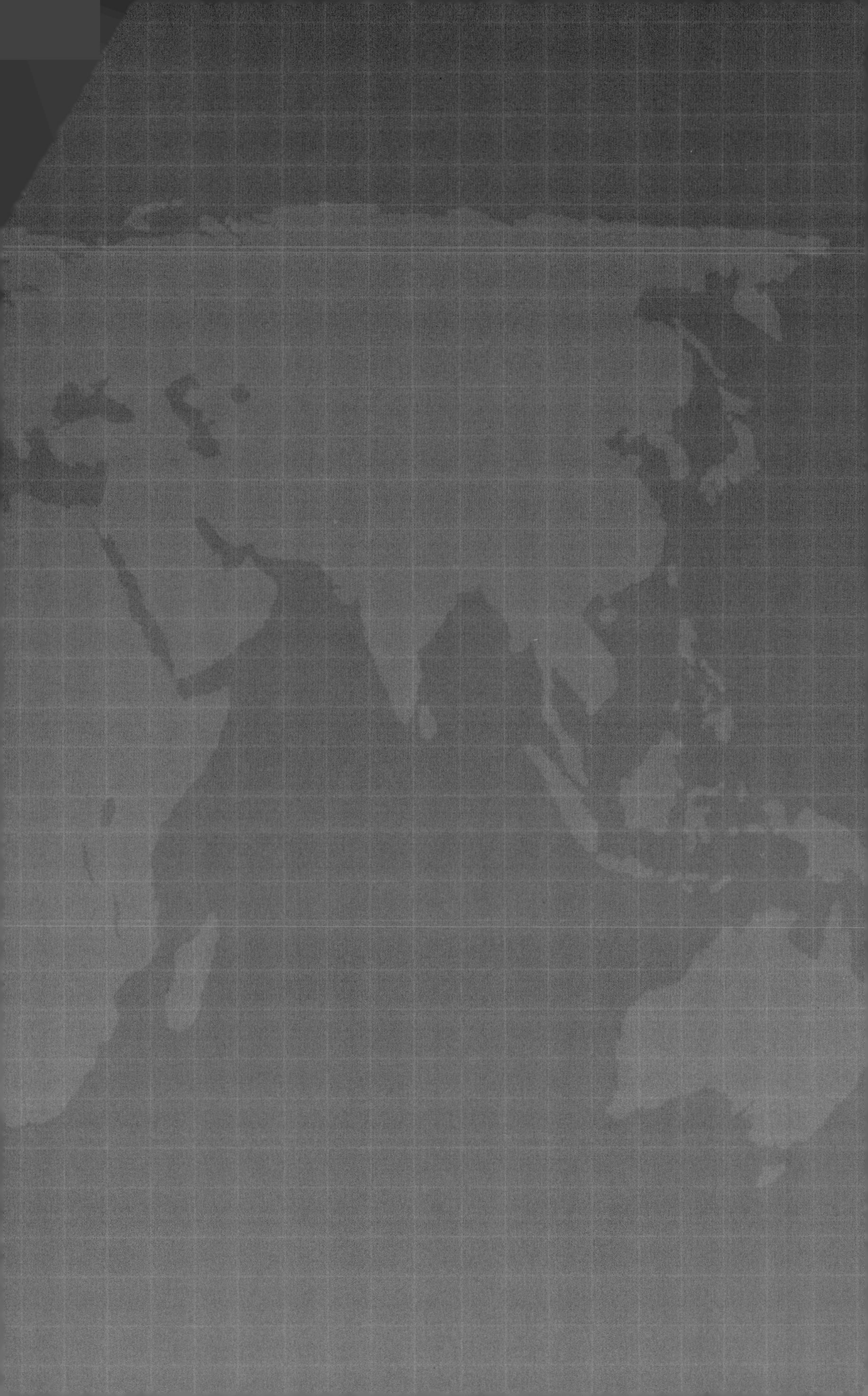

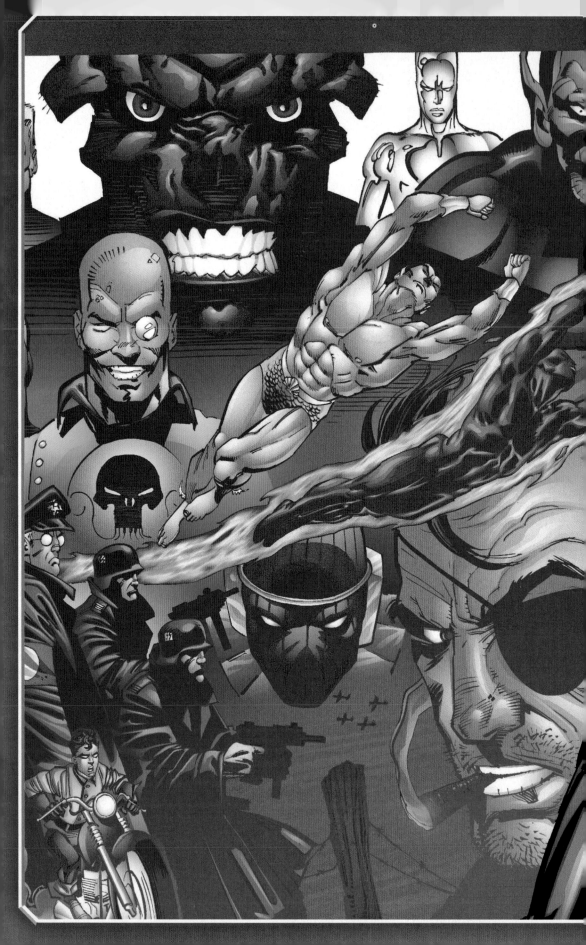

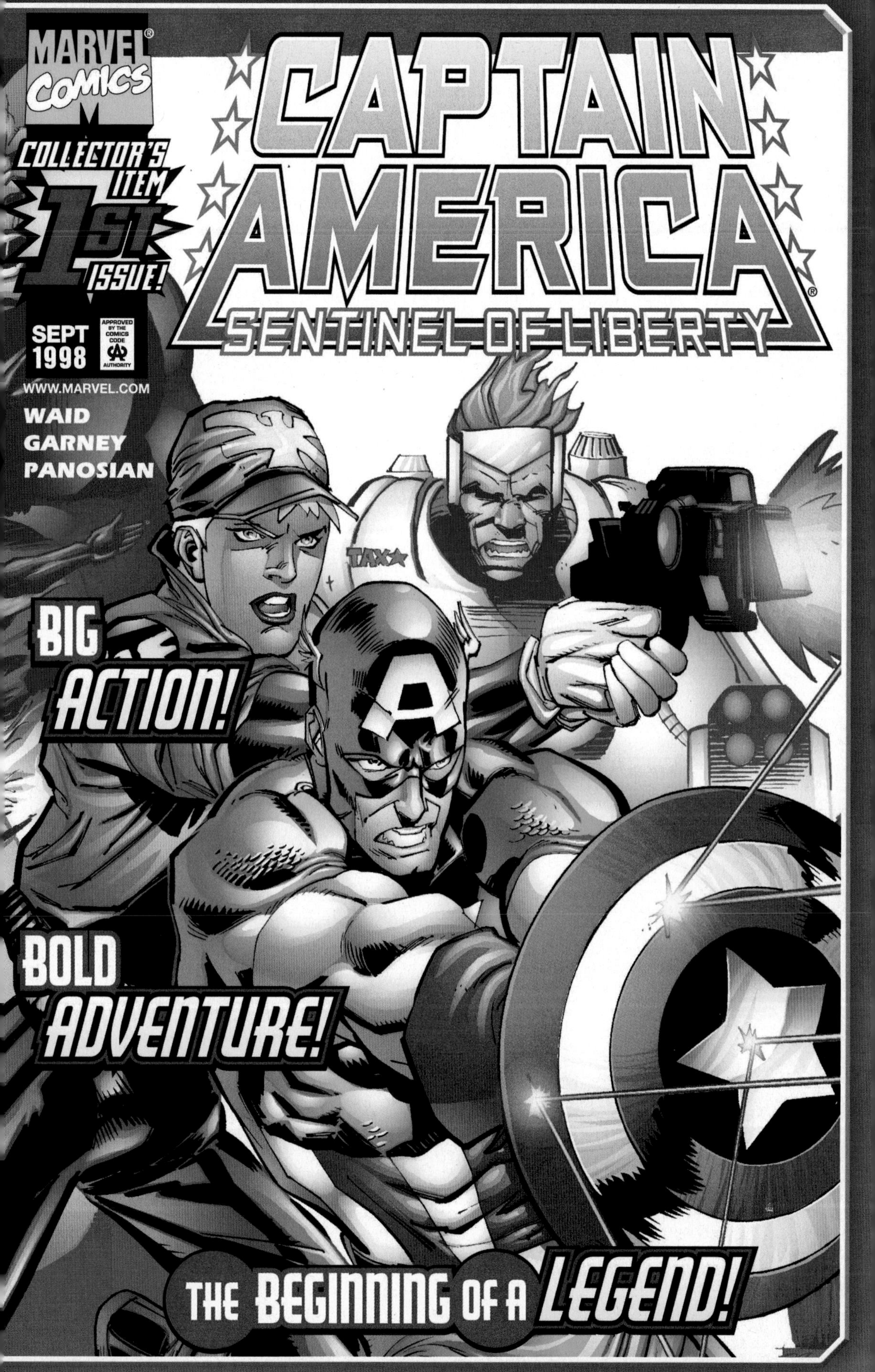
MARVEL® COMICS
CAPTAIN AMERICA®
SENTINEL OF LIBERTY
COLLECTOR'S ITEM 1ST ISSUE!
SEPT 1998
APPROVED BY THE COMICS CODE AUTHORITY
WWW.MARVEL.COM
WAID
GARNEY
PANOSIAN
BIG ACTION!
BOLD ADVENTURE!
THE BEGINNING OF A LEGEND!

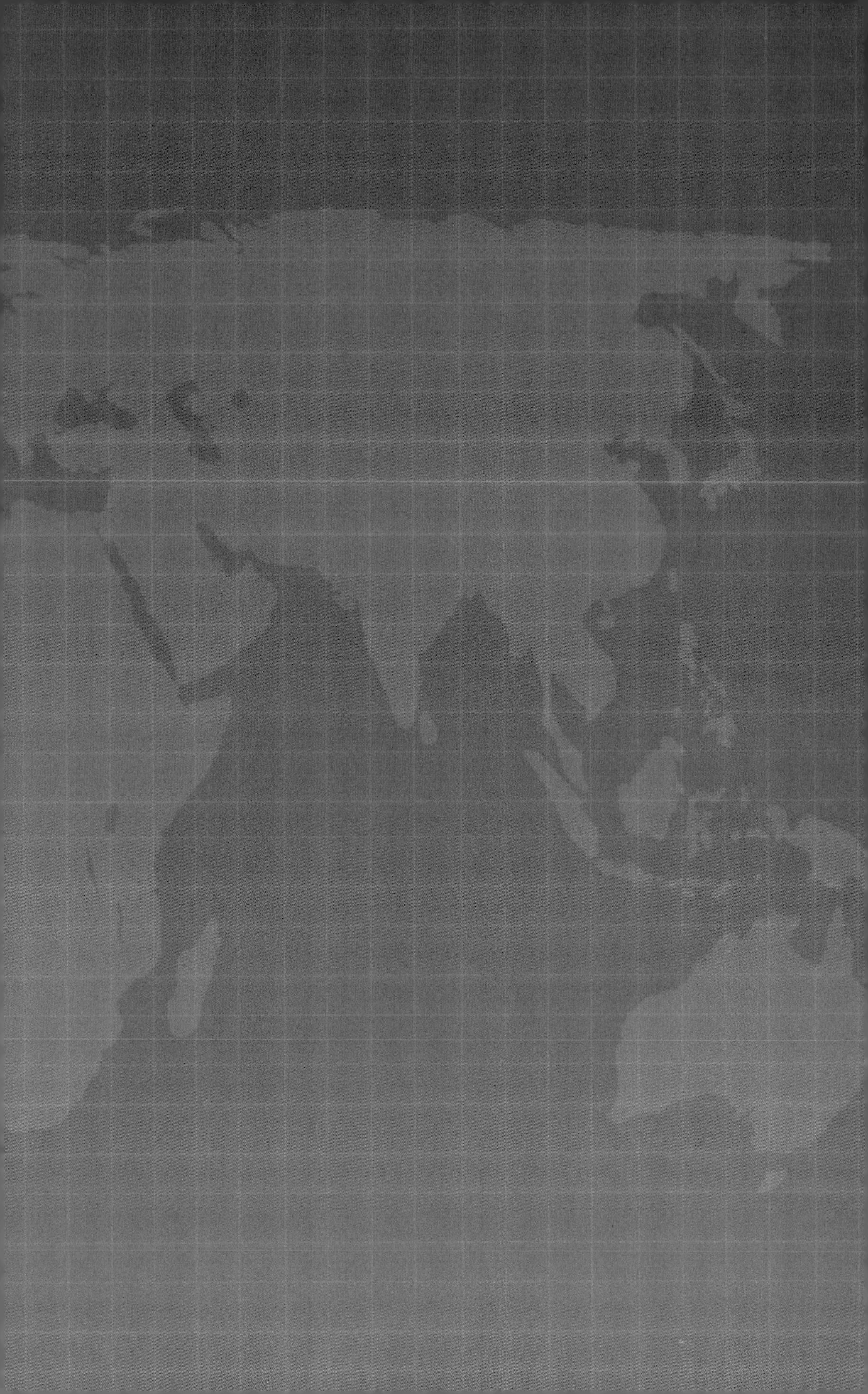

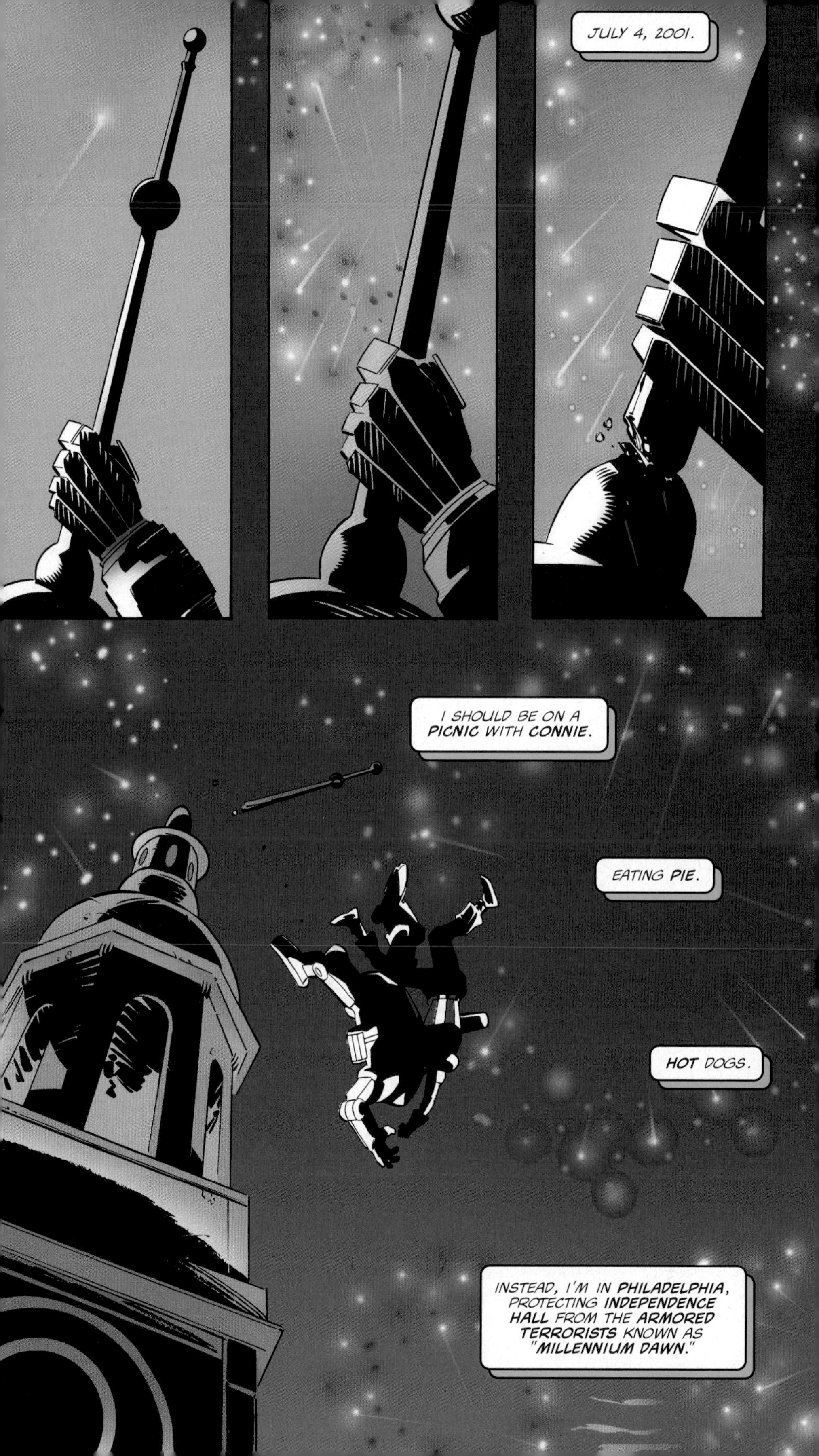
JULY 4, 2001.
I SHOULD BE ON A PICNIC WITH CONNIE.
EATING PIE.
HOT DOGS.
INSTEAD, I'M IN PHILADELPHIA, PROTECTING INDEPENDENCE HALL FROM THE ARMORED TERRORISTS KNOWN AS "MILLENNIUM DAWN."

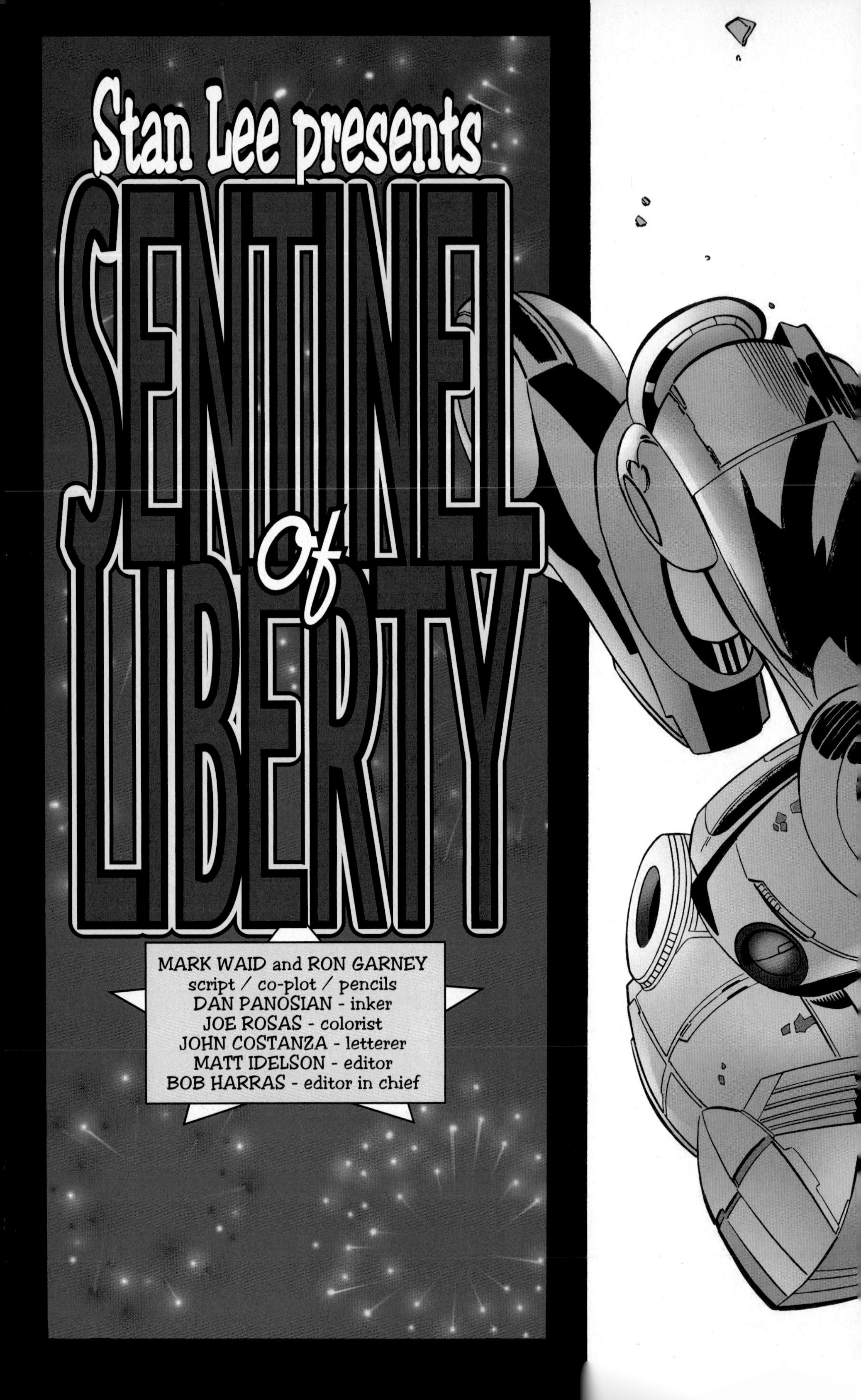

Stan Lee presents
SENTINEL of LIBERTY
MARK WAID and RON GARNEY
script / co-plot / pencils
DAN PANOSIAN - inker
JOE ROSAS - colorist
JOHN COSTANZA - letterer
MATT IDELSON - editor
BOB HARRAS - editor in chief

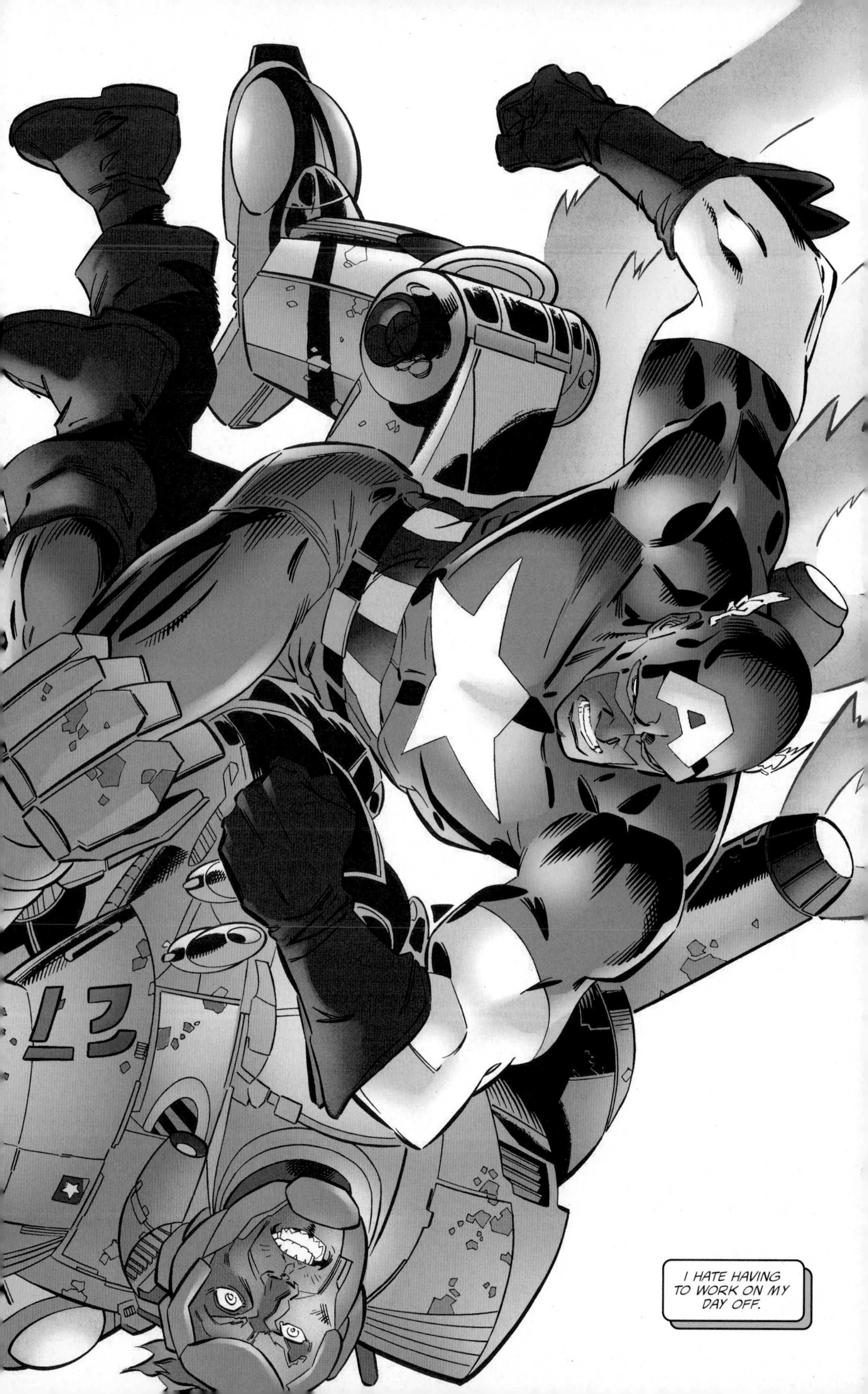
I HATE HAVING TO WORK ON MY DAY OFF.

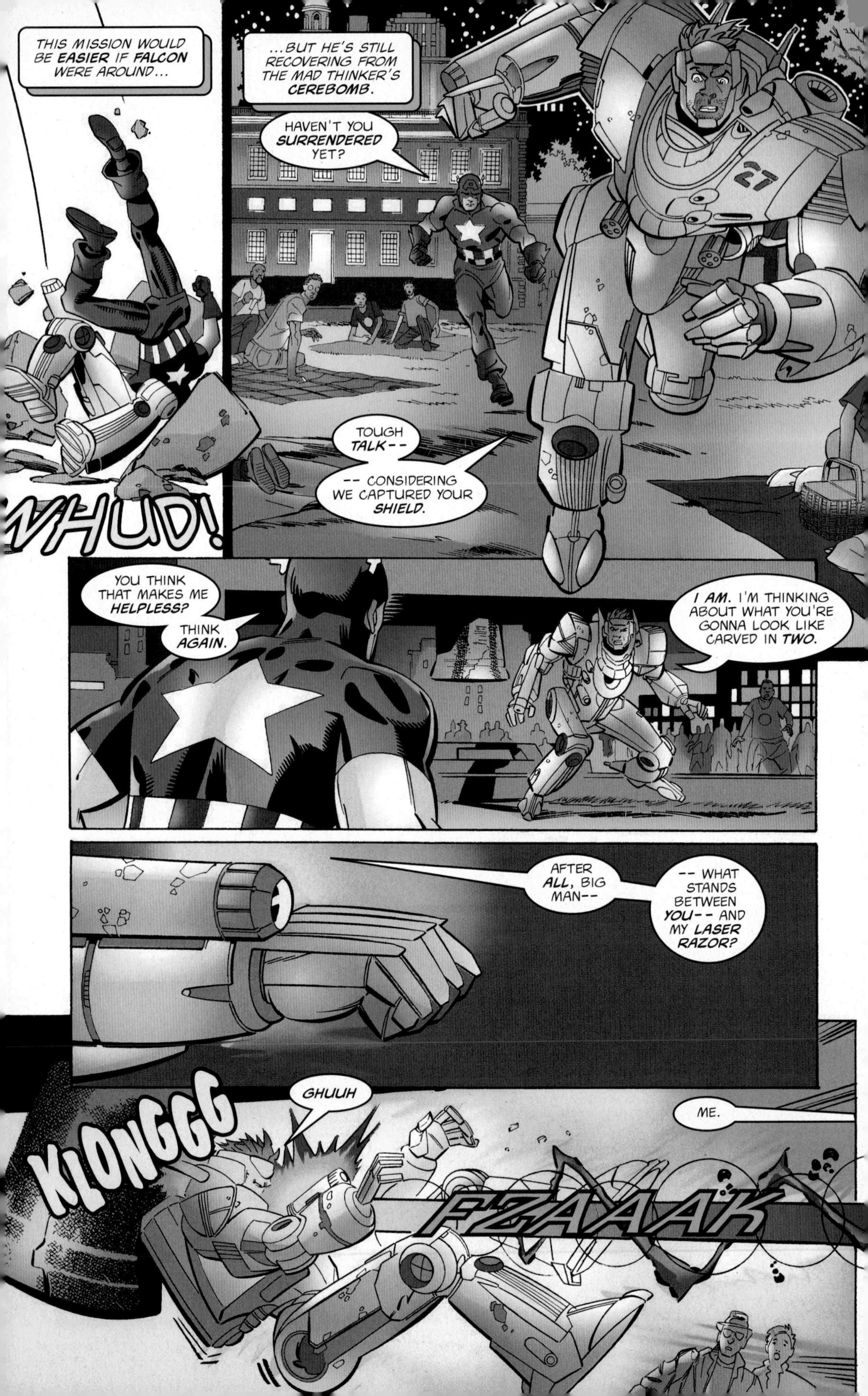
THIS MISSION WOULD BE EASIER IF FALCON WERE AROUND...
WHUD!
...BUT HE'S STILL RECOVERING FROM THE MAD THINKER'S CEREBOMB.
HAVEN'T YOU SURRENDERED YET?
27
TOUGH TALK--
-- CONSIDERING WE CAPTURED YOUR SHIELD.
YOU THINK THAT MAKES ME HELPLESS?
THINK AGAIN.
I AM. I'M THINKING ABOUT WHAT YOU'RE GONNA LOOK LIKE CARVED IN TWO.
AFTER ALL, BIG MAN--
-- WHAT STANDS BETWEEN YOU-- AND MY LASER RAZOR?
KLONGGG
GHUUH
ME.
FZAAAAK

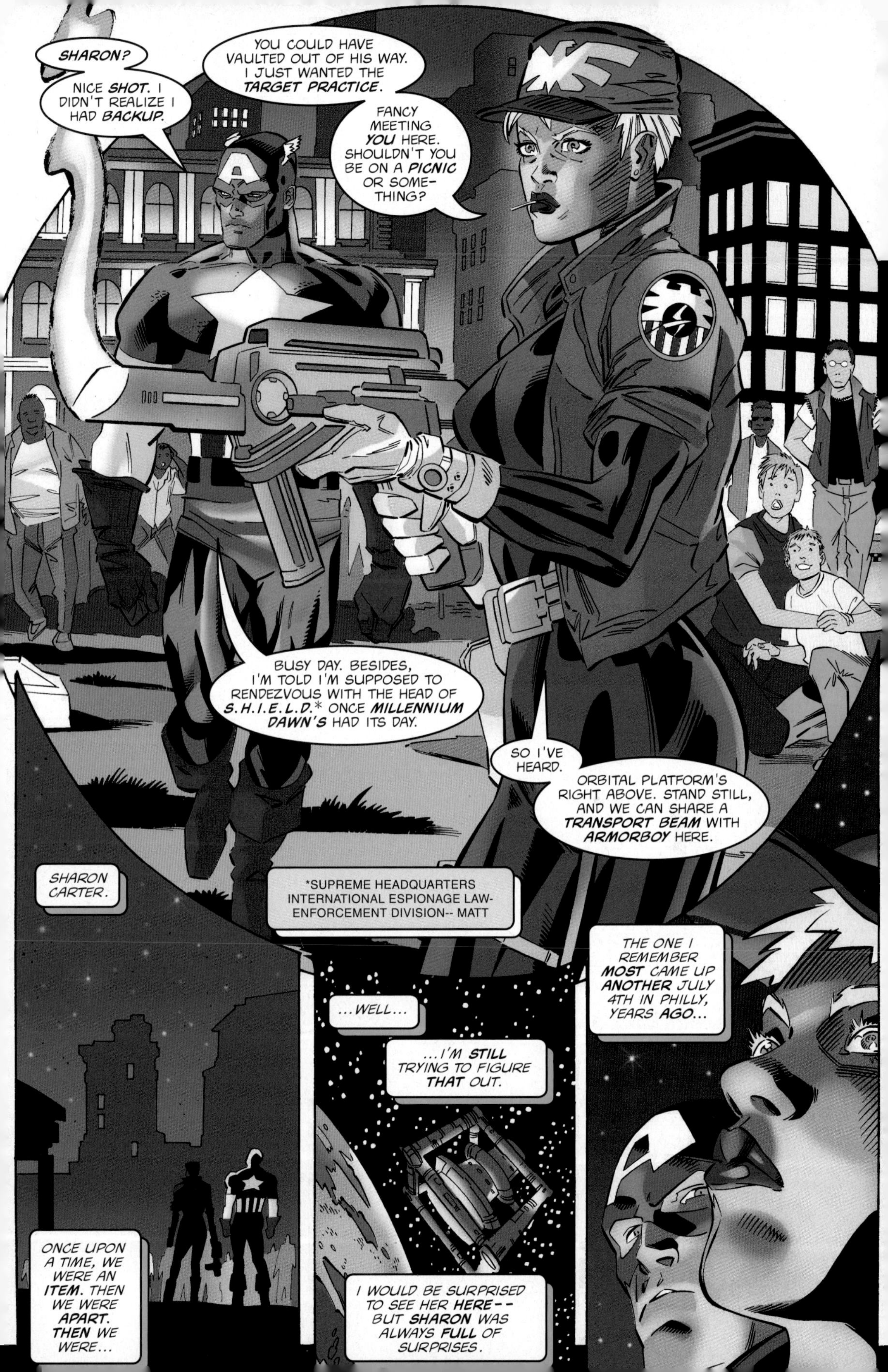
SHARON?
NICE SHOT. I DIDN'T REALIZE I HAD BACKUP.
YOU COULD HAVE VAULTED OUT OF HIS WAY. I JUST WANTED THE TARGET PRACTICE.
FANCY MEETING YOU HERE. SHOULDN'T YOU BE ON A PICNIC OR SOME-THING?
BUSY DAY. BESIDES, I'M TOLD I'M SUPPOSED TO RENDEZVOUS WITH THE HEAD OF S.H.I.E.L.D.* ONCE MILLENNIUM DAWN'S HAD ITS DAY.
SO I'VE HEARD.
ORBITAL PLATFORM'S RIGHT ABOVE. STAND STILL, AND WE CAN SHARE A TRANSPORT BEAM WITH ARMORBOY HERE.
SHARON CARTER.
*SUPREME HEADQUARTERS INTERNATIONAL ESPIONAGE LAW-ENFORCEMENT DIVISION-- MATT
ONCE UPON A TIME, WE WERE AN ITEM. THEN WE WERE APART. THEN WE WERE...
...WELL...
...I'M STILL TRYING TO FIGURE THAT OUT.
I WOULD BE SURPRISED TO SEE HER HERE-- BUT SHARON WAS ALWAYS FULL OF SURPRISES.
THE ONE I REMEMBER MOST CAME UP ANOTHER JULY 4TH IN PHILLY, YEARS AGO...

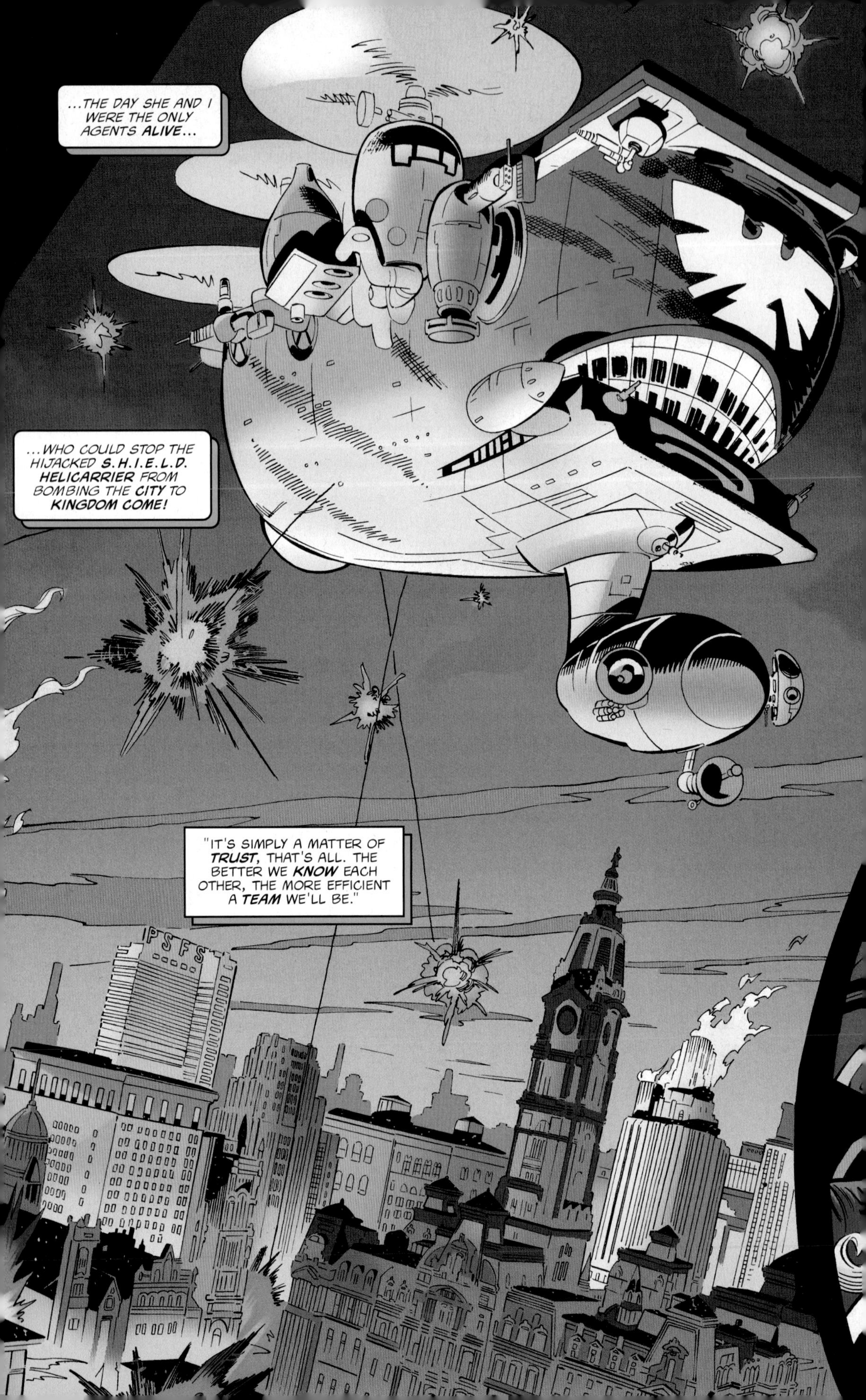
...THE DAY SHE AND I WERE THE ONLY AGENTS ALIVE...
...WHO COULD STOP THE HIJACKED S.H.I.E.L.D. HELICARRIER FROM BOMBING THE CITY TO KINGDOM COME!
"IT'S SIMPLY A MATTER OF TRUST, THAT'S ALL. THE BETTER WE KNOW EACH OTHER, THE MORE EFFICIENT A TEAM WE'LL BE."
PSFS

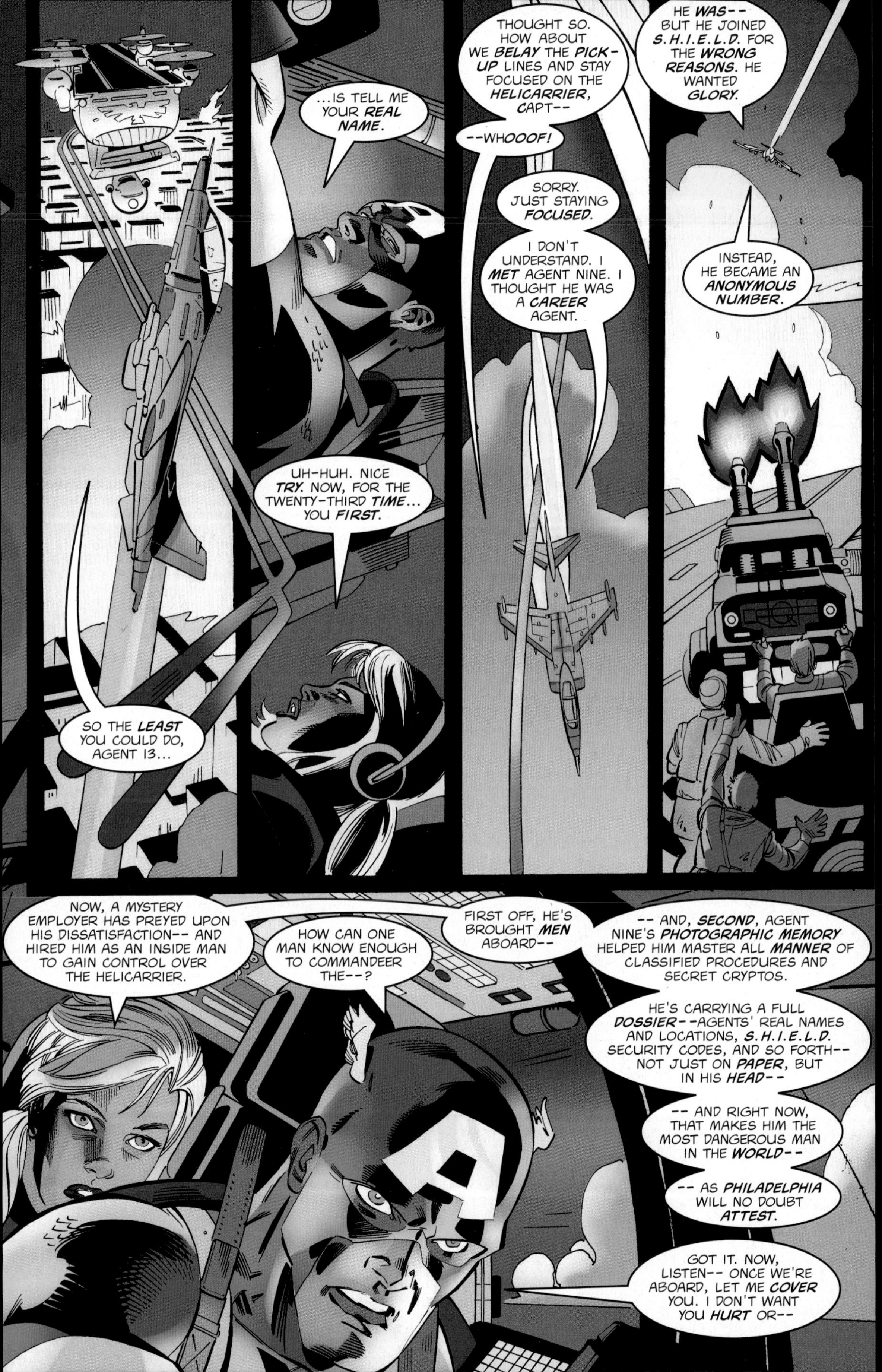
SO THE LEAST YOU COULD DO, AGENT 13...
...IS TELL ME YOUR REAL NAME.
UH-HUH. NICE TRY. NOW, FOR THE TWENTY-THIRD TIME... YOU FIRST.
THOUGHT SO. HOW ABOUT WE BELAY THE PICK-UP LINES AND STAY FOCUSED ON THE HELICARRIER, CAPT--
--WHOOOF!
SORRY. JUST STAYING FOCUSED.
I DON'T UNDERSTAND. I MET AGENT NINE. I THOUGHT HE WAS A CAREER AGENT.
HE WAS-- BUT HE JOINED S.H.I.E.L.D. FOR THE WRONG REASONS. HE WANTED GLORY.
INSTEAD, HE BECAME AN ANONYMOUS NUMBER.
NOW, A MYSTERY EMPLOYER HAS PREYED UPON HIS DISSATISFACTION-- AND HIRED HIM AS AN INSIDE MAN TO GAIN CONTROL OVER THE HELICARRIER.
HOW CAN ONE MAN KNOW ENOUGH TO COMMANDEER THE--?
FIRST OFF, HE'S BROUGHT MEN ABOARD--
-- AND, SECOND, AGENT NINE'S PHOTOGRAPHIC MEMORY HELPED HIM MASTER ALL MANNER OF CLASSIFIED PROCEDURES AND SECRET CRYPTOS.
HE'S CARRYING A FULL DOSSIER--AGENTS' REAL NAMES AND LOCATIONS, S.H.I.E.L.D. SECURITY CODES, AND SO FORTH-- NOT JUST ON PAPER, BUT IN HIS HEAD--
-- AND RIGHT NOW, THAT MAKES HIM THE MOST DANGEROUS MAN IN THE WORLD--
-- AS PHILADELPHIA WILL NO DOUBT ATTEST.
GOT IT. NOW, LISTEN-- ONCE WE'RE ABOARD, LET ME COVER YOU. I DON'T WANT YOU HURT OR--

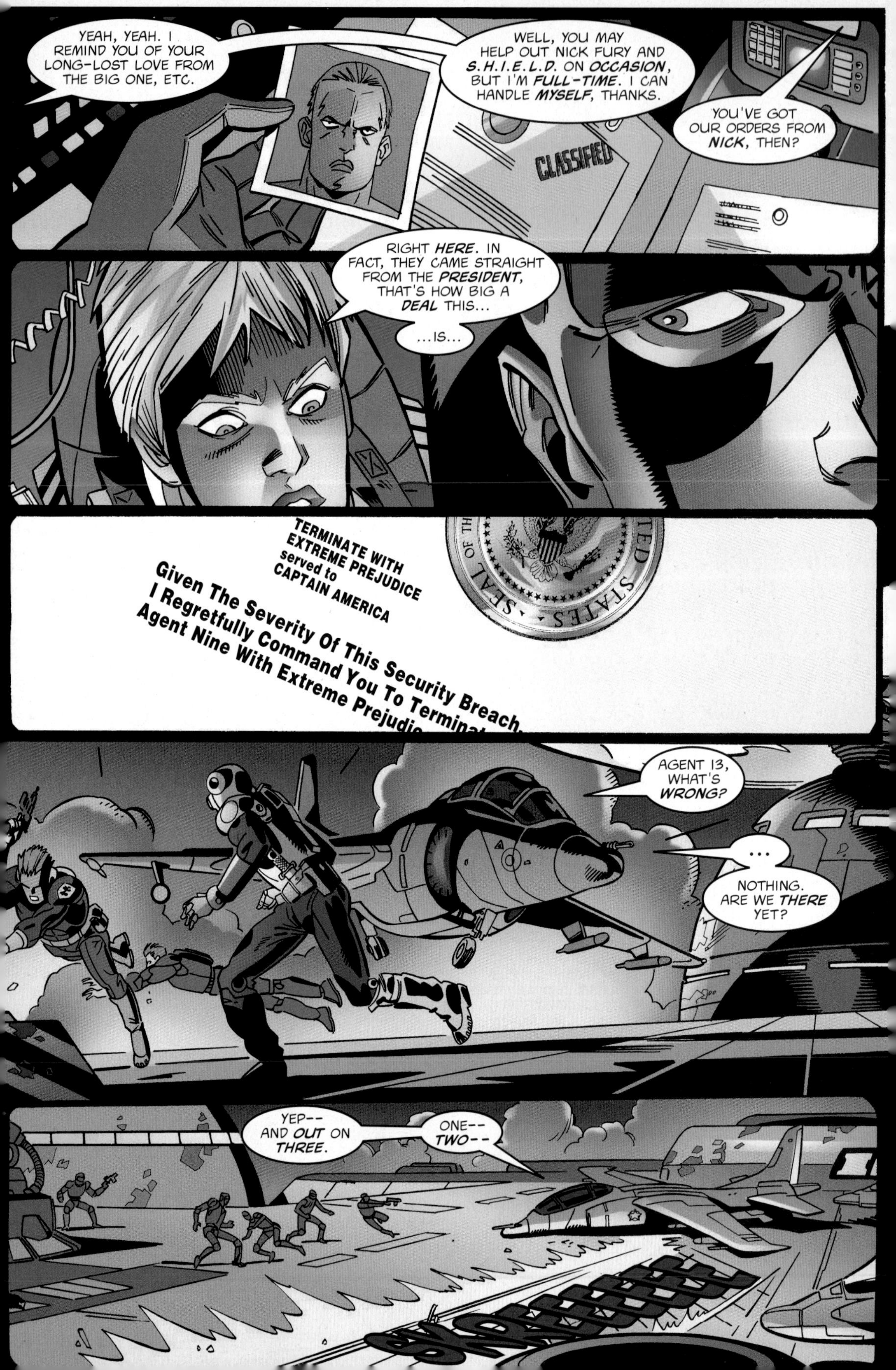
YEAH, YEAH. I REMIND YOU OF YOUR LONG-LOST LOVE FROM THE BIG ONE, ETC.
WELL, YOU MAY HELP OUT NICK FURY AND S.H.I.E.L.D. ON OCCASION, BUT I'M FULL-TIME. I CAN HANDLE MYSELF, THANKS.
CLASSIFIED
YOU'VE GOT OUR ORDERS FROM NICK, THEN?
RIGHT HERE. IN FACT, THEY CAME STRAIGHT FROM THE PRESIDENT, THAT'S HOW BIG A DEAL THIS...
...IS...
TERMINATE WITH EXTREME PREJUDICE served to CAPTAIN AMERICA
Given The Severity Of This Security Breach, I Regretfully Command You To Terminat
Agent Nine With Extreme Prejudic
SEAL OF THE PRESIDENT OF THE UNITED STATES
AGENT 13, WHAT'S WRONG?
...
NOTHING. ARE WE THERE YET?
YEP-- AND OUT ON THREE.
ONE-- TWO--
SKREEEE

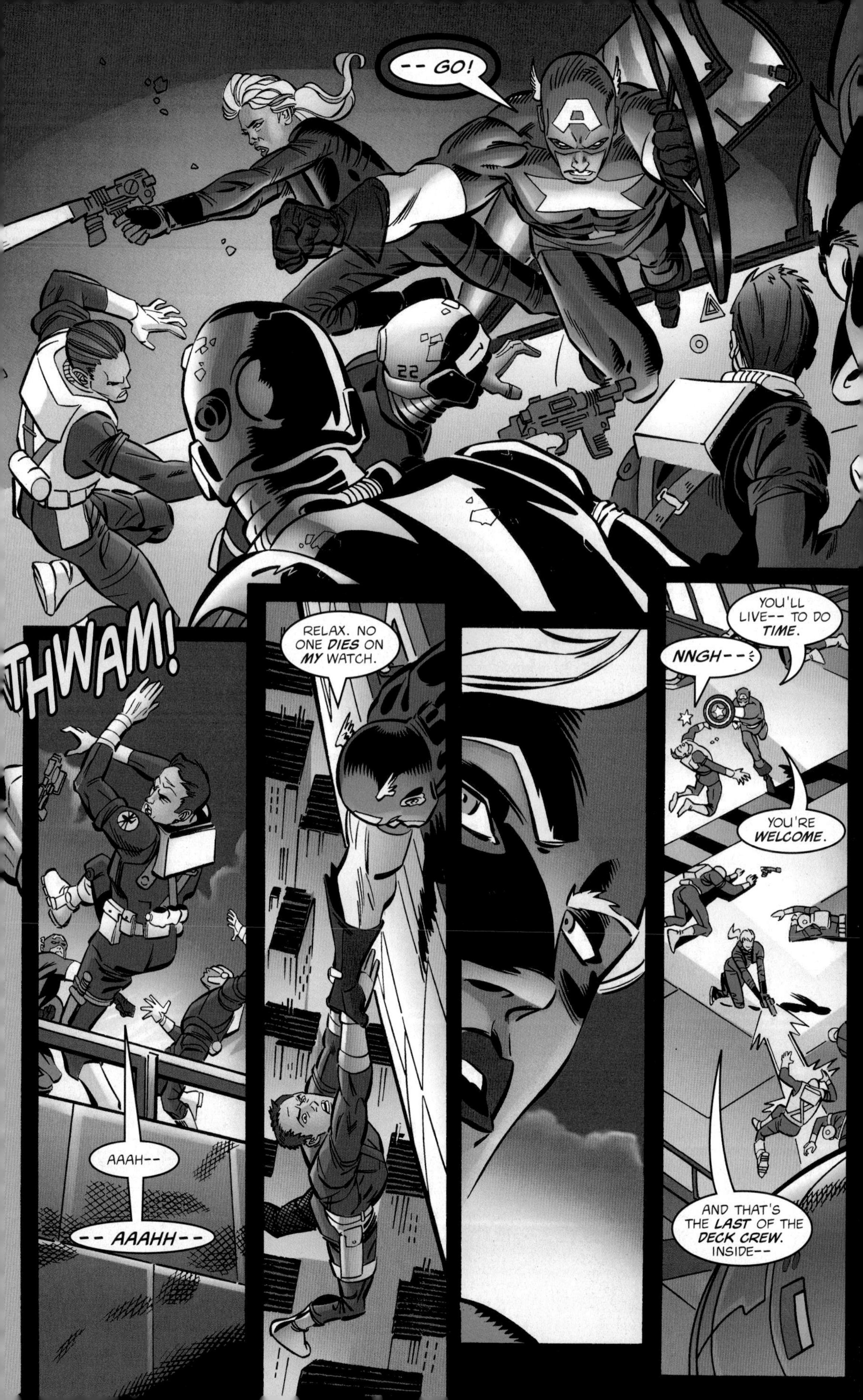
-- GO!
THWAM!
AAAH--
-- AAAHH--
RELAX. NO ONE DIES ON MY WATCH.
YOU'LL LIVE-- TO DO TIME.
NNGH--
YOU'RE WELCOME.
AND THAT'S THE LAST OF THE DECK CREW. INSIDE--

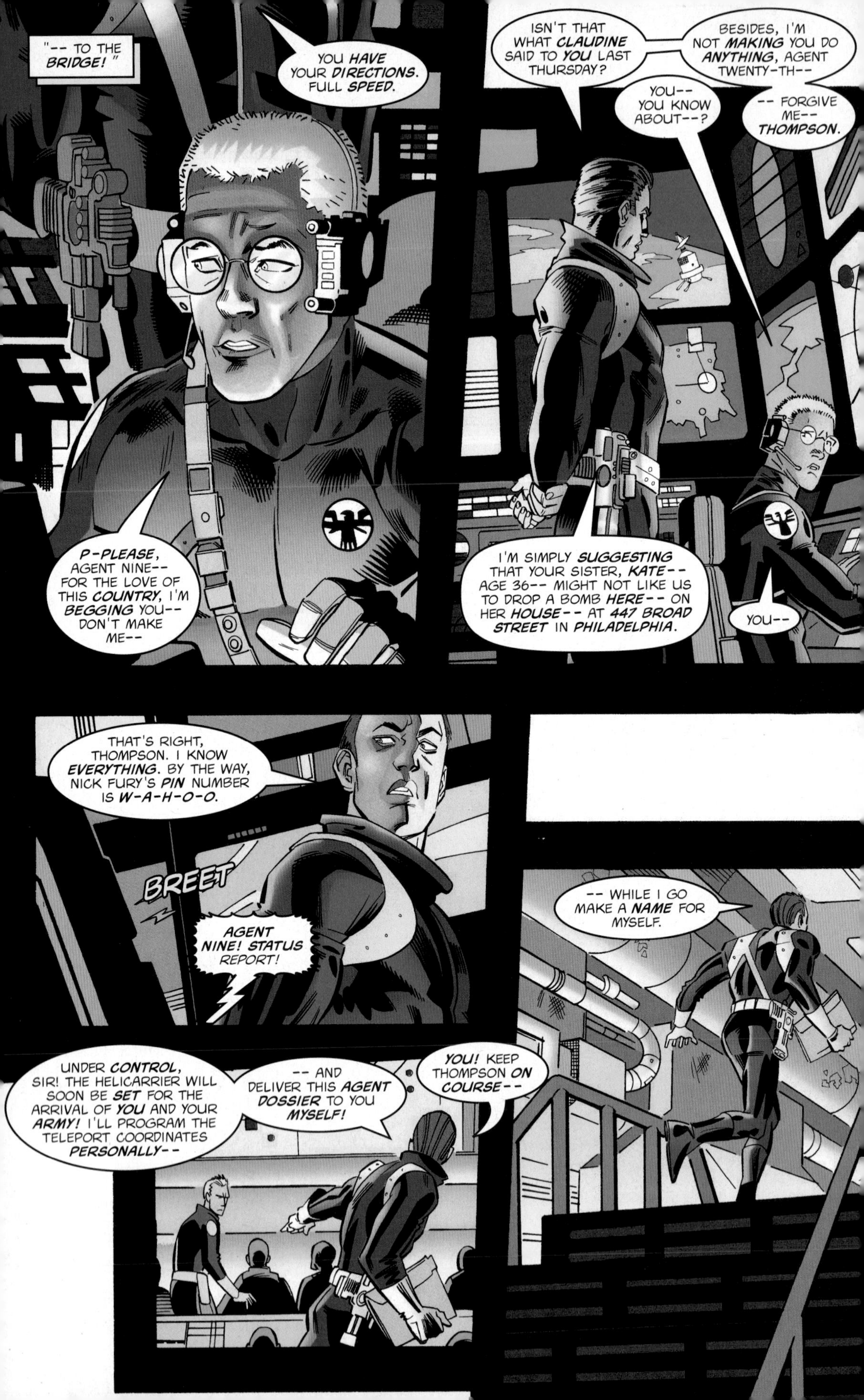
"-- TO THE BRIDGE!"
YOU HAVE YOUR DIRECTIONS. FULL SPEED.
P-PLEASE, AGENT NINE-- FOR THE LOVE OF THIS COUNTRY, I'M BEGGING YOU-- DON'T MAKE ME--
ISN'T THAT WHAT CLAUDINE SAID TO YOU LAST THURSDAY?
BESIDES, I'M NOT MAKING YOU DO ANYTHING, AGENT TWENTY-TH--
YOU-- YOU KNOW ABOUT--?
-- FORGIVE ME-- THOMPSON.
I'M SIMPLY SUGGESTING THAT YOUR SISTER, KATE-- AGE 36-- MIGHT NOT LIKE US TO DROP A BOMB HERE-- ON HER HOUSE-- AT 447 BROAD STREET IN PHILADELPHIA.
YOU--
THAT'S RIGHT, THOMPSON. I KNOW EVERYTHING. BY THE WAY, NICK FURY'S PIN NUMBER IS W-A-H-O-O.
BREET
AGENT NINE! STATUS REPORT!
UNDER CONTROL, SIR! THE HELICARRIER WILL SOON BE SET FOR THE ARRIVAL OF YOU AND YOUR ARMY! I'LL PROGRAM THE TELEPORT COORDINATES PERSONALLY--
-- AND DELIVER THIS AGENT DOSSIER TO YOU MYSELF!
YOU! KEEP THOMPSON ON COURSE--
-- WHILE I GO MAKE A NAME FOR MYSELF.

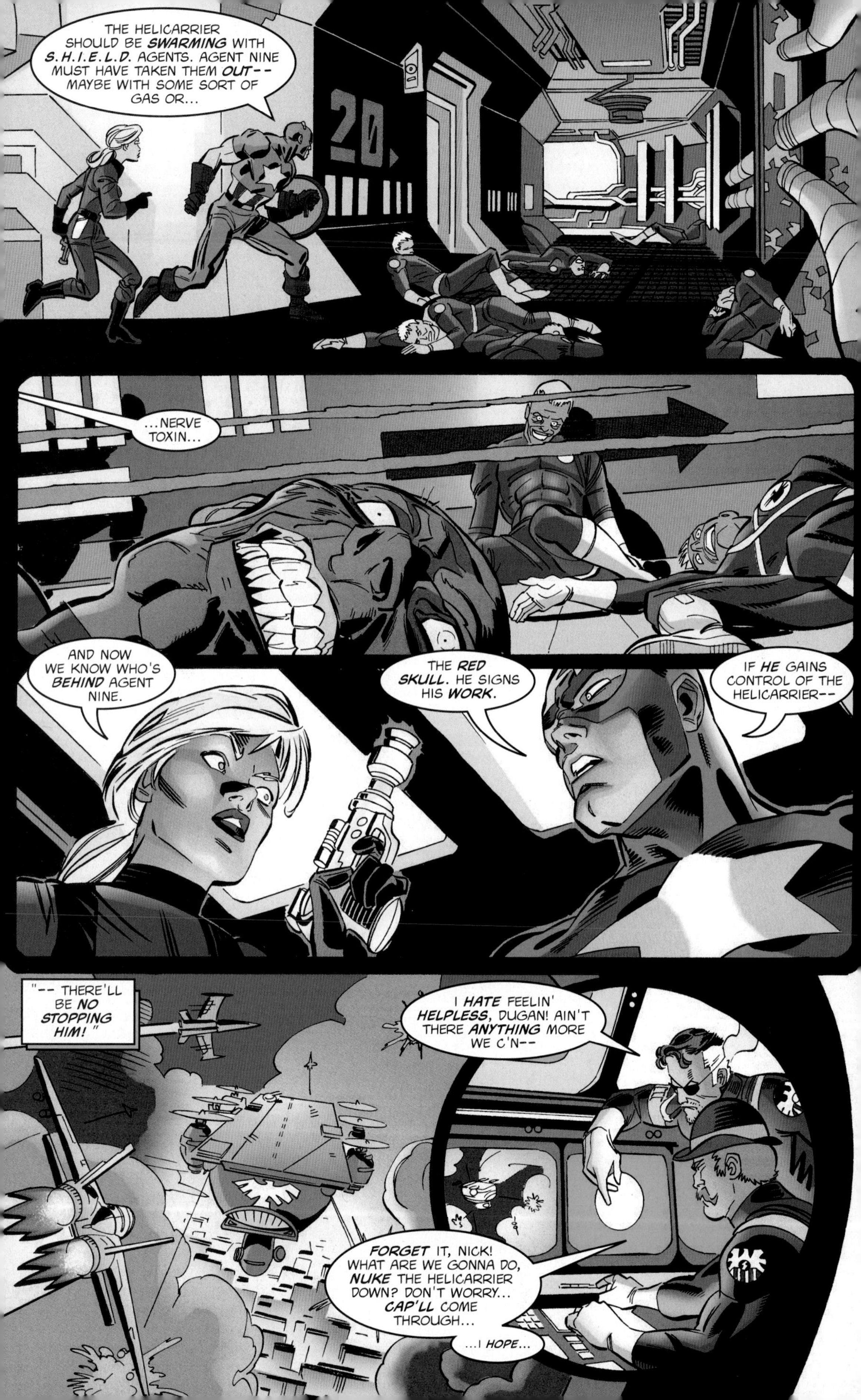
THE HELICARRIER SHOULD BE SWARMING WITH S.H.I.E.L.D. AGENTS. AGENT NINE MUST HAVE TAKEN THEM OUT-- MAYBE WITH SOME SORT OF GAS OR...
20
...NERVE TOXIN...
AND NOW WE KNOW WHO'S BEHIND AGENT NINE.
THE RED SKULL. HE SIGNS HIS WORK.
IF HE GAINS CONTROL OF THE HELICARRIER--
"-- THERE'LL BE NO STOPPING HIM!"
I HATE FEELIN' HELPLESS, DUGAN! AIN'T THERE ANYTHING MORE WE C'N--
FORGET IT, NICK! WHAT ARE WE GONNA DO, NUKE THE HELICARRIER DOWN? DON'T WORRY... CAP'LL COME THROUGH...
...I HOPE...

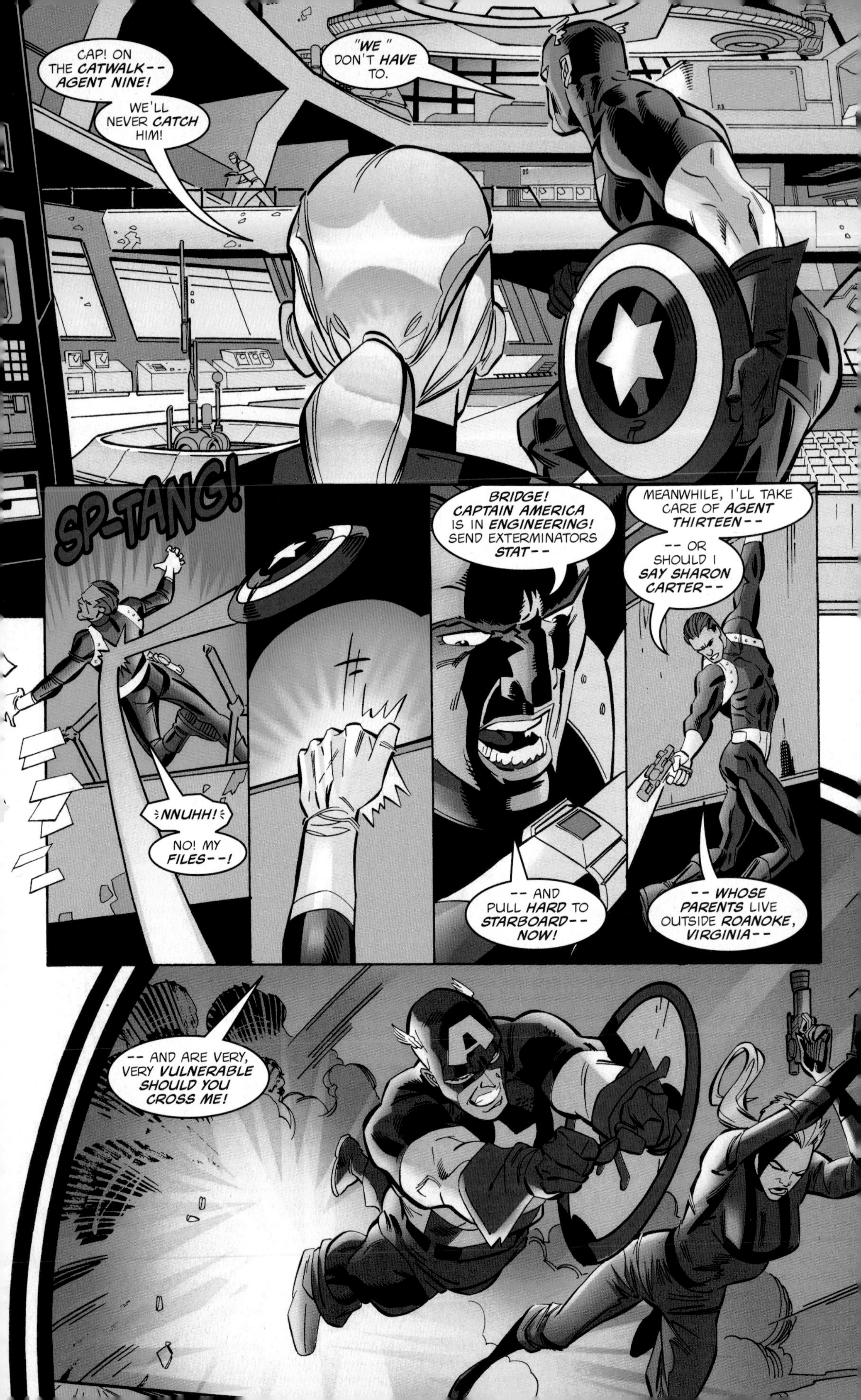
CAP! ON THE CATWALK-- AGENT NINE!
WE'LL NEVER CATCH HIM!
"WE" DON'T HAVE TO.
SP-TANG!
NNUHH!
NO! MY FILES--!
BRIDGE! CAPTAIN AMERICA IS IN ENGINEERING! SEND EXTERMINATORS STAT--
-- AND PULL HARD TO STARBOARD-- NOW!
MEANWHILE, I'LL TAKE CARE OF AGENT THIRTEEN--
-- OR SHOULD I SAY SHARON CARTER--
-- WHOSE PARENTS LIVE OUTSIDE ROANOKE, VIRGINIA--
-- AND ARE VERY, VERY VULNERABLE SHOULD YOU CROSS ME!

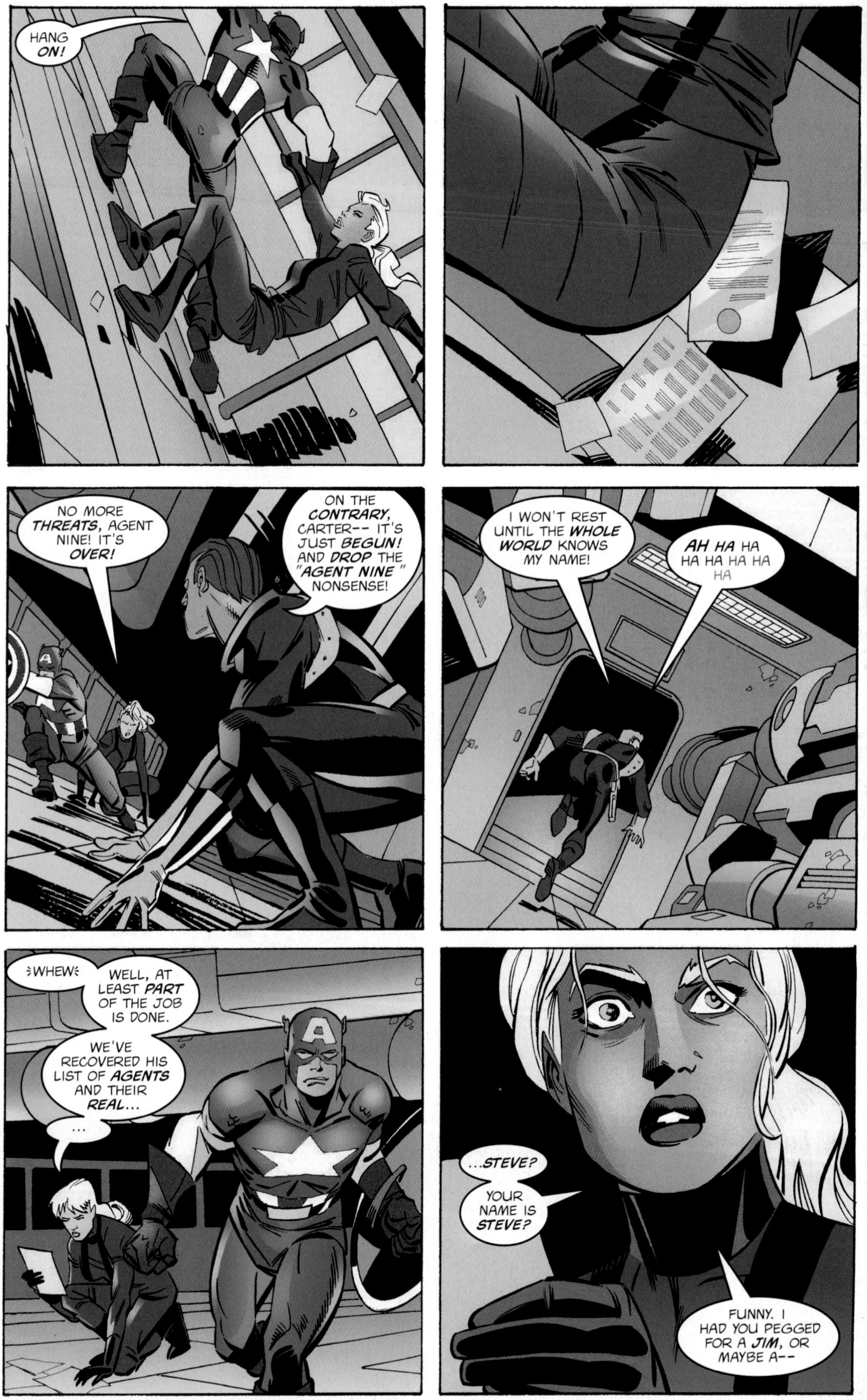
HANG ON!
NO MORE THREATS, AGENT NINE! IT'S OVER!
ON THE CONTRARY, CARTER-- IT'S JUST BEGUN! AND DROP THE "AGENT NINE" NONSENSE!
I WON'T REST UNTIL THE WHOLE WORLD KNOWS MY NAME!
AH HA HA HA HA HA HA HA
WHEW
WELL, AT LEAST PART OF THE JOB IS DONE.
WE'VE RECOVERED HIS LIST OF AGENTS AND THEIR REAL...
...
...STEVE?
YOUR NAME IS STEVE?
FUNNY. I HAD YOU PEGGED FOR A JIM, OR MAYBE A--

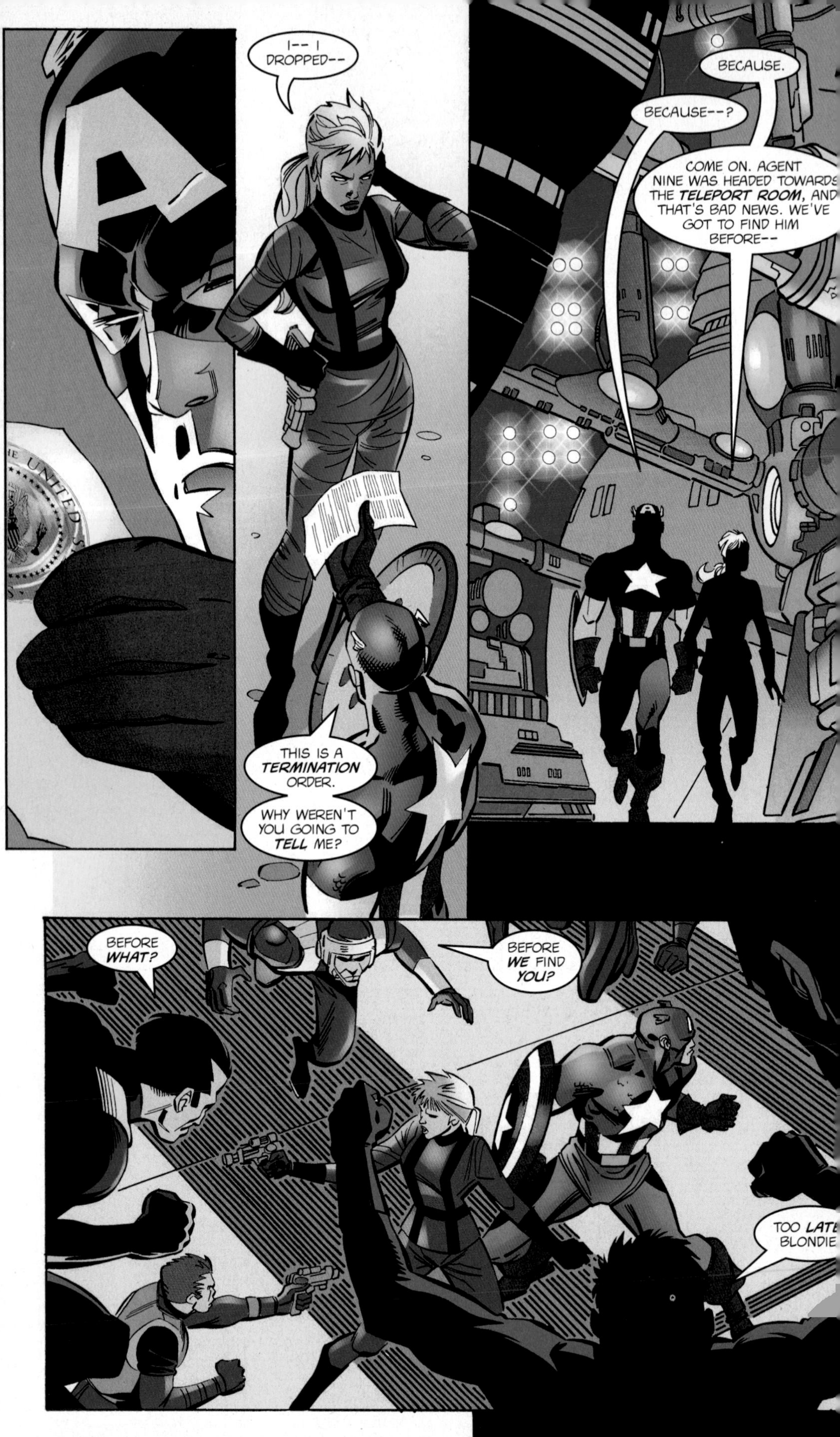
I-- I DROPPED--
THIS IS A TERMINATION ORDER.
WHY WEREN'T YOU GOING TO TELL ME?
BECAUSE--?
BECAUSE.
COME ON. AGENT NINE WAS HEADED TOWARDS THE TELEPORT ROOM, AND THAT'S BAD NEWS. WE'VE GOT TO FIND HIM BEFORE--
BEFORE WHAT?
BEFORE WE FIND YOU?
TOO LATE BLONDIE

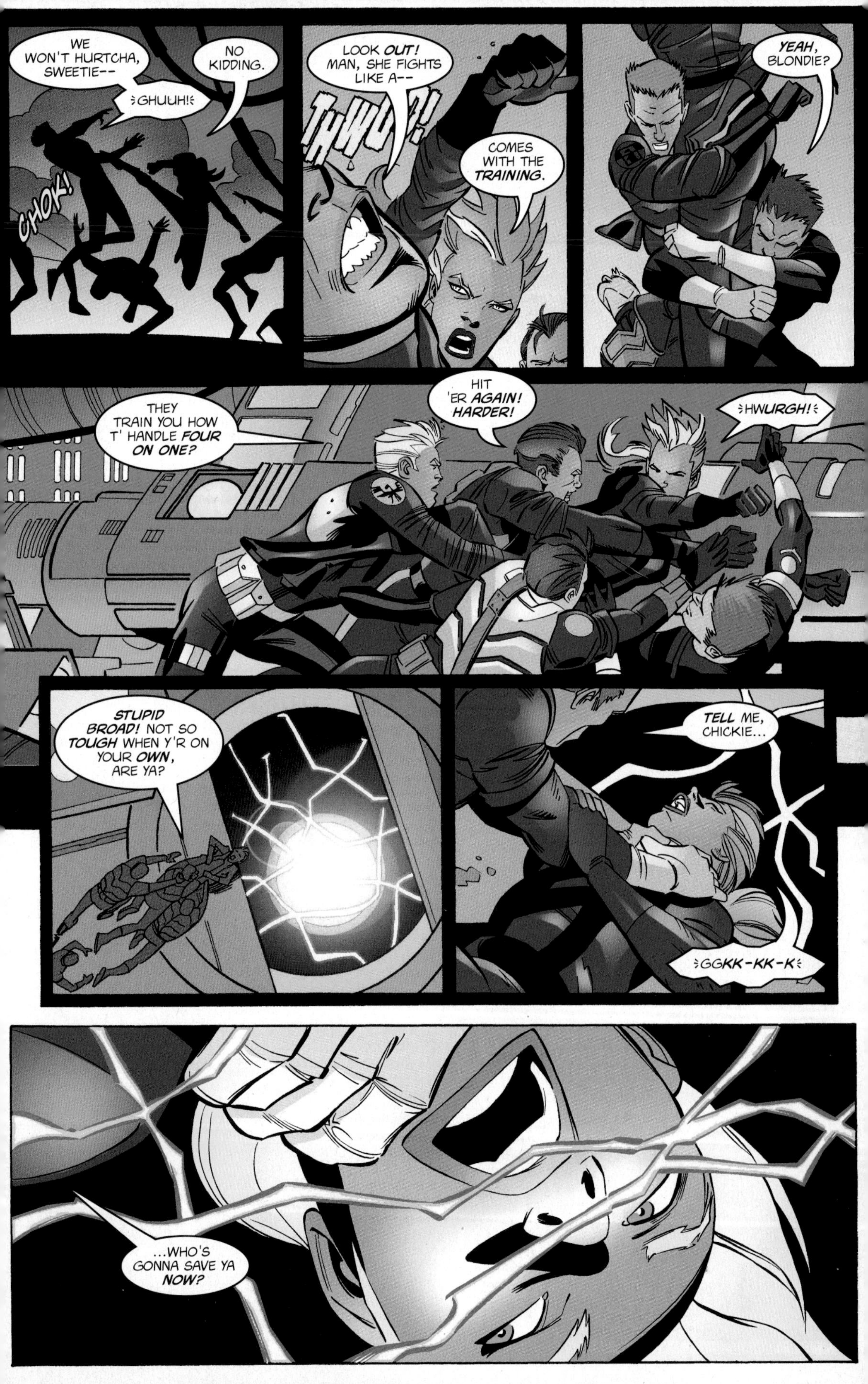
WE WON'T HURTCHA, SWEETIE--
GHUUH!
NO KIDDING.
CHOK!
LOOK OUT! MAN, SHE FIGHTS LIKE A--
THWUD?!
COMES WITH THE TRAINING.
YEAH, BLONDIE?
THEY TRAIN YOU HOW T' HANDLE FOUR ON ONE?
HIT 'ER AGAIN! HARDER!
HWURGH!
STUPID BROAD! NOT SO TOUGH WHEN Y'R ON YOUR OWN, ARE YA?
TELL ME, CHICKIE...
GGKK-KK-K
...WHO'S GONNA SAVE YA NOW?

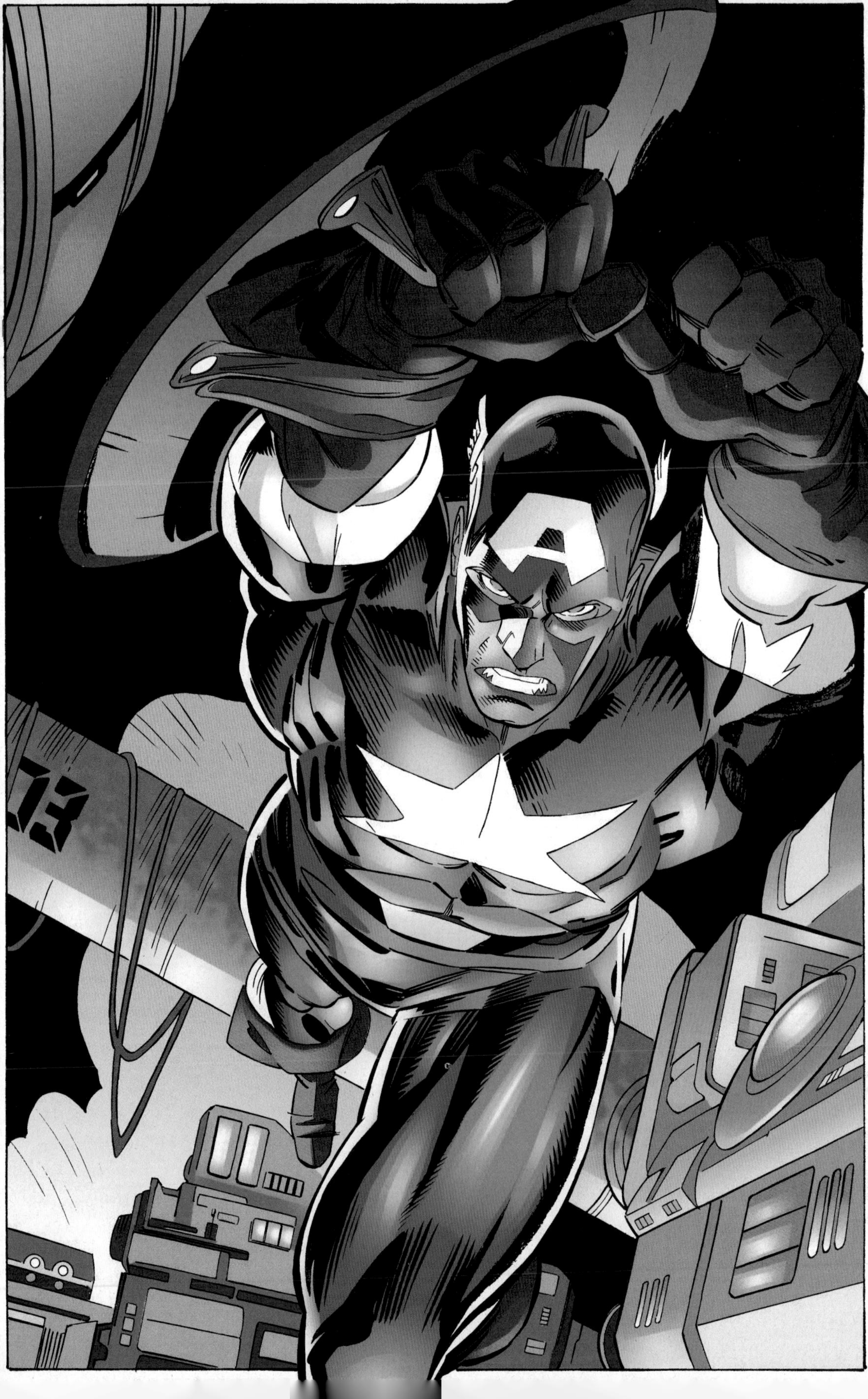

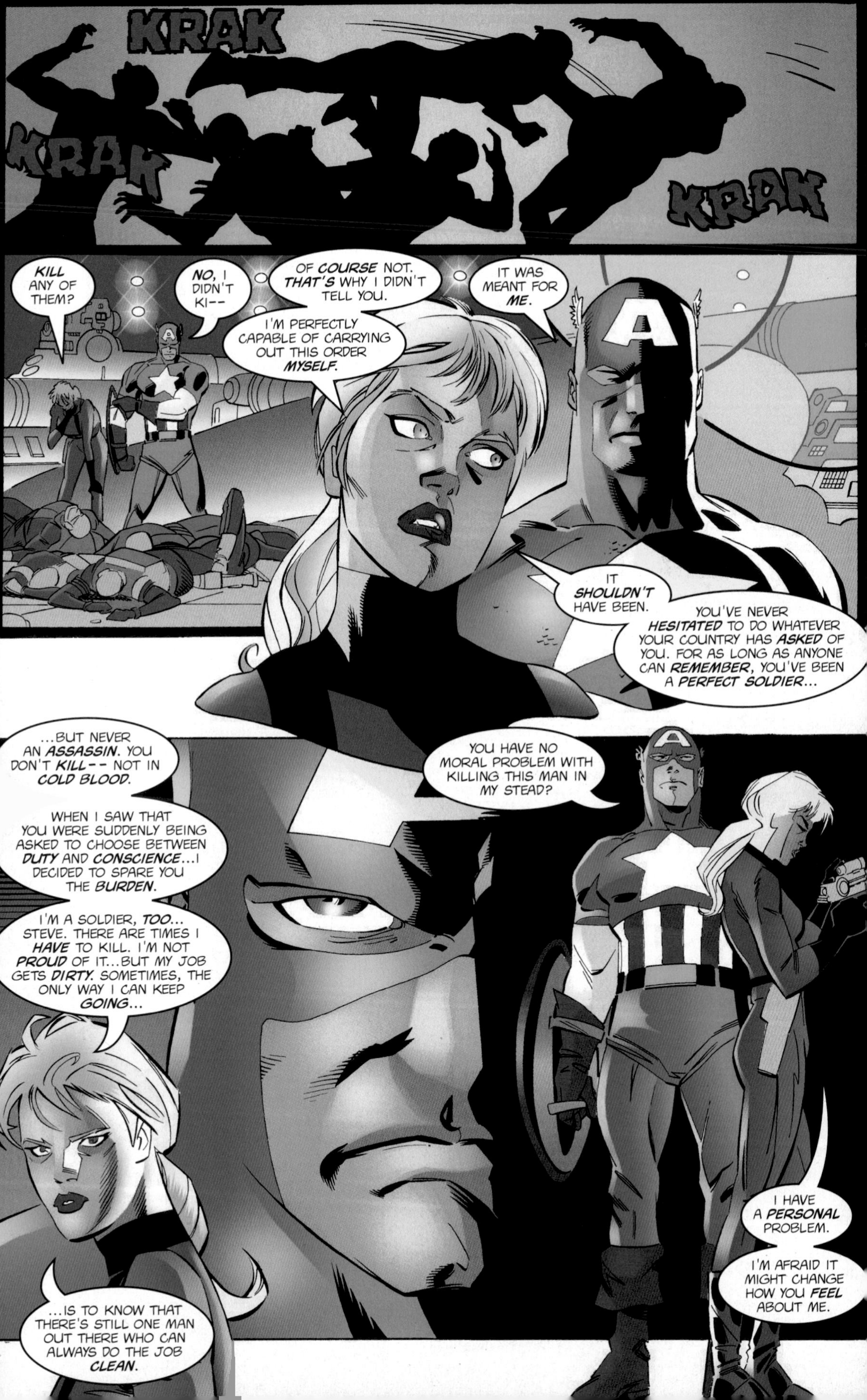
KRAK
KRAK
KRAK
KILL ANY OF THEM?
NO, I DIDN'T KI--
OF COURSE NOT. THAT'S WHY I DIDN'T TELL YOU.
I'M PERFECTLY CAPABLE OF CARRYING OUT THIS ORDER MYSELF.
IT WAS MEANT FOR ME.
IT SHOULDN'T HAVE BEEN.
YOU'VE NEVER HESITATED TO DO WHATEVER YOUR COUNTRY HAS ASKED OF YOU. FOR AS LONG AS ANYONE CAN REMEMBER, YOU'VE BEEN A PERFECT SOLDIER...
...BUT NEVER AN ASSASSIN. YOU DON'T KILL-- NOT IN COLD BLOOD.
WHEN I SAW THAT YOU WERE SUDDENLY BEING ASKED TO CHOOSE BETWEEN DUTY AND CONSCIENCE...I DECIDED TO SPARE YOU THE BURDEN.
I'M A SOLDIER, TOO... STEVE. THERE ARE TIMES I HAVE TO KILL. I'M NOT PROUD OF IT...BUT MY JOB GETS DIRTY. SOMETIMES, THE ONLY WAY I CAN KEEP GOING...
...IS TO KNOW THAT THERE'S STILL ONE MAN OUT THERE WHO CAN ALWAYS DO THE JOB CLEAN.
YOU HAVE NO MORAL PROBLEM WITH KILLING THIS MAN IN MY STEAD?
I HAVE A PERSONAL PROBLEM.
I'M AFRAID IT MIGHT CHANGE HOW YOU FEEL ABOUT ME.

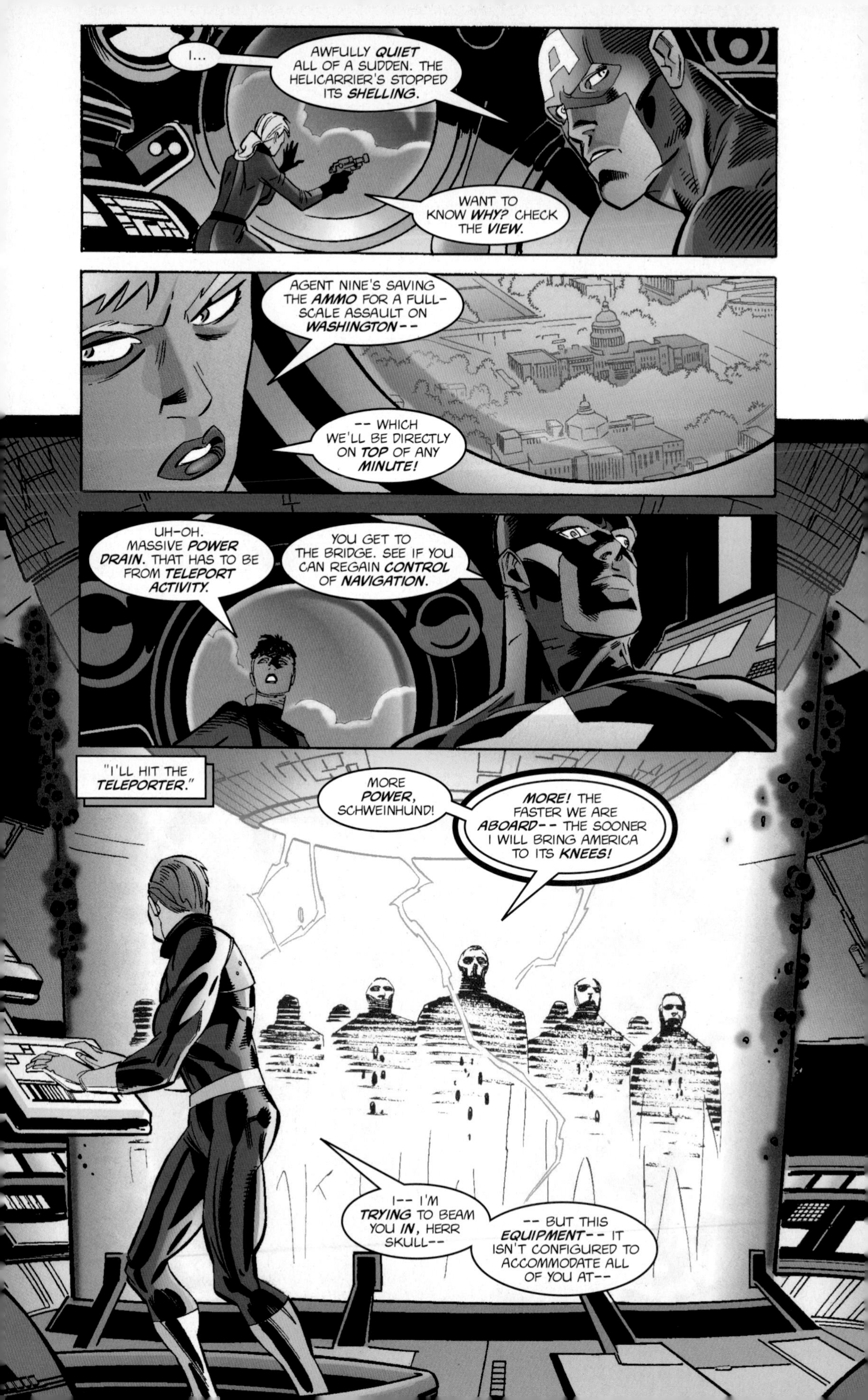
I...
AWFULLY QUIET ALL OF A SUDDEN. THE HELICARRIER'S STOPPED ITS SHELLING.
WANT TO KNOW WHY? CHECK THE VIEW.
AGENT NINE'S SAVING THE AMMO FOR A FULL-SCALE ASSAULT ON WASHINGTON--
-- WHICH WE'LL BE DIRECTLY ON TOP OF ANY MINUTE!
UH-OH. MASSIVE POWER DRAIN. THAT HAS TO BE FROM TELEPORT ACTIVITY.
YOU GET TO THE BRIDGE. SEE IF YOU CAN REGAIN CONTROL OF NAVIGATION.
"I'LL HIT THE TELEPORTER."
MORE POWER, SCHWEINHUND!
MORE! THE FASTER WE ARE ABOARD-- THE SOONER I WILL BRING AMERICA TO ITS KNEES!
I-- I'M TRYING TO BEAM YOU IN, HERR SKULL--
-- BUT THIS EQUIPMENT-- IT ISN'T CONFIGURED TO ACCOMMODATE ALL OF YOU AT--

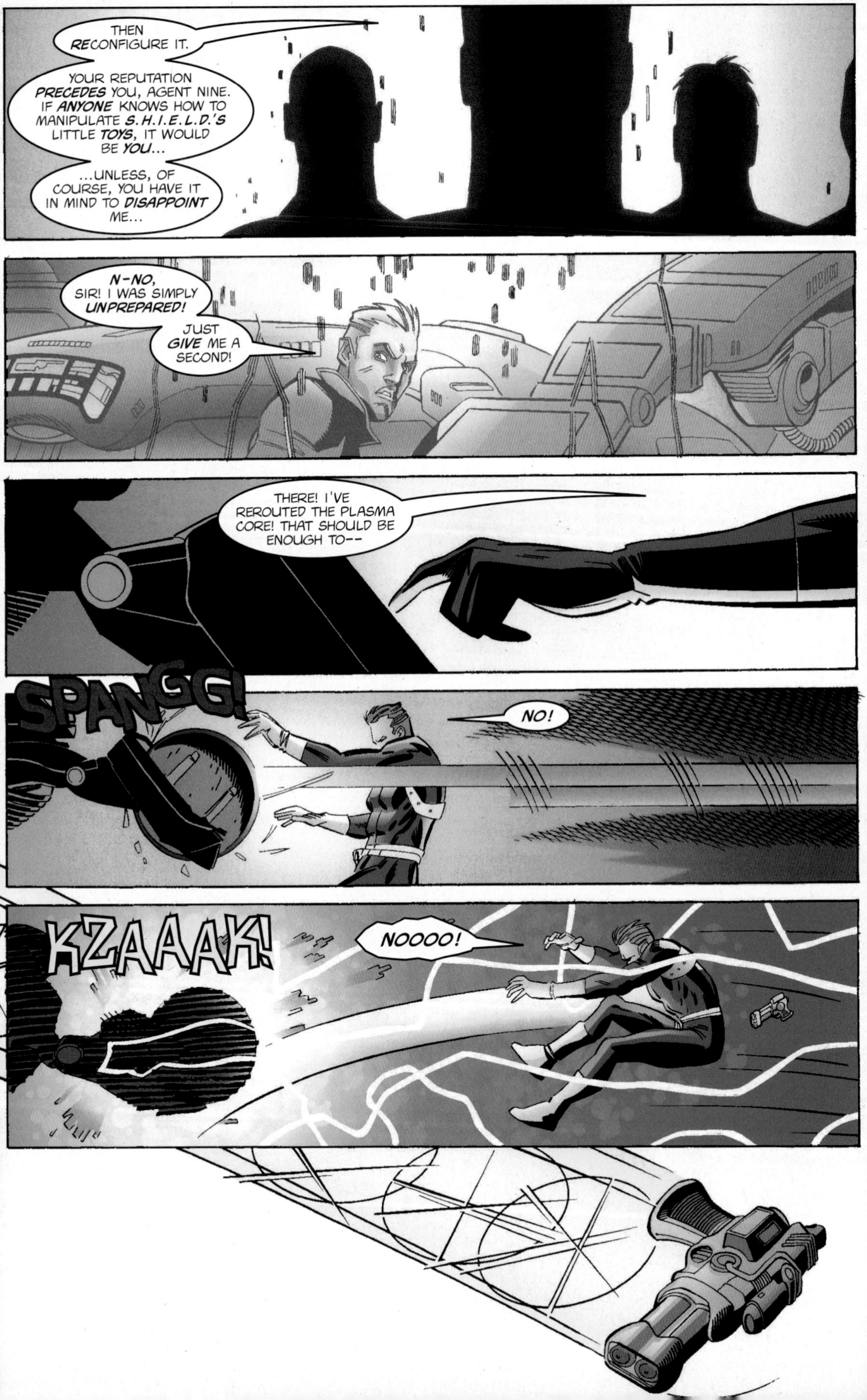
THEN RECONFIGURE IT.
YOUR REPUTATION PRECEDES YOU, AGENT NINE. IF ANYONE KNOWS HOW TO MANIPULATE S.H.I.E.L.D.'S LITTLE TOYS, IT WOULD BE YOU...
...UNLESS, OF COURSE, YOU HAVE IT IN MIND TO DISAPPOINT ME...
N-NO, SIR! I WAS SIMPLY UNPREPARED!
JUST GIVE ME A SECOND!
THERE! I'VE REROUTED THE PLASMA CORE! THAT SHOULD BE ENOUGH TO--
SPANGG!
NO!
KZAAAK!
NOOOO!

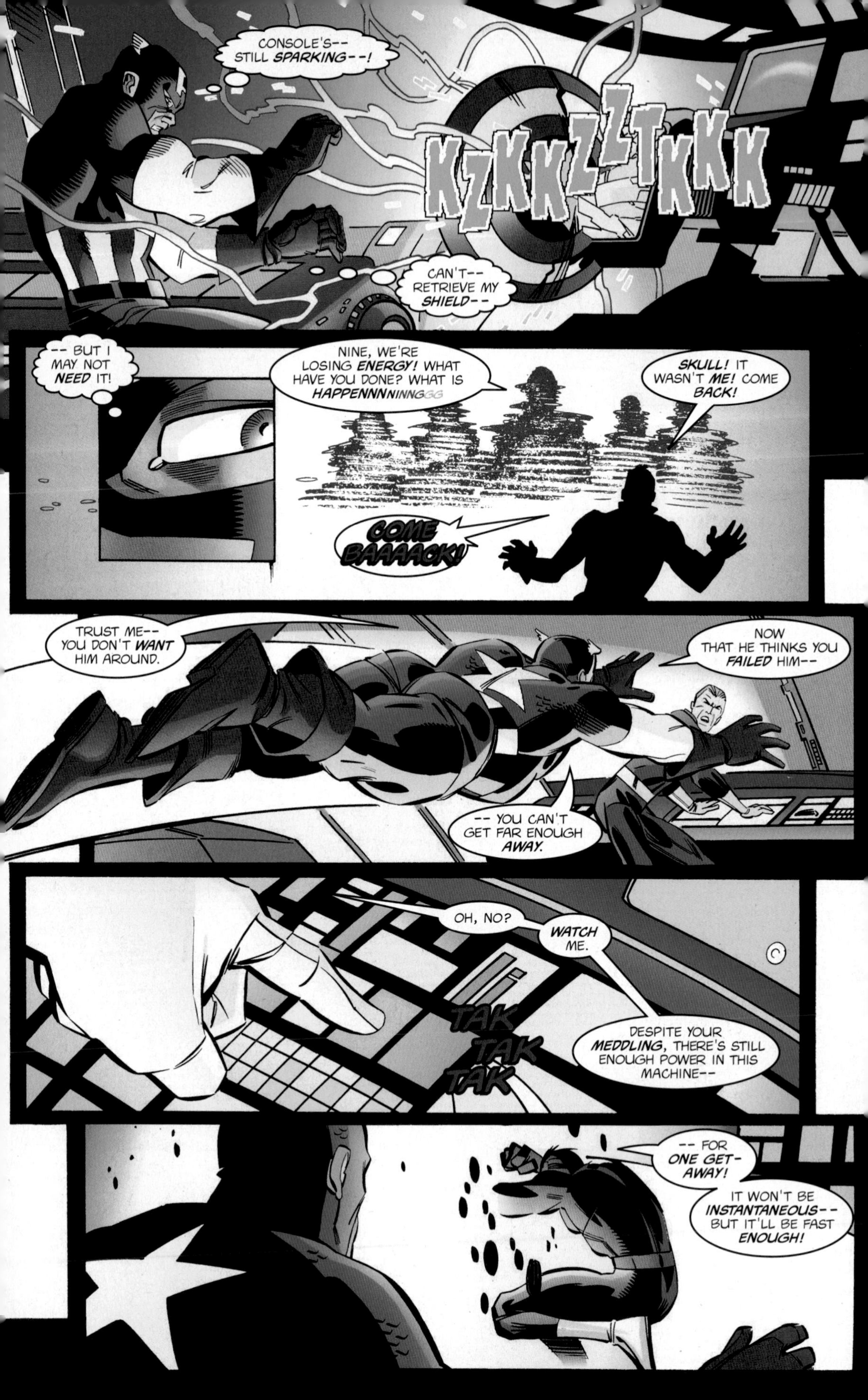
CONSOLE'S-- STILL SPARKING--!
KZKKKZZZTKKK
CAN'T-- RETRIEVE MY SHIELD--
-- BUT I MAY NOT NEED IT!
NINE, WE'RE LOSING ENERGY! WHAT HAVE YOU DONE? WHAT IS HAPPENNNNINNGGG
SKULL! IT WASN'T ME! COME BACK!
COME BAAAACK!
TRUST ME-- YOU DON'T WANT HIM AROUND.
NOW THAT HE THINKS YOU FAILED HIM--
-- YOU CAN'T GET FAR ENOUGH AWAY.
OH, NO?
WATCH ME.
TAK TAK TAK
DESPITE YOUR MEDDLING, THERE'S STILL ENOUGH POWER IN THIS MACHINE--
-- FOR ONE GET-AWAY!
IT WON'T BE INSTANTANEOUS-- BUT IT'LL BE FAST ENOUGH!

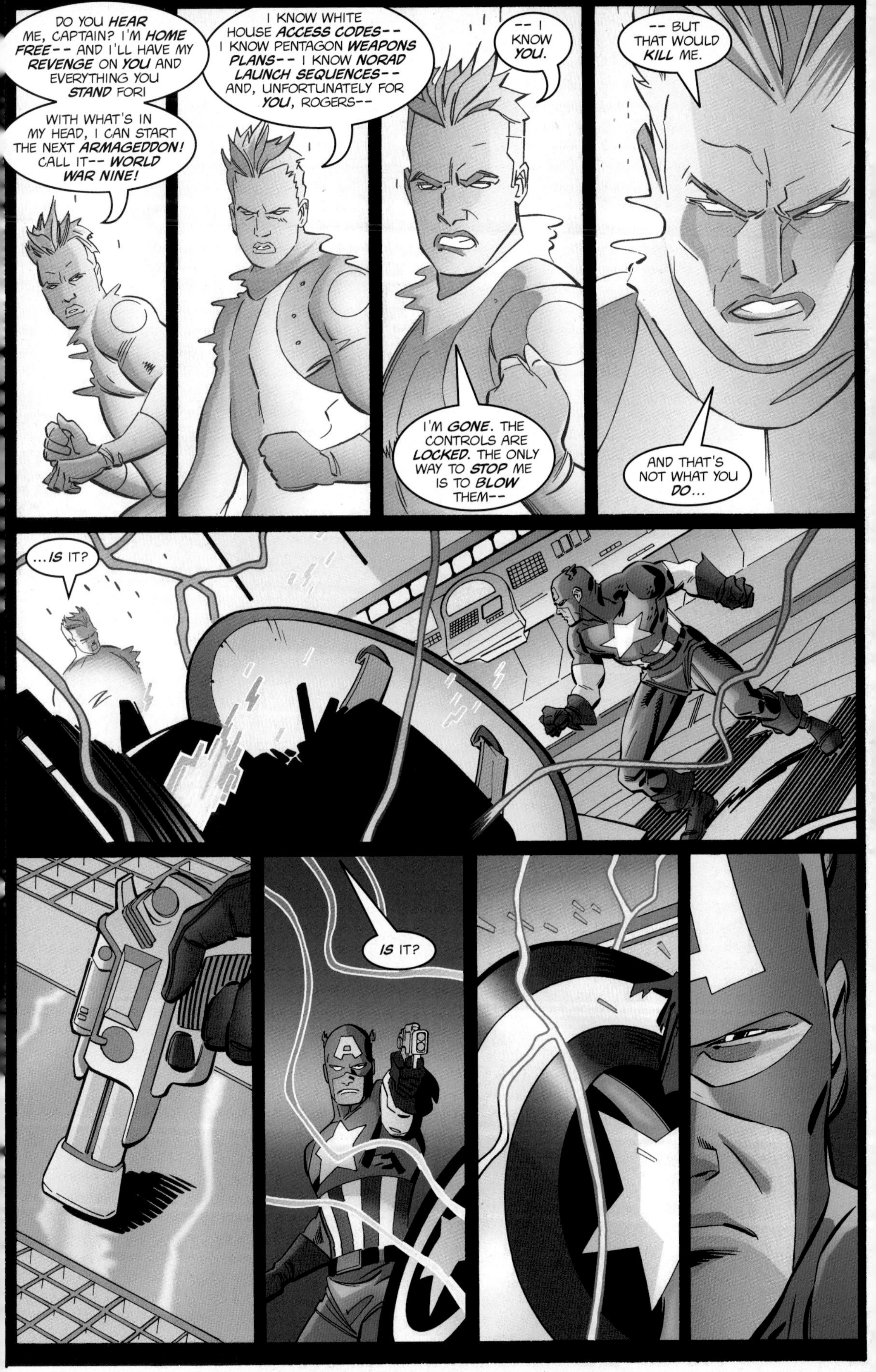
DO YOU HEAR ME, CAPTAIN? I'M HOME FREE-- AND I'LL HAVE MY REVENGE ON YOU AND EVERYTHING YOU STAND FOR!
WITH WHAT'S IN MY HEAD, I CAN START THE NEXT ARMAGEDDON! CALL IT-- WORLD WAR NINE!
I KNOW WHITE HOUSE ACCESS CODES-- I KNOW PENTAGON WEAPONS PLANS-- I KNOW NORAD LAUNCH SEQUENCES-- AND, UNFORTUNATELY FOR YOU, ROGERS--
-- I KNOW YOU.
I'M GONE. THE CONTROLS ARE LOCKED. THE ONLY WAY TO STOP ME IS TO BLOW THEM--
-- BUT THAT WOULD KILL ME.
AND THAT'S NOT WHAT YOU DO...
...IS IT?
IS IT?

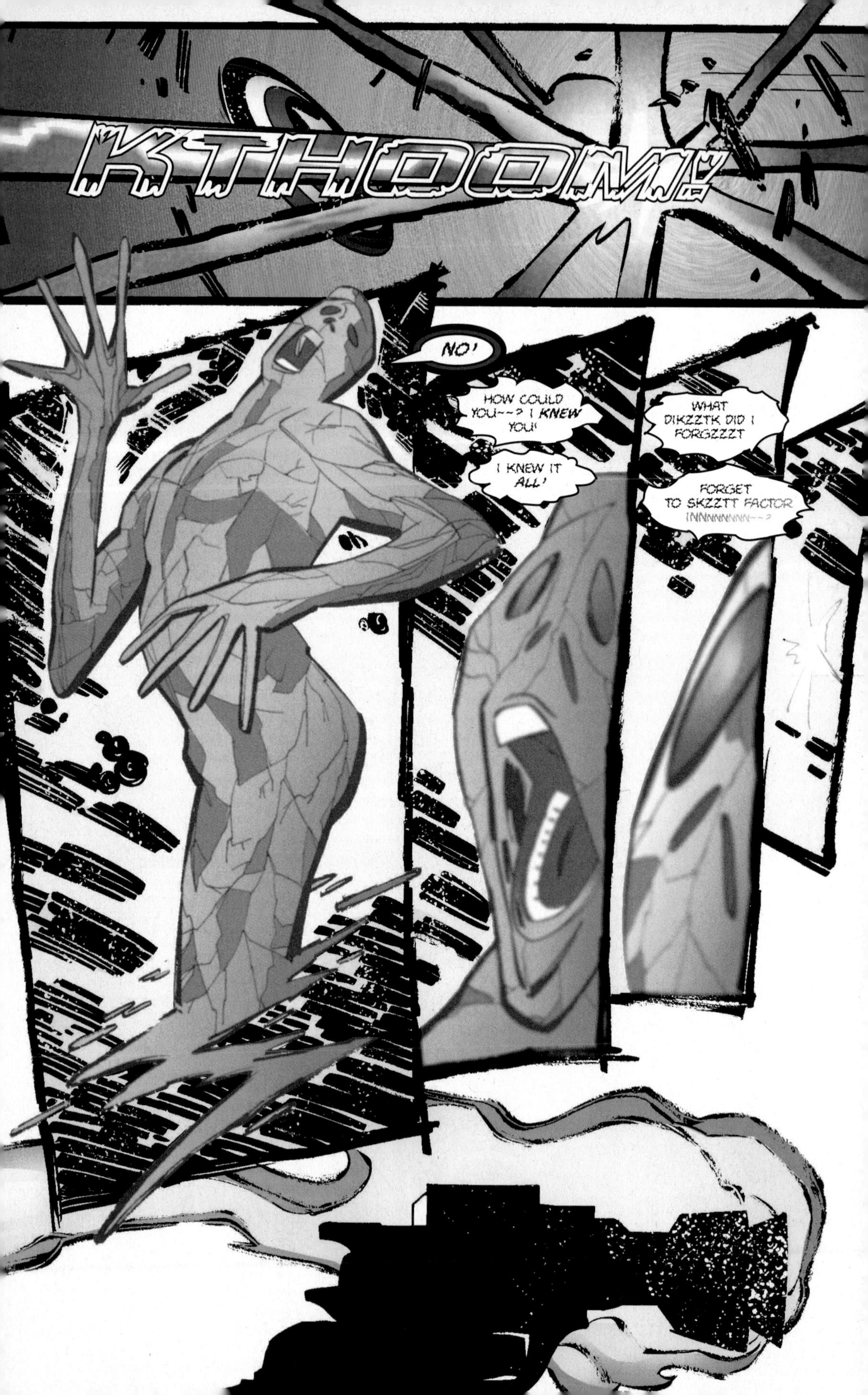
KTHOOM!
NO!
HOW COULD YOU--? I KNEW YOU!
I KNEW IT ALL!
WHAT DIKZZTK DID I FORGZZZT
FORGET TO SKZZTT FACTOR INNNNNNNN--?

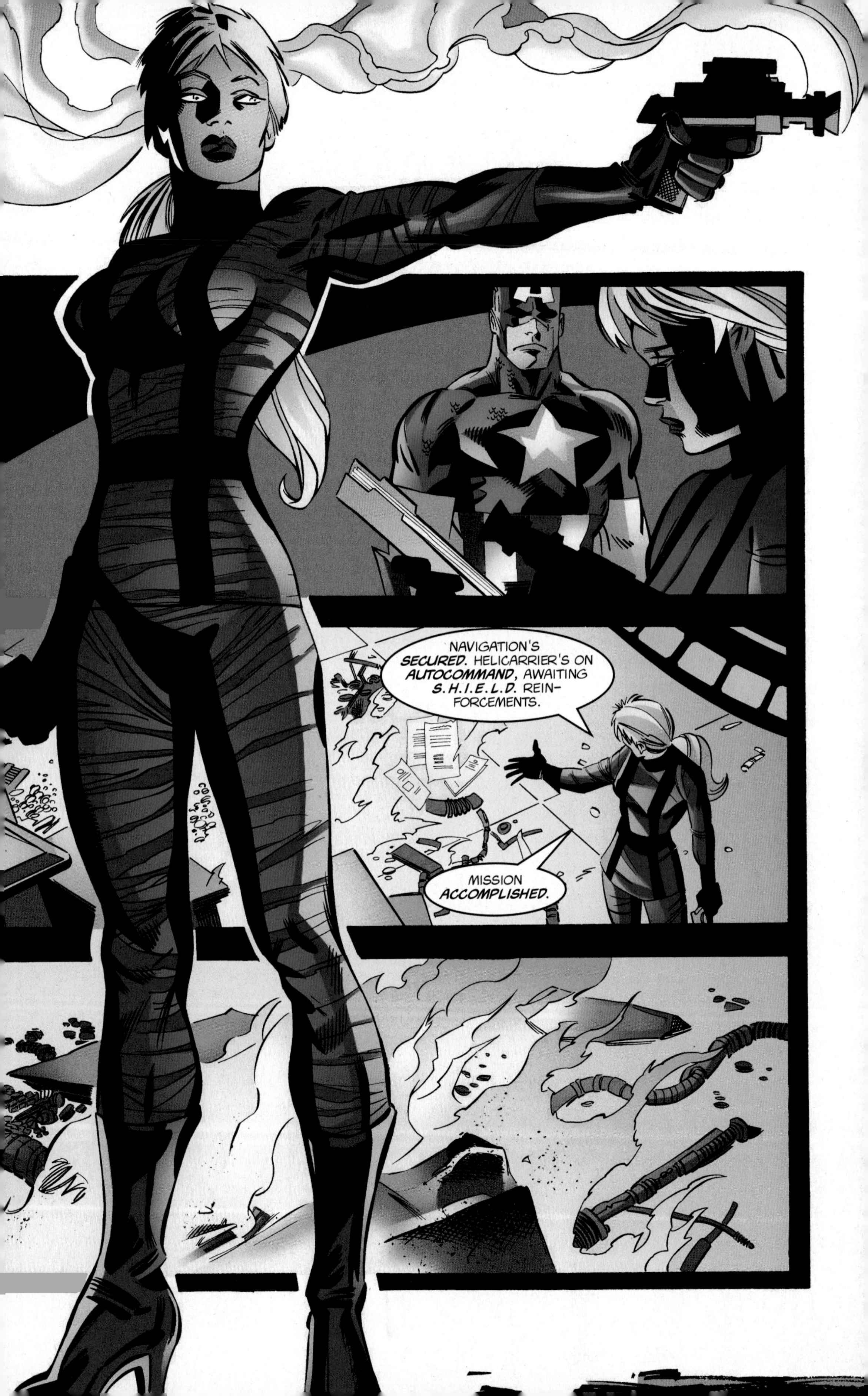
NAVIGATION'S SECURED. HELICARRIER'S ON AUTOCOMMAND, AWAITING S.H.I.E.L.D. REIN-FORCEMENTS.
MISSION ACCOMPLISHED.

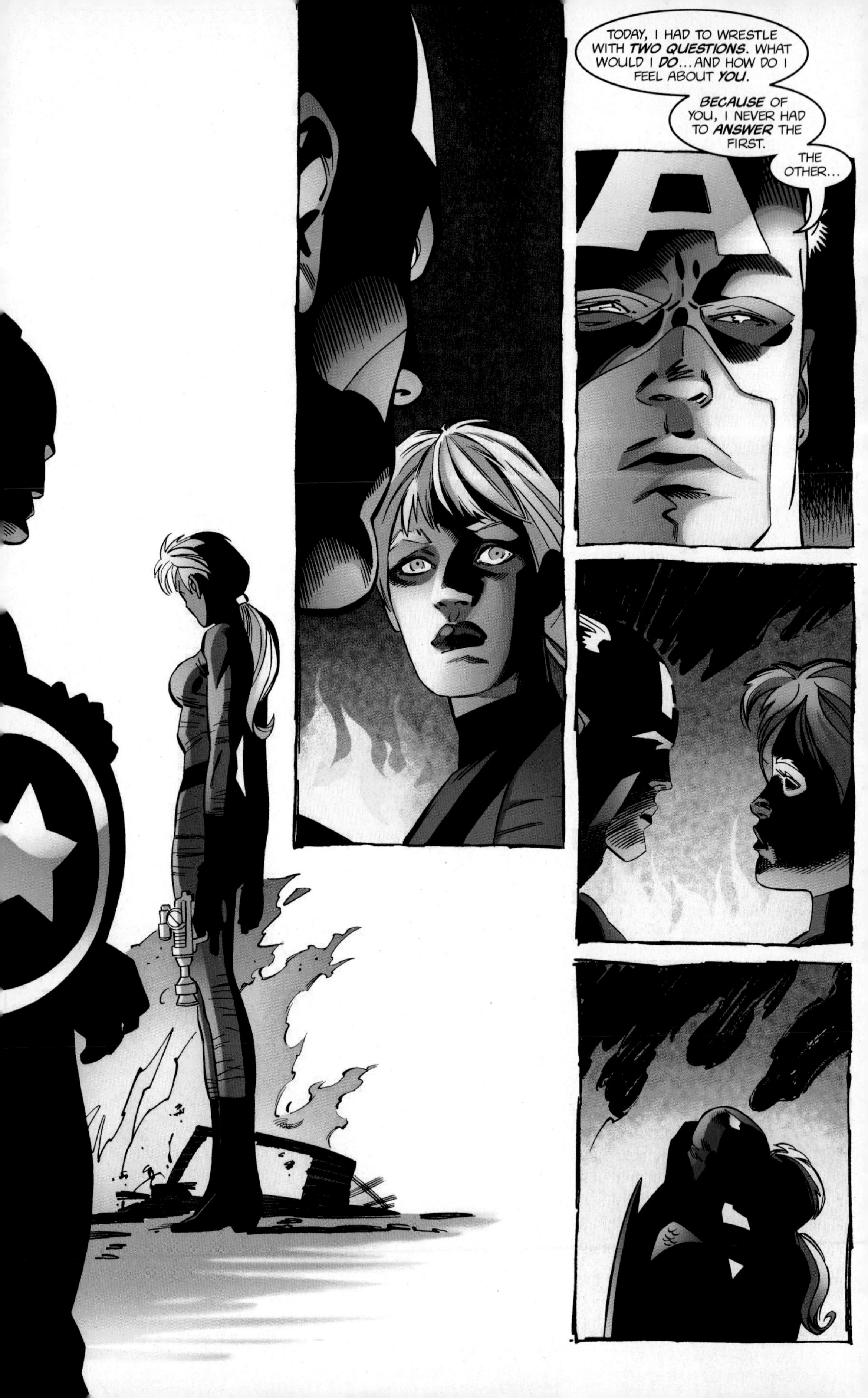
TODAY, I HAD TO WRESTLE WITH TWO QUESTIONS. WHAT WOULD I DO...AND HOW DO I FEEL ABOUT YOU.
BECAUSE OF YOU, I NEVER HAD TO ANSWER THE FIRST.
THE OTHER...

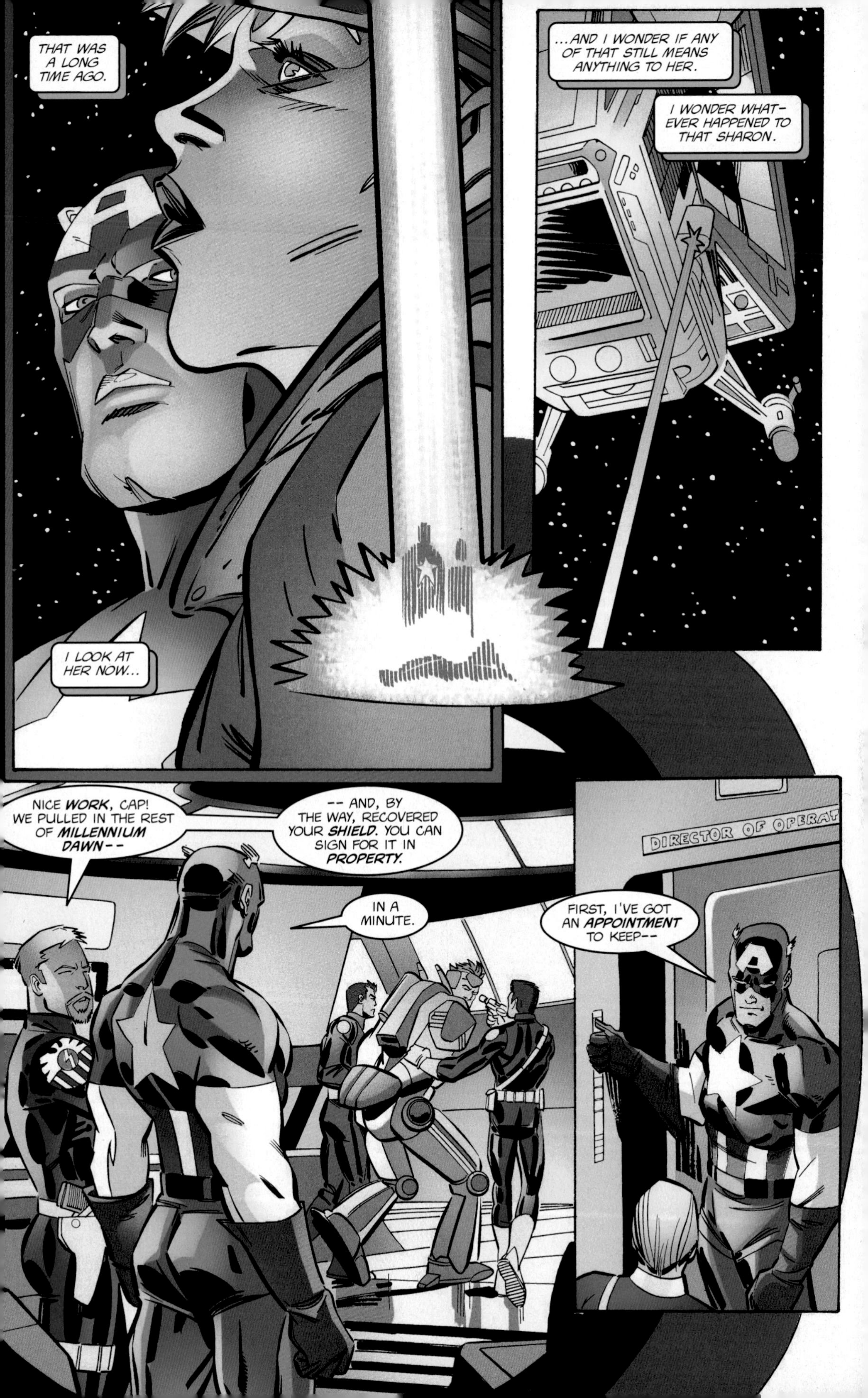
THAT WAS A LONG TIME AGO.
I LOOK AT HER NOW...
...AND I WONDER IF ANY OF THAT STILL MEANS ANYTHING TO HER.
I WONDER WHATEVER HAPPENED TO THAT SHARON.
NICE WORK, CAP! WE PULLED IN THE REST OF MILLENNIUM DAWN--
-- AND, BY THE WAY, RECOVERED YOUR SHIELD. YOU CAN SIGN FOR IT IN PROPERTY.
IN A MINUTE.
DIRECTOR OF OPERAT
FIRST, I'VE GOT AN APPOINTMENT TO KEEP--

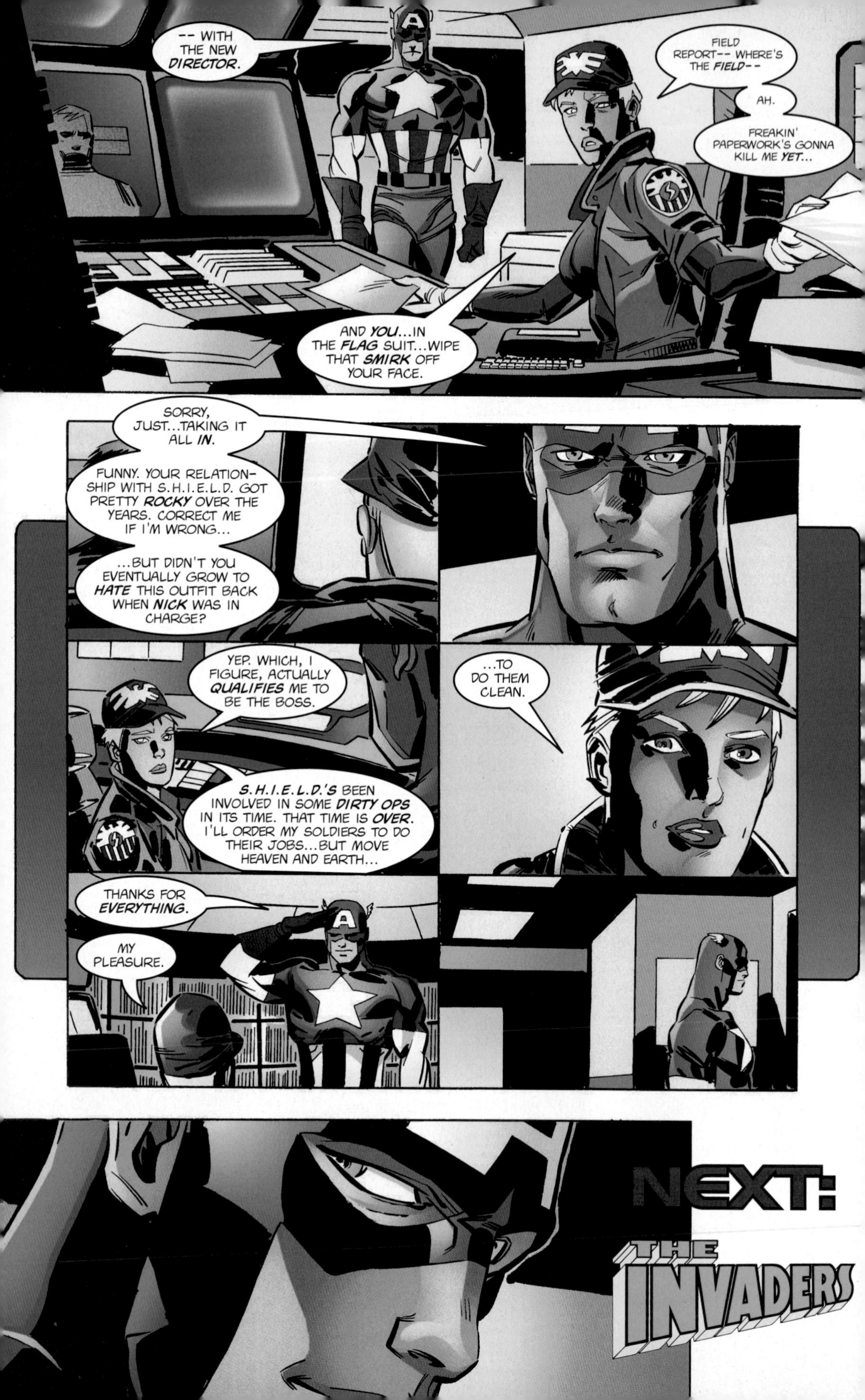
-- WITH THE NEW DIRECTOR.
FIELD REPORT-- WHERE'S THE FIELD--
AH.
FREAKIN' PAPERWORK'S GONNA KILL ME YET...
AND YOU...IN THE FLAG SUIT...WIPE THAT SMIRK OFF YOUR FACE.
SORRY, JUST...TAKING IT ALL IN.
FUNNY. YOUR RELATIONSHIP WITH S.H.I.E.L.D. GOT PRETTY ROCKY OVER THE YEARS. CORRECT ME IF I'M WRONG...
...BUT DIDN'T YOU EVENTUALLY GROW TO HATE THIS OUTFIT BACK WHEN NICK WAS IN CHARGE?
YEP. WHICH, I FIGURE, ACTUALLY QUALIFIES ME TO BE THE BOSS.
S.H.I.E.L.D.'S BEEN INVOLVED IN SOME DIRTY OPS IN ITS TIME. THAT TIME IS OVER. I'LL ORDER MY SOLDIERS TO DO THEIR JOBS...BUT MOVE HEAVEN AND EARTH...
...TO DO THEM CLEAN.
THANKS FOR EVERYTHING.
MY PLEASURE.
NEXT:
THE INVADERS

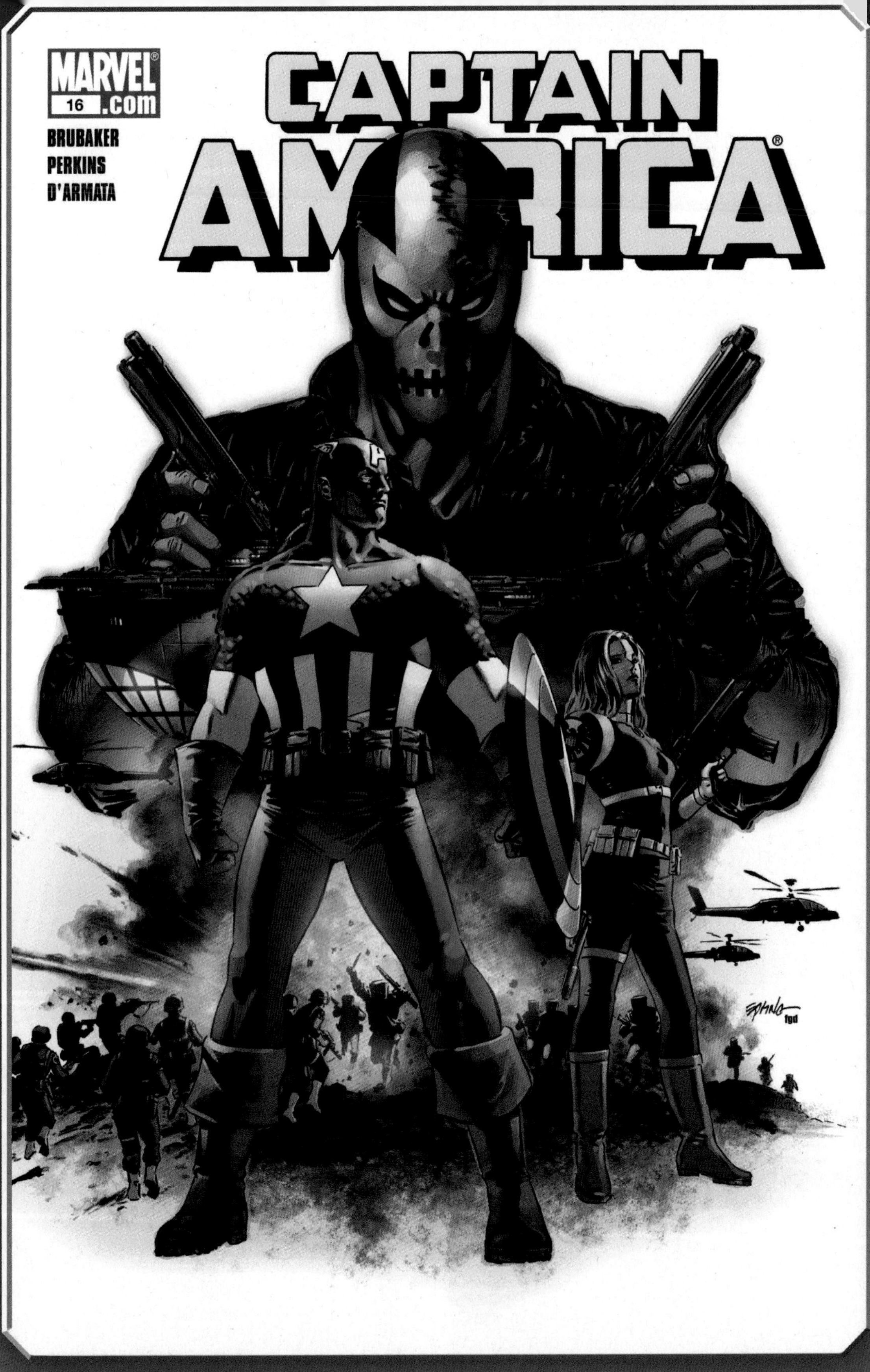
MARVEL
16 .com
BRUBAKER
PERKINS
D'ARMATA
CAPTAIN AMERICA

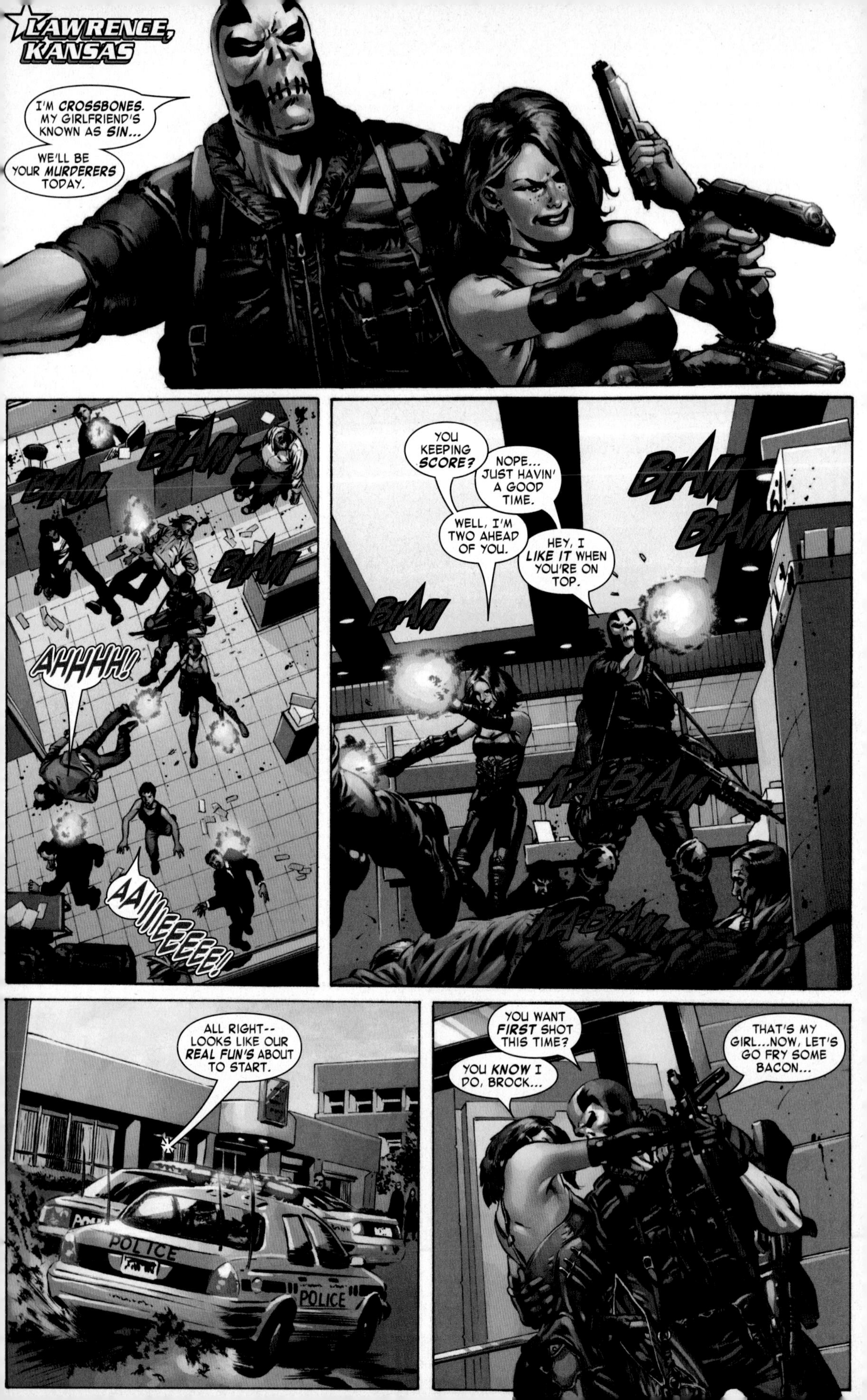
LAWRENCE, KANSAS
I'M CROSSBONES. MY GIRLFRIEND'S KNOWN AS SIN...
WE'LL BE YOUR MURDERERS TODAY.
BLAM
BLAM
BLAM
AHHHH!
AAIIIEEEEEE!
YOU KEEPING SCORE?
NOPE... JUST HAVIN' A GOOD TIME.
WELL, I'M TWO AHEAD OF YOU.
HEY, I LIKE IT WHEN YOU'RE ON TOP.
BLAM
BLAM
BLAM
KA-BLAM
KA-BLAM
ALL RIGHT-- LOOKS LIKE OUR REAL FUN'S ABOUT TO START.
POLICE
POLICE
YOU WANT FIRST SHOT THIS TIME?
YOU KNOW I DO, BROCK...
THAT'S MY GIRL...NOW, LET'S GO FRY SOME BACON...

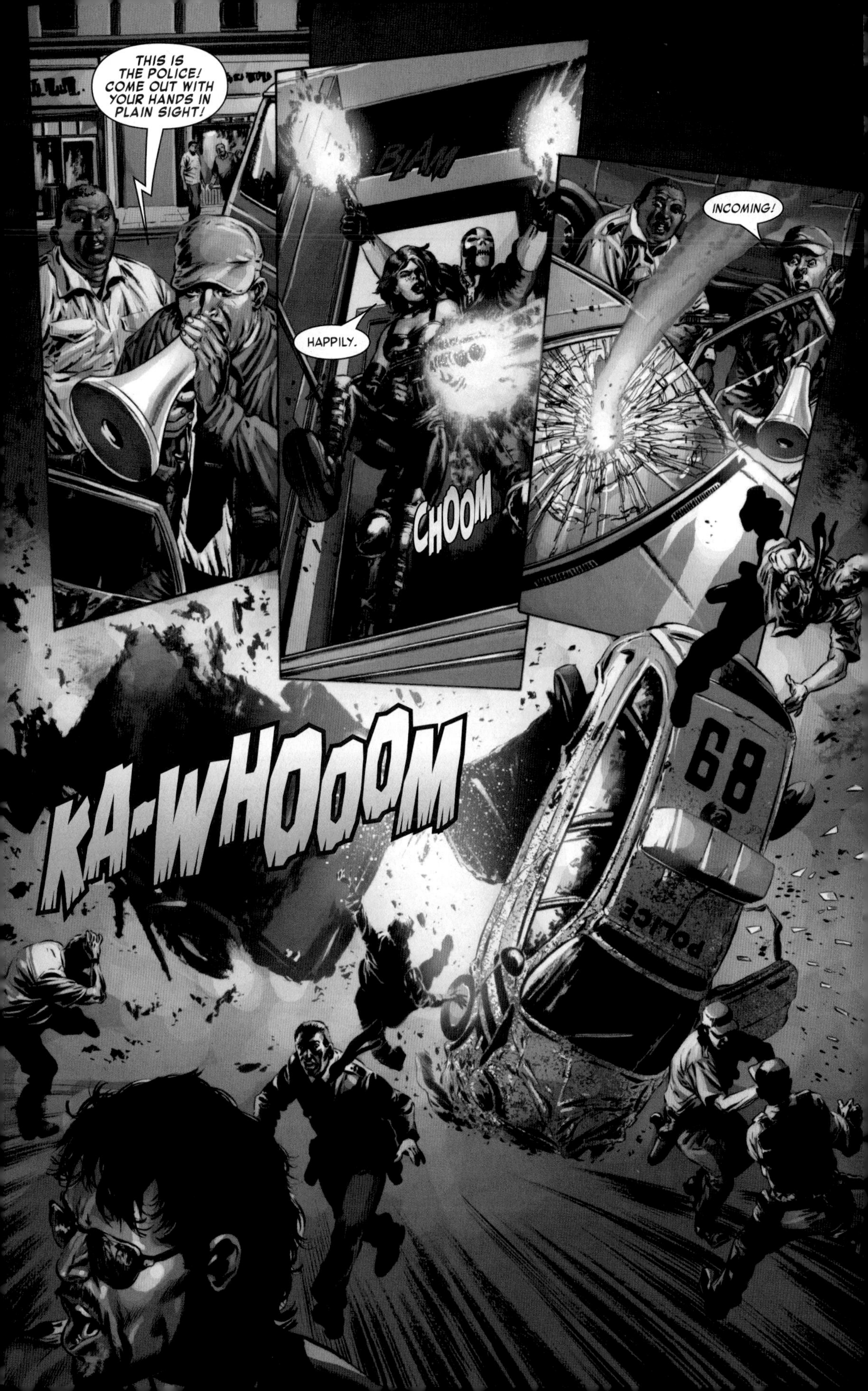
THIS IS THE POLICE! COME OUT WITH YOUR HANDS IN PLAIN SIGHT!
BLAM
HAPPILY.
CHOOM
INCOMING!
KA-WHOOOM
68
POLICE

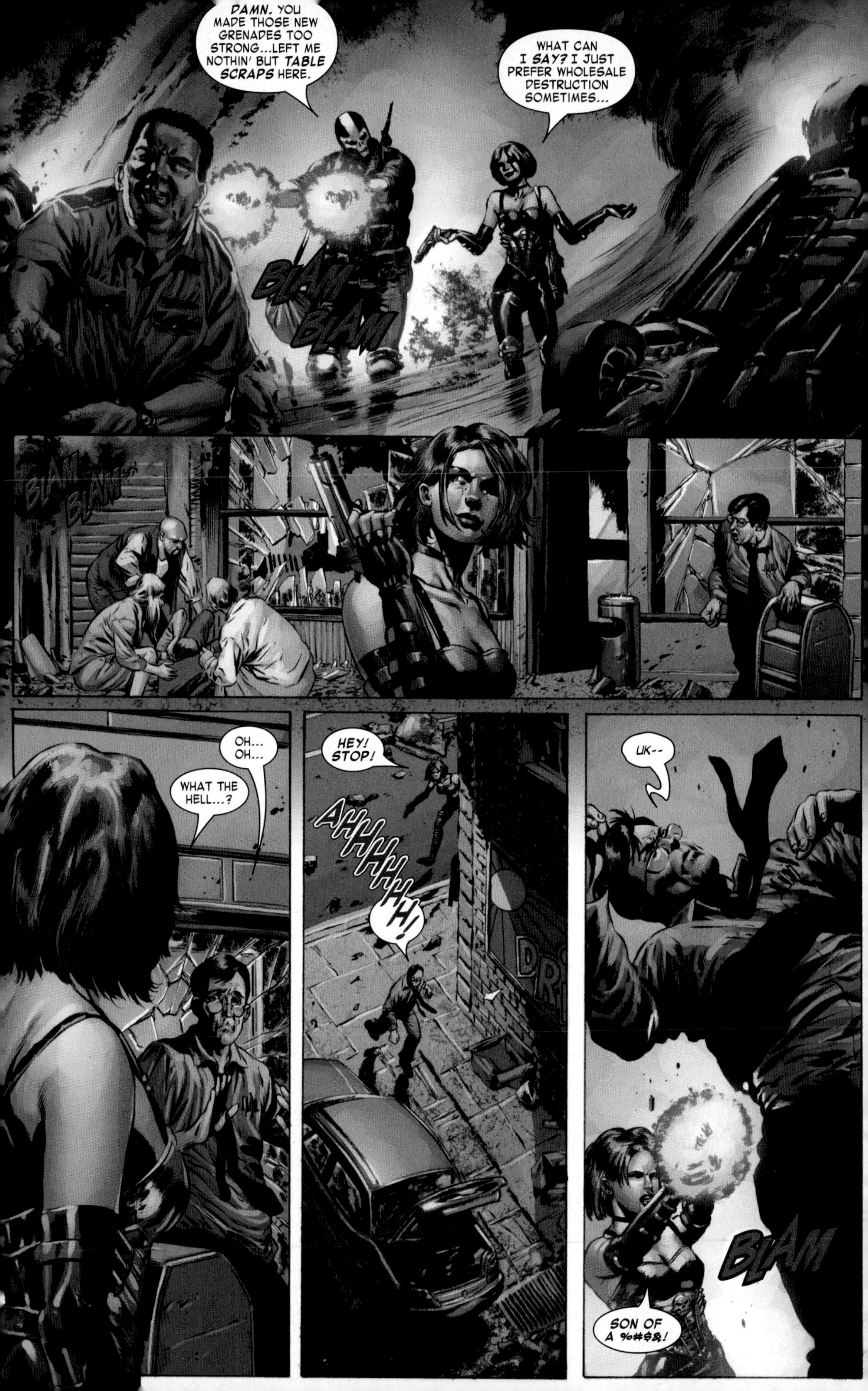
DAMN. YOU MADE THOSE NEW GRENADES TOO STRONG...LEFT ME NOTHIN' BUT TABLE SCRAPS HERE.
WHAT CAN I SAY? I JUST PREFER WHOLESALE DESTRUCTION SOMETIMES...
BLAM BLAM
BLAM BLAM
OH... OH...
WHAT THE HELL...?
HEY! STOP!
AHHHHHH!
UK--
BLAM
SON OF A %#$&!

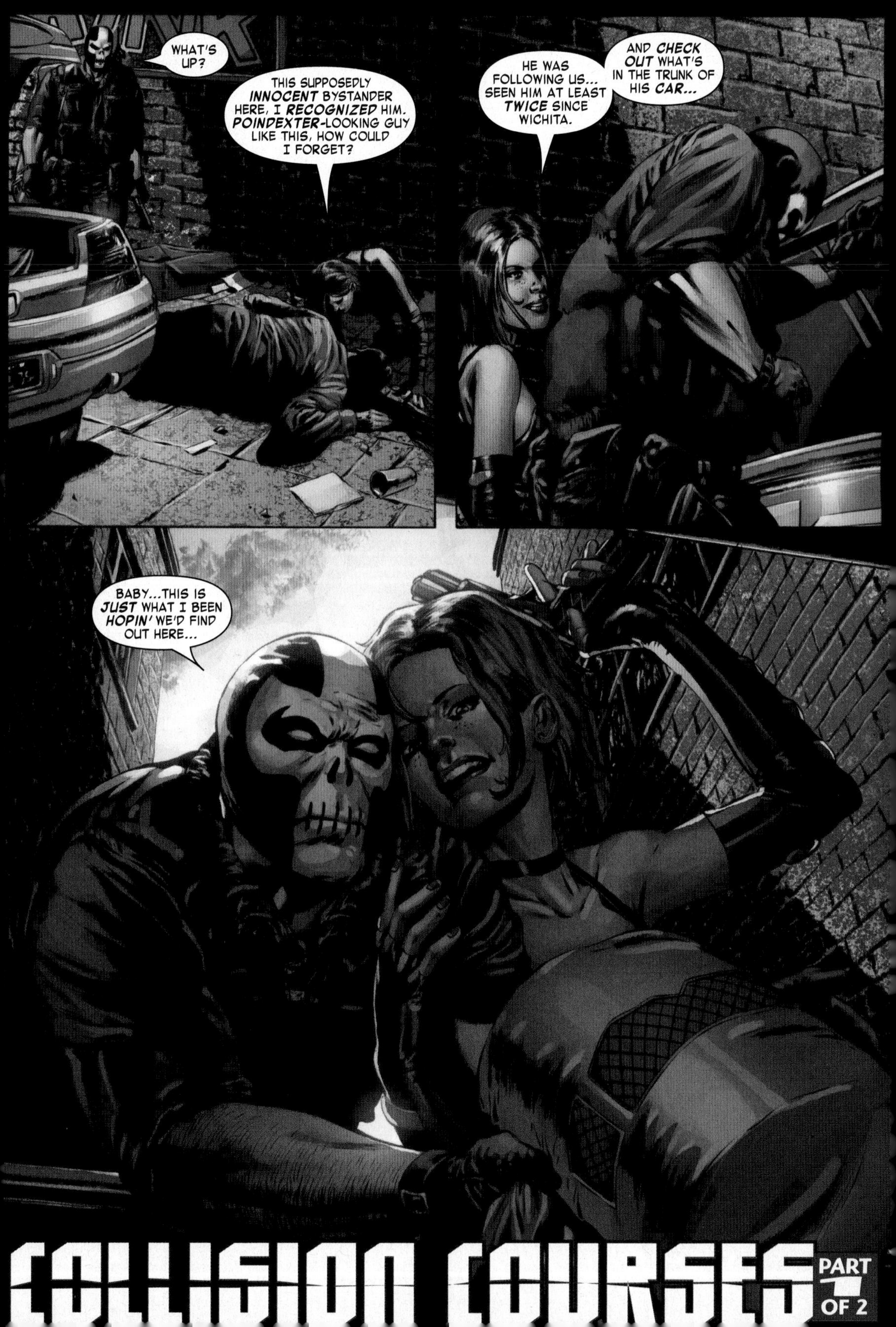
WHAT'S UP?
THIS SUPPOSEDLY INNOCENT BYSTANDER HERE, I RECOGNIZED HIM. POINDEXTER-LOOKING GUY LIKE THIS, HOW COULD I FORGET?
HE WAS FOLLOWING US... SEEN HIM AT LEAST TWICE SINCE WICHITA.
AND CHECK OUT WHAT'S IN THE TRUNK OF HIS CAR...
BABY...THIS IS JUST WHAT I BEEN HOPIN' WE'D FIND OUT HERE...
COLLISION COURSES
PART 1 OF 2

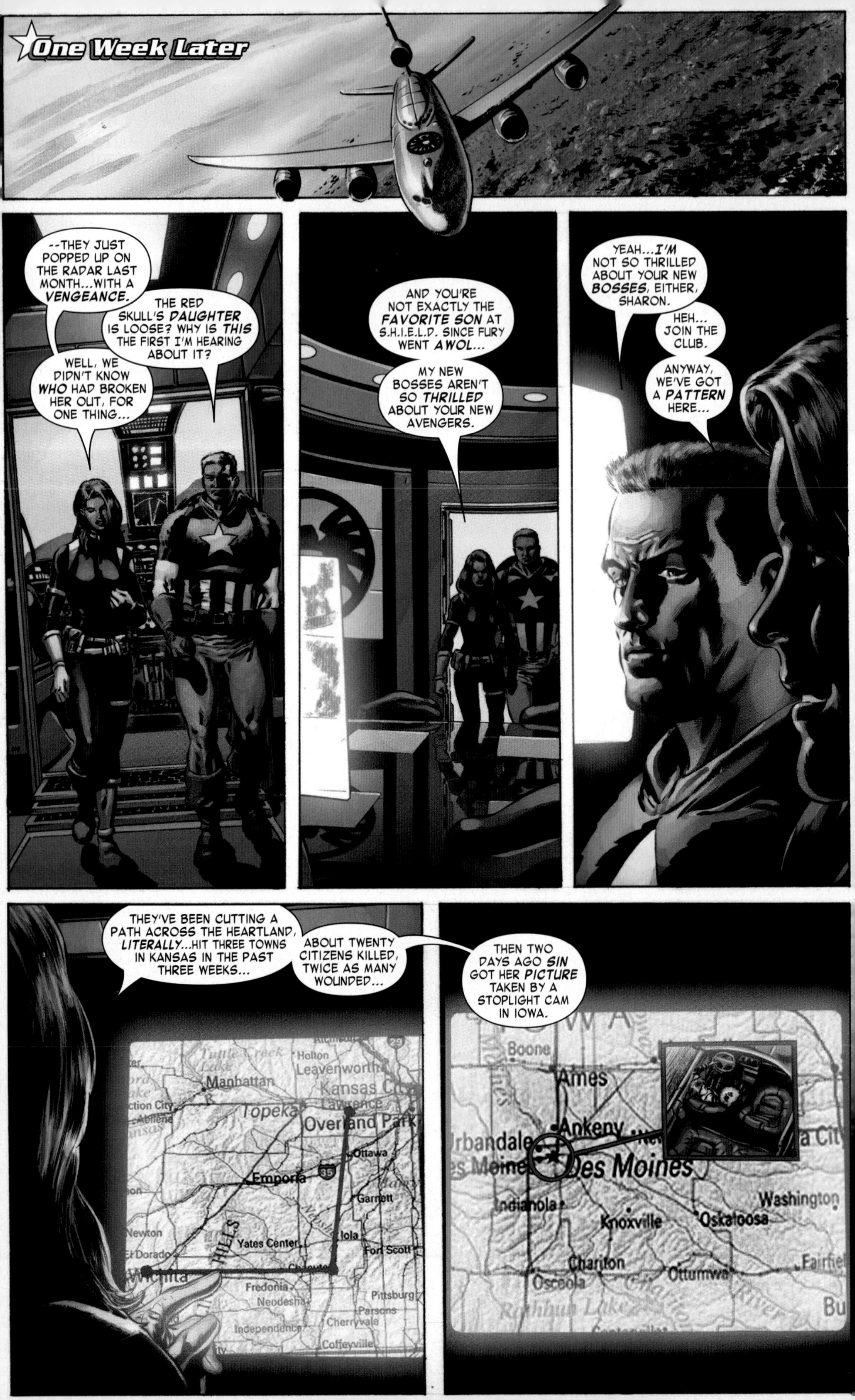
One Week Later
--THEY JUST POPPED UP ON THE RADAR LAST MONTH...WITH A VENGEANCE.
THE RED SKULL'S DAUGHTER IS LOOSE? WHY IS THIS THE FIRST I'M HEARING ABOUT IT?
WELL, WE DIDN'T KNOW WHO HAD BROKEN HER OUT, FOR ONE THING...
AND YOU'RE NOT EXACTLY THE FAVORITE SON AT S.H.I.E.L.D. SINCE FURY WENT AWOL...
MY NEW BOSSES AREN'T SO THRILLED ABOUT YOUR NEW AVENGERS.
YEAH...I'M NOT SO THRILLED ABOUT YOUR NEW BOSSES, EITHER, SHARON.
HEH... JOIN THE CLUB.
ANYWAY, WE'VE GOT A PATTERN HERE...
THEY'VE BEEN CUTTING A PATH ACROSS THE HEARTLAND, LITERALLY...HIT THREE TOWNS IN KANSAS IN THE PAST THREE WEEKS...
ABOUT TWENTY CITIZENS KILLED, TWICE AS MANY WOUNDED...
THEN TWO DAYS AGO SIN GOT HER PICTURE TAKEN BY A STOPLIGHT CAM IN IOWA.
Holton
Leavenworth
Manhattan
Kansas City
Topeka
Lawrence
Overland Park
Ottawa
Emporia
35
Garnett
Newton
Yates Center
Iola
Fort Scott
El Dorado
Wichita
Chanute
Fredonia
Neodesha
Pittsburg
Parsons
Independence
Cherryvale
Coffeyville
Boone
Ames
Ankeny
Urbandale
Des Moines
Indianola
Knoxville
Oskaloosa
Washington
Chariton
Ottumwa
Osceola

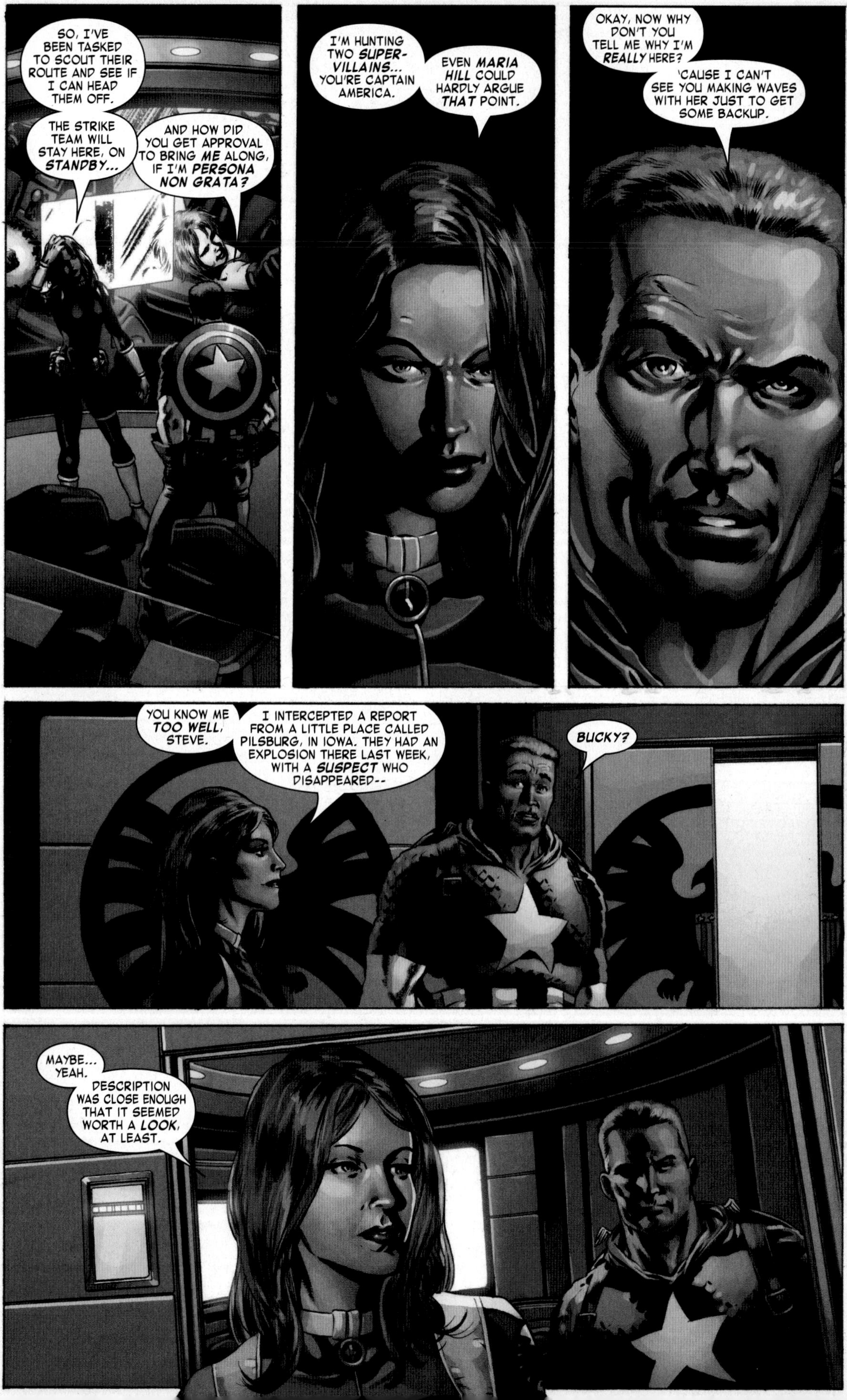

SO, I'VE BEEN TASKED TO SCOUT THEIR ROUTE AND SEE IF I CAN HEAD THEM OFF.
THE STRIKE TEAM WILL STAY HERE, ON STANDBY...
AND HOW DID YOU GET APPROVAL TO BRING ME ALONG, IF I'M PERSONA NON GRATA?
I'M HUNTING TWO SUPER-VILLAINS... YOU'RE CAPTAIN AMERICA.
EVEN MARIA HILL COULD HARDLY ARGUE THAT POINT.
OKAY, NOW WHY DON'T YOU TELL ME WHY I'M REALLY HERE?
'CAUSE I CAN'T SEE YOU MAKING WAVES WITH HER JUST TO GET SOME BACKUP.
YOU KNOW ME TOO WELL, STEVE.
I INTERCEPTED A REPORT FROM A LITTLE PLACE CALLED PILSBURG, IN IOWA. THEY HAD AN EXPLOSION THERE LAST WEEK, WITH A SUSPECT WHO DISAPPEARED--
BUCKY?
MAYBE... YEAH.
DESCRIPTION WAS CLOSE ENOUGH THAT IT SEEMED WORTH A LOOK, AT LEAST.

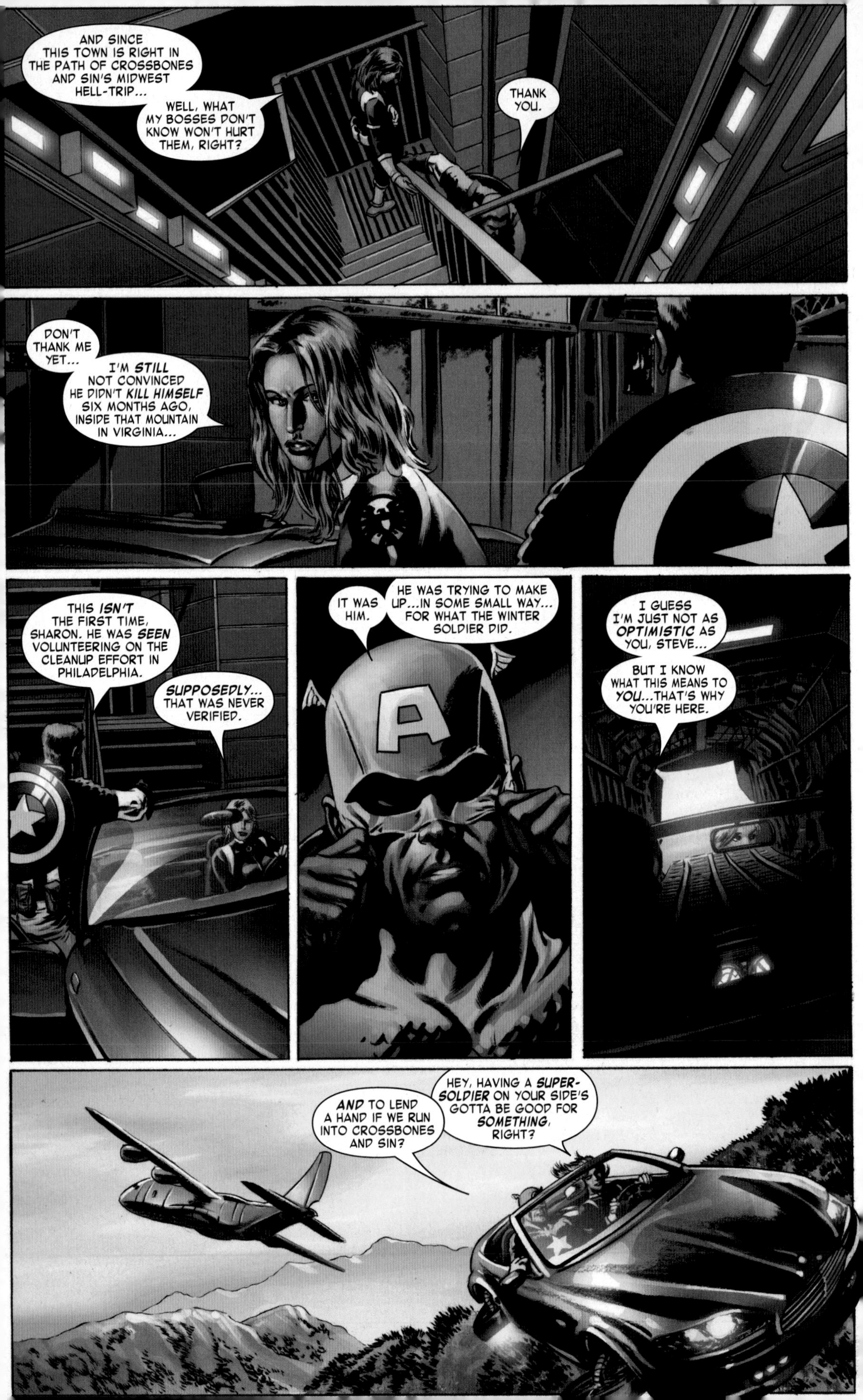
AND SINCE THIS TOWN IS RIGHT IN THE PATH OF CROSSBONES AND SIN'S MIDWEST HELL-TRIP...
WELL, WHAT MY BOSSES DON'T KNOW WON'T HURT THEM, RIGHT?
THANK YOU.
DON'T THANK ME YET...
I'M STILL NOT CONVINCED HE DIDN'T KILL HIMSELF SIX MONTHS AGO, INSIDE THAT MOUNTAIN IN VIRGINIA...
THIS ISN'T THE FIRST TIME, SHARON. HE WAS SEEN VOLUNTEERING ON THE CLEANUP EFFORT IN PHILADELPHIA.
SUPPOSEDLY... THAT WAS NEVER VERIFIED.
IT WAS HIM.
HE WAS TRYING TO MAKE UP...IN SOME SMALL WAY... FOR WHAT THE WINTER SOLDIER DID.
I GUESS I'M JUST NOT AS OPTIMISTIC AS YOU, STEVE...
BUT I KNOW WHAT THIS MEANS TO YOU...THAT'S WHY YOU'RE HERE.
AND TO LEND A HAND IF WE RUN INTO CROSSBONES AND SIN?
HEY, HAVING A SUPER-SOLDIER ON YOUR SIDE'S GOTTA BE GOOD FOR SOMETHING, RIGHT?

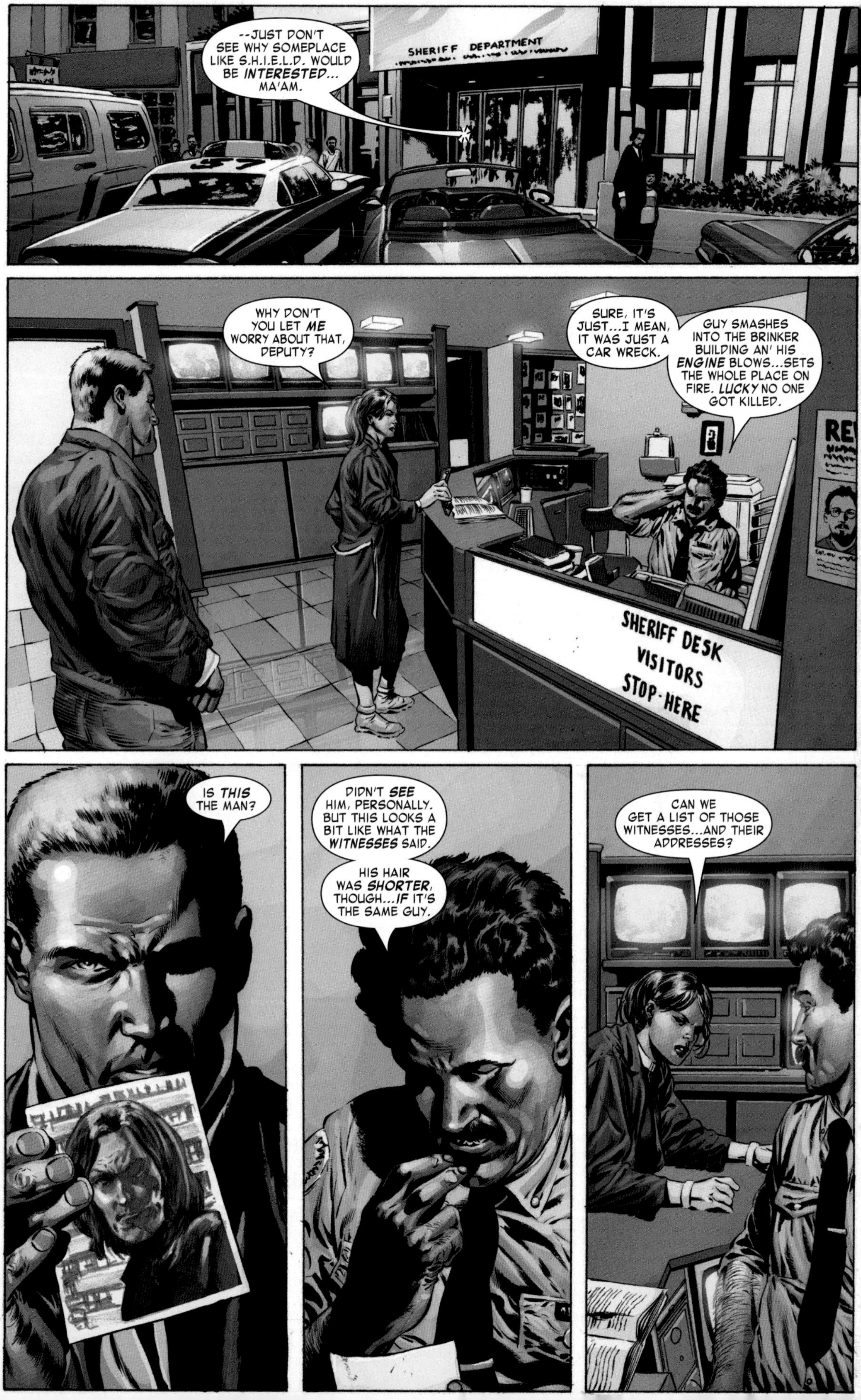
--JUST DON'T SEE WHY SOMEPLACE LIKE S.H.I.E.L.D. WOULD BE INTERESTED... MA'AM.
SHERIFF DEPARTMENT
WHY DON'T YOU LET ME WORRY ABOUT THAT, DEPUTY?
SURE, IT'S JUST...I MEAN, IT WAS JUST A CAR WRECK.
GUY SMASHES INTO THE BRINKER BUILDING AN' HIS ENGINE BLOWS...SETS THE WHOLE PLACE ON FIRE. LUCKY NO ONE GOT KILLED.
SHERIFF DESK VISITORS STOP-HERE
IS THIS THE MAN?
DIDN'T SEE HIM, PERSONALLY. BUT THIS LOOKS A BIT LIKE WHAT THE WITNESSES SAID.
HIS HAIR WAS SHORTER, THOUGH...IF IT'S THE SAME GUY.
CAN WE GET A LIST OF THOSE WITNESSES...AND THEIR ADDRESSES?

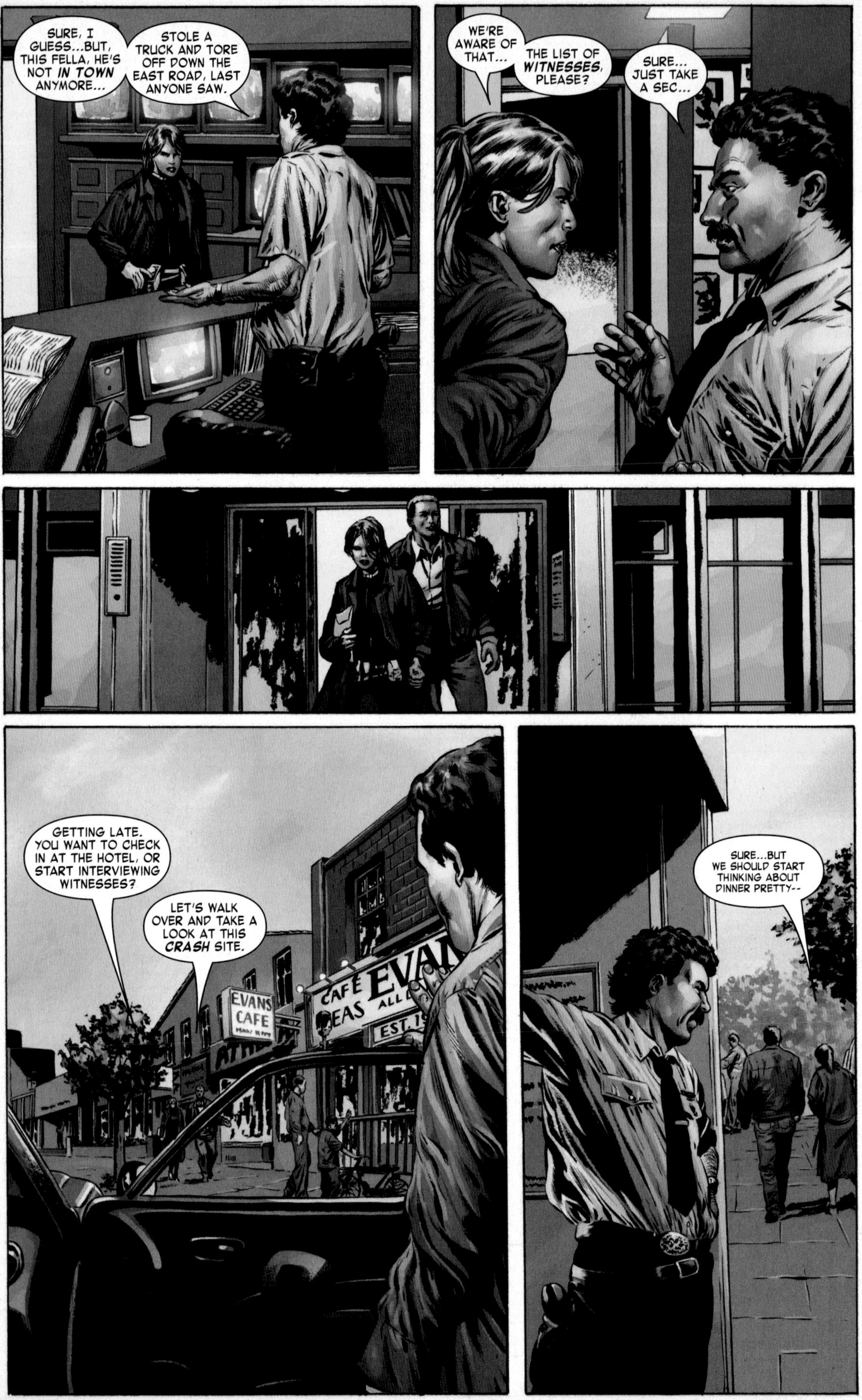
SURE, I GUESS...BUT, THIS FELLA, HE'S NOT *IN TOWN* ANYMORE...
STOLE A TRUCK AND TORE OFF DOWN THE EAST ROAD, LAST ANYONE SAW.
WE'RE AWARE OF THAT...
THE LIST OF *WITNESSES*, PLEASE?
SURE... JUST TAKE A SEC...
GETTING LATE. YOU WANT TO CHECK IN AT THE HOTEL, OR START INTERVIEWING WITNESSES?
LET'S WALK OVER AND TAKE A LOOK AT THIS *CRASH* SITE.
EVANS CAFE
SURE...BUT WE SHOULD START THINKING ABOUT DINNER PRETTY--

BRINKER BUILDING
UNDER CONSTRUCTION

DANGER
DO NOT ENTER

OKAY...ARE YOU THINKING THE SAME THING *I* AM?

LIKE, HOW THE HELL DOES A TOWN *THIS SMALL* START RECONSTRUCTING A BURNED-DOWN BUILDING THIS QUICKLY?

YEAH.

PILSBURG FOUNDERS DAY

FAMILY STORE

FAMILY STORE

Laverne+Shirley CLOTHING

AND IT'S MORE THAN THAT...JUST LOOK AT THIS PLACE. THERE'S NO FACTORY, NO ECONOMY TO SPEAK OF...

BUT IT'S DOING PRETTY WELL FOR SMALL-TOWN AMERICA IN THE 21ST CENTURY.

SOMETHING'S GOING ON HERE.

DEFINITELY.

IT'S NO *COINCIDENCE* BUCK WAS HERE.

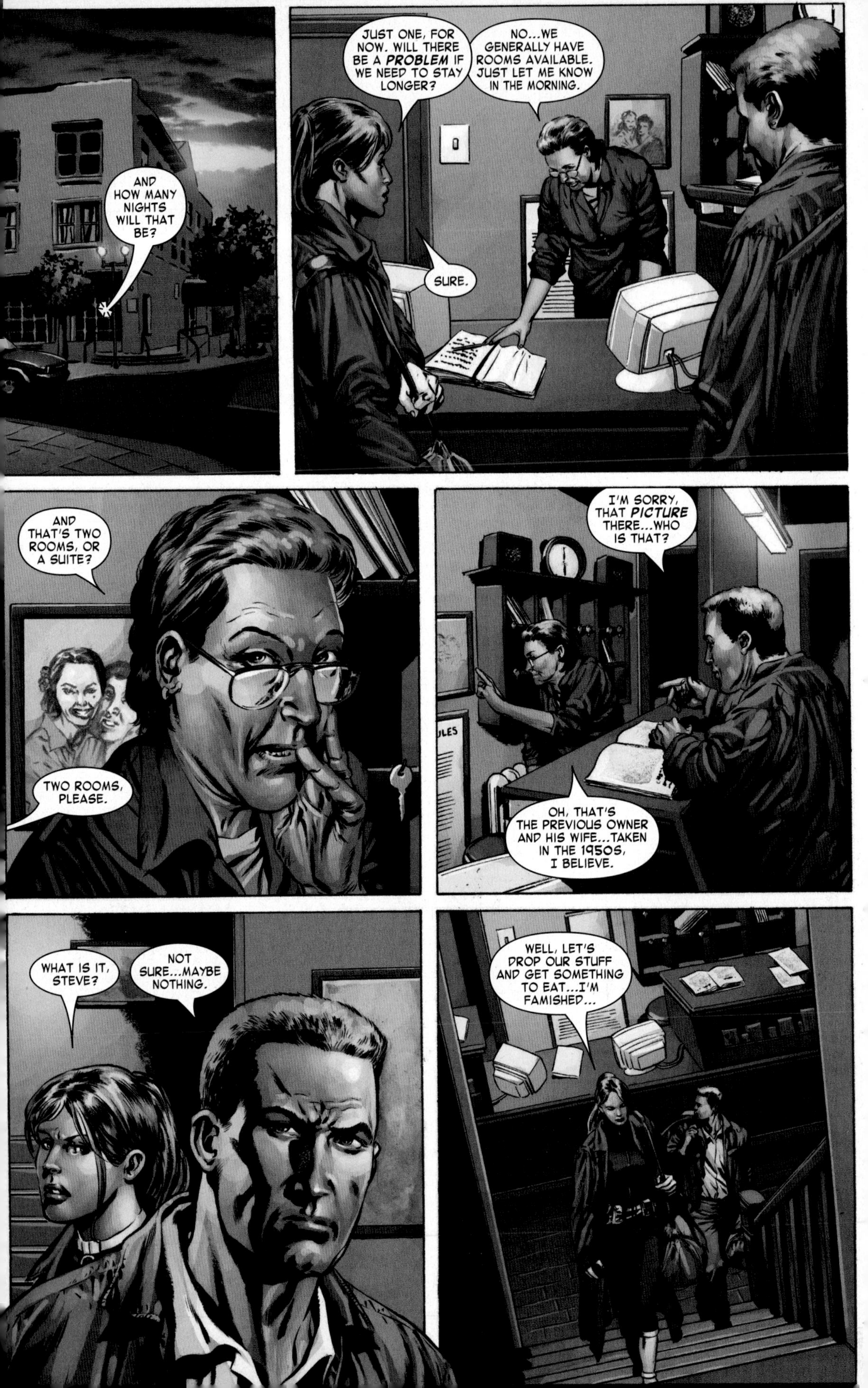
AND HOW MANY NIGHTS WILL THAT BE?
JUST ONE, FOR NOW. WILL THERE BE A PROBLEM IF WE NEED TO STAY LONGER?
NO...WE GENERALLY HAVE ROOMS AVAILABLE. JUST LET ME KNOW IN THE MORNING.
SURE.
AND THAT'S TWO ROOMS, OR A SUITE?
TWO ROOMS, PLEASE.
I'M SORRY, THAT PICTURE THERE...WHO IS THAT?
OH, THAT'S THE PREVIOUS OWNER AND HIS WIFE...TAKEN IN THE 1950S, I BELIEVE.
WHAT IS IT, STEVE?
NOT SURE...MAYBE NOTHING.
WELL, LET'S DROP OUR STUFF AND GET SOMETHING TO EAT...I'M FAMISHED...

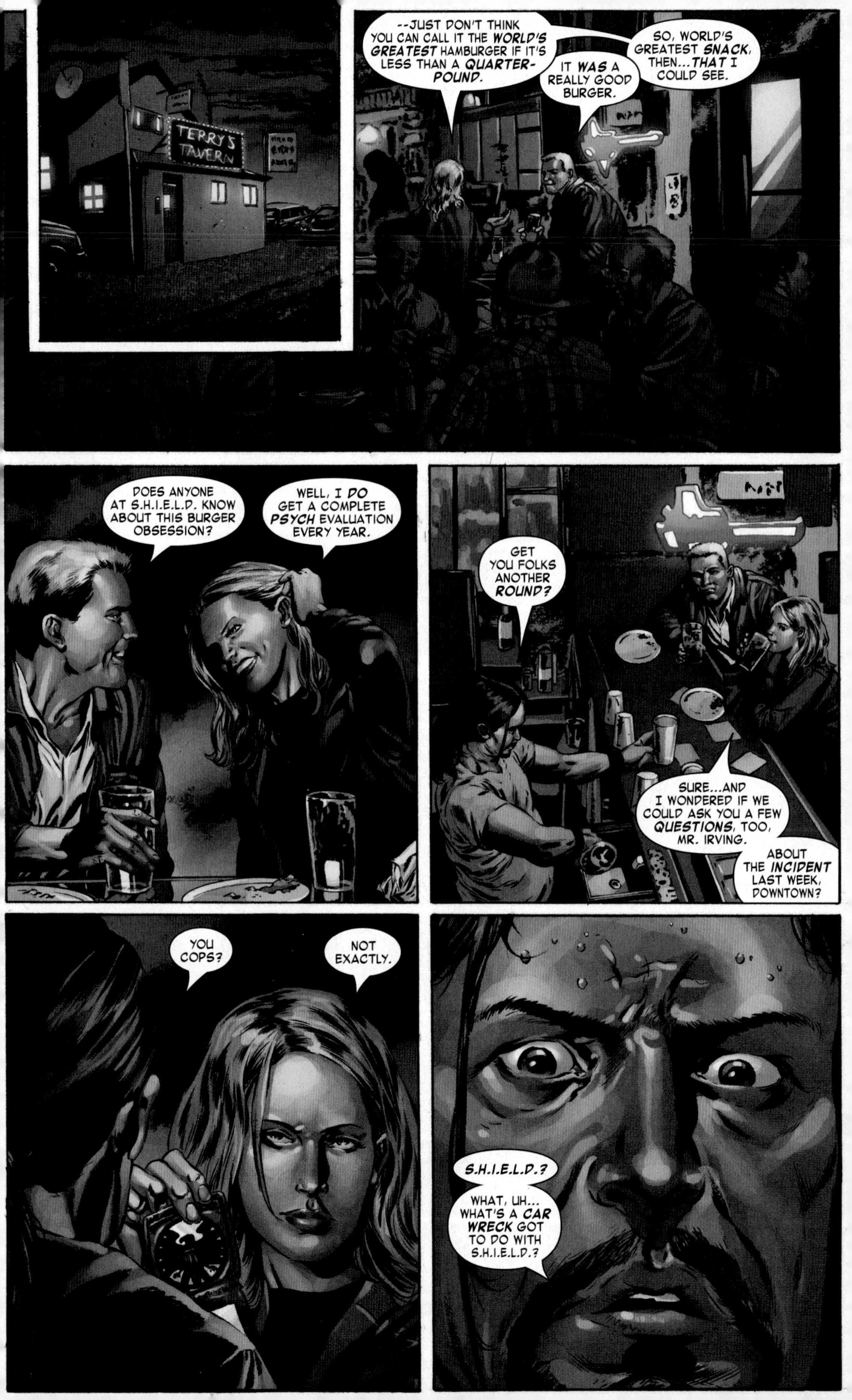
TERRY'S TAVERN
--JUST DON'T THINK YOU CAN CALL IT THE WORLD'S GREATEST HAMBURGER IF IT'S LESS THAN A QUARTER-POUND.
IT WAS A REALLY GOOD BURGER.
SO, WORLD'S GREATEST SNACK, THEN...THAT I COULD SEE.
DOES ANYONE AT S.H.I.E.L.D. KNOW ABOUT THIS BURGER OBSESSION?
WELL, I DO GET A COMPLETE PSYCH EVALUATION EVERY YEAR.
GET YOU FOLKS ANOTHER ROUND?
SURE...AND I WONDERED IF WE COULD ASK YOU A FEW QUESTIONS, TOO, MR. IRVING.
ABOUT THE INCIDENT LAST WEEK, DOWNTOWN?
YOU COPS?
NOT EXACTLY.
S.H.I.E.L.D.?
WHAT, UH... WHAT'S A CAR WRECK GOT TO DO WITH S.H.I.E.L.D.?

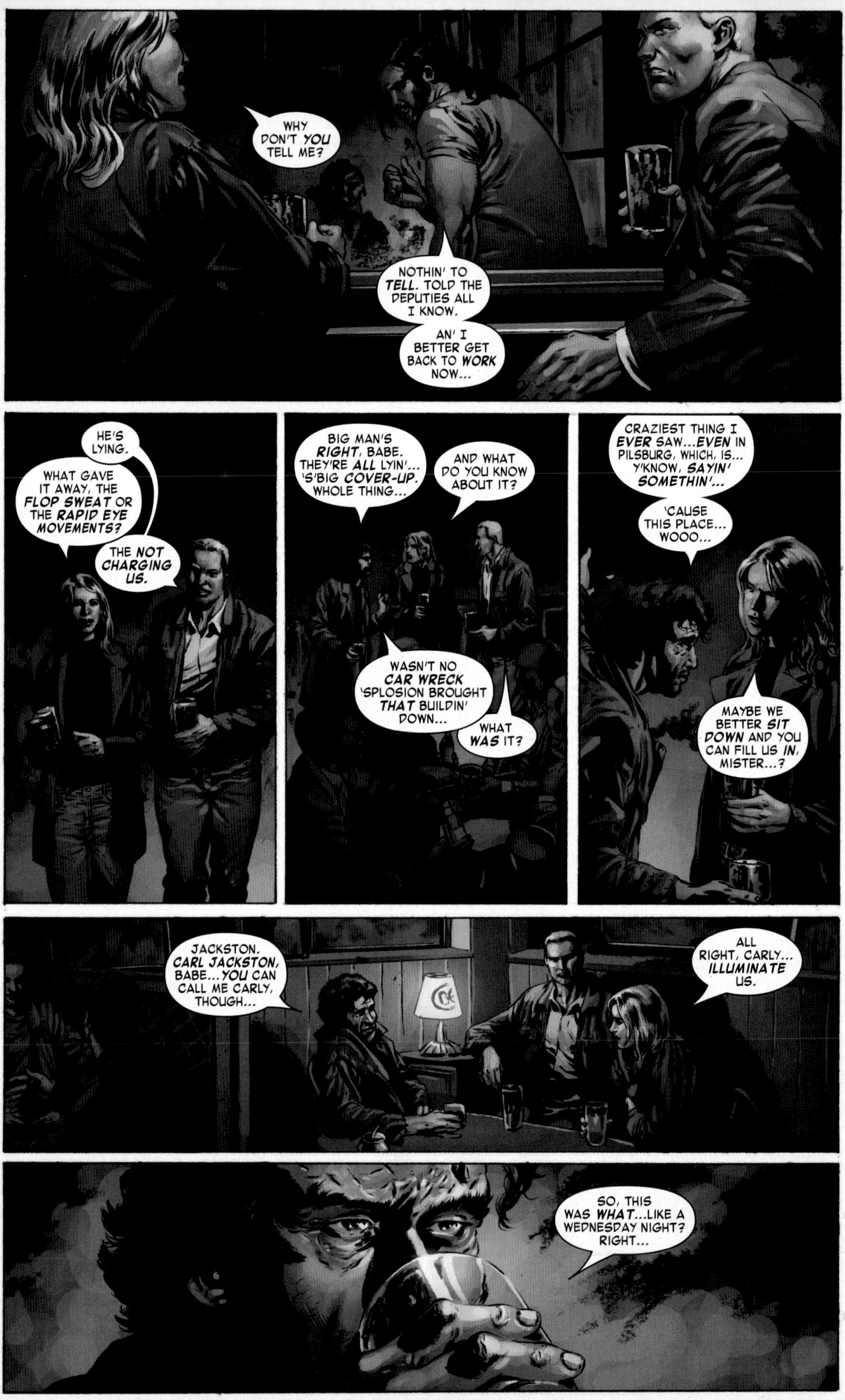
WHY DON'T YOU TELL ME?
NOTHIN' TO TELL. TOLD THE DEPUTIES ALL I KNOW.
AN' I BETTER GET BACK TO WORK NOW...
HE'S LYING.
WHAT GAVE IT AWAY, THE FLOP SWEAT OR THE RAPID EYE MOVEMENTS?
THE NOT CHARGING US.
BIG MAN'S RIGHT, BABE. THEY'RE ALL LYIN'... 'S'BIG COVER-UP. WHOLE THING...
AND WHAT DO YOU KNOW ABOUT IT?
WASN'T NO CAR WRECK 'SPLOSION BROUGHT THAT BUILDIN' DOWN...
WHAT WAS IT?
CRAZIEST THING I EVER SAW...EVEN IN PILSBURG, WHICH, IS... Y'KNOW, SAYIN' SOMETHIN'...
'CAUSE THIS PLACE... WOOO...
MAYBE WE BETTER SIT DOWN AND YOU CAN FILL US IN, MISTER...?
JACKSTON. CARL JACKSTON, BABE...YOU CAN CALL ME CARLY, THOUGH...
ALL RIGHT, CARLY... ILLUMINATE US.
SO, THIS WAS WHAT...LIKE A WEDNESDAY NIGHT? RIGHT...

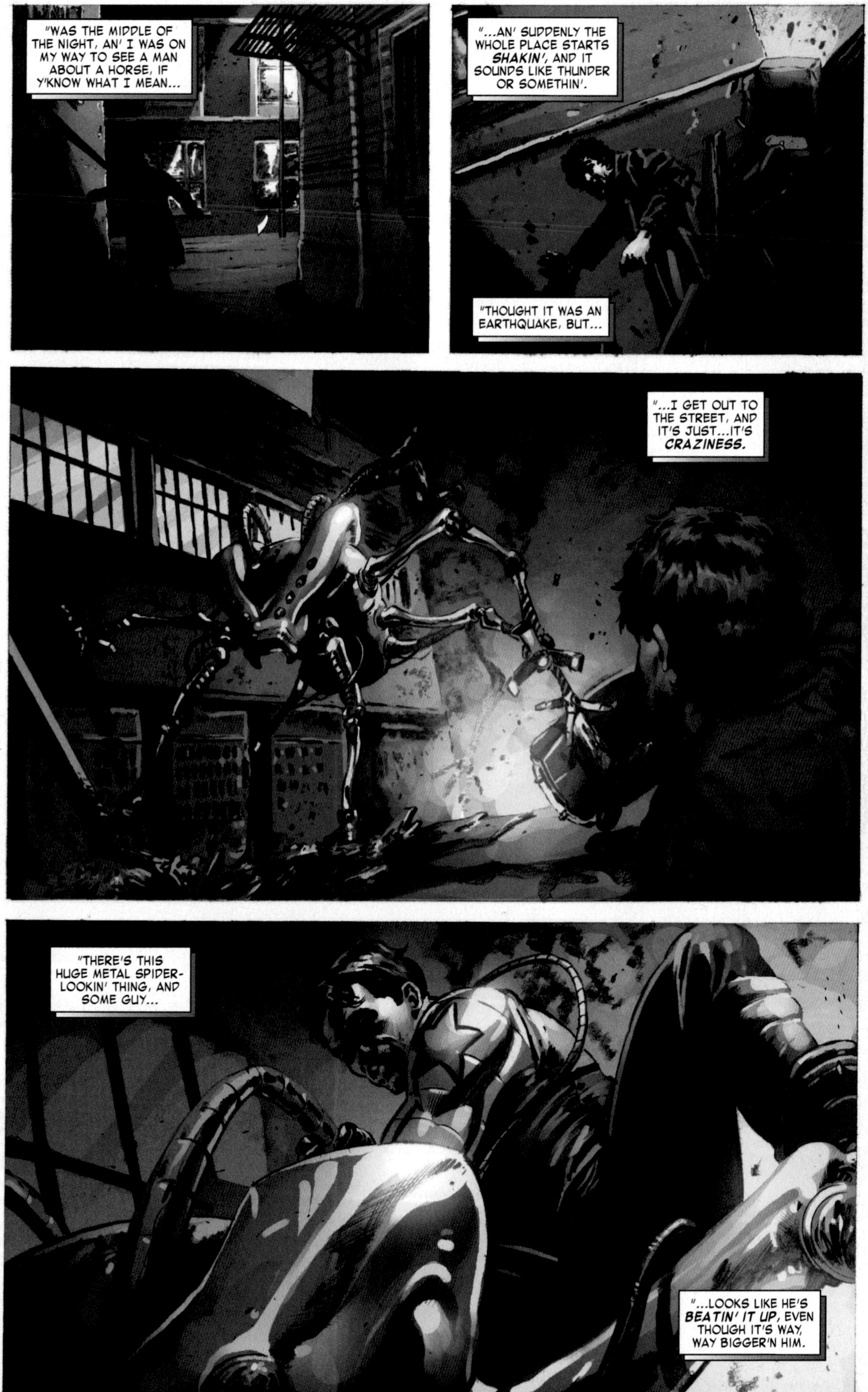
"WAS THE MIDDLE OF THE NIGHT, AN' I WAS ON MY WAY TO SEE A MAN ABOUT A HORSE, IF Y'KNOW WHAT I MEAN...
"...AN' SUDDENLY THE WHOLE PLACE STARTS SHAKIN', AND IT SOUNDS LIKE THUNDER OR SOMETHIN'.
"THOUGHT IT WAS AN EARTHQUAKE, BUT...
"...I GET OUT TO THE STREET, AND IT'S JUST...IT'S CRAZINESS.
"THERE'S THIS HUGE METAL SPIDER-LOOKIN' THING, AND SOME GUY...
"...LOOKS LIKE HE'S BEATIN' IT UP, EVEN THOUGH IT'S WAY, WAY BIGGER'N HIM.

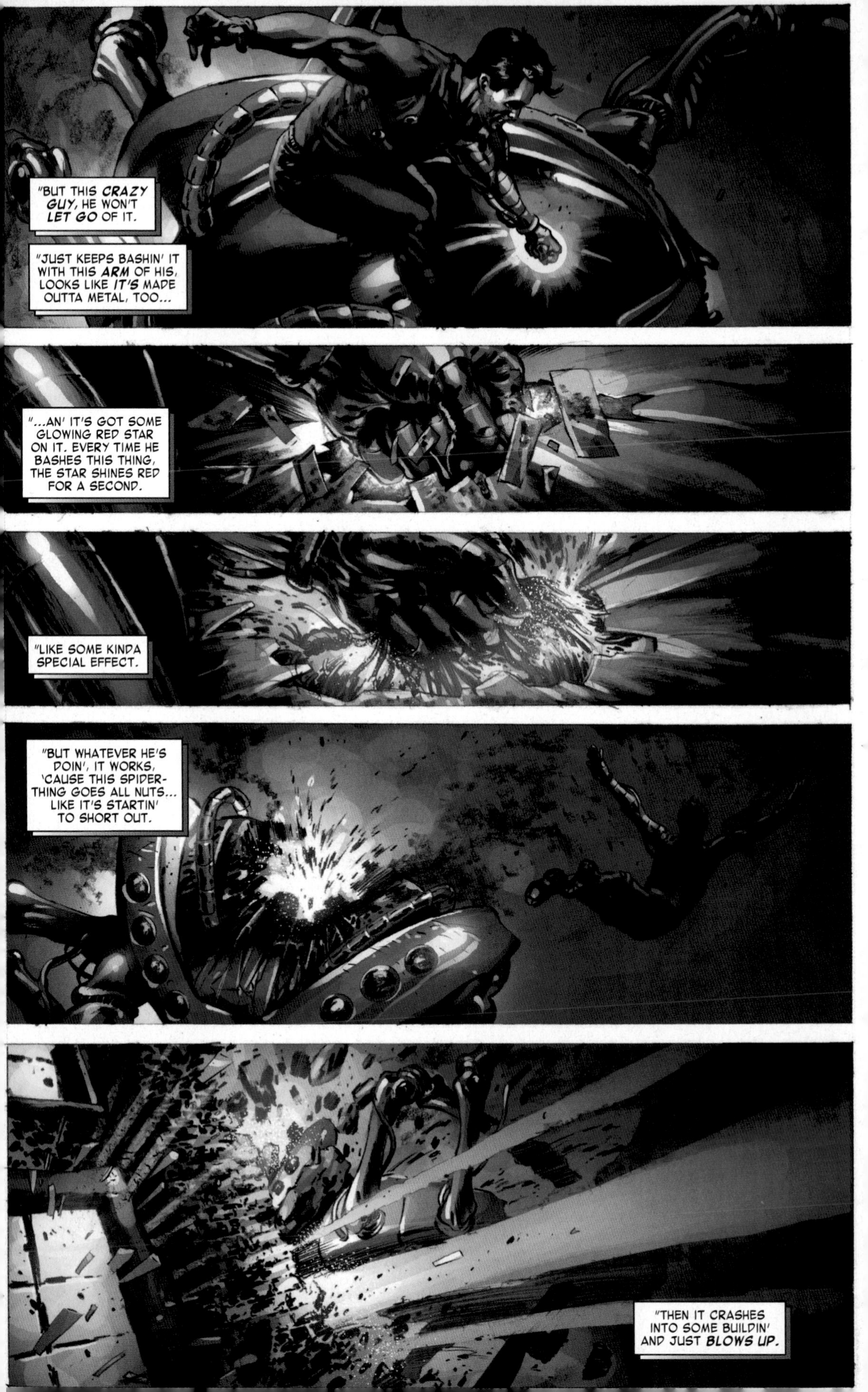
"BUT THIS *CRAZY GUY,* HE WON'T *LET GO* OF IT.
"JUST KEEPS BASHIN' IT WITH THIS *ARM* OF HIS, LOOKS LIKE *IT'S* MADE OUTTA METAL, TOO...
"...AN' IT'S GOT SOME GLOWING RED STAR ON IT. EVERY TIME HE BASHES THIS THING, THE STAR SHINES RED FOR A SECOND.
"LIKE SOME KINDA SPECIAL EFFECT.
"BUT WHATEVER HE'S DOIN', IT WORKS, 'CAUSE THIS SPIDER-THING GOES ALL NUTS... LIKE IT'S STARTIN' TO SHORT OUT.
"THEN IT CRASHES INTO SOME BUILDIN' AND JUST *BLOWS UP.*

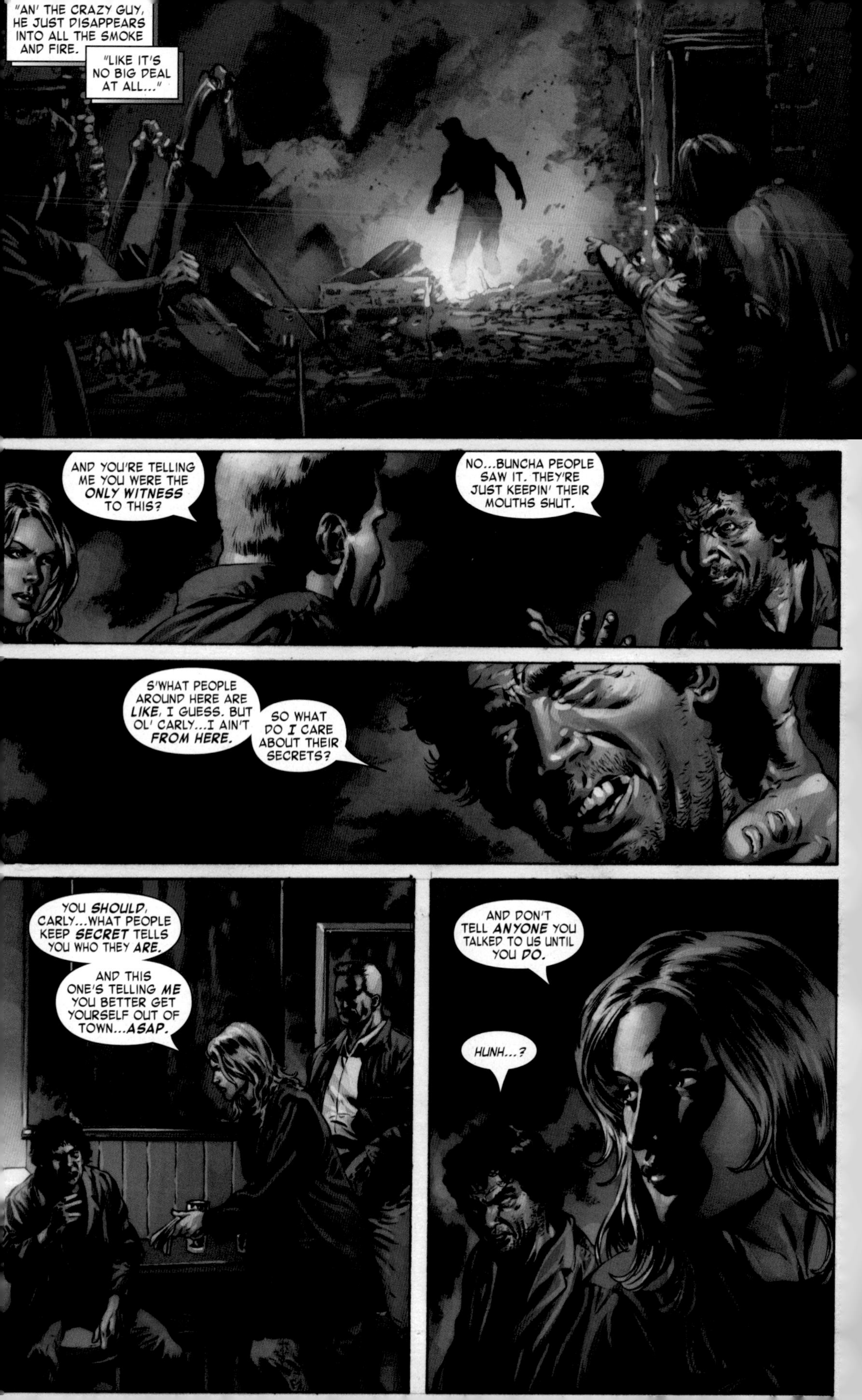
"AN' THE CRAZY GUY, HE JUST DISAPPEARS INTO ALL THE SMOKE AND FIRE.
"LIKE IT'S NO BIG DEAL AT ALL..."
AND YOU'RE TELLING ME YOU WERE THE ONLY WITNESS TO THIS?
NO...BUNCHA PEOPLE SAW IT. THEY'RE JUST KEEPIN' THEIR MOUTHS SHUT.
S'WHAT PEOPLE AROUND HERE ARE LIKE, I GUESS. BUT OL' CARLY...I AIN'T FROM HERE.
SO WHAT DO I CARE ABOUT THEIR SECRETS?
YOU SHOULD, CARLY...WHAT PEOPLE KEEP SECRET TELLS YOU WHO THEY ARE.
AND THIS ONE'S TELLING ME YOU BETTER GET YOURSELF OUT OF TOWN...ASAP.
AND DON'T TELL ANYONE YOU TALKED TO US UNTIL YOU DO.
HUNH...?

OKAY...THIS PLACE IS OFFICIALLY MOVED TO THE TOP OF MY SUSPICIOUS LIST.

BUCKY FIGHTING A GIANT METAL SPIDER? WHAT DO YOU THINK ABOUT THAT?

I MEAN, THAT GUY WASN'T THE MOST RELIABLE OF WITNESSES, BUT...UH...

...STEVE?

HE'S ALIVE.

HE'S ALIVE!

WAA-- HEY!

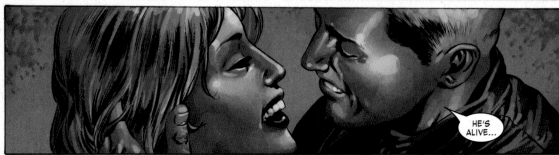

HE'S ALIVE...

HEY... ARE YOU DRUNK?

I DON'T GET DRUNK. I CAN'T...

I'M JUST HAPPY...

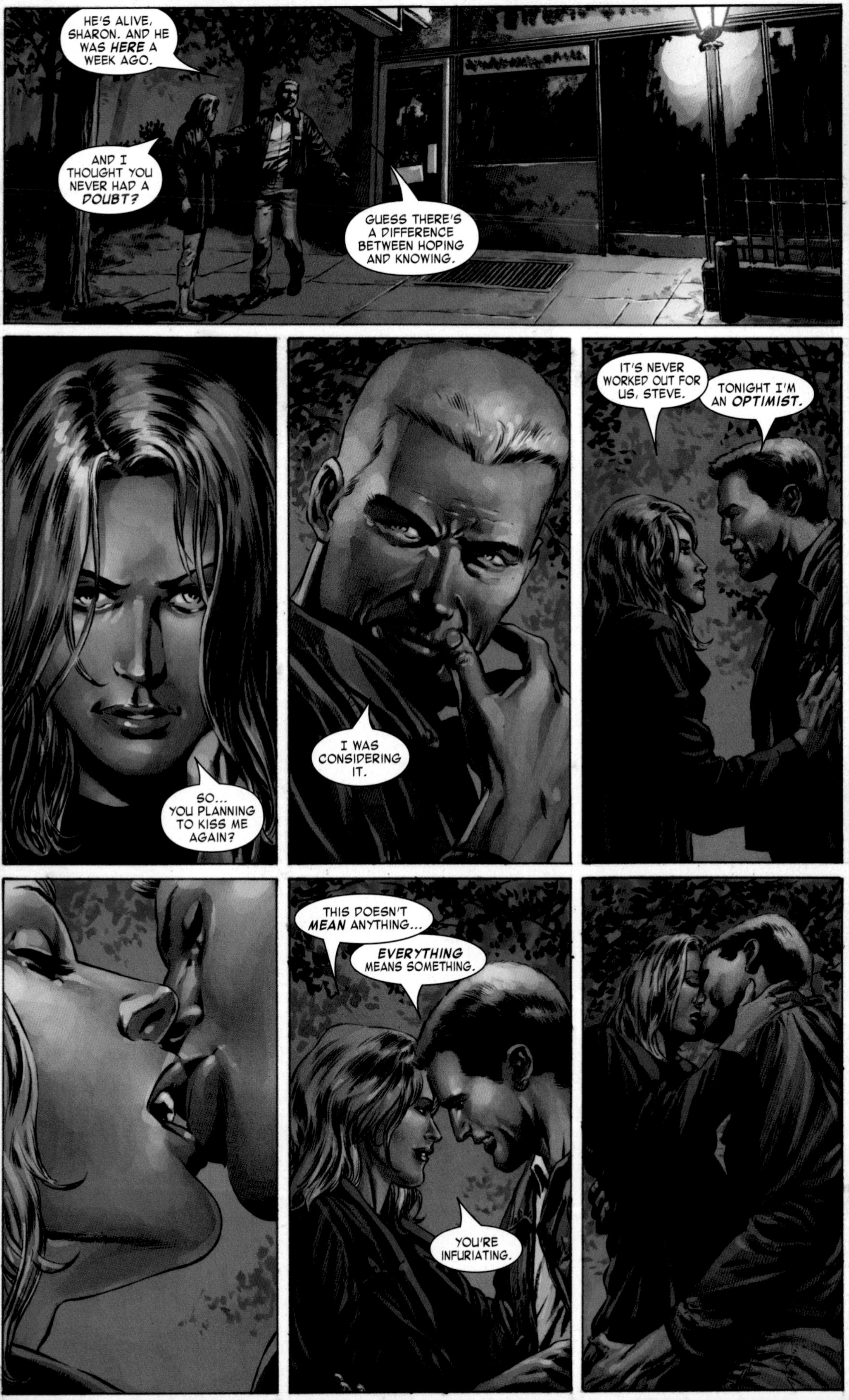

HE'S ALIVE, SHARON. AND HE WAS HERE A WEEK AGO.
AND I THOUGHT YOU NEVER HAD A DOUBT?
GUESS THERE'S A DIFFERENCE BETWEEN HOPING AND KNOWING.
SO... YOU PLANNING TO KISS ME AGAIN?
I WAS CONSIDERING IT.
IT'S NEVER WORKED OUT FOR US, STEVE.
TONIGHT I'M AN OPTIMIST.
THIS DOESN'T MEAN ANYTHING...
EVERYTHING MEANS SOMETHING.
YOU'RE INFURIATING.

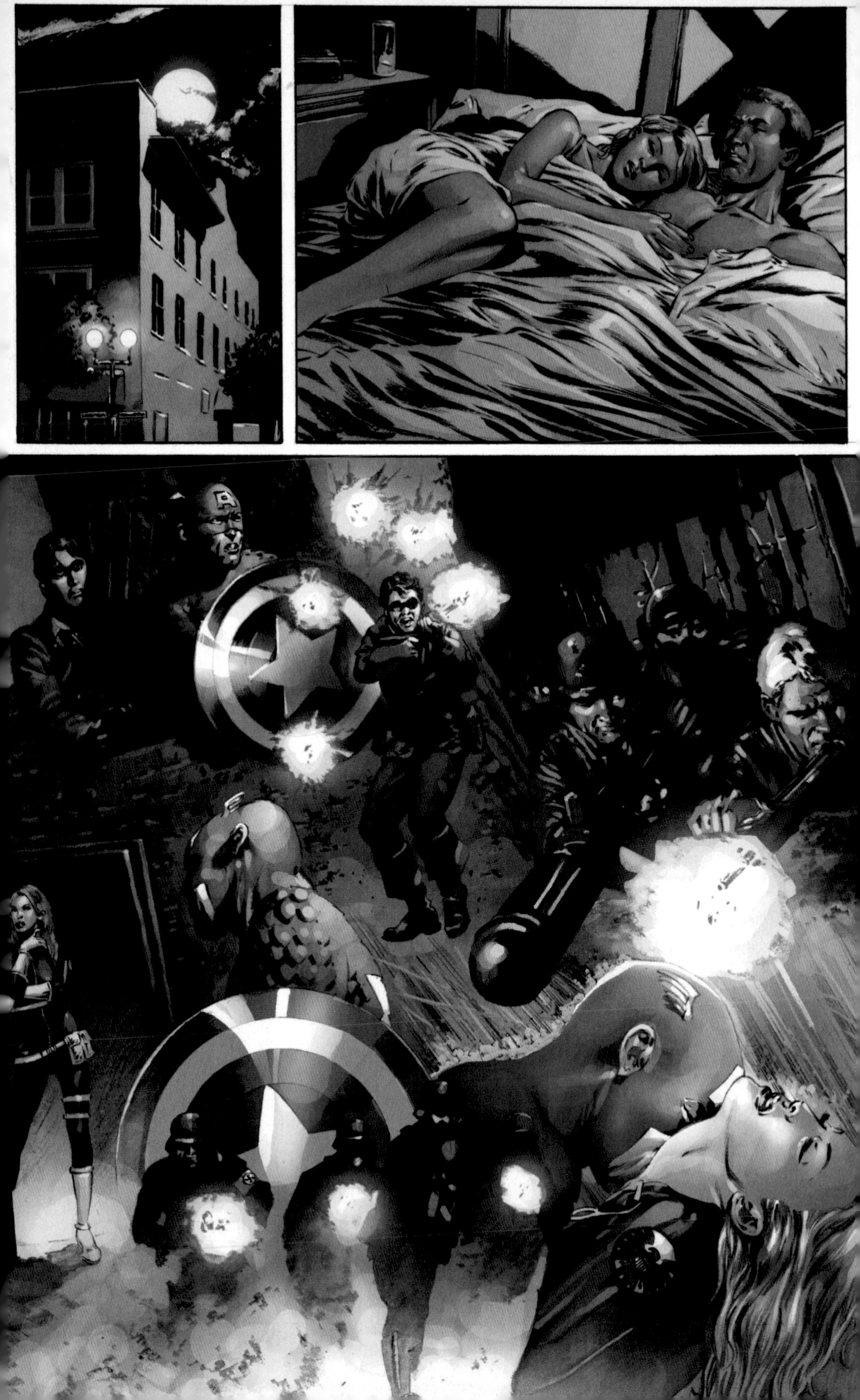

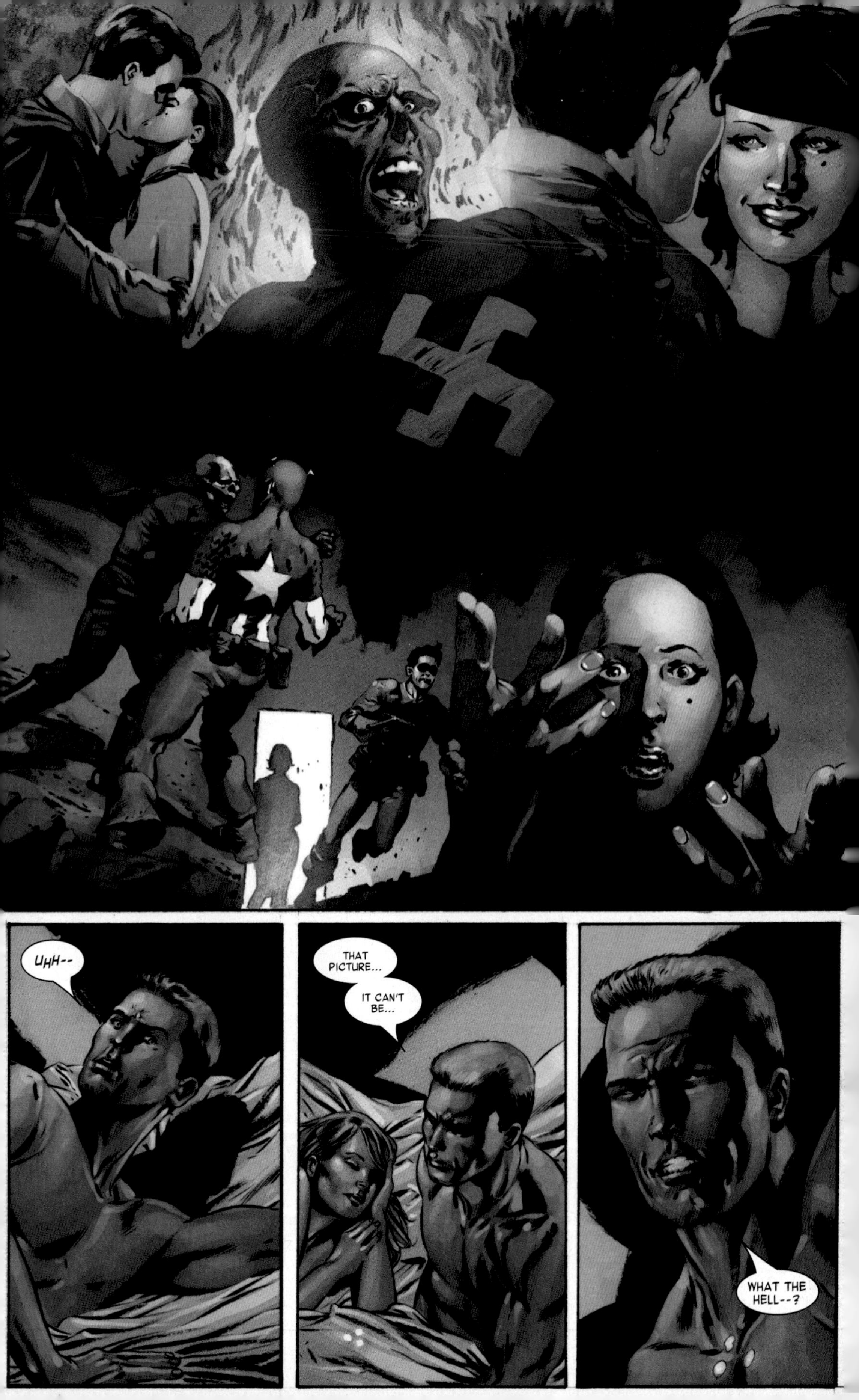
UHH--
THAT PICTURE...
IT CAN'T BE...
WHAT THE HELL--?

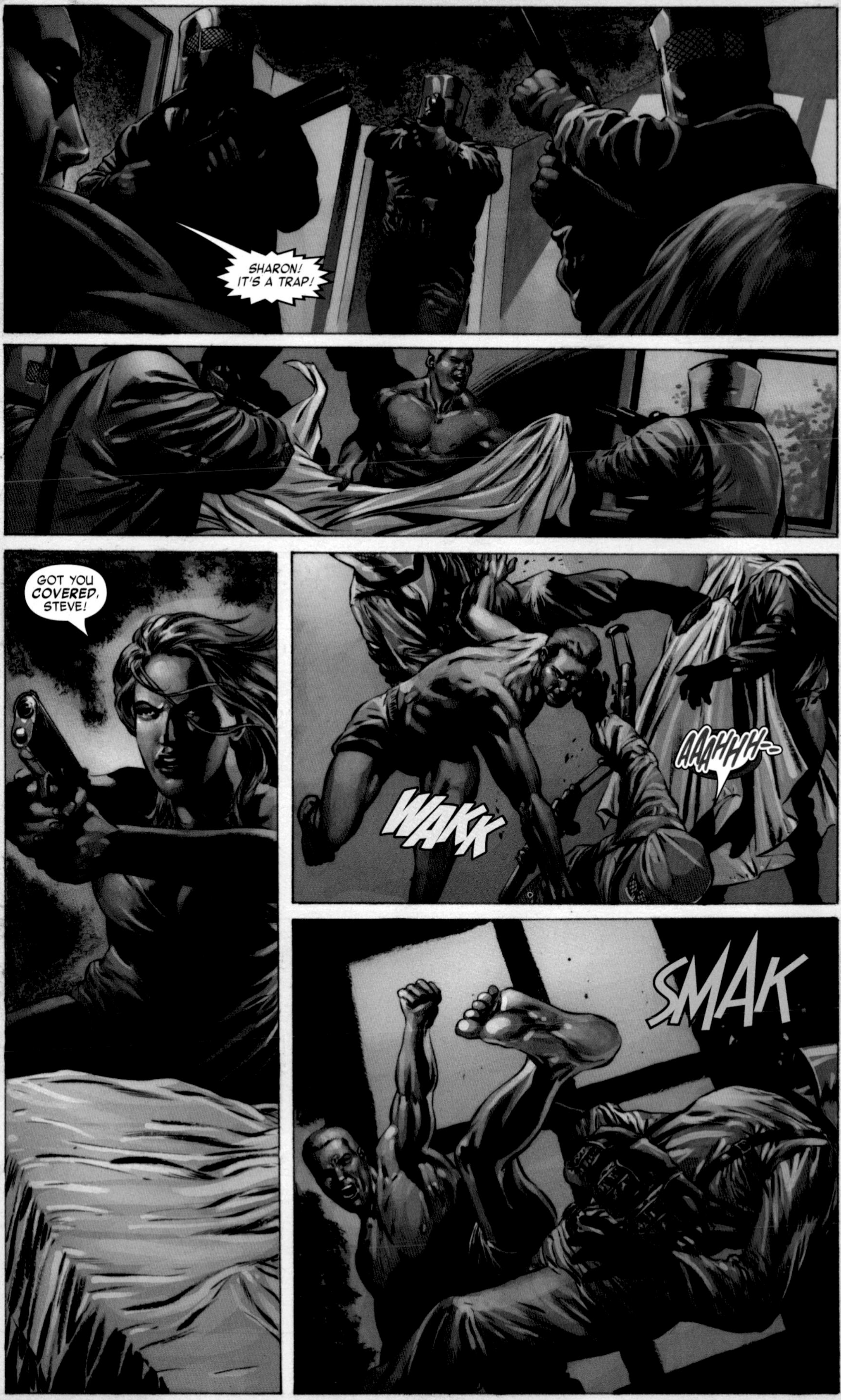
SHARON! IT'S A TRAP!
GOT YOU COVERED, STEVE!
WAKK
AAAHHH-
SMAK

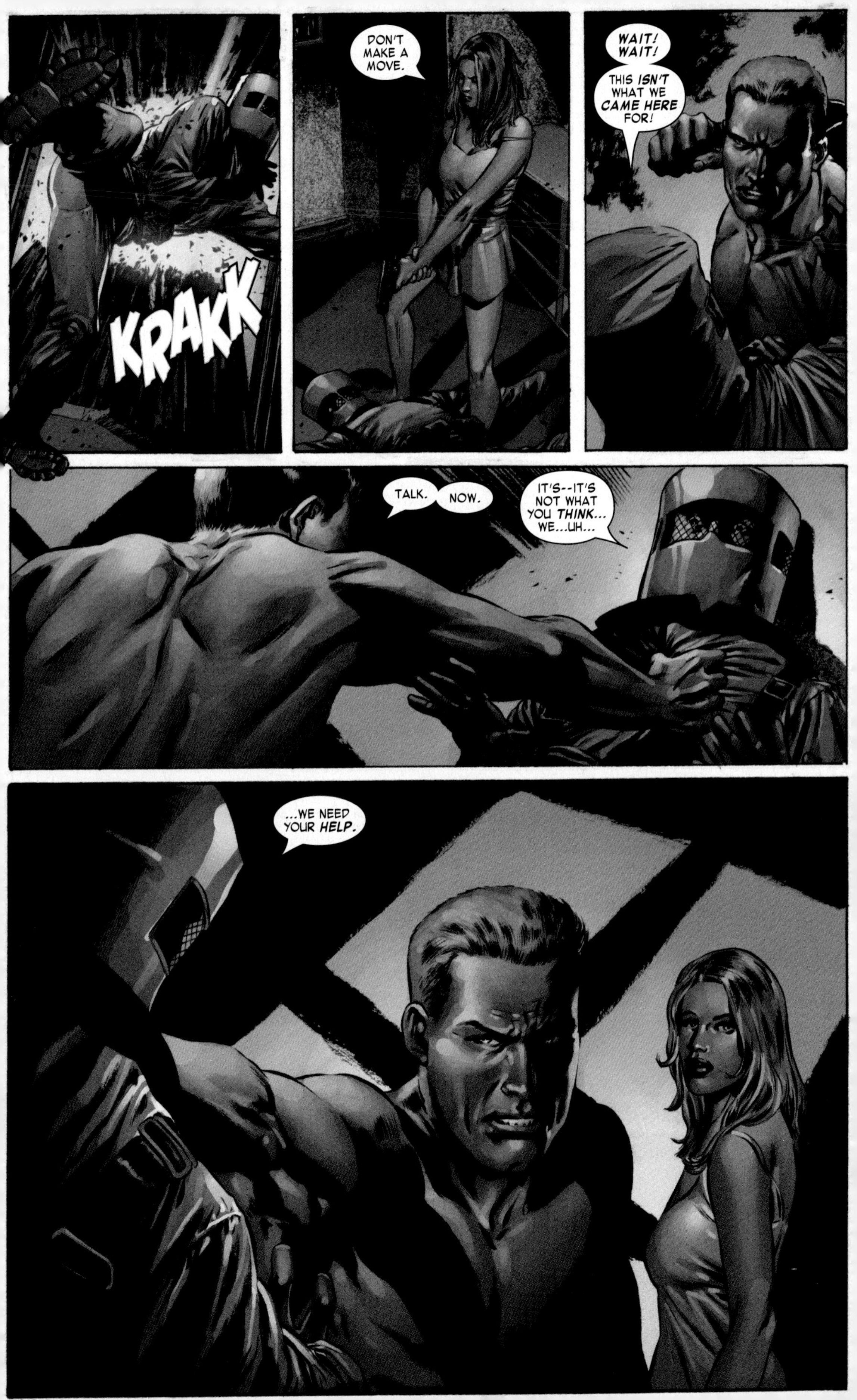
KRAKK
DON'T MAKE A MOVE.
WAIT! WAIT!
THIS ISN'T WHAT WE CAME HERE FOR!
TALK.
NOW.
IT'S--IT'S NOT WHAT YOU THINK... WE...UH...
...WE NEED YOUR HELP.

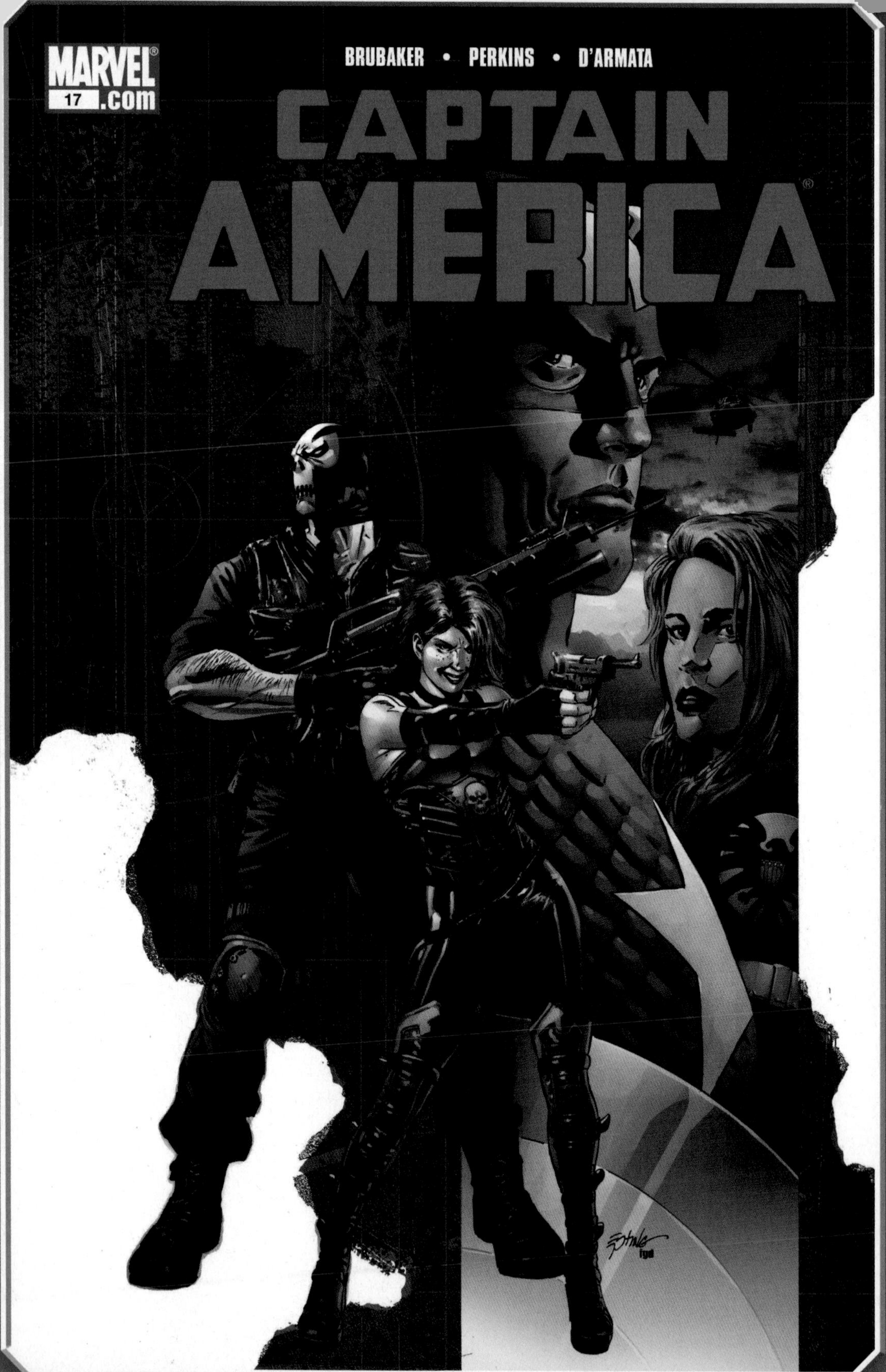
MARVEL
17 .com
BRUBAKER • PERKINS • D'ARMATA
CAPTAIN AMERICA

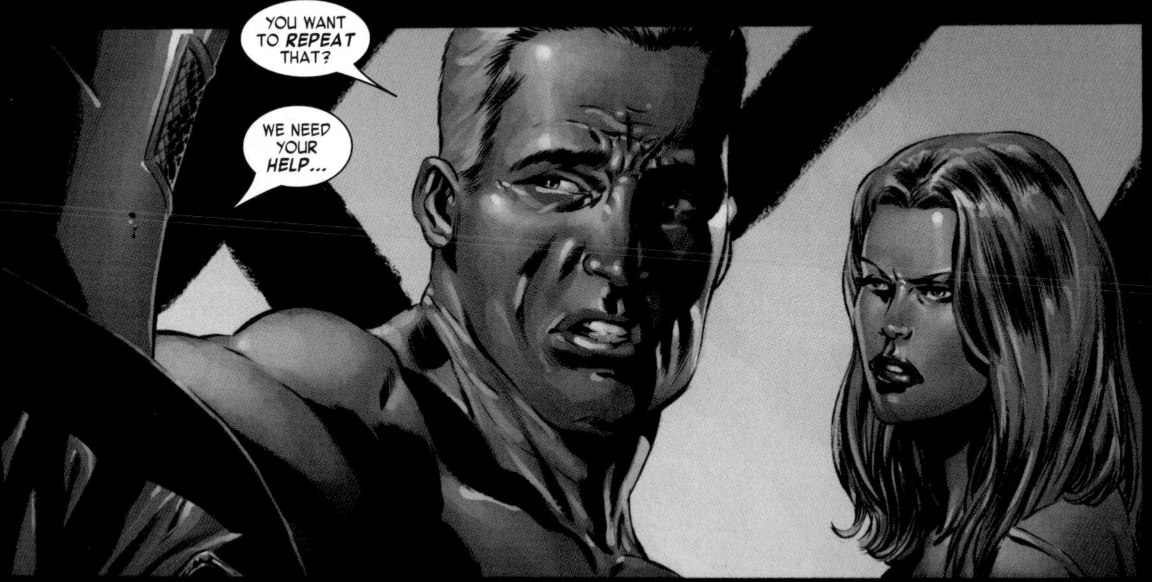
YOU WANT TO REPEAT THAT?
WE NEED YOUR HELP...

COLLISION COURSES PART 2 OF 2

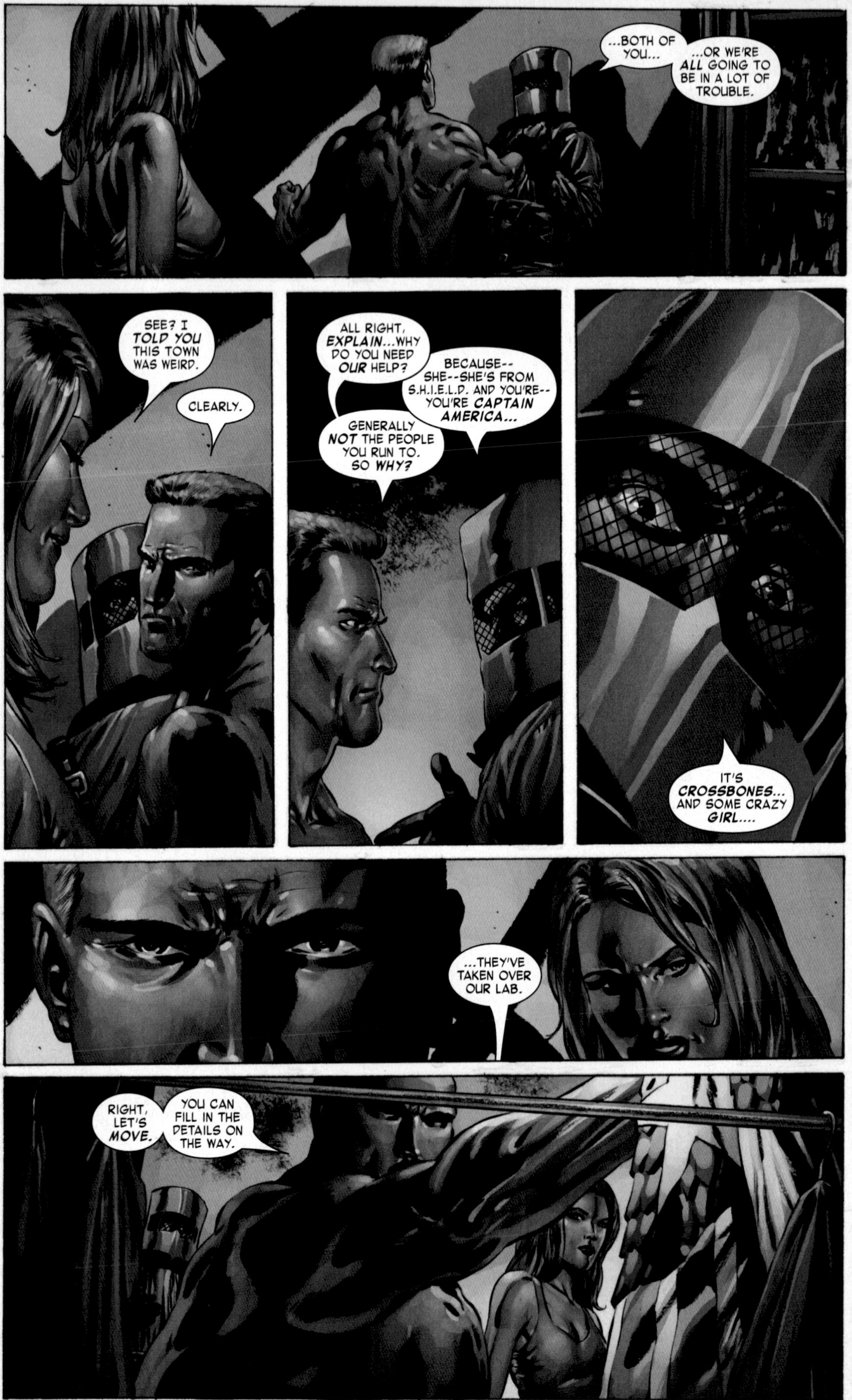
...BOTH OF YOU...
...OR WE'RE ALL GOING TO BE IN A LOT OF TROUBLE.
SEE? I TOLD YOU THIS TOWN WAS WEIRD.
CLEARLY.
ALL RIGHT, EXPLAIN...WHY DO YOU NEED OUR HELP?
GENERALLY NOT THE PEOPLE YOU RUN TO. SO WHY?
BECAUSE-- SHE--SHE'S FROM S.H.I.E.L.D. AND YOU'RE-- YOU'RE CAPTAIN AMERICA...
IT'S CROSSBONES... AND SOME CRAZY GIRL....
...THEY'VE TAKEN OVER OUR LAB.
RIGHT, LET'S MOVE.
YOU CAN FILL IN THE DETAILS ON THE WAY.

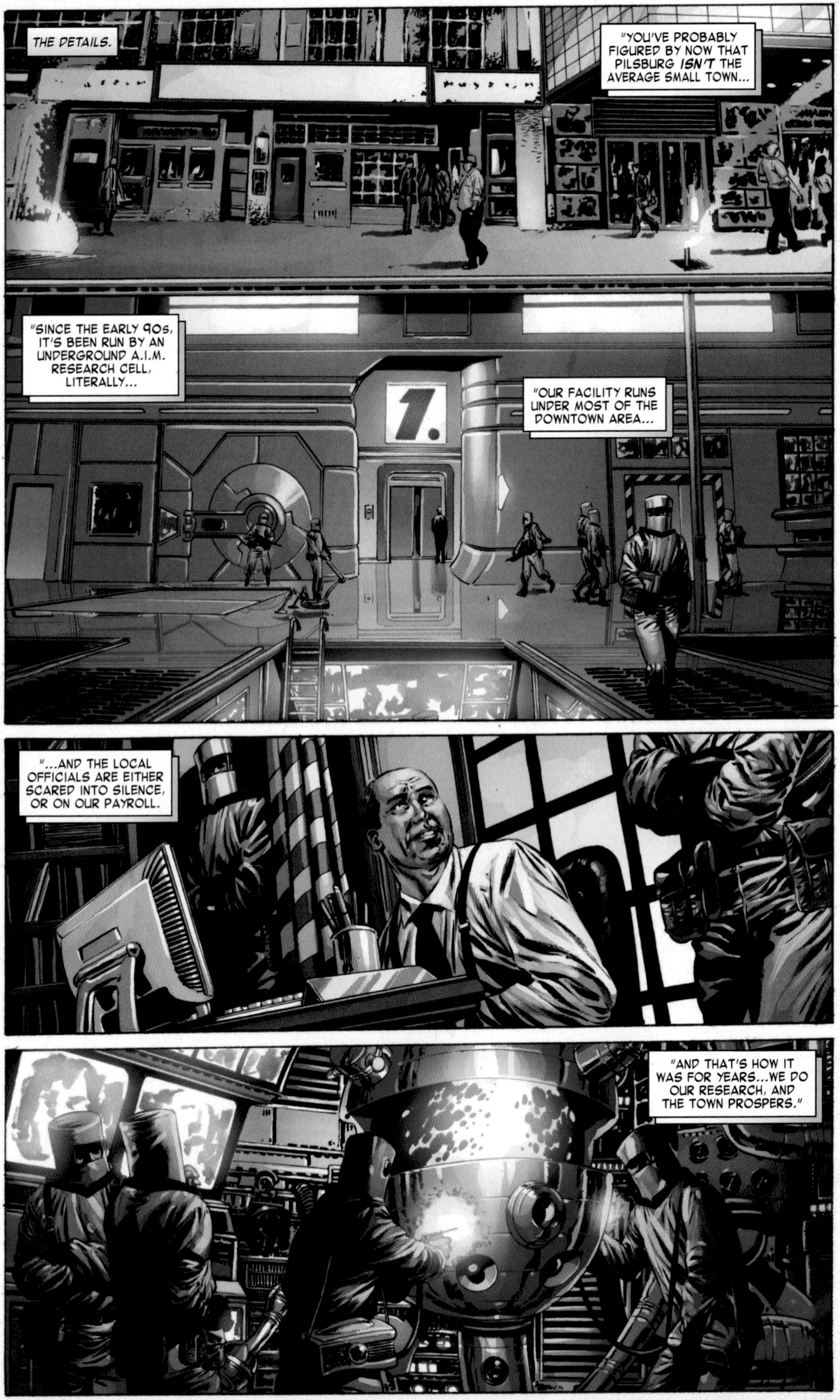
THE DETAILS.
"YOU'VE PROBABLY FIGURED BY NOW THAT PILSBURG *ISN'T* THE AVERAGE SMALL TOWN...
"SINCE THE EARLY 90s, IT'S BEEN RUN BY AN UNDERGROUND A.I.M. RESEARCH CELL, LITERALLY...
1.
"OUR FACILITY RUNS UNDER MOST OF THE DOWNTOWN AREA...
"...AND THE LOCAL OFFICIALS ARE EITHER SCARED INTO SILENCE, OR ON OUR PAYROLL.
"AND THAT'S HOW IT WAS FOR YEARS...WE DO OUR RESEARCH, AND THE TOWN PROSPERS."

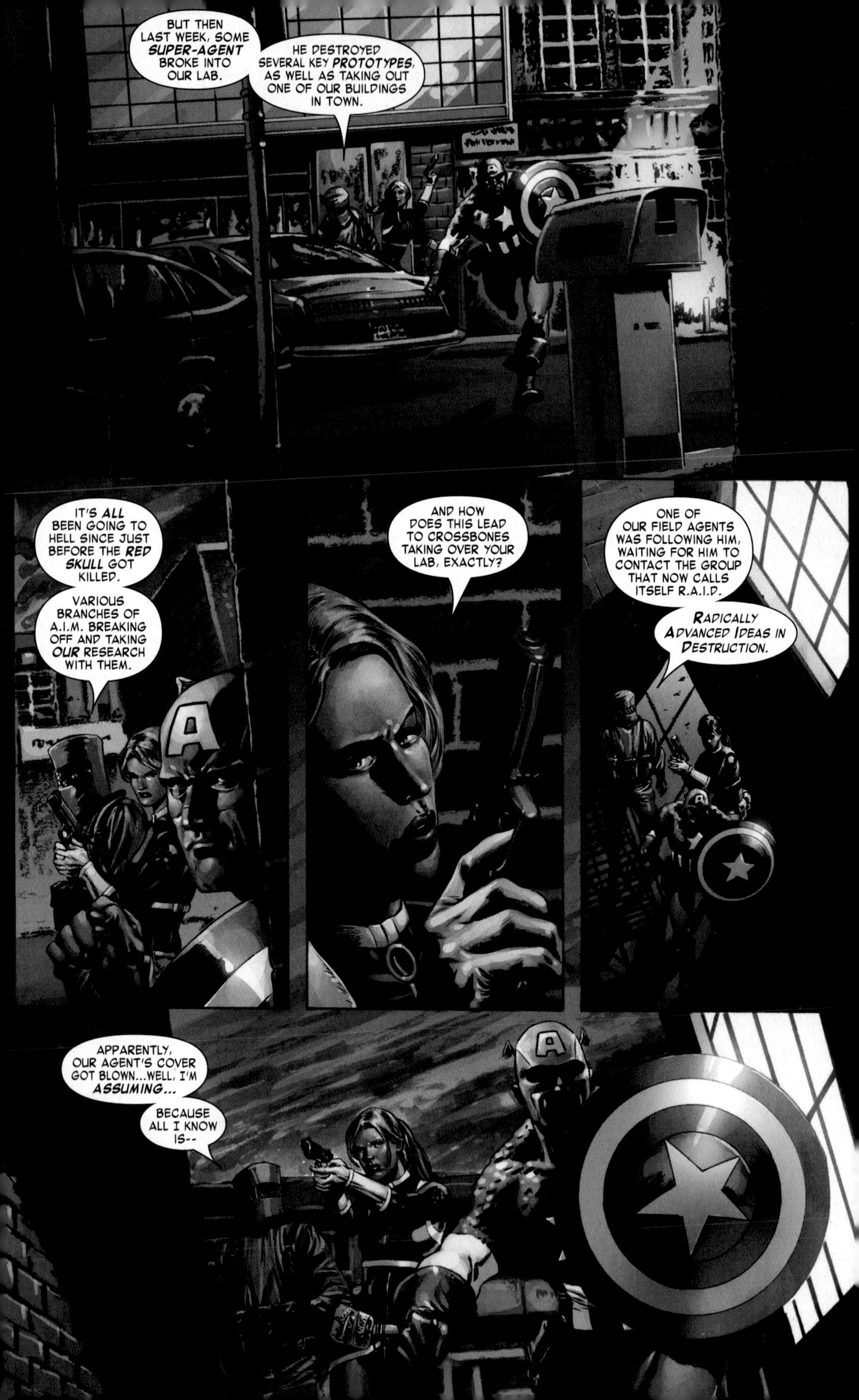
BUT THEN LAST WEEK, SOME *SUPER-AGENT* BROKE INTO OUR LAB.
HE DESTROYED SEVERAL KEY *PROTOTYPES*, AS WELL AS TAKING OUT ONE OF OUR BUILDINGS IN TOWN.
IT'S *ALL* BEEN GOING TO HELL SINCE JUST BEFORE THE *RED SKULL* GOT KILLED.
VARIOUS BRANCHES OF A.I.M. BREAKING OFF AND TAKING *OUR* RESEARCH WITH THEM.
AND HOW DOES THIS LEAD TO CROSSBONES TAKING OVER YOUR LAB, EXACTLY?
ONE OF OUR FIELD AGENTS WAS FOLLOWING HIM, WAITING FOR HIM TO CONTACT THE GROUP THAT NOW CALLS ITSELF R.A.I.D.
RADICALLY ADVANCED IDEAS IN DESTRUCTION.
APPARENTLY, OUR AGENT'S COVER GOT BLOWN...WELL, I'M *ASSUMING...*
BECAUSE ALL I KNOW IS--

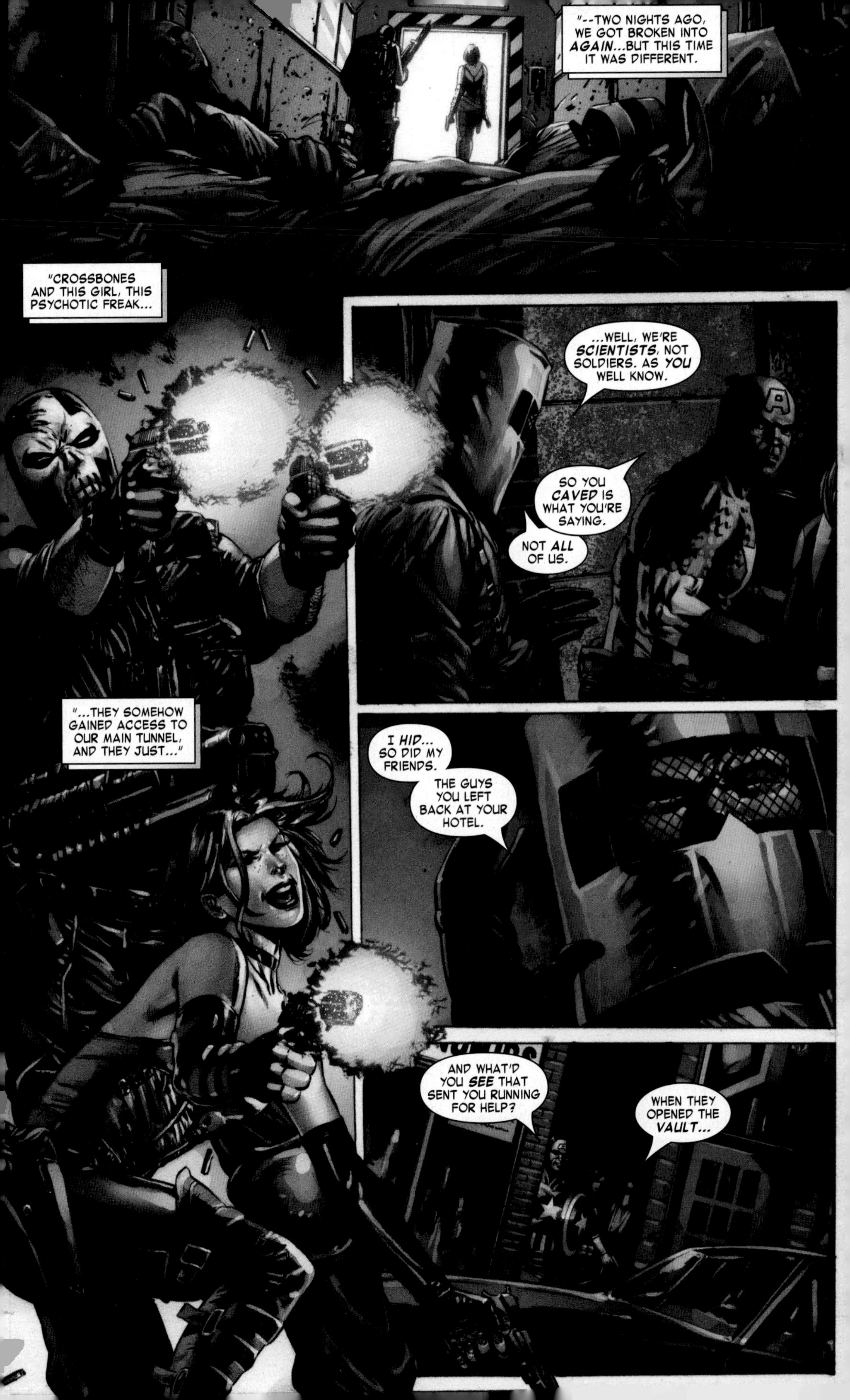
"--TWO NIGHTS AGO, WE GOT BROKEN INTO AGAIN...BUT THIS TIME IT WAS DIFFERENT.
"CROSSBONES AND THIS GIRL, THIS PSYCHOTIC FREAK...
...WELL, WE'RE SCIENTISTS, NOT SOLDIERS. AS YOU WELL KNOW.
SO YOU CAVED IS WHAT YOU'RE SAYING.
NOT ALL OF US.
"...THEY SOMEHOW GAINED ACCESS TO OUR MAIN TUNNEL, AND THEY JUST..."
I HID... SO DID MY FRIENDS.
THE GUYS YOU LEFT BACK AT YOUR HOTEL.
AND WHAT'D YOU SEE THAT SENT YOU RUNNING FOR HELP?
WHEN THEY OPENED THE VAULT...

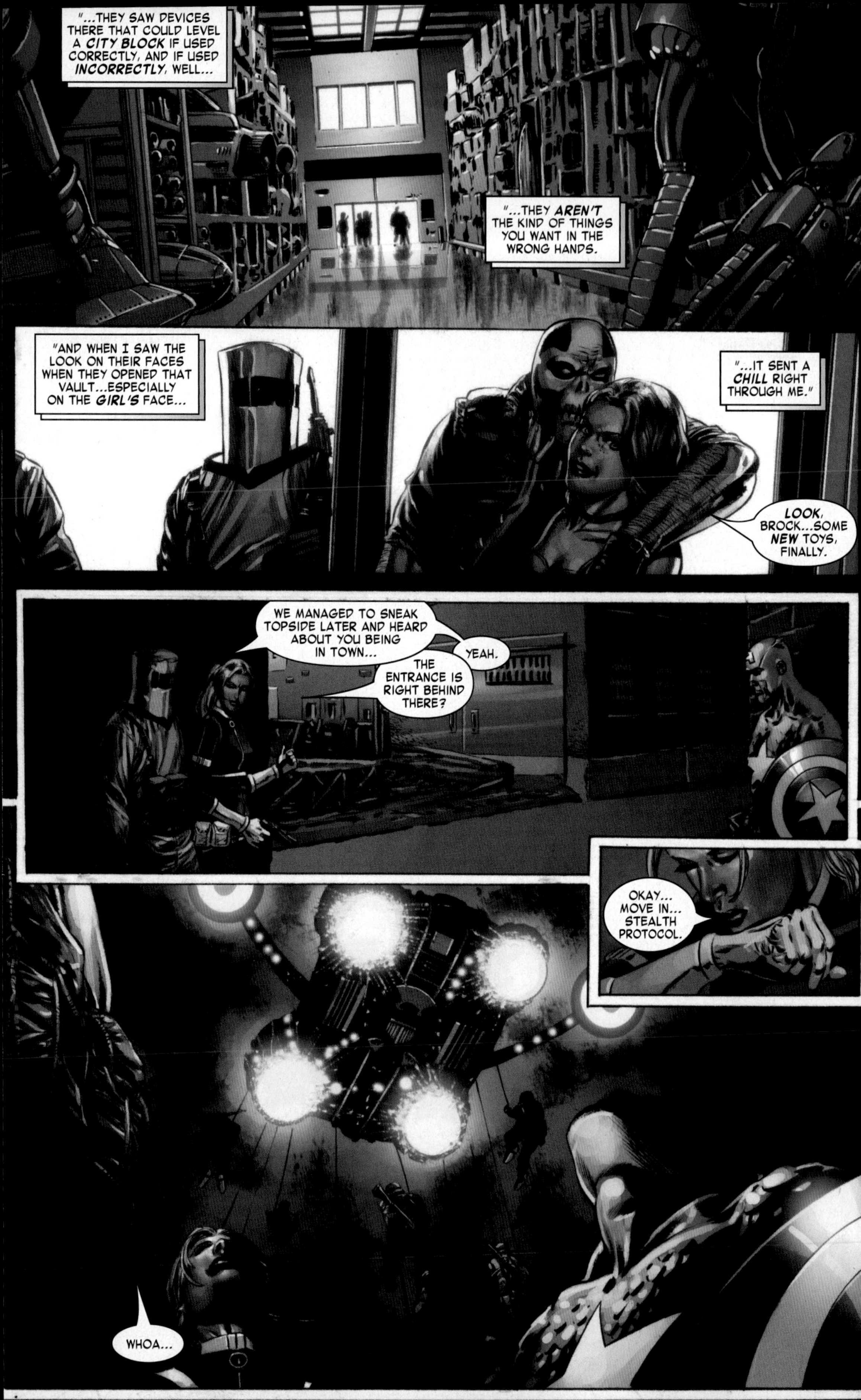
"...THEY SAW DEVICES THERE THAT COULD LEVEL A CITY BLOCK IF USED CORRECTLY, AND IF USED INCORRECTLY, WELL...
"...THEY AREN'T THE KIND OF THINGS YOU WANT IN THE WRONG HANDS.
"AND WHEN I SAW THE LOOK ON THEIR FACES WHEN THEY OPENED THAT VAULT...ESPECIALLY ON THE GIRL'S FACE...
"...IT SENT A CHILL RIGHT THROUGH ME."
LOOK, BROCK...SOME NEW TOYS, FINALLY.
WE MANAGED TO SNEAK TOPSIDE LATER AND HEARD ABOUT YOU BEING IN TOWN...
YEAH.
THE ENTRANCE IS RIGHT BEHIND THERE?
OKAY... MOVE IN... STEALTH PROTOCOL.
WHOA...

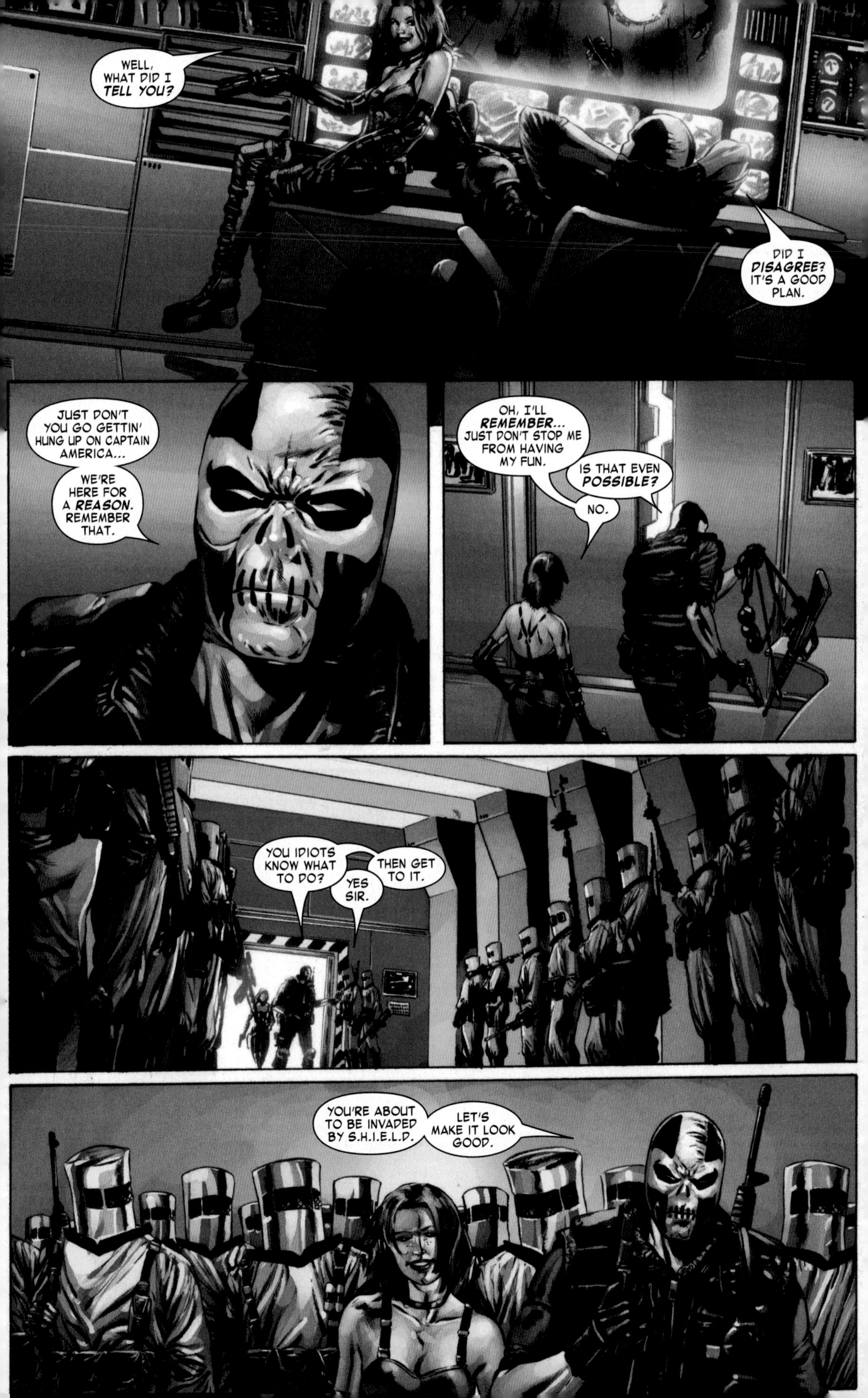
WELL, WHAT DID I *TELL YOU?*
DID I *DISAGREE?* IT'S A GOOD PLAN.
JUST DON'T YOU GO GETTIN' HUNG UP ON CAPTAIN AMERICA...
WE'RE HERE FOR A *REASON.* REMEMBER THAT.
OH, I'LL *REMEMBER...* JUST DON'T STOP ME FROM HAVING MY FUN.
IS THAT EVEN *POSSIBLE?*
NO.
YOU IDIOTS KNOW WHAT TO DO?
YES SIR.
THEN GET TO IT.
YOU'RE ABOUT TO BE INVADED BY S.H.I.E.L.D.
LET'S MAKE IT LOOK GOOD.

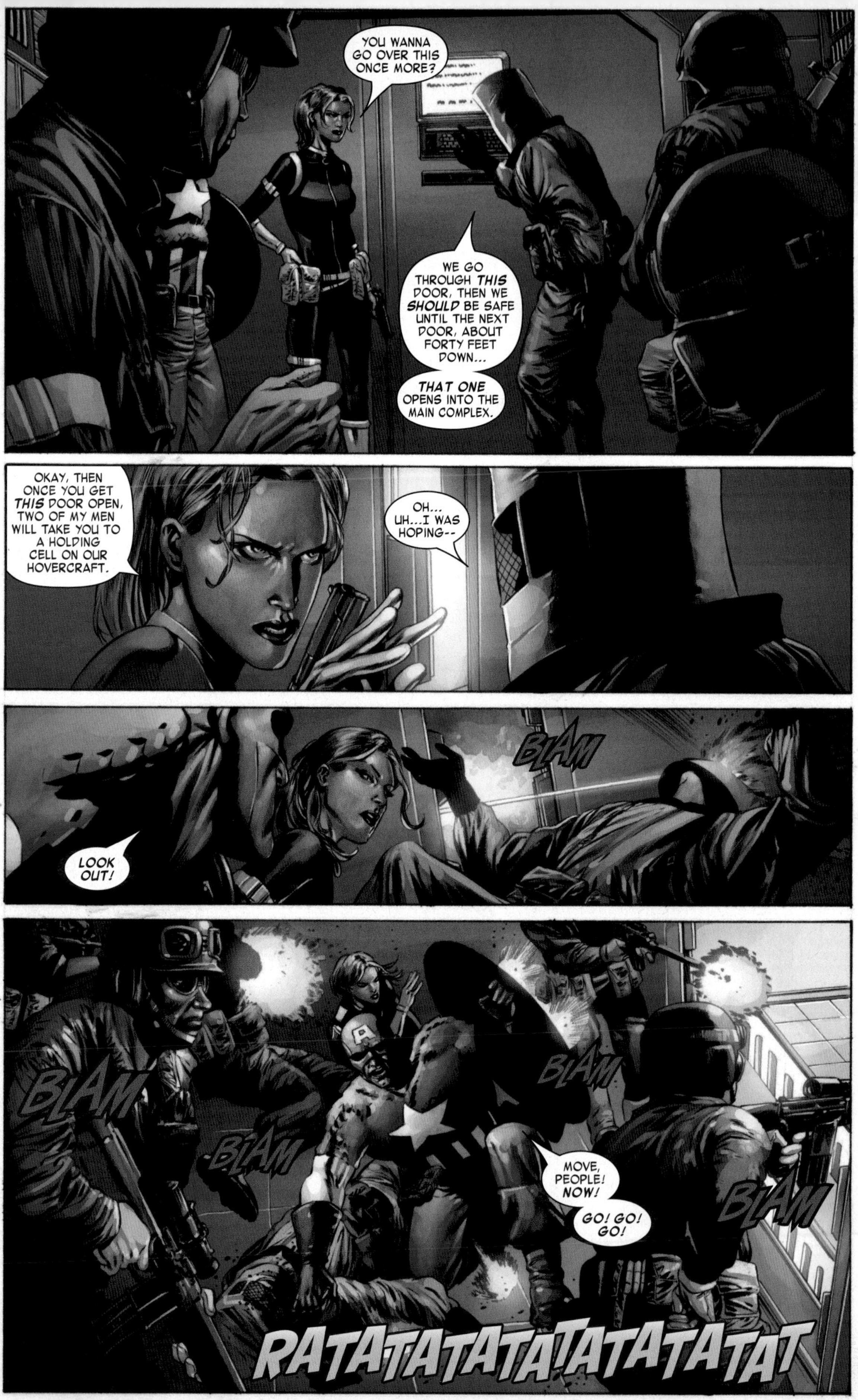
YOU WANNA GO OVER THIS ONCE MORE?
WE GO THROUGH THIS DOOR, THEN WE SHOULD BE SAFE UNTIL THE NEXT DOOR, ABOUT FORTY FEET DOWN...
THAT ONE OPENS INTO THE MAIN COMPLEX.
OKAY, THEN ONCE YOU GET THIS DOOR OPEN, TWO OF MY MEN WILL TAKE YOU TO A HOLDING CELL ON OUR HOVERCRAFT.
OH... UH...I WAS HOPING--
BLAM
LOOK OUT!
BLAM
BLAM
BLAM
MOVE, PEOPLE! NOW!
GO! GO! GO!
BLAM
RATATATATATATATATATAT

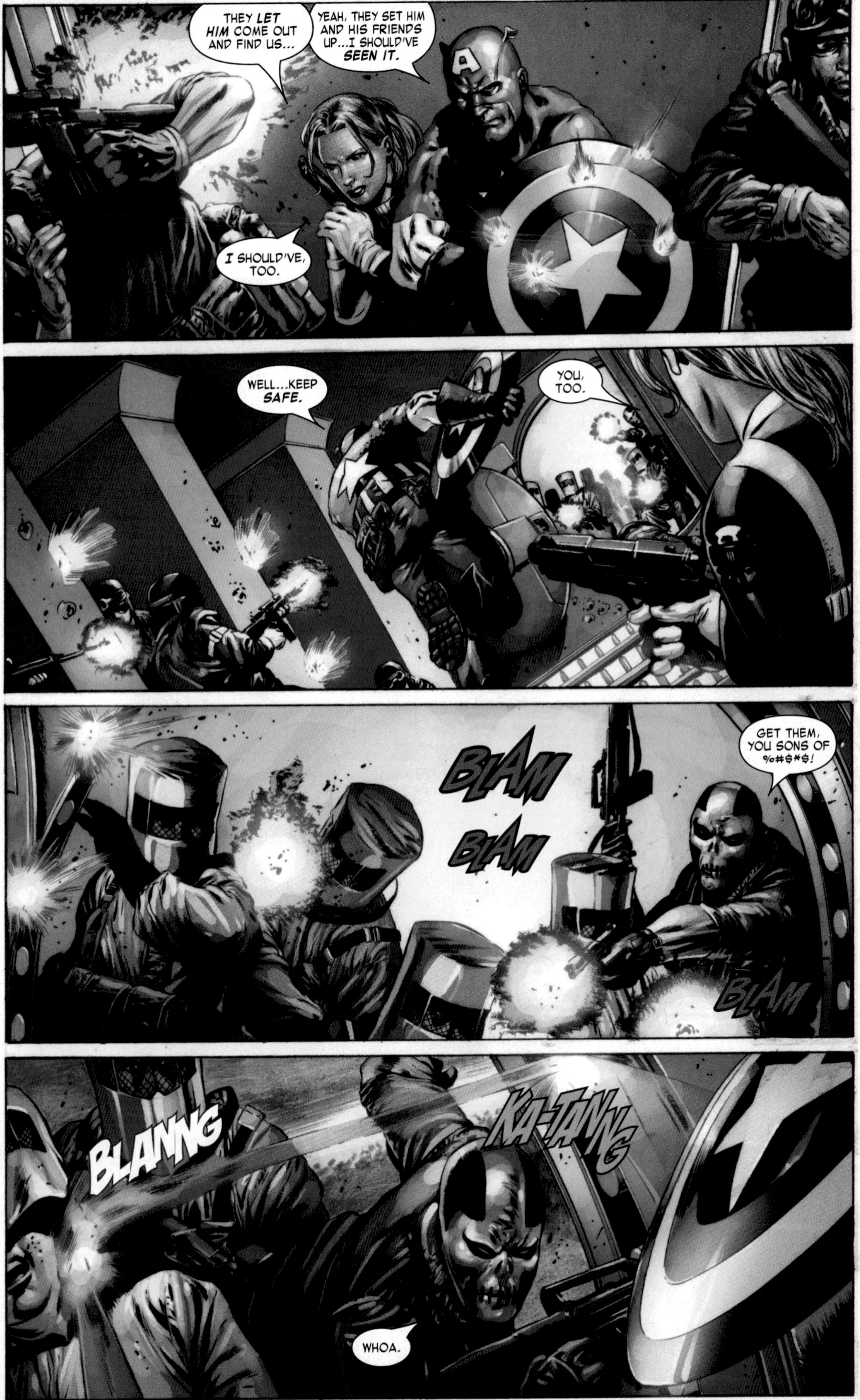
THEY LET HIM COME OUT AND FIND US...
YEAH, THEY SET HIM AND HIS FRIENDS UP...I SHOULD'VE SEEN IT.
I SHOULD'VE, TOO.
WELL...KEEP SAFE.
YOU, TOO.
BLAM
BLAM
GET THEM, YOU SONS OF %#$*$!
BLAM
BLANNG
KA-TANNG
WHOA.

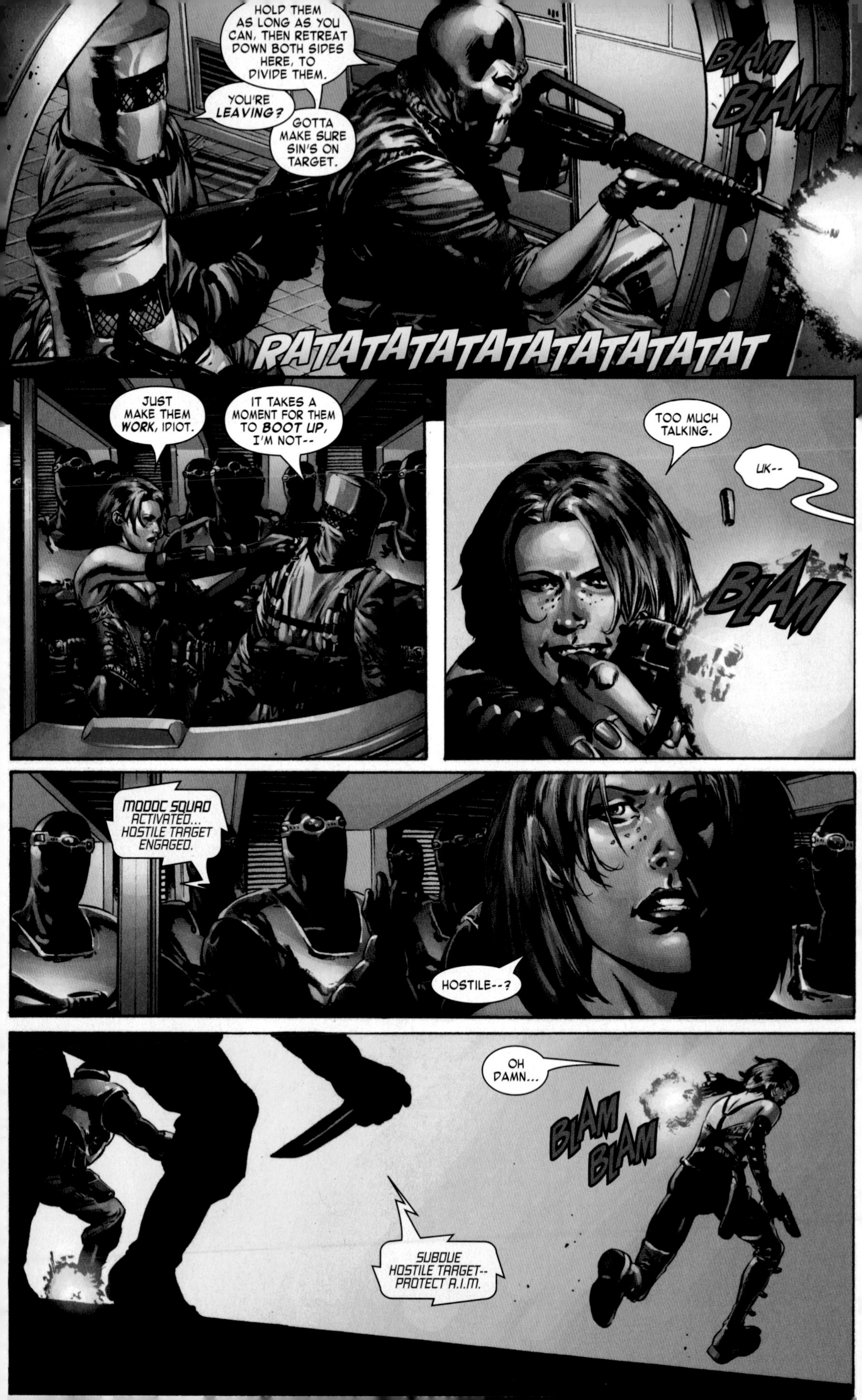
HOLD THEM AS LONG AS YOU CAN, THEN RETREAT DOWN BOTH SIDES HERE, TO DIVIDE THEM.
YOU'RE LEAVING?
GOTTA MAKE SURE SIN'S ON TARGET.
BLAM BLAM
RATATATATATATATATATATAT
JUST MAKE THEM WORK, IDIOT.
IT TAKES A MOMENT FOR THEM TO BOOT UP, I'M NOT--
TOO MUCH TALKING.
UK--
BLAM
MODOC SQUAD ACTIVATED... HOSTILE TARGET ENGAGED.
HOSTILE--?
OH DAMN...
BLAM BLAM
SUBDUE HOSTILE TARGET-- PROTECT A.I.M.

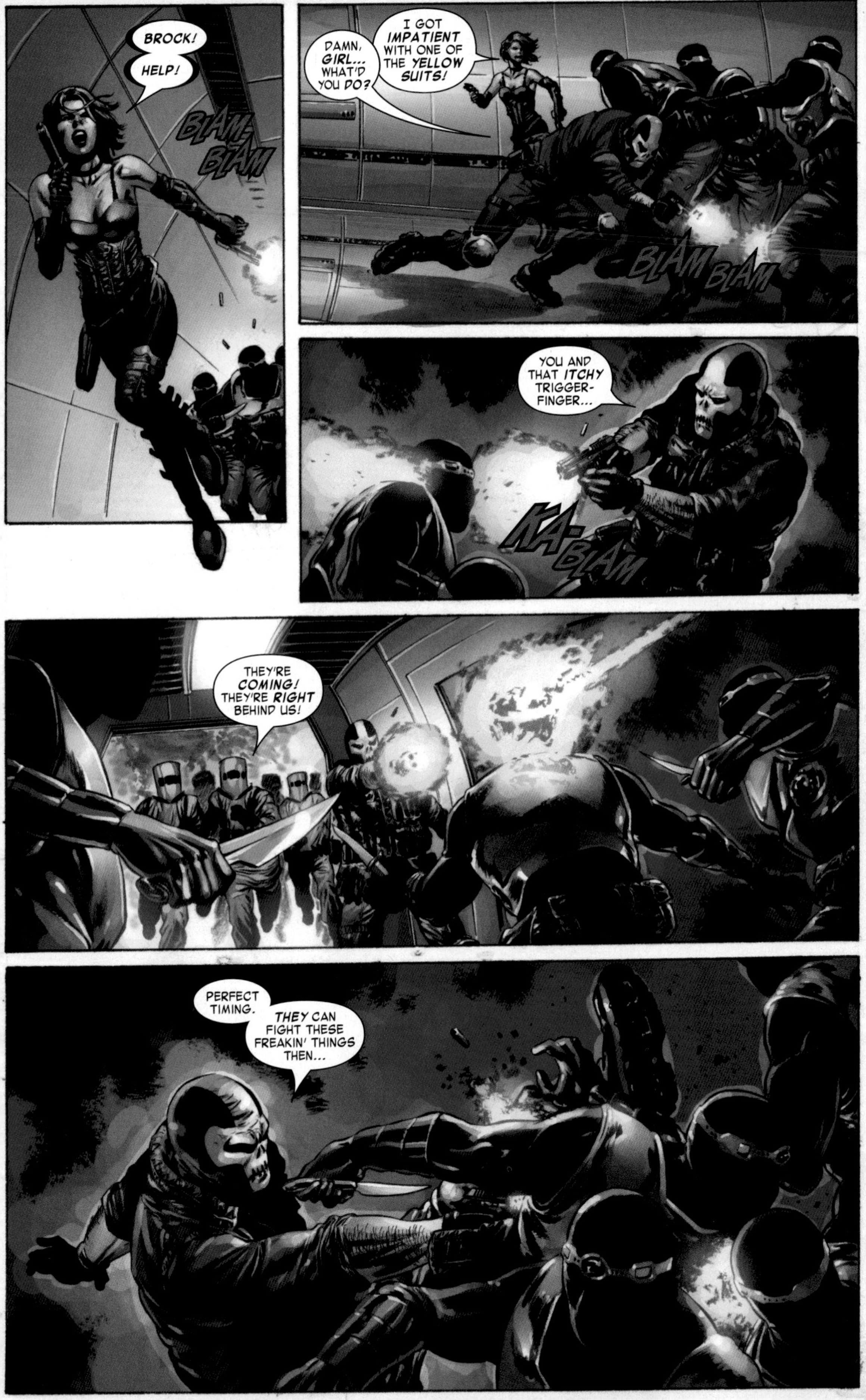
BROCK!
HELP!
BLAM-BLAM
DAMN, GIRL... WHAT'D YOU DO?
I GOT IMPATIENT WITH ONE OF THE YELLOW SUITS!
BLAM BLAM
YOU AND THAT ITCHY TRIGGER-FINGER...
KA-BLAM
THEY'RE COMING! THEY'RE RIGHT BEHIND US!
PERFECT TIMING.
THEY CAN FIGHT THESE FREAKIN' THINGS THEN...

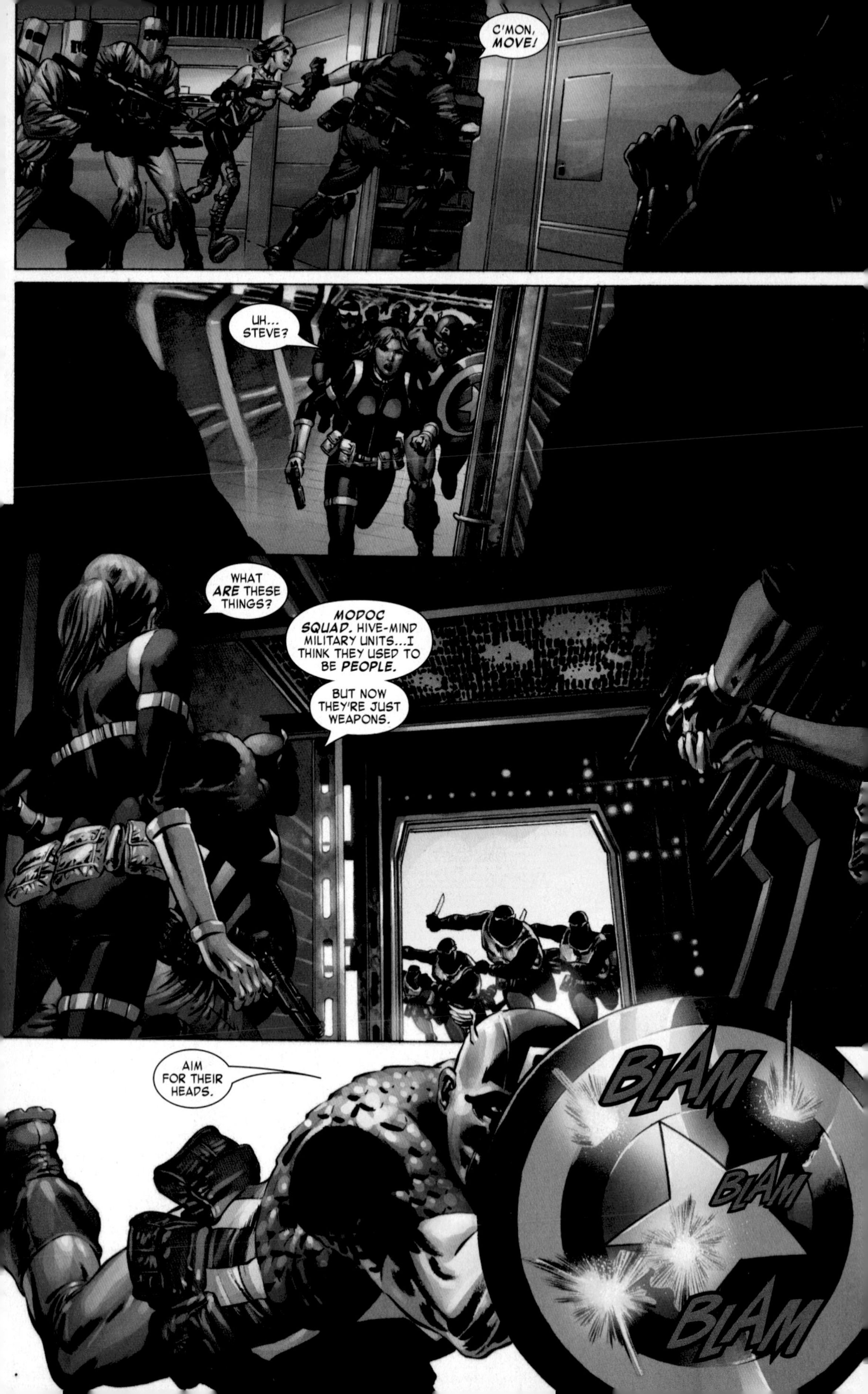
C'MON, MOVE!
UH... STEVE?
WHAT ARE THESE THINGS?
MODOC SQUAD. HIVE-MIND MILITARY UNITS...I THINK THEY USED TO BE PEOPLE.
BUT NOW THEY'RE JUST WEAPONS.
AIM FOR THEIR HEADS.
BLAM
BLAM
BLAM

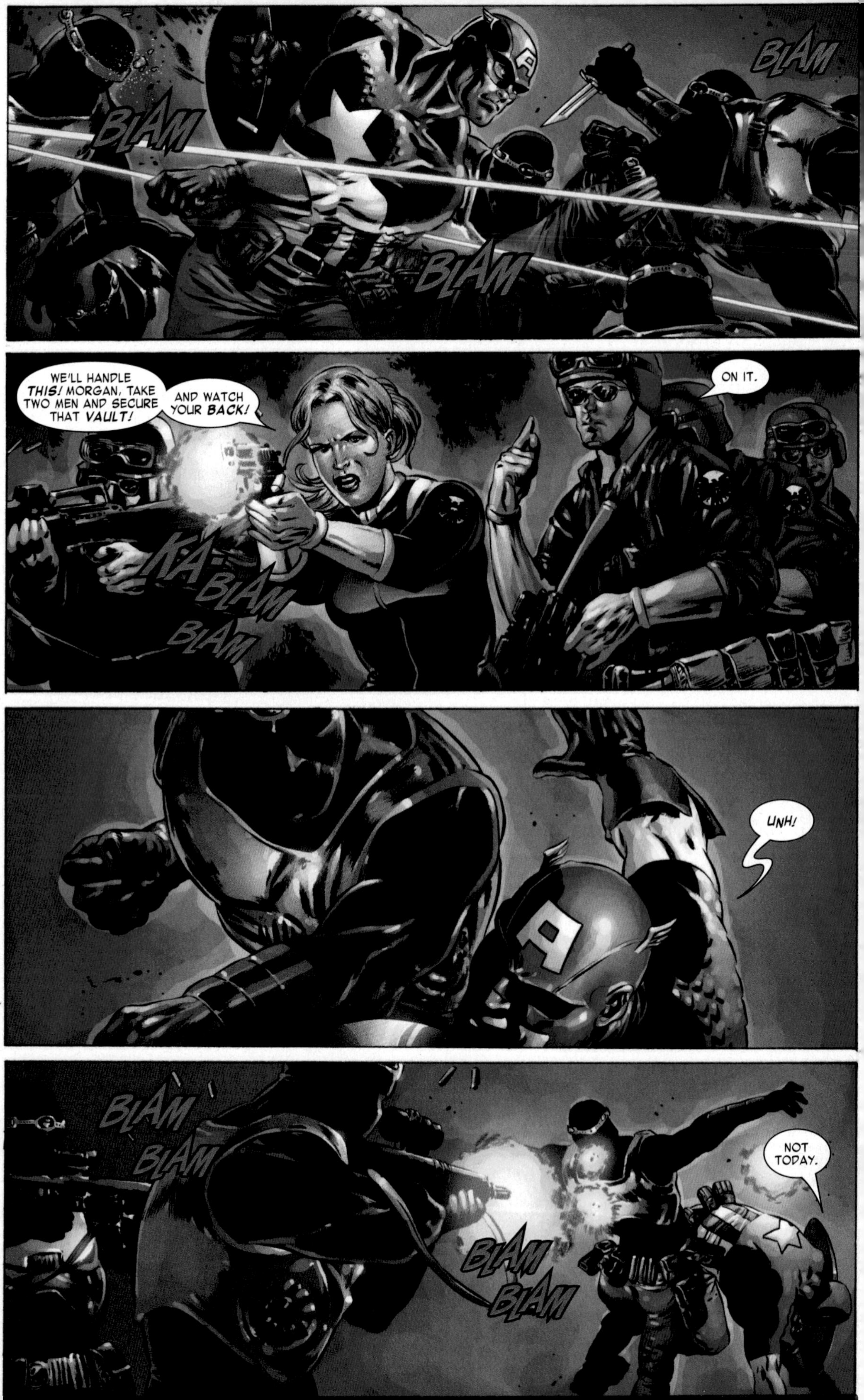
BLAM
BLAM
BLAM
WE'LL HANDLE THIS! MORGAN, TAKE TWO MEN AND SECURE THAT VAULT!
AND WATCH YOUR BACK!
ON IT.
KA-BLAM
BLAM
UNH!
BLAM
BLAM
BLAM
BLAM
NOT TODAY.

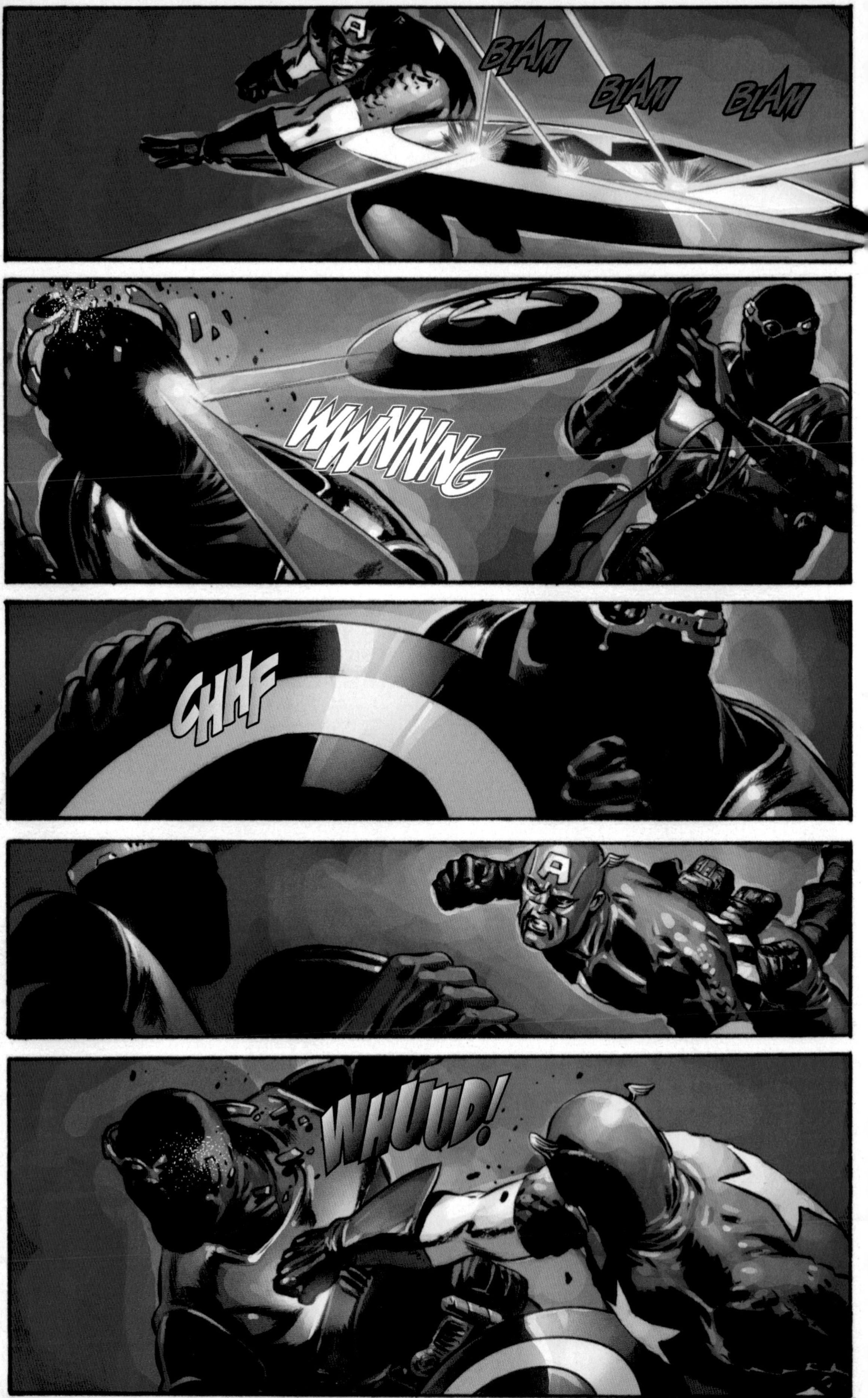
BLAM
BLAM
BLAM
WWNNNG
CHHF
WHUUD!

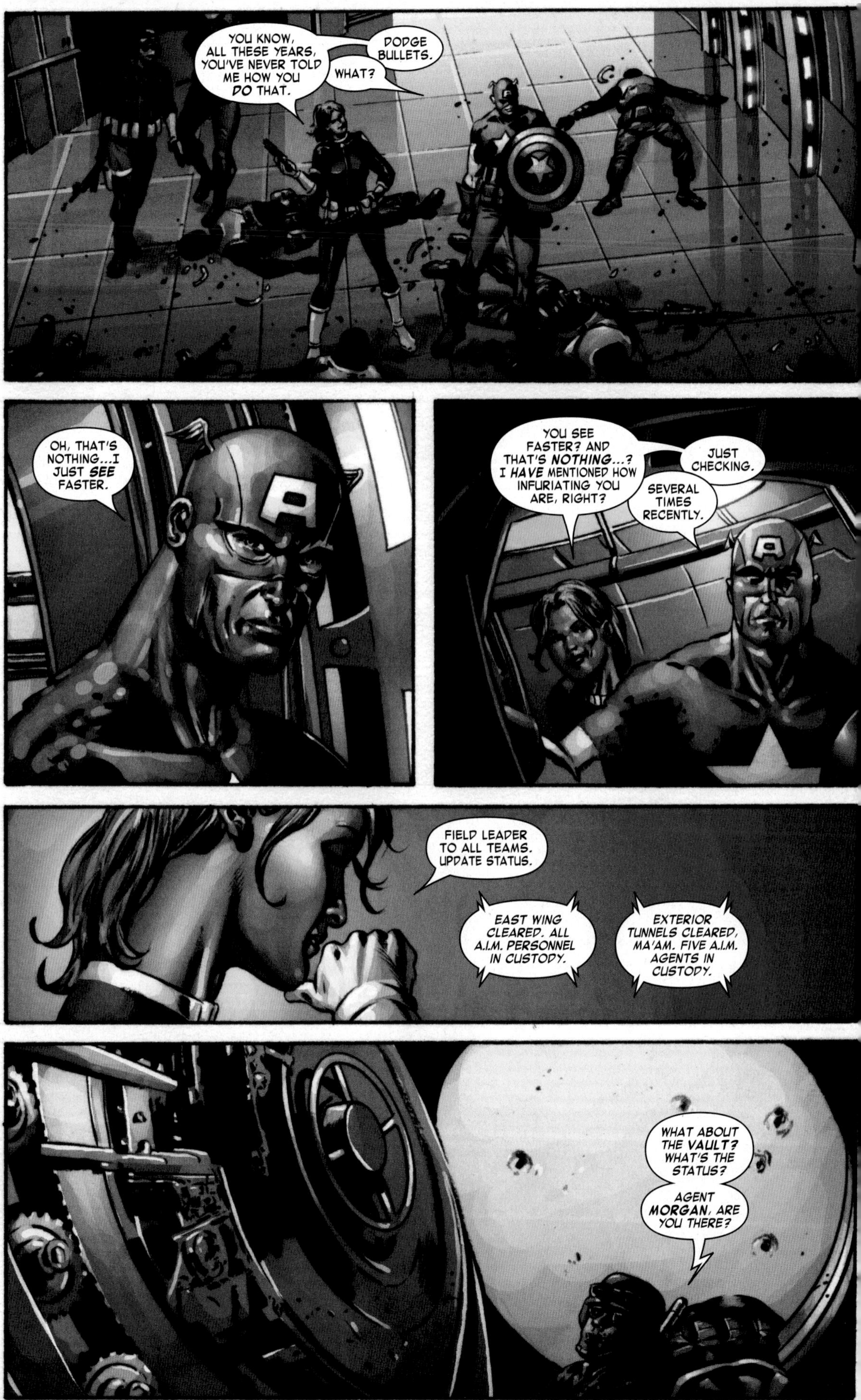
YOU KNOW, ALL THESE YEARS, YOU'VE NEVER TOLD ME HOW YOU DO THAT.
WHAT?
DODGE BULLETS.
OH, THAT'S NOTHING...I JUST SEE FASTER.
YOU SEE FASTER? AND THAT'S NOTHING...? I HAVE MENTIONED HOW INFURIATING YOU ARE, RIGHT?
SEVERAL TIMES RECENTLY.
JUST CHECKING.
FIELD LEADER TO ALL TEAMS. UPDATE STATUS.
EAST WING CLEARED. ALL A.I.M. PERSONNEL IN CUSTODY.
EXTERIOR TUNNELS CLEARED, MA'AM. FIVE A.I.M. AGENTS IN CUSTODY.
WHAT ABOUT THE VAULT? WHAT'S THE STATUS?
AGENT MORGAN, ARE YOU THERE?

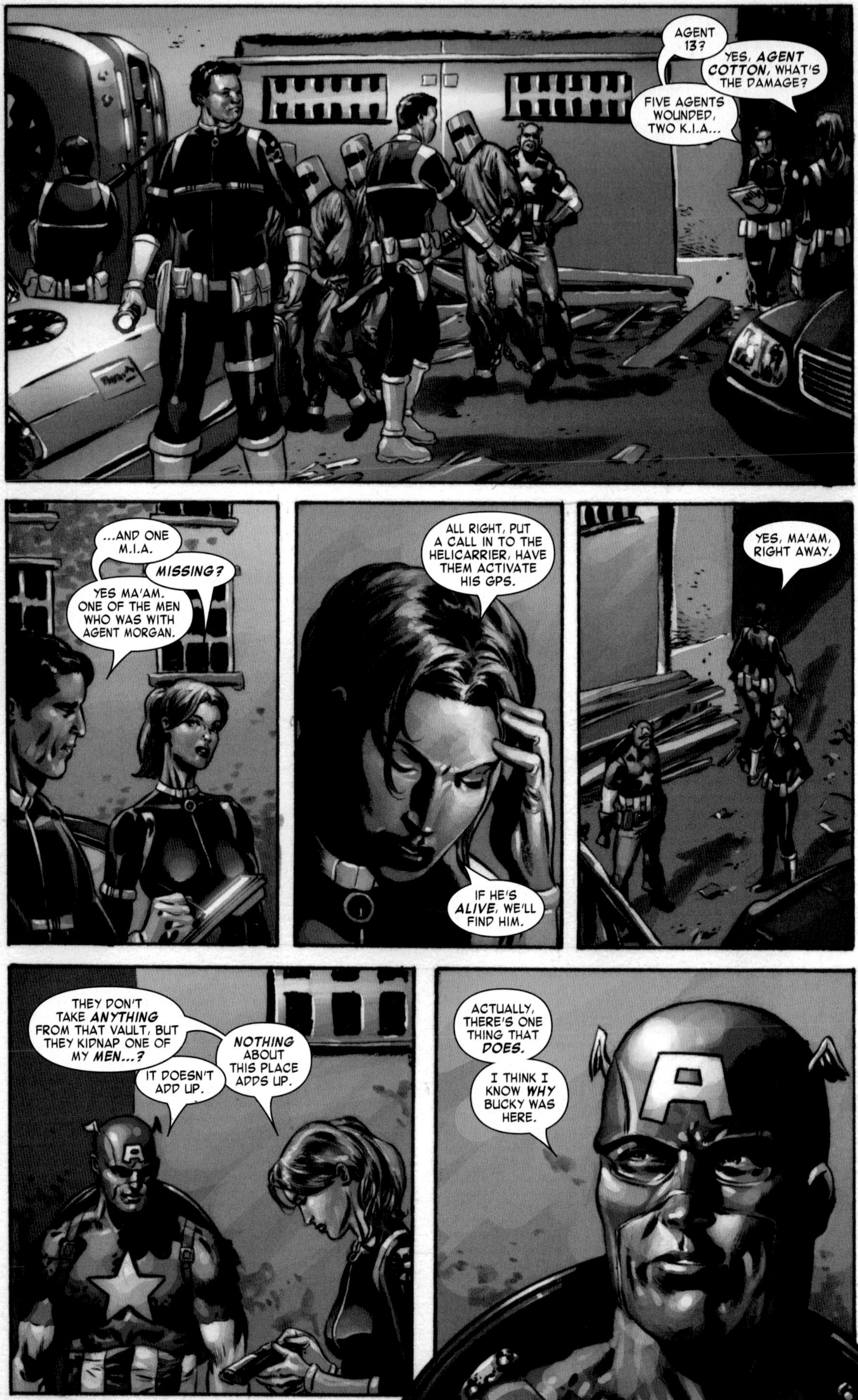
AGENT 13?
YES, AGENT COTTON, WHAT'S THE DAMAGE?
FIVE AGENTS WOUNDED, TWO K.I.A...
...AND ONE M.I.A.
MISSING?
YES MA'AM. ONE OF THE MEN WHO WAS WITH AGENT MORGAN.
ALL RIGHT, PUT A CALL IN TO THE HELICARRIER, HAVE THEM ACTIVATE HIS GPS.
IF HE'S ALIVE, WE'LL FIND HIM.
YES, MA'AM, RIGHT AWAY.
THEY DON'T TAKE ANYTHING FROM THAT VAULT, BUT THEY KIDNAP ONE OF MY MEN...?
IT DOESN'T ADD UP.
NOTHING ABOUT THIS PLACE ADDS UP.
ACTUALLY, THERE'S ONE THING THAT DOES.
I THINK I KNOW WHY BUCKY WAS HERE.

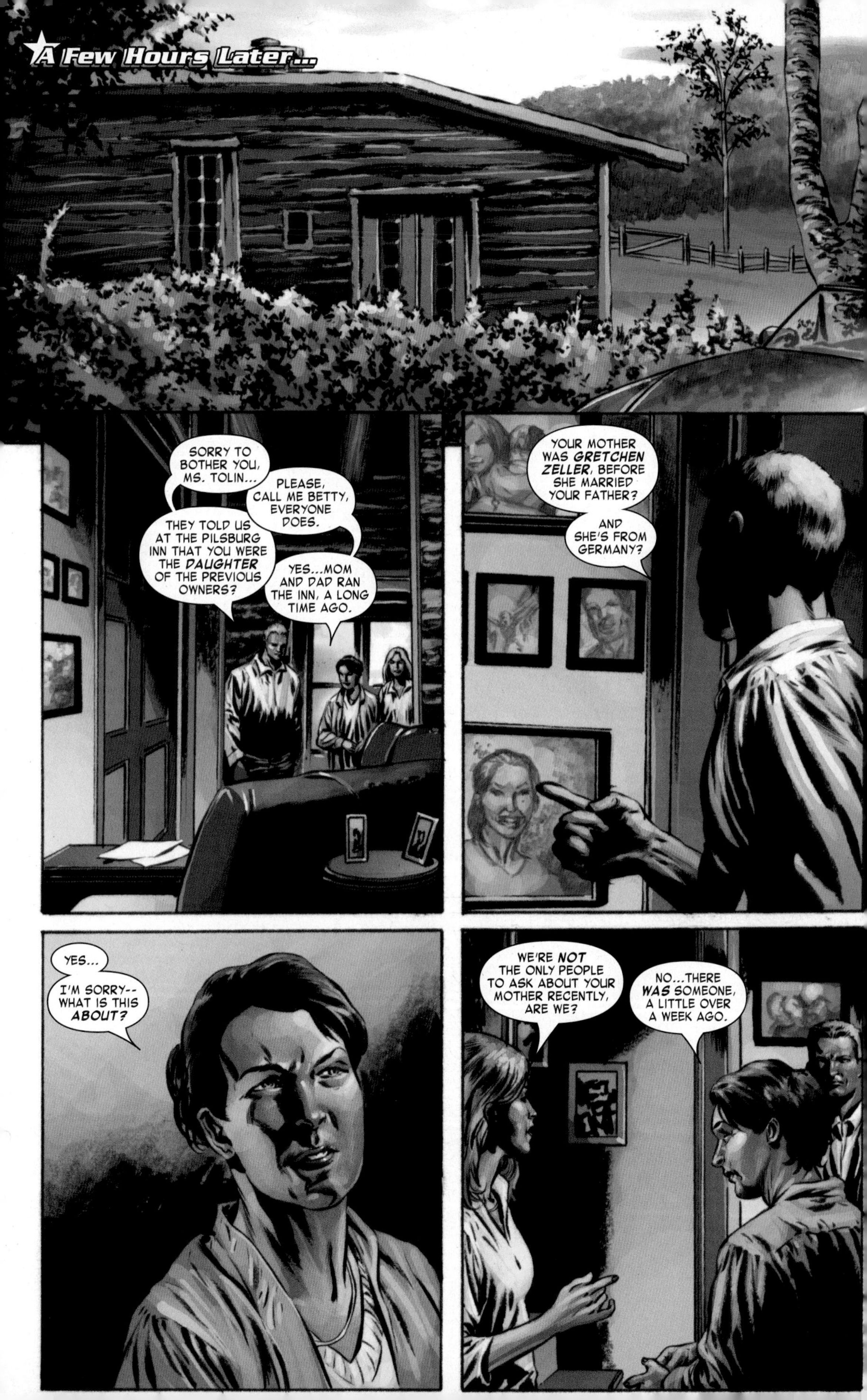
A Few Hours Later...
SORRY TO BOTHER YOU, MS. TOLIN...
THEY TOLD US AT THE PILSBURG INN THAT YOU WERE THE DAUGHTER OF THE PREVIOUS OWNERS?
PLEASE, CALL ME BETTY, EVERYONE DOES.
YES...MOM AND DAD RAN THE INN, A LONG TIME AGO.
YOUR MOTHER WAS GRETCHEN ZELLER, BEFORE SHE MARRIED YOUR FATHER?
AND SHE'S FROM GERMANY?
YES...
I'M SORRY-- WHAT IS THIS ABOUT?
WE'RE NOT THE ONLY PEOPLE TO ASK ABOUT YOUR MOTHER RECENTLY, ARE WE?
NO...THERE WAS SOMEONE, A LITTLE OVER A WEEK AGO.

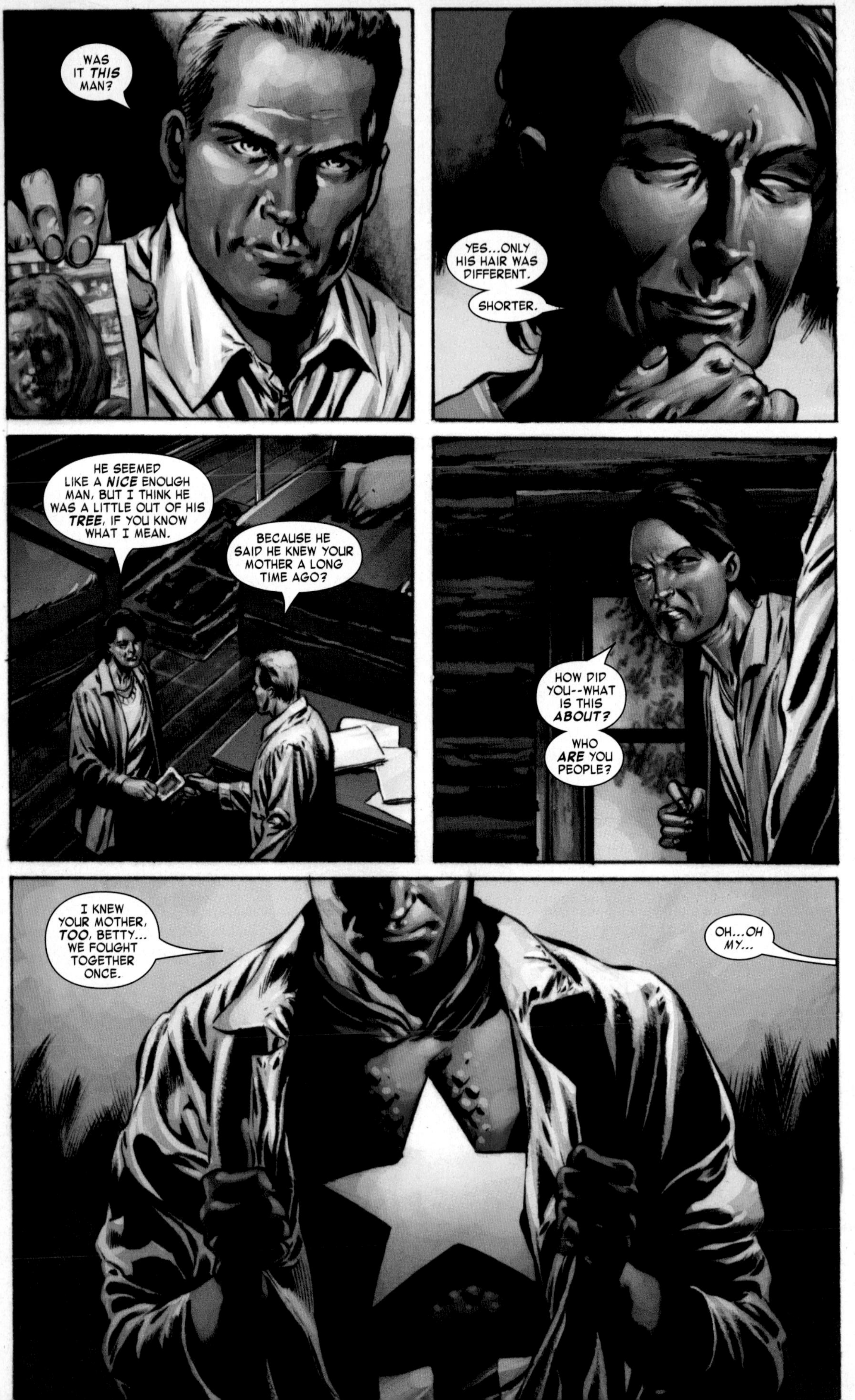
WAS IT THIS MAN?
YES...ONLY HIS HAIR WAS DIFFERENT.
SHORTER.
HE SEEMED LIKE A NICE ENOUGH MAN, BUT I THINK HE WAS A LITTLE OUT OF HIS TREE, IF YOU KNOW WHAT I MEAN.
BECAUSE HE SAID HE KNEW YOUR MOTHER A LONG TIME AGO?
HOW DID YOU--WHAT IS THIS ABOUT?
WHO ARE YOU PEOPLE?
I KNEW YOUR MOTHER, TOO, BETTY... WE FOUGHT TOGETHER ONCE.
OH...OH MY...

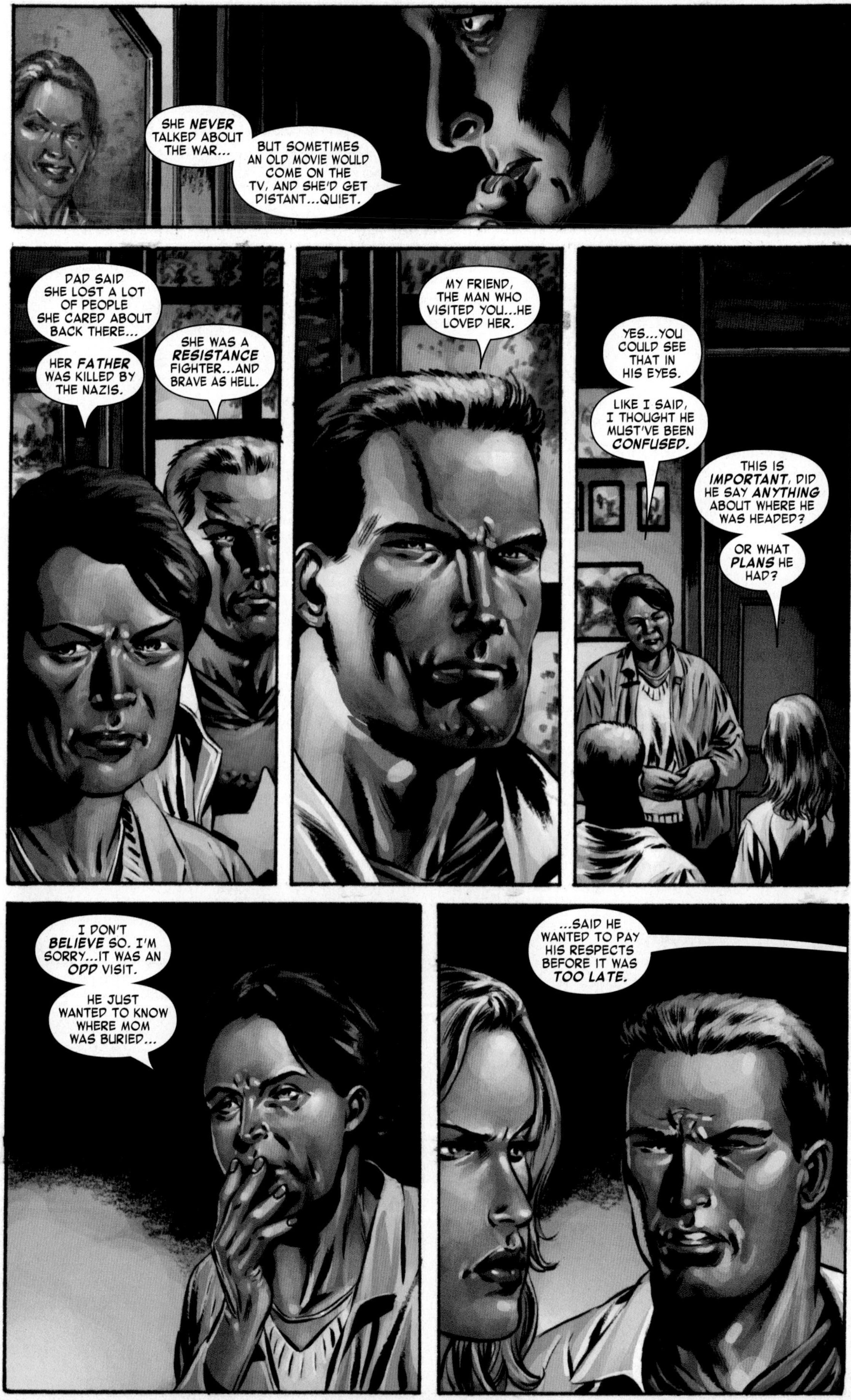

SHE *NEVER* TALKED ABOUT THE WAR...
BUT SOMETIMES AN OLD MOVIE WOULD COME ON THE TV, AND SHE'D GET DISTANT...QUIET.
DAD SAID SHE LOST A LOT OF PEOPLE SHE CARED ABOUT BACK THERE...
HER *FATHER* WAS KILLED BY THE NAZIS.
SHE WAS A *RESISTANCE* FIGHTER...AND BRAVE AS HELL.
MY FRIEND, THE MAN WHO VISITED YOU...HE LOVED HER.
YES...YOU COULD SEE THAT IN HIS EYES.
LIKE I SAID, I THOUGHT HE MUST'VE BEEN *CONFUSED.*
THIS IS *IMPORTANT*, DID HE SAY *ANYTHING* ABOUT WHERE HE WAS HEADED?
OR WHAT *PLANS* HE HAD?
I DON'T *BELIEVE* SO. I'M SORRY...IT WAS AN *ODD* VISIT.
HE JUST WANTED TO KNOW WHERE MOM WAS BURIED...
...SAID HE WANTED TO PAY HIS RESPECTS BEFORE IT WAS *TOO LATE.*

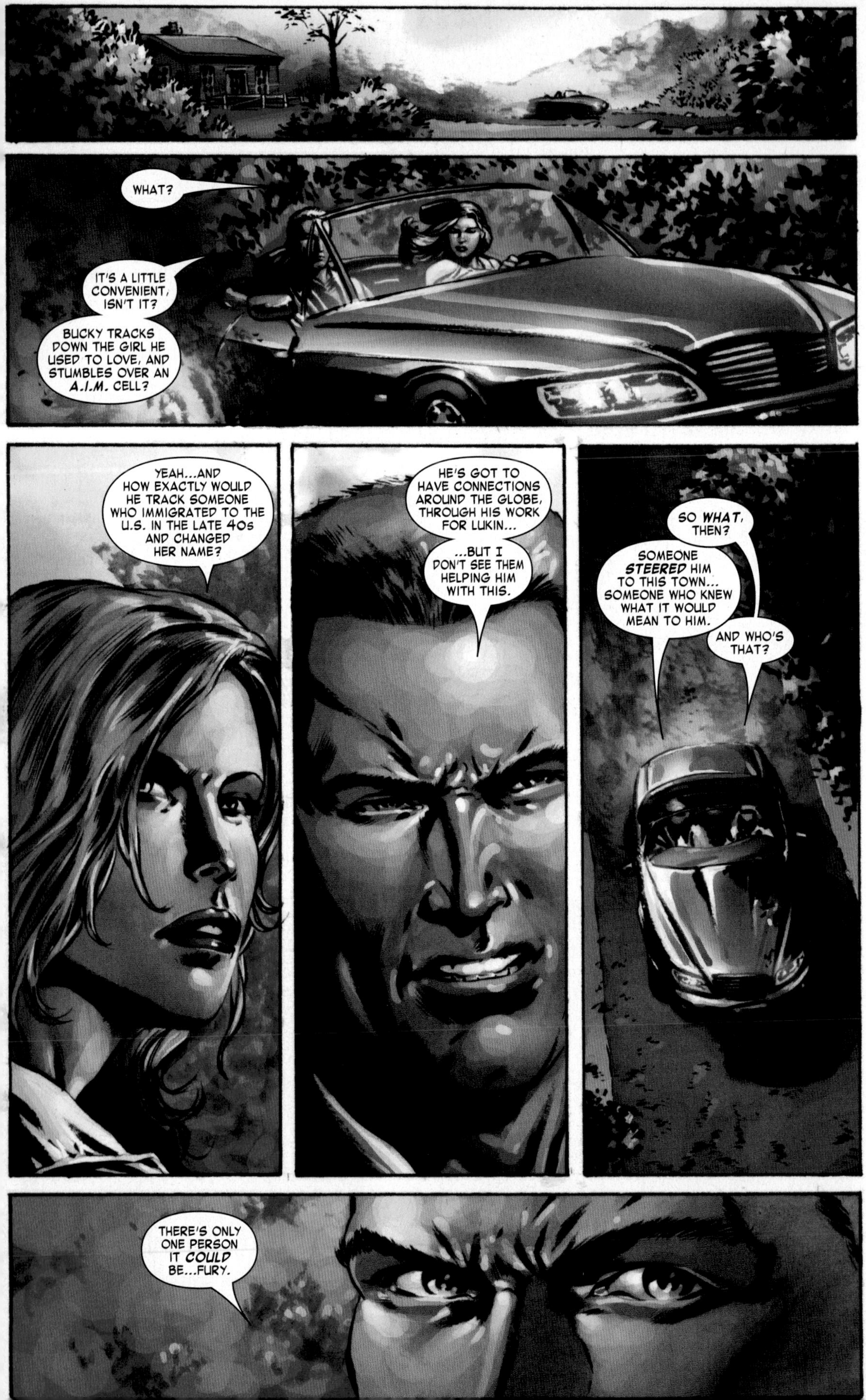
WHAT?
IT'S A LITTLE CONVENIENT, ISN'T IT?
BUCKY TRACKS DOWN THE GIRL HE USED TO LOVE, AND STUMBLES OVER AN A.I.M. CELL?
YEAH...AND HOW EXACTLY WOULD HE TRACK SOMEONE WHO IMMIGRATED TO THE U.S. IN THE LATE 40s AND CHANGED HER NAME?
HE'S GOT TO HAVE CONNECTIONS AROUND THE GLOBE, THROUGH HIS WORK FOR LUKIN...
...BUT I DON'T SEE THEM HELPING HIM WITH THIS.
SO WHAT, THEN?
SOMEONE STEERED HIM TO THIS TOWN... SOMEONE WHO KNEW WHAT IT WOULD MEAN TO HIM.
AND WHO'S THAT?
THERE'S ONLY ONE PERSON IT COULD BE...FURY.

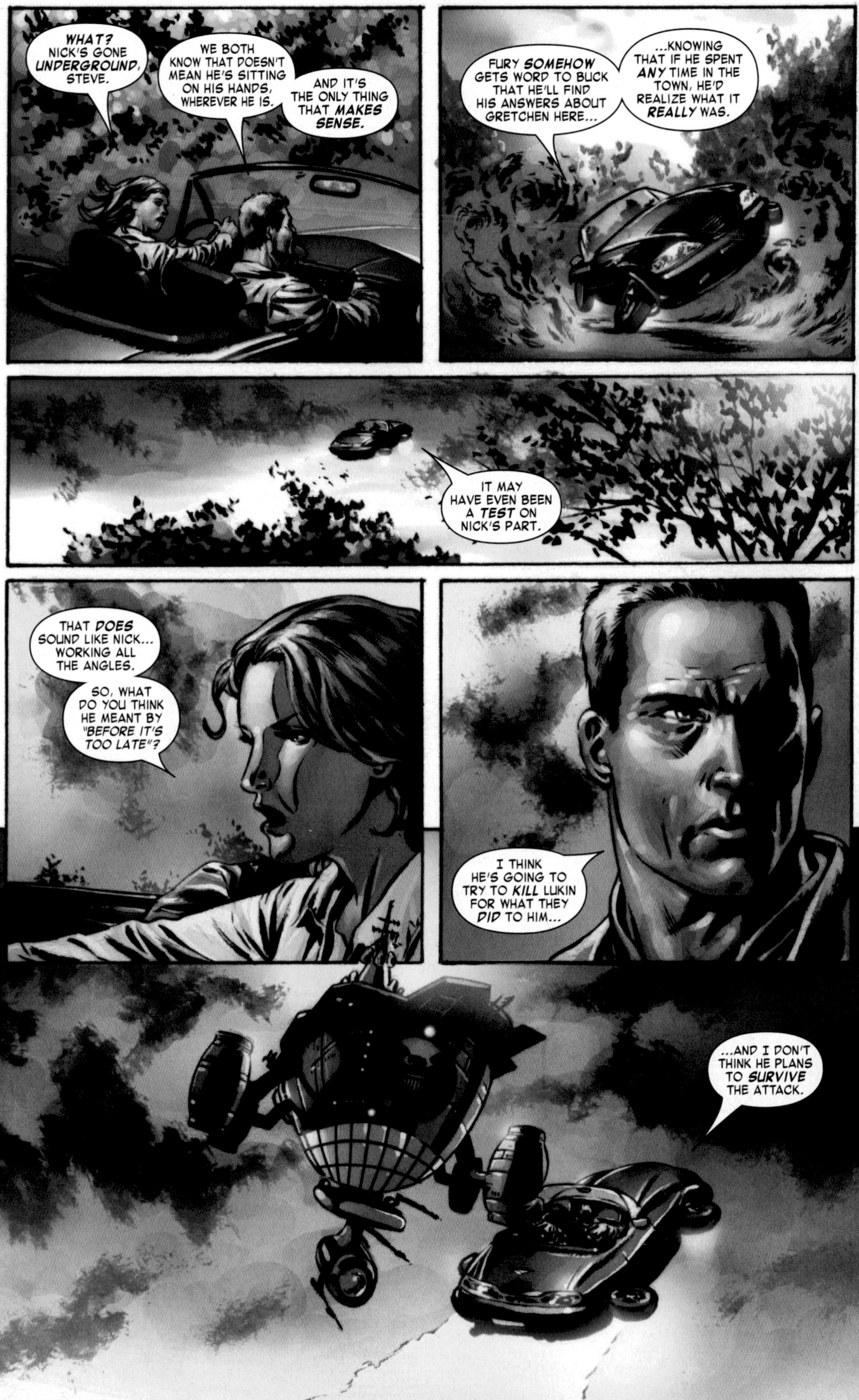
WHAT? NICK'S GONE UNDERGROUND, STEVE.
WE BOTH KNOW THAT DOESN'T MEAN HE'S SITTING ON HIS HANDS, WHEREVER HE IS.
AND IT'S THE ONLY THING THAT MAKES SENSE.
FURY SOMEHOW GETS WORD TO BUCK THAT HE'LL FIND HIS ANSWERS ABOUT GRETCHEN HERE...
...KNOWING THAT IF HE SPENT ANY TIME IN THE TOWN, HE'D REALIZE WHAT IT REALLY WAS.
IT MAY HAVE EVEN BEEN A TEST ON NICK'S PART.
THAT DOES SOUND LIKE NICK... WORKING ALL THE ANGLES.
SO, WHAT DO YOU THINK HE MEANT BY "BEFORE IT'S TOO LATE"?
I THINK HE'S GOING TO TRY TO KILL LUKIN FOR WHAT THEY DID TO HIM...
...AND I DON'T THINK HE PLANS TO SURVIVE THE ATTACK.

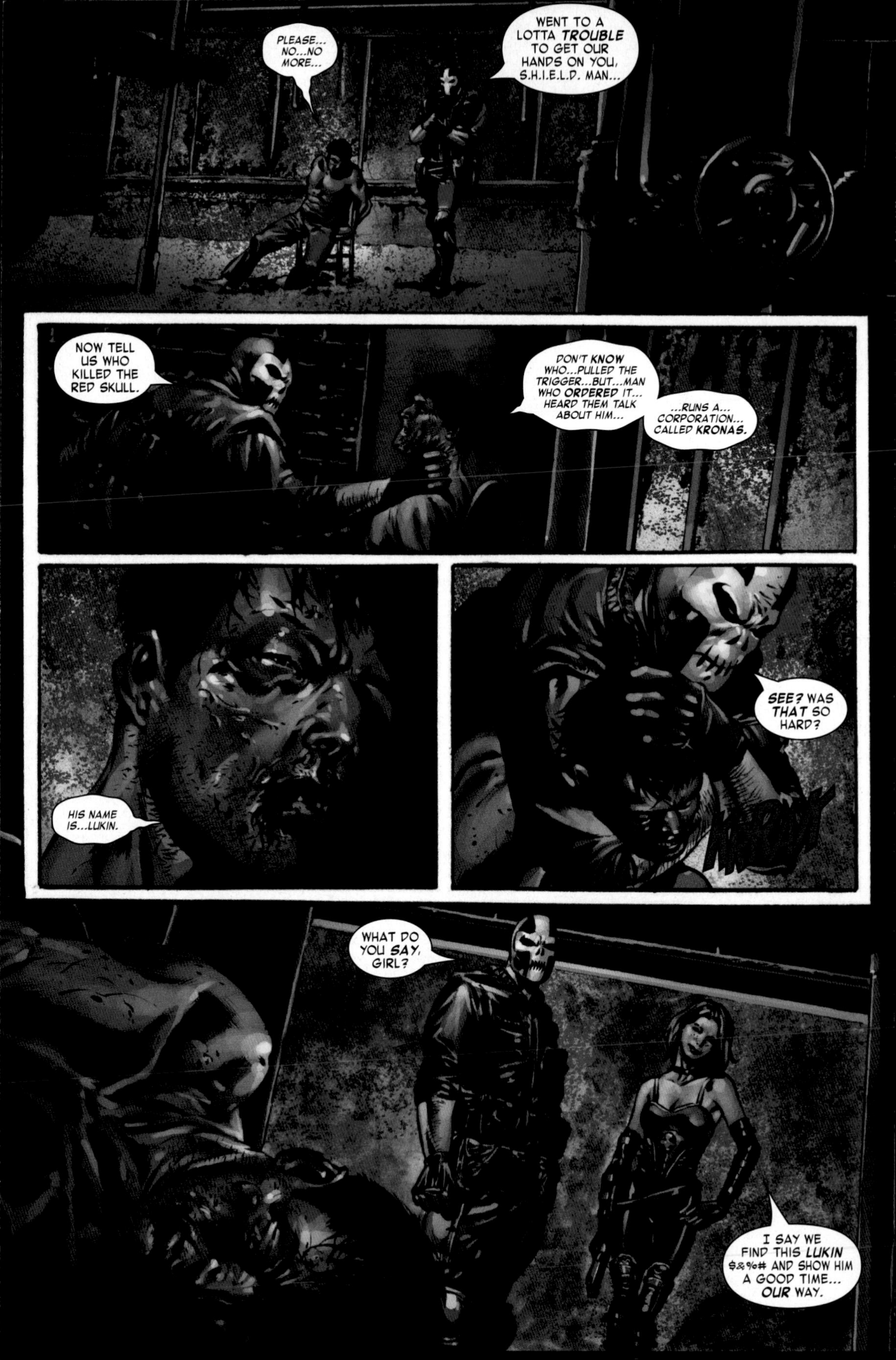

PLEASE... NO...NO MORE...
WENT TO A LOTTA TROUBLE TO GET OUR HANDS ON YOU, S.H.I.E.L.D. MAN...
NOW TELL US WHO KILLED THE RED SKULL.
DON'T KNOW WHO...PULLED THE TRIGGER...BUT...MAN WHO ORDERED IT... HEARD THEM TALK ABOUT HIM...
...RUNS A... CORPORATION... CALLED KRONAS.
HIS NAME IS...LUKIN.
SEE? WAS THAT SO HARD?
WHAT DO YOU SAY, GIRL?
I SAY WE FIND THIS LUKIN $&%# AND SHOW HIM A GOOD TIME... OUR WAY.

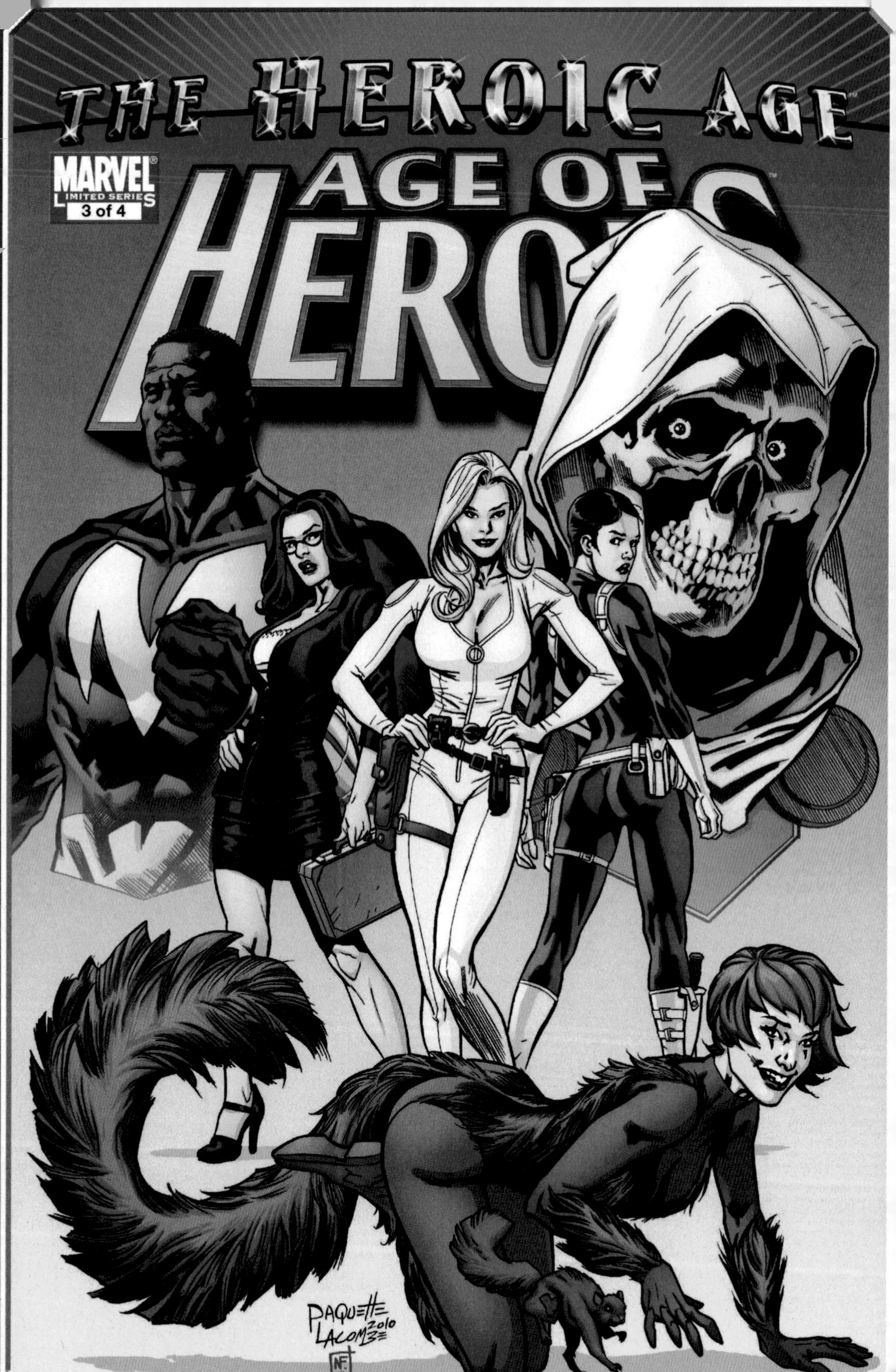

THE HEROIC AGE
MARVEL
LIMITED SERIES
3 of 4
AGE OF
HERO
PAQUETTE
LACOMBE 2010

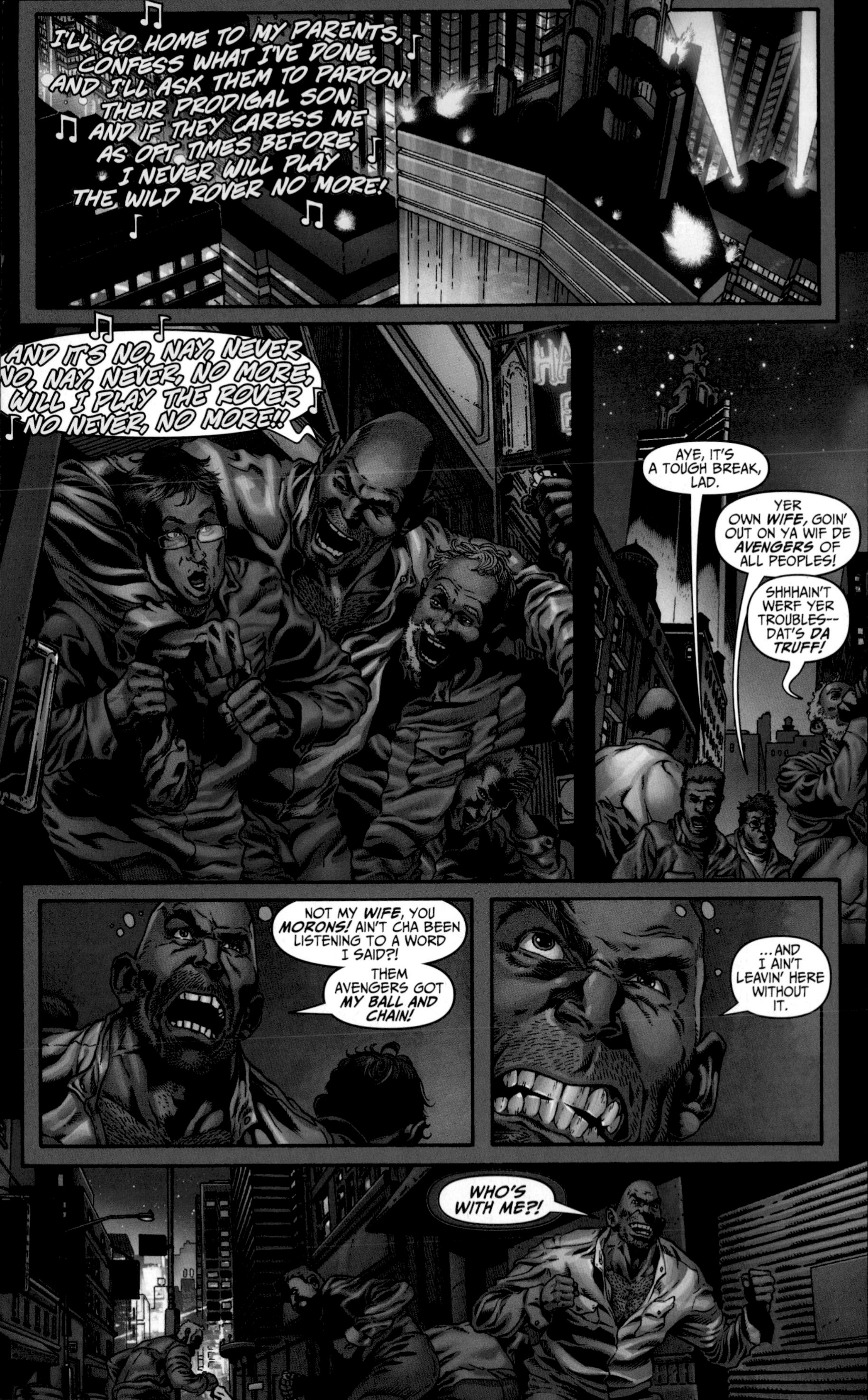
I'LL GO HOME TO MY PARENTS, CONFESS WHAT I'VE DONE, AND I'LL ASK THEM TO PARDON THEIR PRODIGAL SON. AND IF THEY CARESS ME AS OFT TIMES BEFORE, I NEVER WILL PLAY THE WILD ROVER NO MORE!
AND IT'S NO, NAY, NEVER NO, NAY, NEVER, NO MORE, WILL I PLAY THE ROVER NO NEVER, NO MORE!!
AYE, IT'S A TOUGH BREAK, LAD.
YER OWN WIFE, GOIN' OUT ON YA WIF DE AVENGERS OF ALL PEOPLES!
SHHHAIN'T WERF YER TROUBLES-- DAT'S DA TRUFF!
NOT MY WIFE, YOU MORONS! AIN'T CHA BEEN LISTENING TO A WORD I SAID?!
THEM AVENGERS GOT MY BALL AND CHAIN!
...AND I AIN'T LEAVIN' HERE WITHOUT IT.
WHO'S WITH ME?!

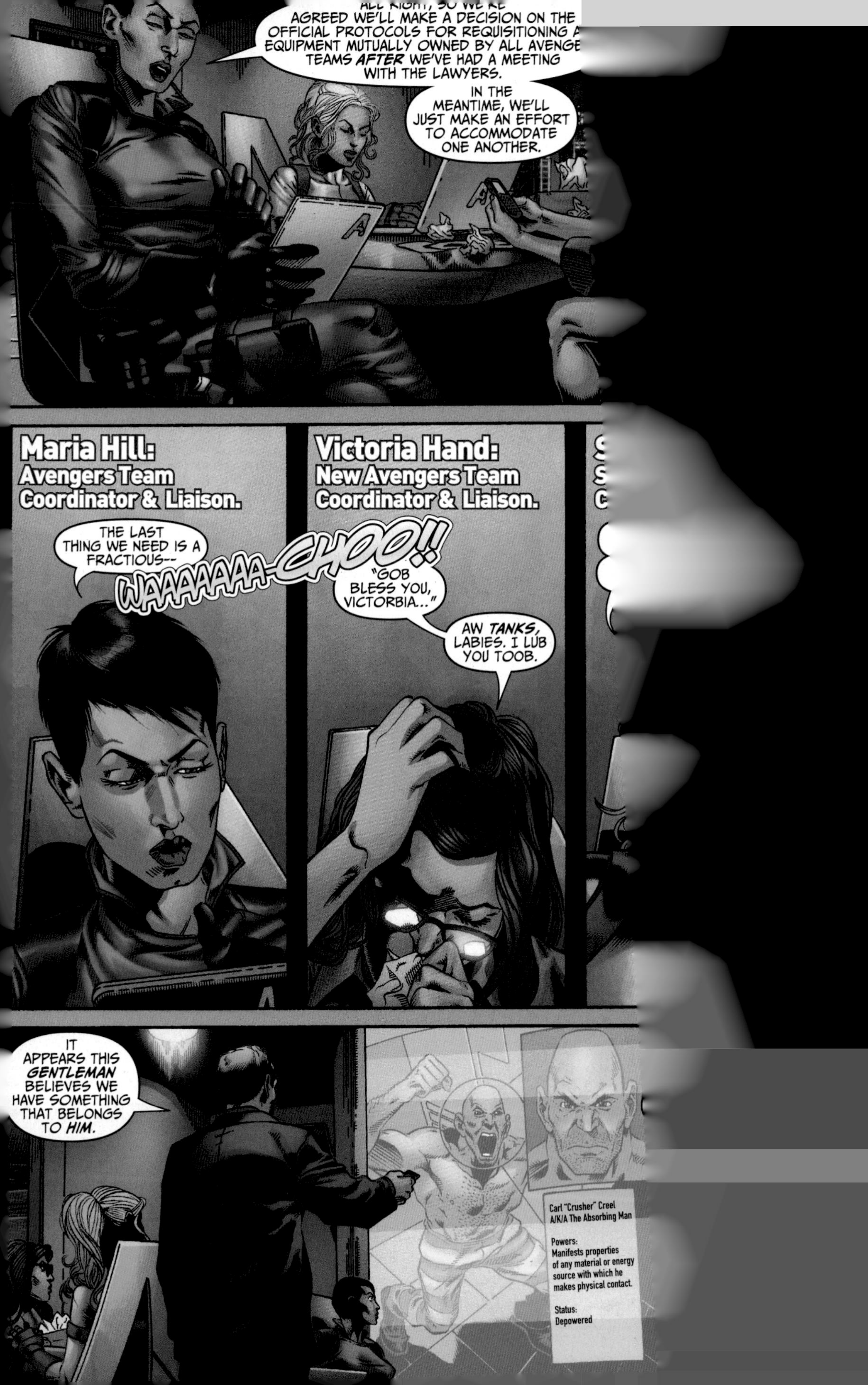
ALL RIGHT, SO WE'RE AGREED WE'LL MAKE A DECISION ON THE OFFICIAL PROTOCOLS FOR REQUISITIONING A EQUIPMENT MUTUALLY OWNED BY ALL AVENGE TEAMS AFTER WE'VE HAD A MEETING WITH THE LAWYERS.
IN THE MEANTIME, WE'LL JUST MAKE AN EFFORT TO ACCOMMODATE ONE ANOTHER.
Maria Hill: Avengers Team Coordinator & Liaison.
THE LAST THING WE NEED IS A FRACTIOUS--
Victoria Hand: New Avengers Team Coordinator & Liaison.
WAAAAAAA-CHOO!!
"GOB BLESS YOU, VICTORBIA..."
AW TANKS, LABIES. I LUB YOU TOOB.
IT APPEARS THIS GENTLEMAN BELIEVES WE HAVE SOMETHING THAT BELONGS TO HIM.
Carl "Crusher" Creel
A/K/A The Absorbing Man
Powers:
Manifests properties of any material or energy source with which he makes physical contact.
Status:
Depowered

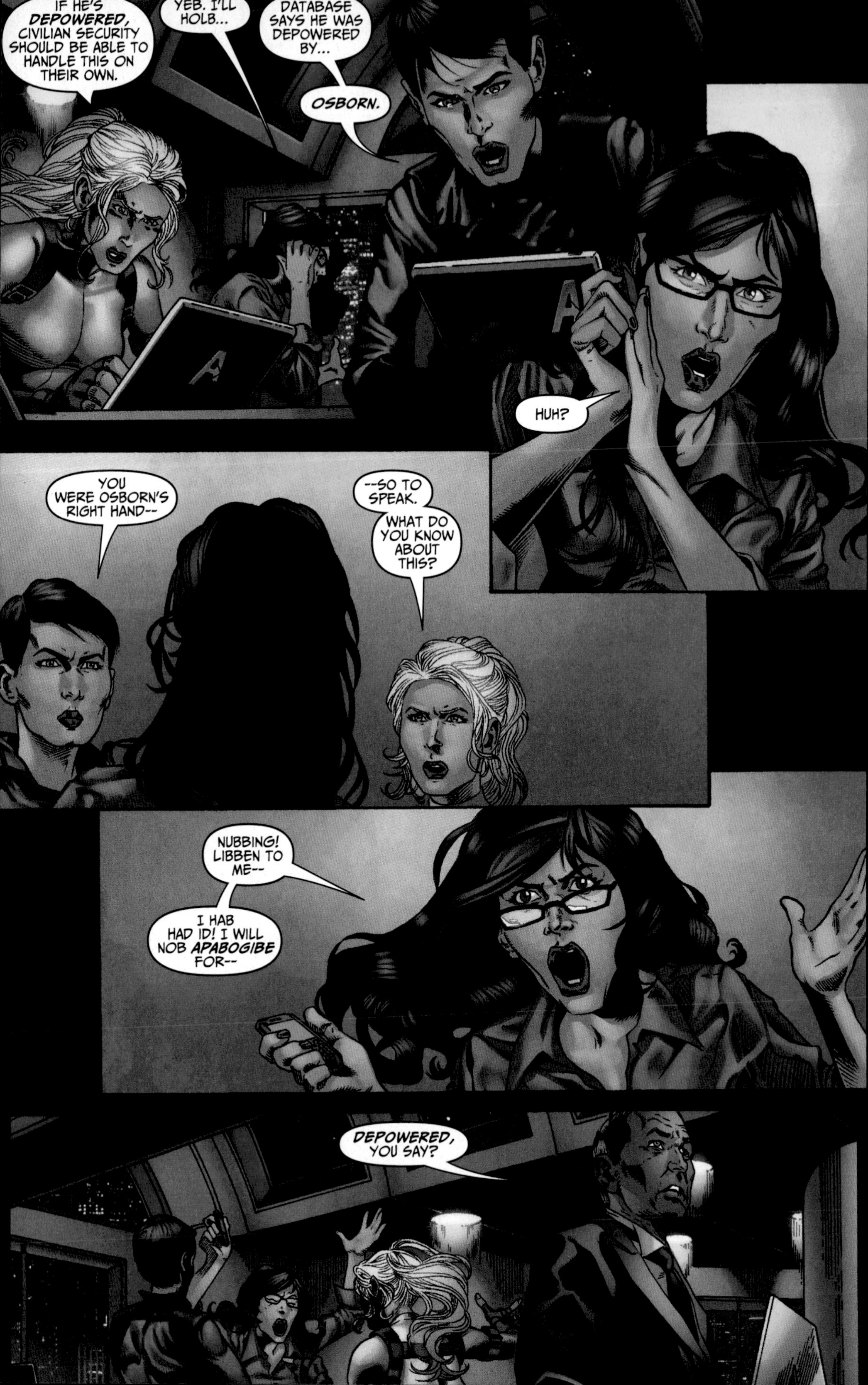

IF HE'S DEPOWERED, CIVILIAN SECURITY SHOULD BE ABLE TO HANDLE THIS ON THEIR OWN.
YEB. I'LL HOLB...
DATABASE SAYS HE WAS DEPOWERED BY...
OSBORN.
HUH?
YOU WERE OSBORN'S RIGHT HAND--
--SO TO SPEAK.
WHAT DO YOU KNOW ABOUT THIS?
NUBBING! LIBBEN TO ME--
I HAB HAD ID! I WILL NOB APABOGIBE FOR--
DEPOWERED, YOU SAY?

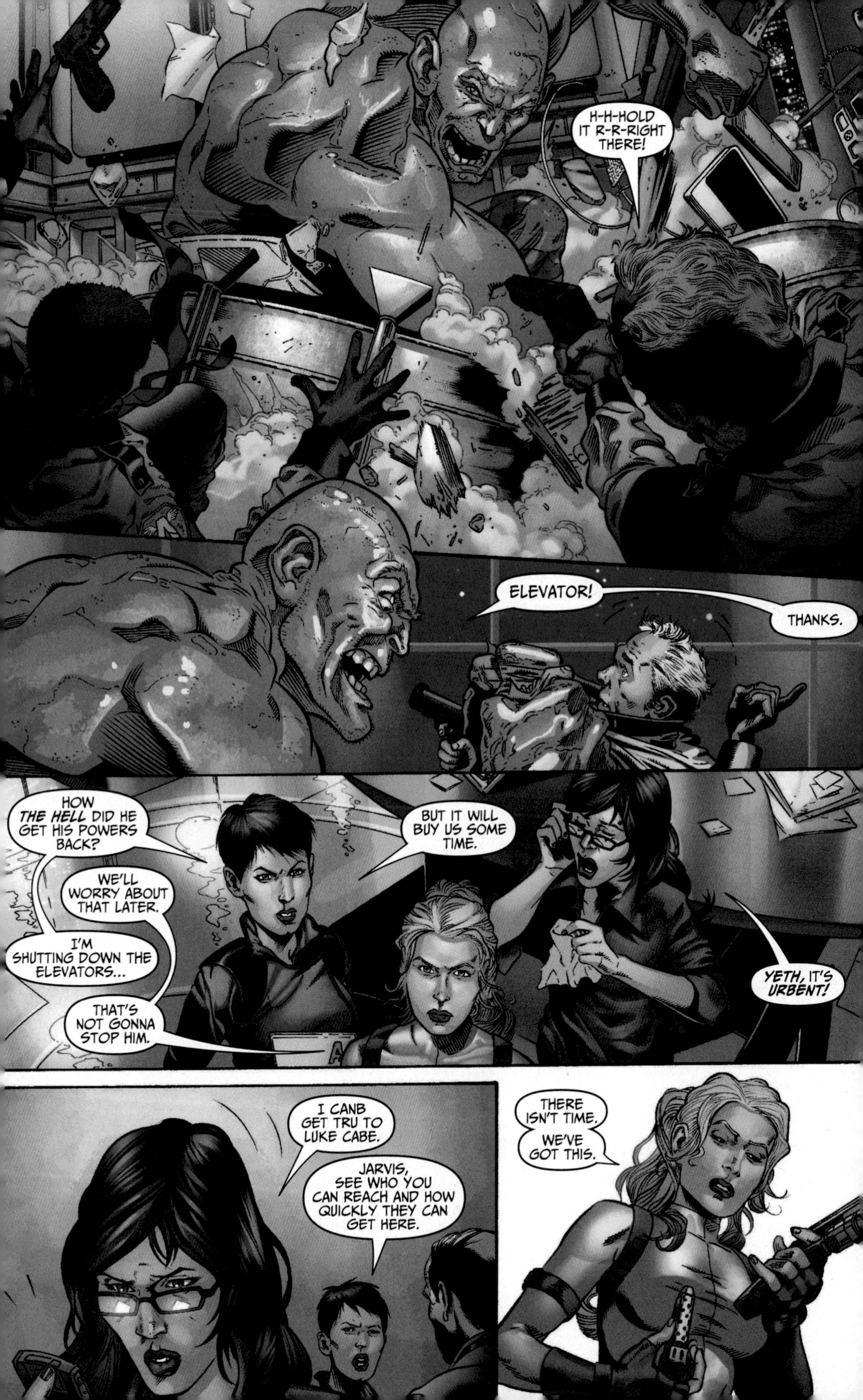
H-H-HOLD IT R-R-RIGHT THERE!
ELEVATOR!
THANKS.
HOW THE HELL DID HE GET HIS POWERS BACK?
WE'LL WORRY ABOUT THAT LATER.
I'M SHUTTING DOWN THE ELEVATORS...
THAT'S NOT GONNA STOP HIM.
BUT IT WILL BUY US SOME TIME.
YETH, IT'S URBENT!
I CANB GET TRU TO LUKE CABE.
JARVIS, SEE WHO YOU CAN REACH AND HOW QUICKLY THEY CAN GET HERE.
THERE ISN'T TIME.
WE'VE GOT THIS.

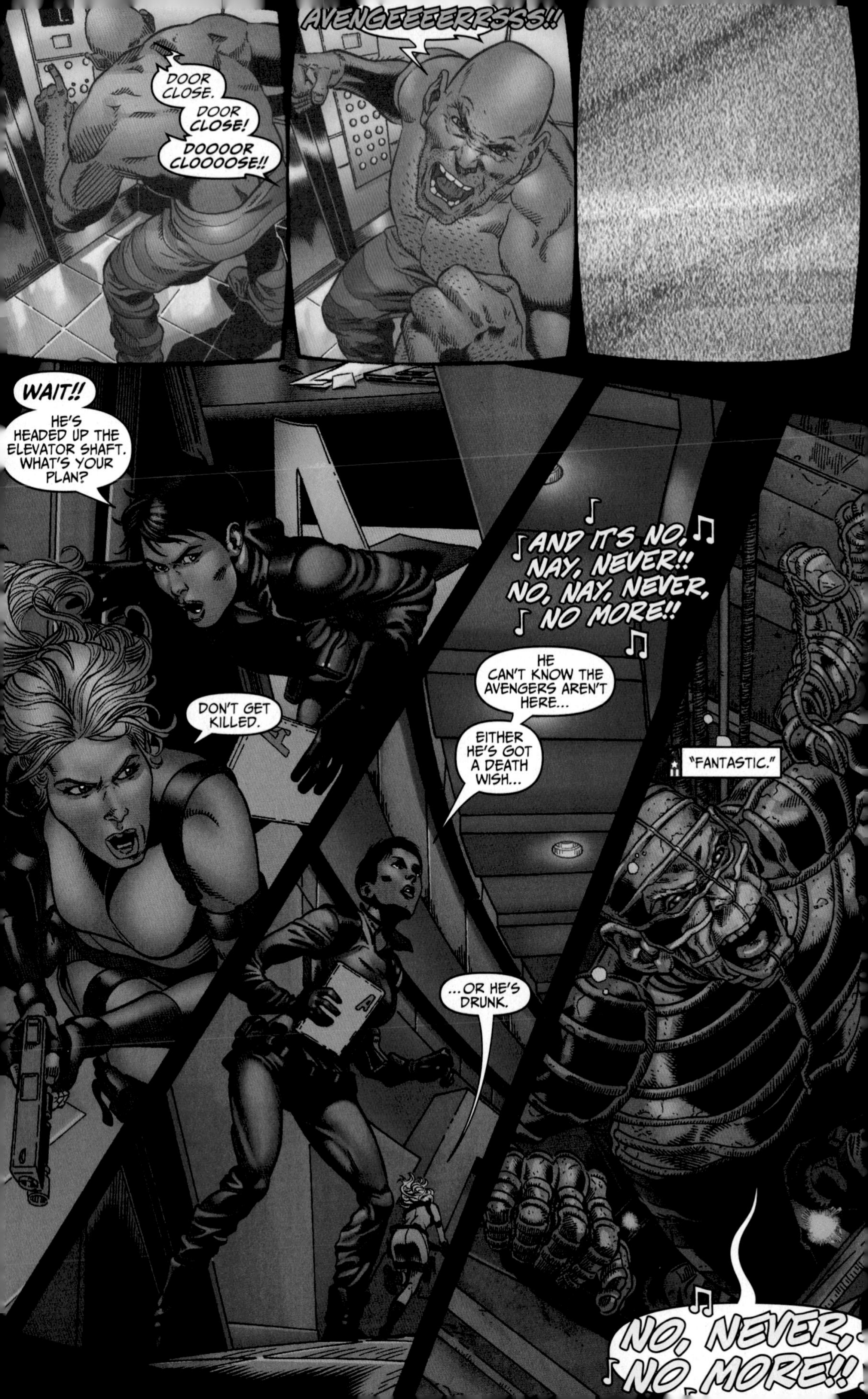
DOOR CLOSE.
DOOR CLOSE!
DOOOOR CLOOOOSE!!
AVENGEEEERRSSS!!
WAIT!!
HE'S HEADED UP THE ELEVATOR SHAFT. WHAT'S YOUR PLAN?
DON'T GET KILLED.
AND IT'S NO, NAY, NEVER!! NO, NAY, NEVER, NO MORE!!
HE CAN'T KNOW THE AVENGERS AREN'T HERE...
EITHER HE'S GOT A DEATH WISH...
...OR HE'S DRUNK.
"FANTASTIC."
NO, NEVER, NO MORE!!

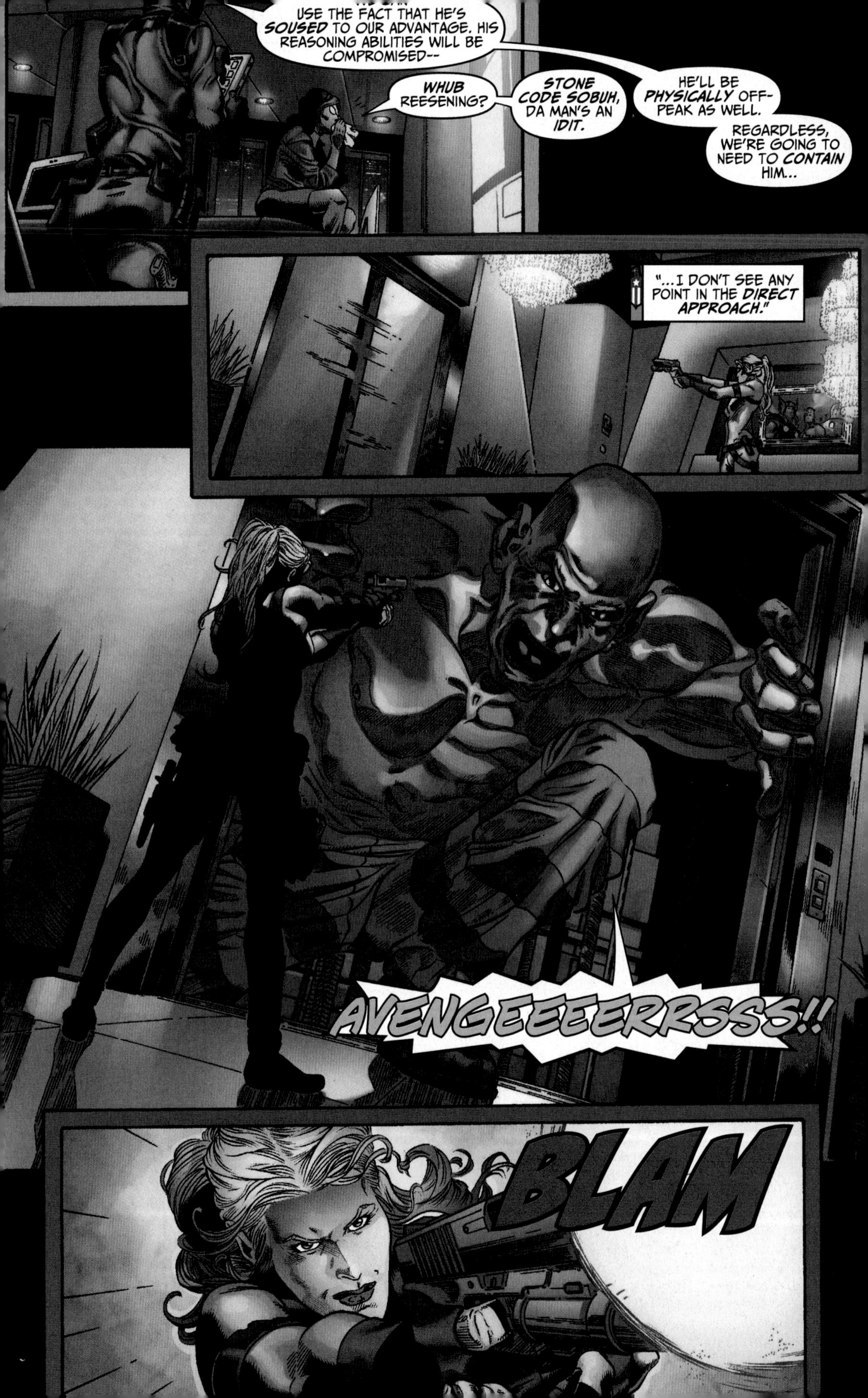
USE THE FACT THAT HE'S SOUSED TO OUR ADVANTAGE. HIS REASONING ABILITIES WILL BE COMPROMISED--
WHUB REESENING?
STONE CODE SOBUH, DA MAN'S AN IDIT.
HE'LL BE PHYSICALLY OFF-PEAK AS WELL.
REGARDLESS, WE'RE GOING TO NEED TO CONTAIN HIM...
"...I DON'T SEE ANY POINT IN THE DIRECT APPROACH."
AVENGEEEEERRSSS!!
BLAM

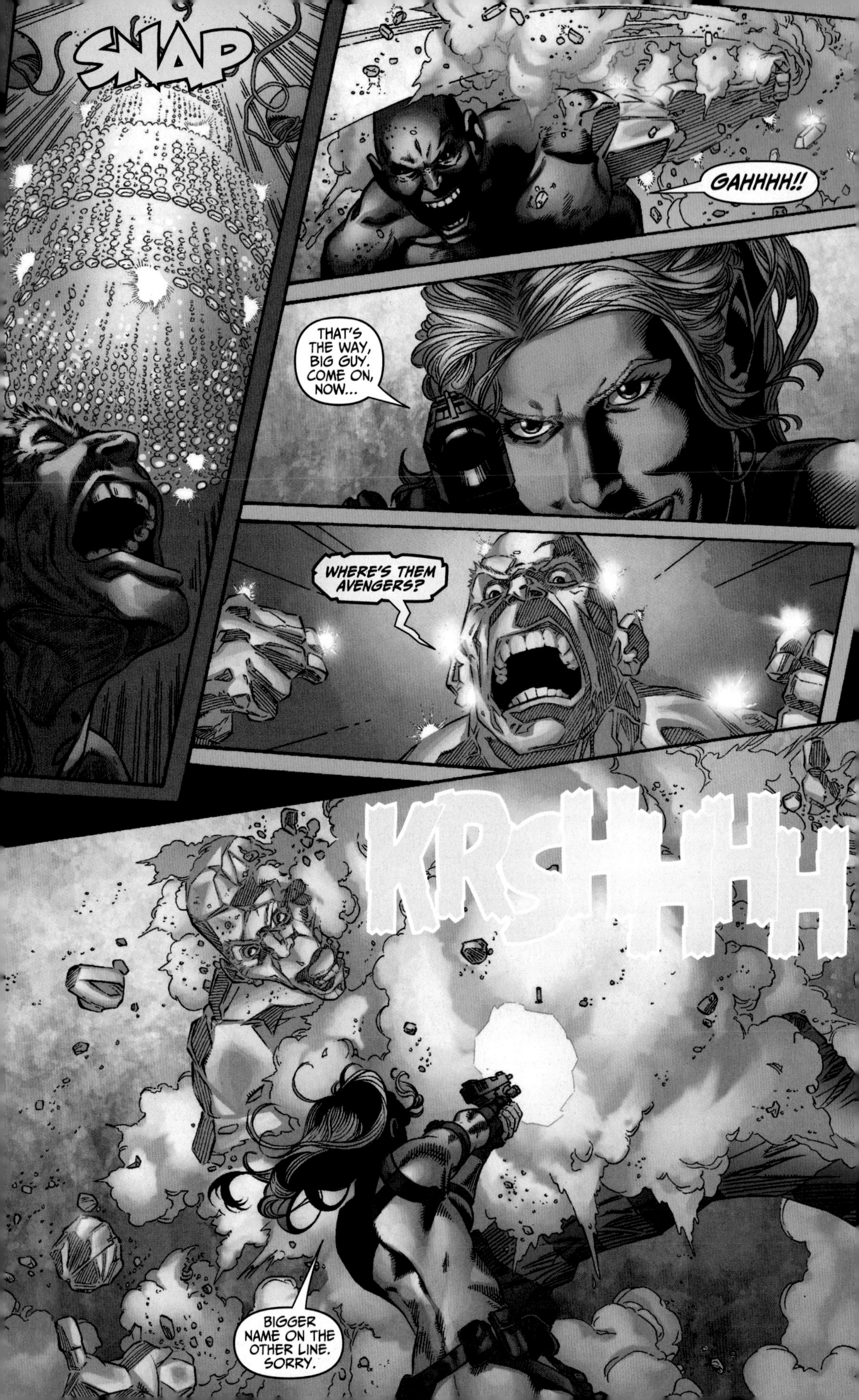
SNAP
GAHHHH!!
THAT'S THE WAY, BIG GUY. COME ON, NOW...
WHERE'S THEM AVENGERS?
KRSHHHH
BIGGER NAME ON THE OTHER LINE. SORRY.

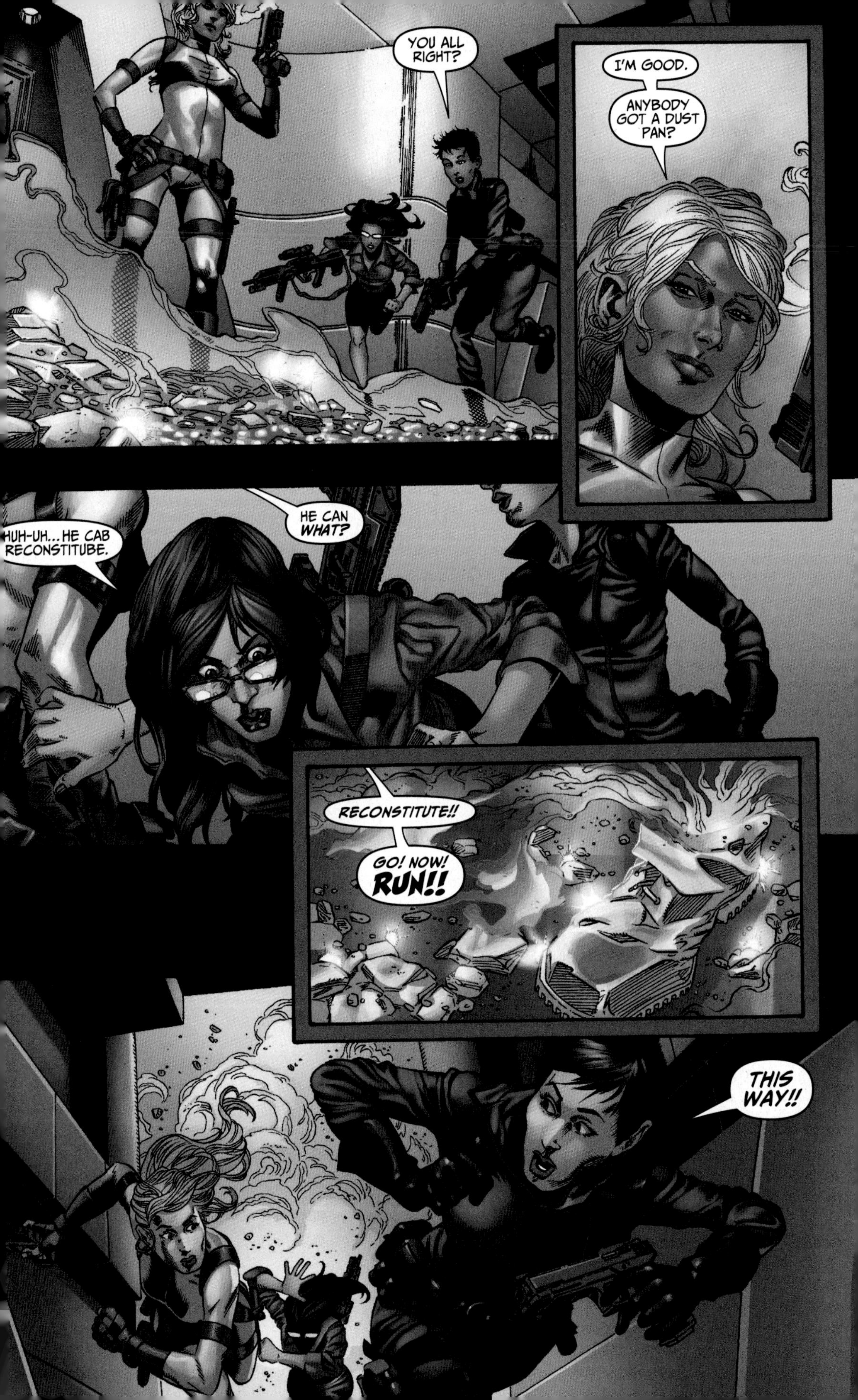
YOU ALL RIGHT?
I'M GOOD.
ANYBODY GOT A DUST PAN?
HE CAN WHAT?
HUH-UH...HE CAB RECONSTITUBE.
RECONSTITUTE!!
GO! NOW! RUN!!
THIS WAY!!

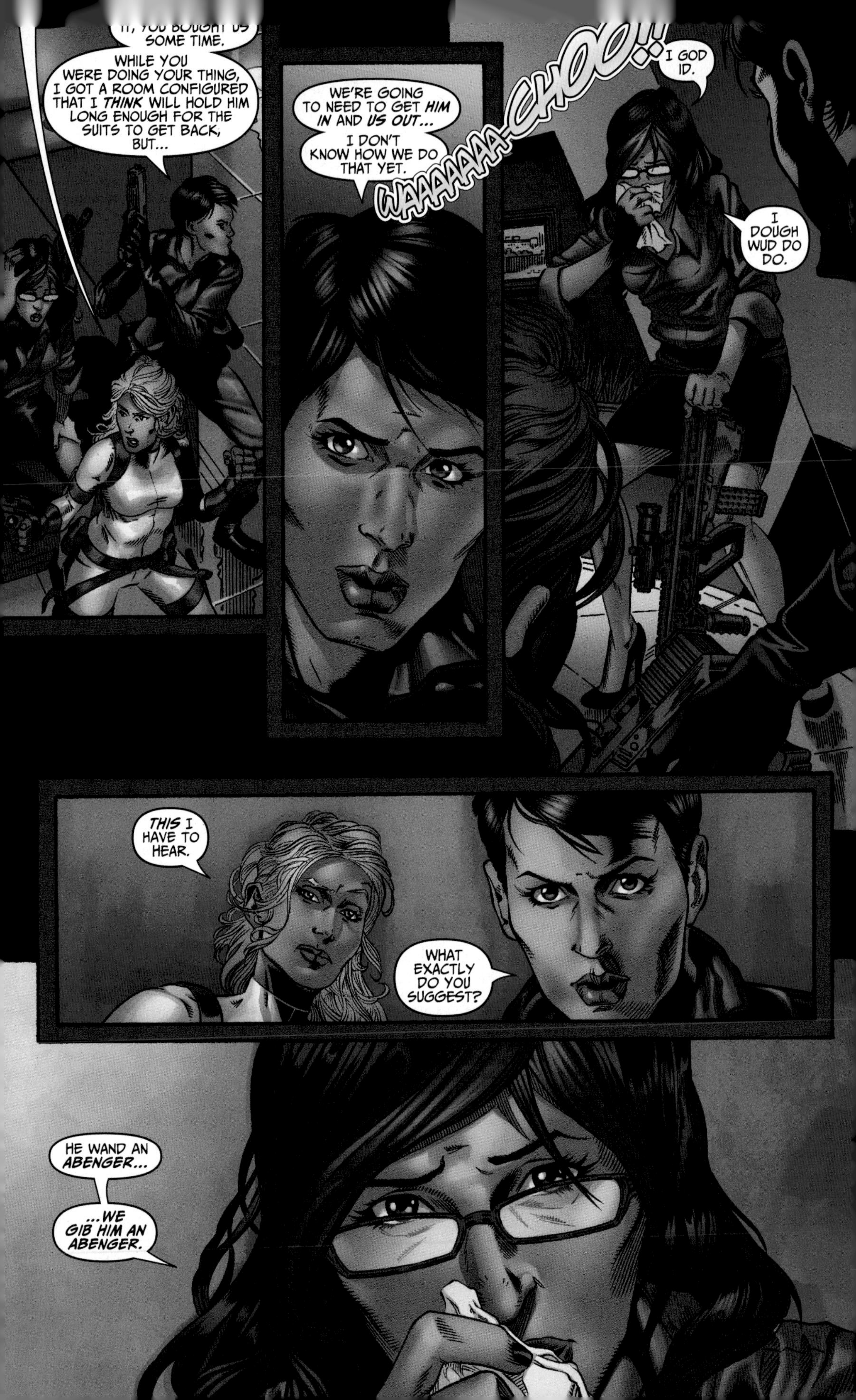
SOME TIME.
WHILE YOU WERE DOING YOUR THING, I GOT A ROOM CONFIGURED THAT I THINK WILL HOLD HIM LONG ENOUGH FOR THE SUITS TO GET BACK, BUT...
WE'RE GOING TO NEED TO GET HIM IN AND US OUT...
I DON'T KNOW HOW WE DO THAT YET.
WAAAAAAA-CHOO!!
I GOD ID.
I DOUGH WUD DO DO.
THIS I HAVE TO HEAR.
WHAT EXACTLY DO YOU SUGGEST?
HE WAND AN ABENGER...
...WE GIB HIM AN ABENGER.

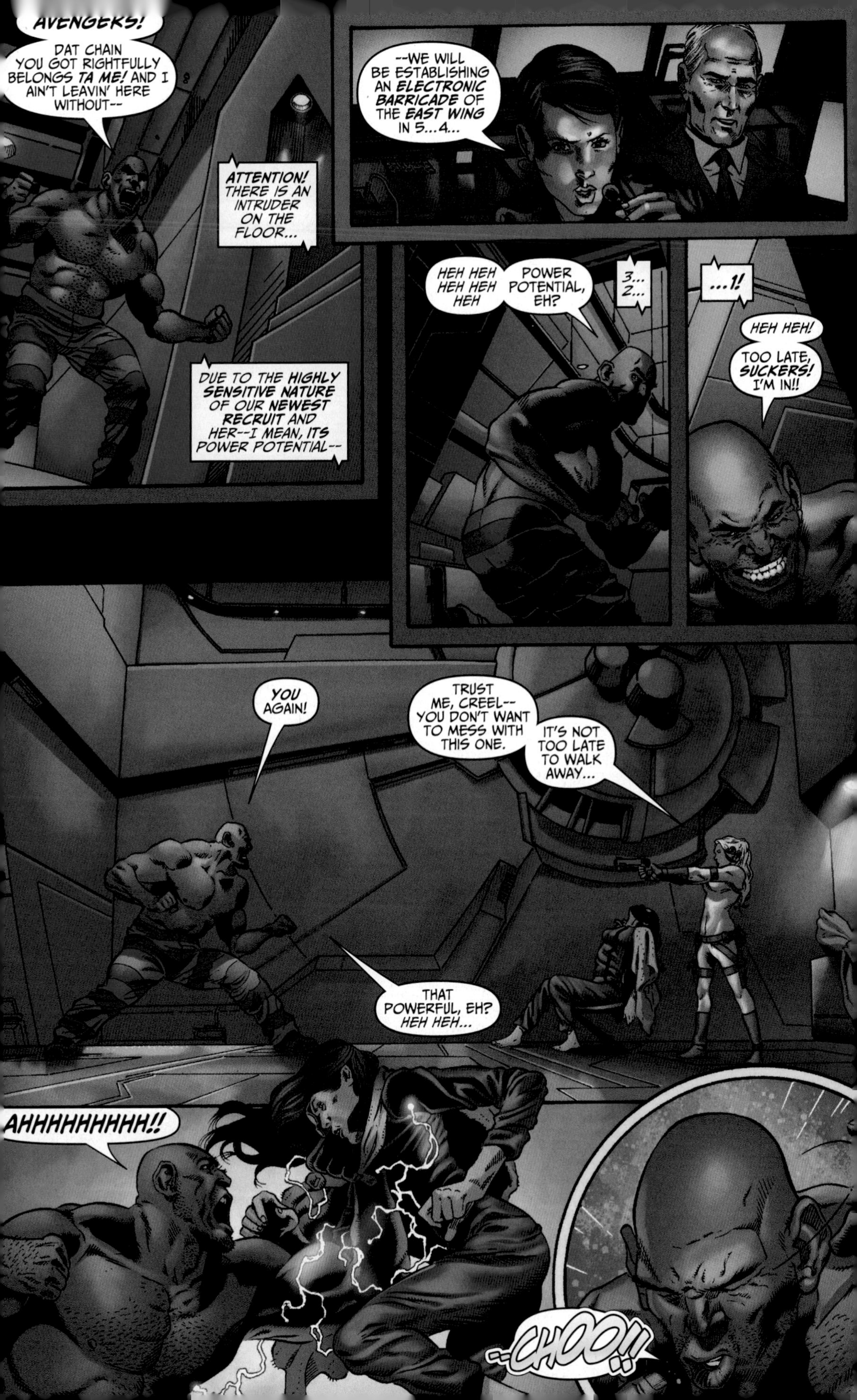
AVENGERS!
DAT CHAIN YOU GOT RIGHTFULLY BELONGS TA ME! AND I AIN'T LEAVIN' HERE WITHOUT--
--WE WILL BE ESTABLISHING AN ELECTRONIC BARRICADE OF THE EAST WING IN 5...4...
ATTENTION! THERE IS AN INTRUDER ON THE FLOOR...
DUE TO THE HIGHLY SENSITIVE NATURE OF OUR NEWEST RECRUIT AND HER--I MEAN, ITS POWER POTENTIAL--
HEH HEH HEH HEH HEH
POWER POTENTIAL, EH?
3... 2...
...1!
HEH HEH!
TOO LATE, SUCKERS! I'M IN!!
YOU AGAIN!
TRUST ME, CREEL-- YOU DON'T WANT TO MESS WITH THIS ONE.
IT'S NOT TOO LATE TO WALK AWAY...
THAT POWERFUL, EH? HEH HEH...
AHHHHHHHHH!!
--CHOO!!

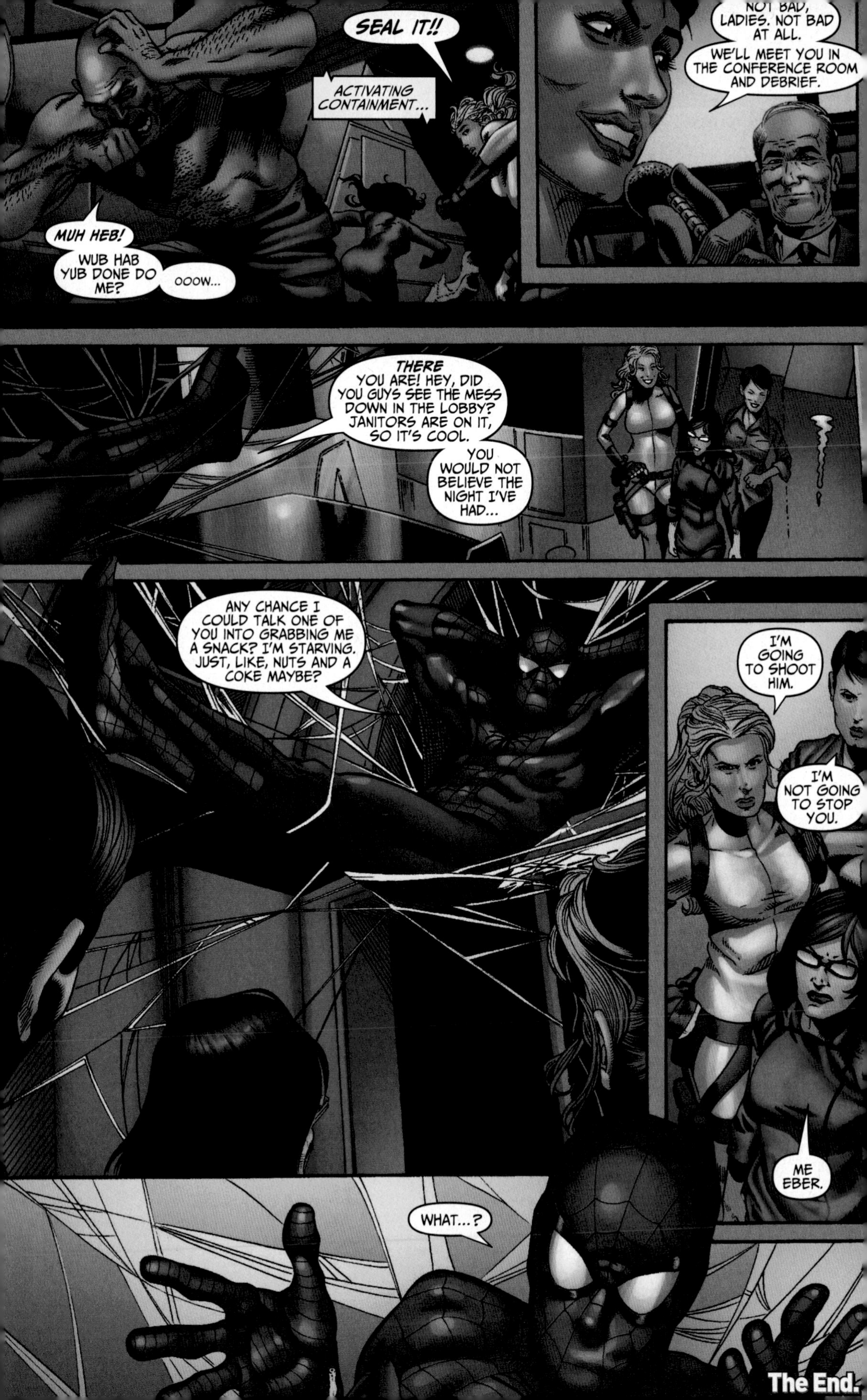
SEAL IT!!
ACTIVATING CONTAINMENT...
MUH HEB!
WUB HAB YUB DONE DO ME?
OOOW...
NOT BAD, LADIES. NOT BAD AT ALL.
WE'LL MEET YOU IN THE CONFERENCE ROOM AND DEBRIEF.
THERE YOU ARE! HEY, DID YOU GUYS SEE THE MESS DOWN IN THE LOBBY? JANITORS ARE ON IT, SO IT'S COOL.
YOU WOULD NOT BELIEVE THE NIGHT I'VE HAD...
ANY CHANCE I COULD TALK ONE OF YOU INTO GRABBING ME A SNACK? I'M STARVING. JUST, LIKE, NUTS AND A COKE MAYBE?
I'M GOING TO SHOOT HIM.
I'M NOT GOING TO STOP YOU.
ME EBER.
WHAT...?
The End.

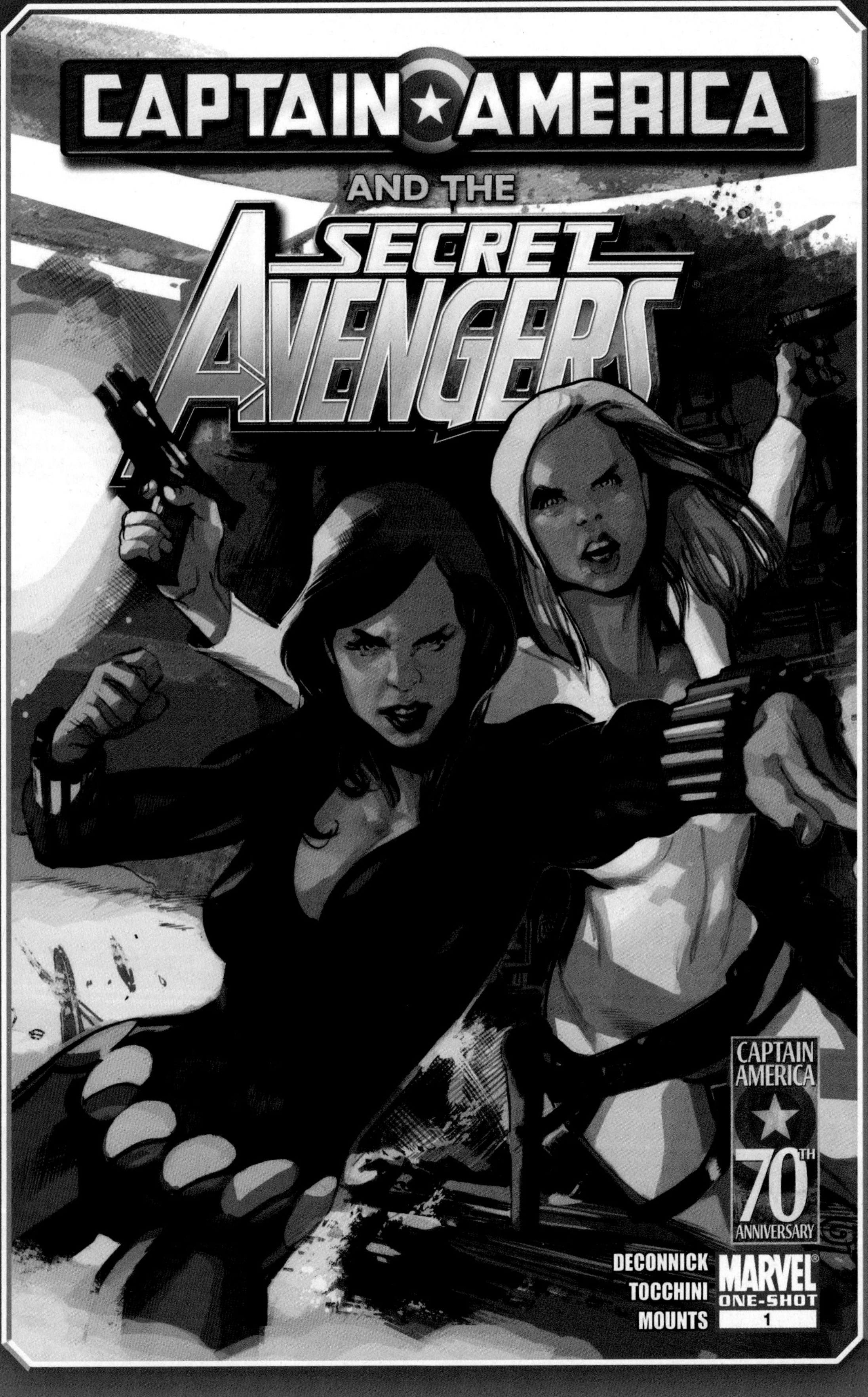

CAPTAIN AMERICA
AND THE
SECRET AVENGERS
CAPTAIN AMERICA
70TH ANNIVERSARY
DECONNICK
TOCCHINI
MOUNTS
MARVEL
ONE-SHOT
1

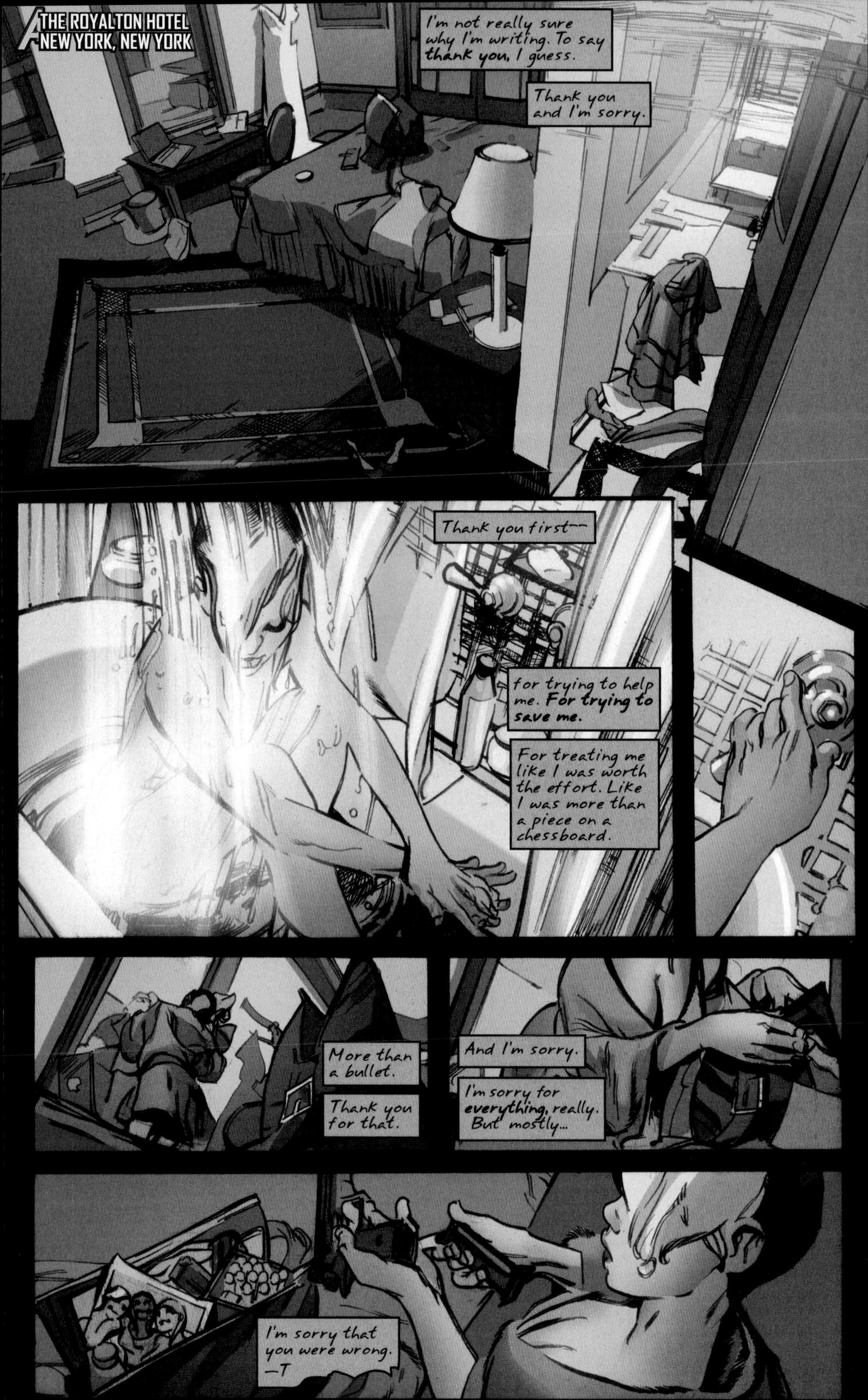
THE ROYALTON HOTEL
NEW YORK, NEW YORK
I'm not really sure why I'm writing. To say thank you, I guess.
Thank you and I'm sorry.
Thank you first--
for trying to help me. For trying to save me.
For treating me like I was worth the effort. Like I was more than a piece on a chessboard.
More than a bullet.
Thank you for that.
And I'm sorry.
I'm sorry for everything, really. But mostly...
I'm sorry that you were wrong.
—T

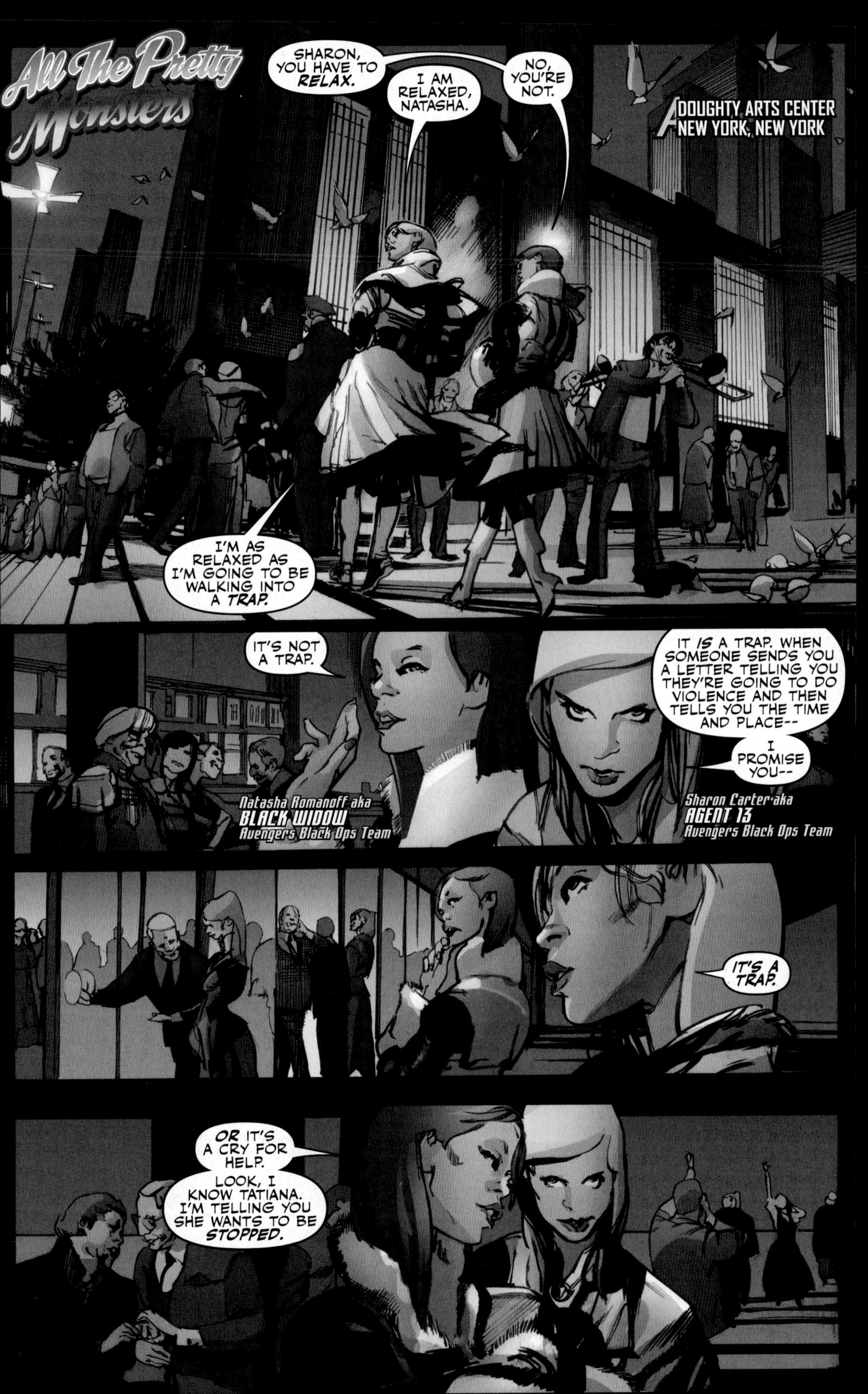
All The Pretty Monsters
SHARON, YOU HAVE TO RELAX.
I AM RELAXED, NATASHA.
NO, YOU'RE NOT.
DOUGHTY ARTS CENTER NEW YORK, NEW YORK
I'M AS RELAXED AS I'M GOING TO BE WALKING INTO A TRAP.
IT'S NOT A TRAP.
IT IS A TRAP. WHEN SOMEONE SENDS YOU A LETTER TELLING YOU THEY'RE GOING TO DO VIOLENCE AND THEN TELLS YOU THE TIME AND PLACE--
I PROMISE YOU--
Natasha Romanoff aka BLACK WIDOW Avengers Black Ops Team
Sharon Carter aka AGENT 13 Avengers Black Ops Team
IT'S A TRAP.
OR IT'S A CRY FOR HELP.
LOOK, I KNOW TATIANA. I'M TELLING YOU SHE WANTS TO BE STOPPED.

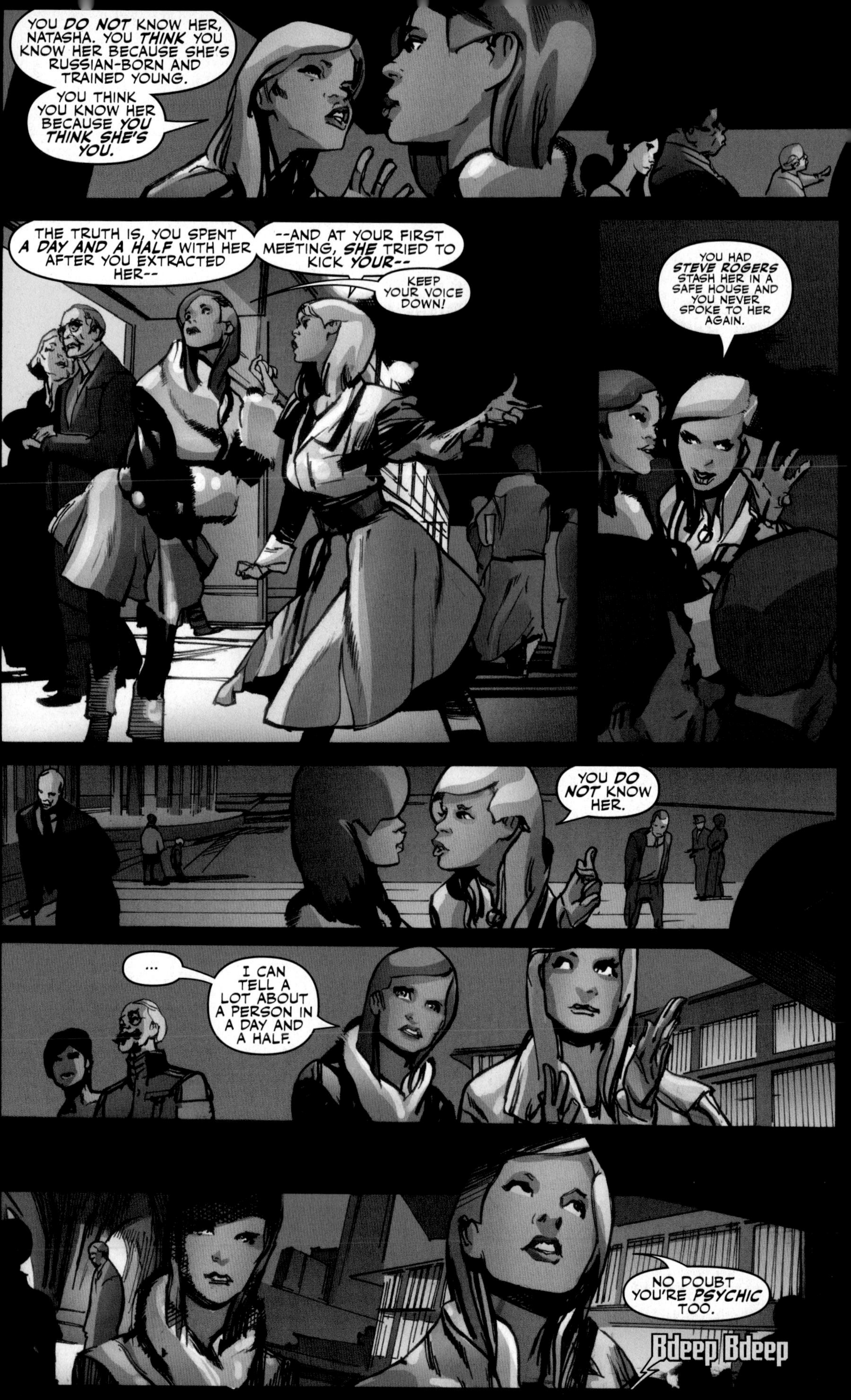
YOU DO NOT KNOW HER, NATASHA. YOU THINK YOU KNOW HER BECAUSE SHE'S RUSSIAN-BORN AND TRAINED YOUNG.
YOU THINK YOU KNOW HER BECAUSE YOU THINK SHE'S YOU.
THE TRUTH IS, YOU SPENT A DAY AND A HALF WITH HER AFTER YOU EXTRACTED HER--
--AND AT YOUR FIRST MEETING, SHE TRIED TO KICK YOUR--
KEEP YOUR VOICE DOWN!
YOU HAD STEVE ROGERS STASH HER IN A SAFE HOUSE AND YOU NEVER SPOKE TO HER AGAIN.
YOU DO NOT KNOW HER.
...
I CAN TELL A LOT ABOUT A PERSON IN A DAY AND A HALF.
NO DOUBT YOU'RE PSYCHIC TOO.
Bdeep Bdeep

13.

SHARON, IT'S STEVE.

WHAT'S THE WORD?

beep beep beep

WARNING
ELECTRONIC
SECURITY SYSTEM

LIFELINE. THEY'RE OSTENSIBLY AN INTERNATIONAL CHARITY FOCUSED ON EDUCATING GIRLS OUT OF POVERTY.

OSTENSIBLY?

INSTEAD OF FUNDING SCHOOLS LOCALLY, THEY WHISK SELECT YOUNG LADIES AWAY AND EDUCATE THEM IN PRIVATE BOARDING SCHOOLS.

Steve Rogers aka
SUPER-SOLDIER
Former Captain America

THE GIRLS ARE *SUPPOSED* TO GO BACK AND BRING CHANGE TO THEIR COMMUNITIES.

BUT THEY DON'T GO BACK.

GENERALLY SPEAKING, NO. THEY DO NOT. INTERPOL'S FLAGGED THEM FOR INQUIRY.

WHAT'S TATIANA GOT AGAINST THEM?

NOT SURE. SEEMS SHE WAS THE RECIPIENT OF ONE OF THEIR SCHOLARSHIPS AT SOME POINT.

beep beep beep

DID YOU BY ANY CHANCE ADVISE THEIR SECURITY OF THE THREAT?

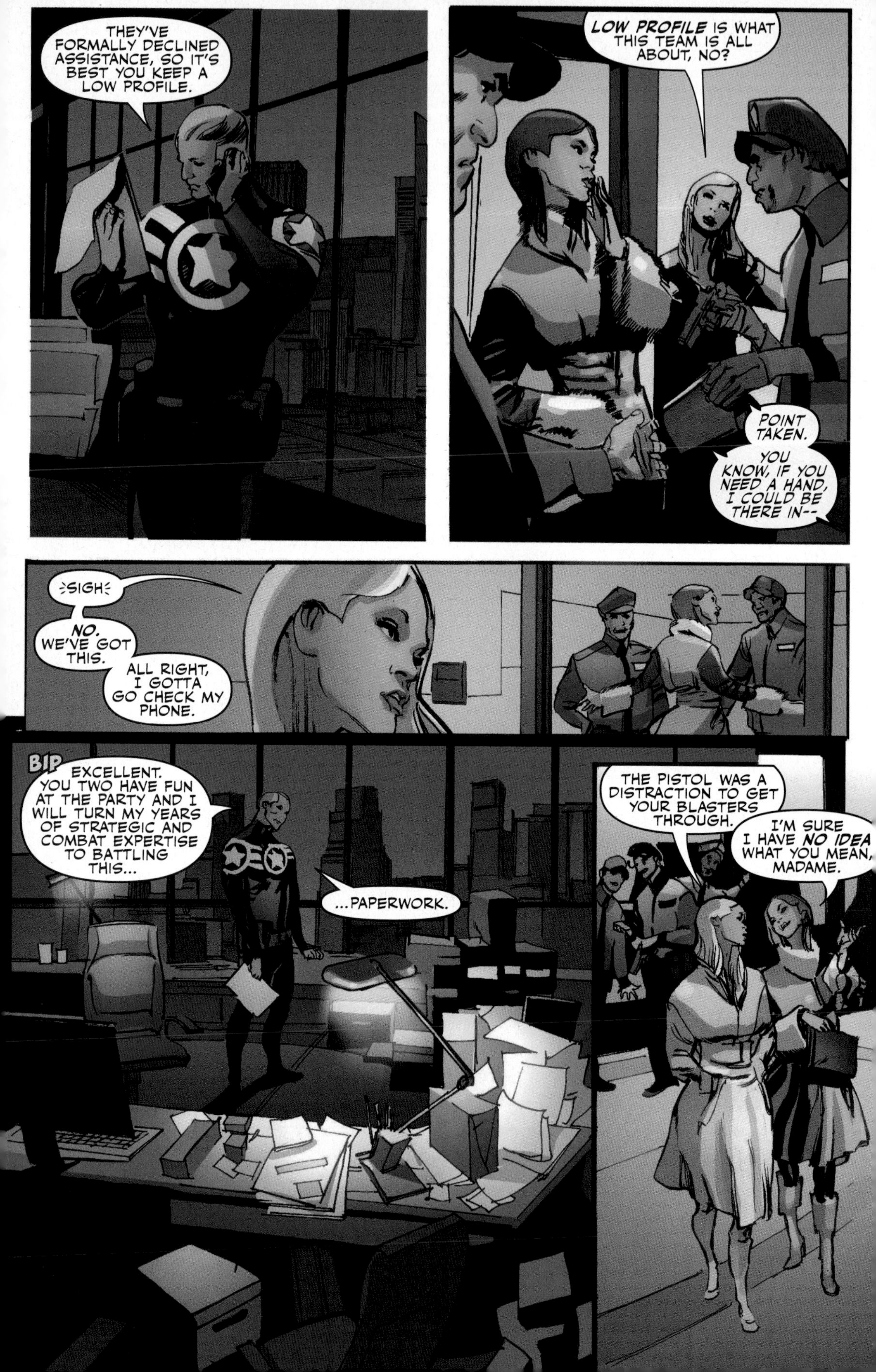

THEY'VE FORMALLY DECLINED ASSISTANCE, SO IT'S BEST YOU KEEP A LOW PROFILE.
LOW PROFILE IS WHAT THIS TEAM IS ALL ABOUT, NO?
POINT TAKEN.
YOU KNOW, IF YOU NEED A HAND, I COULD BE THERE IN--
SIGH
NO. WE'VE GOT THIS.
ALL RIGHT, I GOTTA GO CHECK MY PHONE.
BIP
EXCELLENT. YOU TWO HAVE FUN AT THE PARTY AND I WILL TURN MY YEARS OF STRATEGIC AND COMBAT EXPERTISE TO BATTLING THIS...
...PAPERWORK.
THE PISTOL WAS A DISTRACTION TO GET YOUR BLASTERS THROUGH.
I'M SURE I HAVE NO IDEA WHAT YOU MEAN, MADAME.

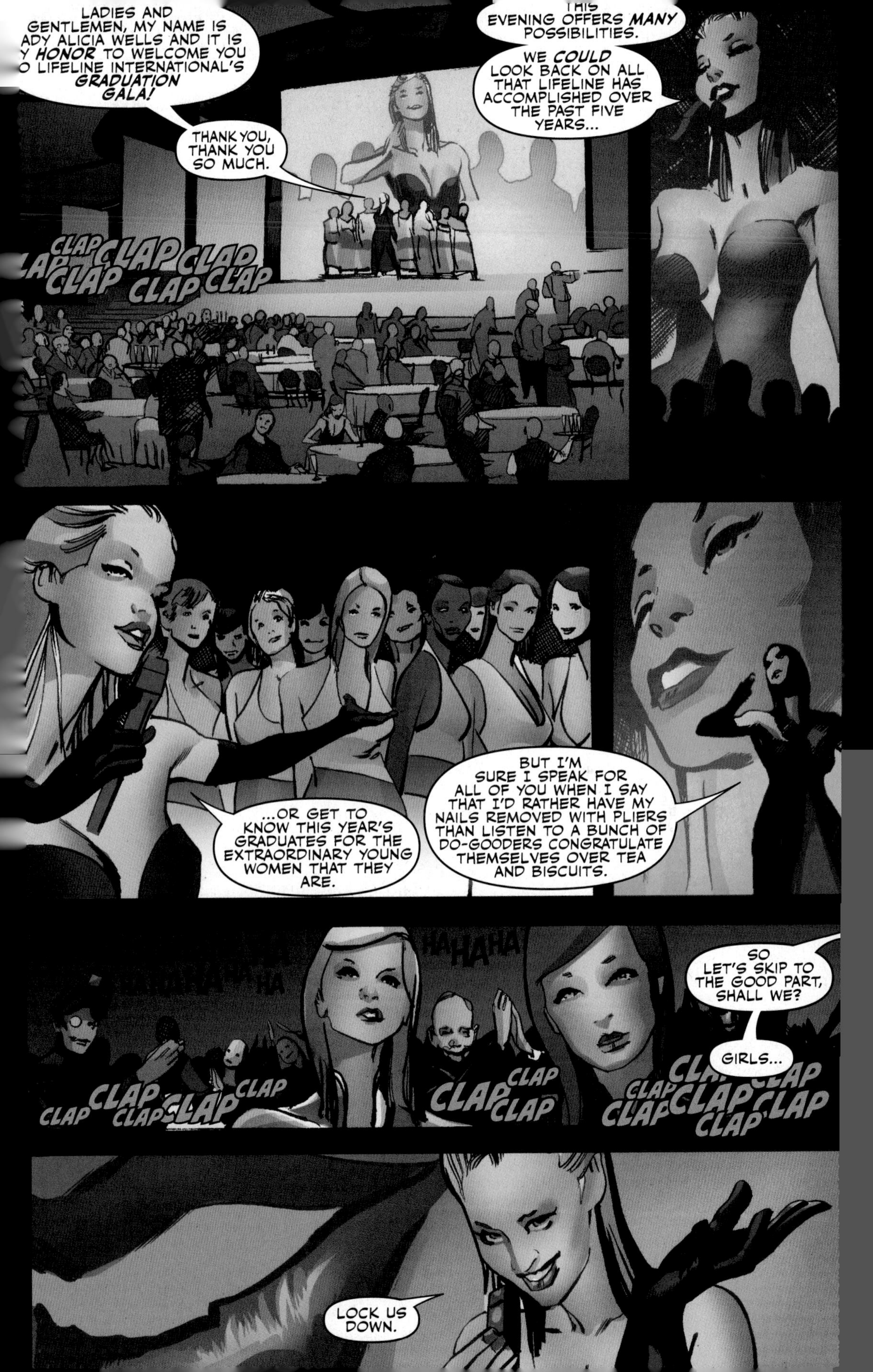

LADIES AND GENTLEMEN, MY NAME IS ADY ALICIA WELLS AND IT IS Y HONOR TO WELCOME YOU O LIFELINE INTERNATIONAL'S GRADUATION GALA!
THANK YOU, THANK YOU SO MUCH.
CLAP CLAP CLAP CLAP CLAP CLAP CLAP
THIS EVENING OFFERS MANY POSSIBILITIES.
WE COULD LOOK BACK ON ALL THAT LIFELINE HAS ACCOMPLISHED OVER THE PAST FIVE YEARS...
...OR GET TO KNOW THIS YEAR'S GRADUATES FOR THE EXTRAORDINARY YOUNG WOMEN THAT THEY ARE.
BUT I'M SURE I SPEAK FOR ALL OF YOU WHEN I SAY THAT I'D RATHER HAVE MY NAILS REMOVED WITH PLIERS THAN LISTEN TO A BUNCH OF DO-GOODERS CONGRATULATE THEMSELVES OVER TEA AND BISCUITS.
HAHAHA HA
SO LET'S SKIP TO THE GOOD PART, SHALL WE?
GIRLS...
CLAP CLAP CLAP CLAP CLAP CLAP CLAP CLAP CLAP CLAP CLAP CLAP CLAP
LOCK US DOWN.

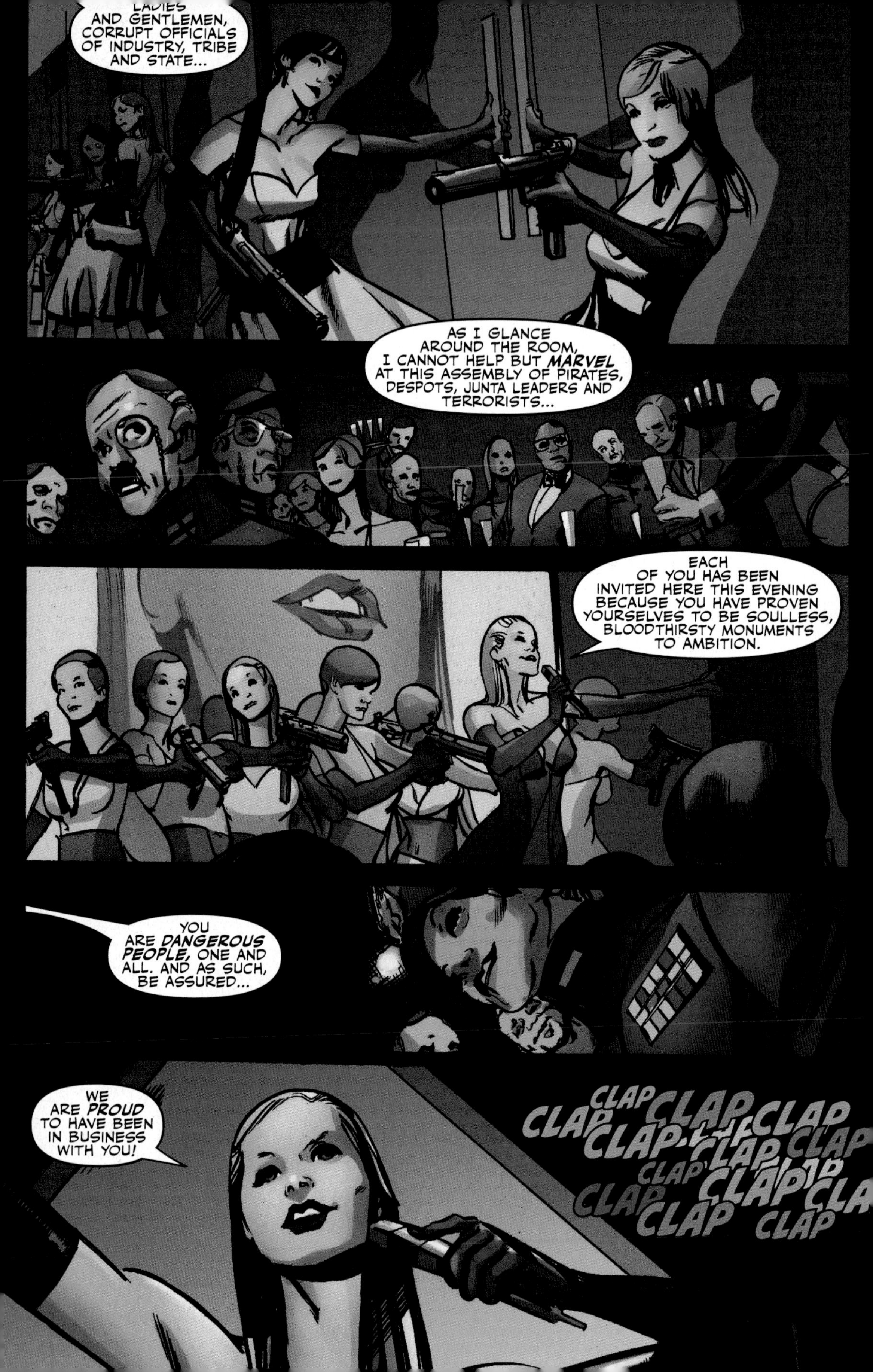
LADIES AND GENTLEMEN, CORRUPT OFFICIALS OF INDUSTRY, TRIBE AND STATE...
AS I GLANCE AROUND THE ROOM, I CANNOT HELP BUT MARVEL AT THIS ASSEMBLY OF PIRATES, DESPOTS, JUNTA LEADERS AND TERRORISTS...
EACH OF YOU HAS BEEN INVITED HERE THIS EVENING BECAUSE YOU HAVE PROVEN YOURSELVES TO BE SOULLESS, BLOODTHIRSTY MONUMENTS TO AMBITION.
YOU ARE DANGEROUS PEOPLE, ONE AND ALL. AND AS SUCH, BE ASSURED...
WE ARE PROUD TO HAVE BEEN IN BUSINESS WITH YOU!
CLAP CLAP CLAP CLAP CLAP CLAP CLAP CLAP CLAP CLAP CLAP CLAP CLAP

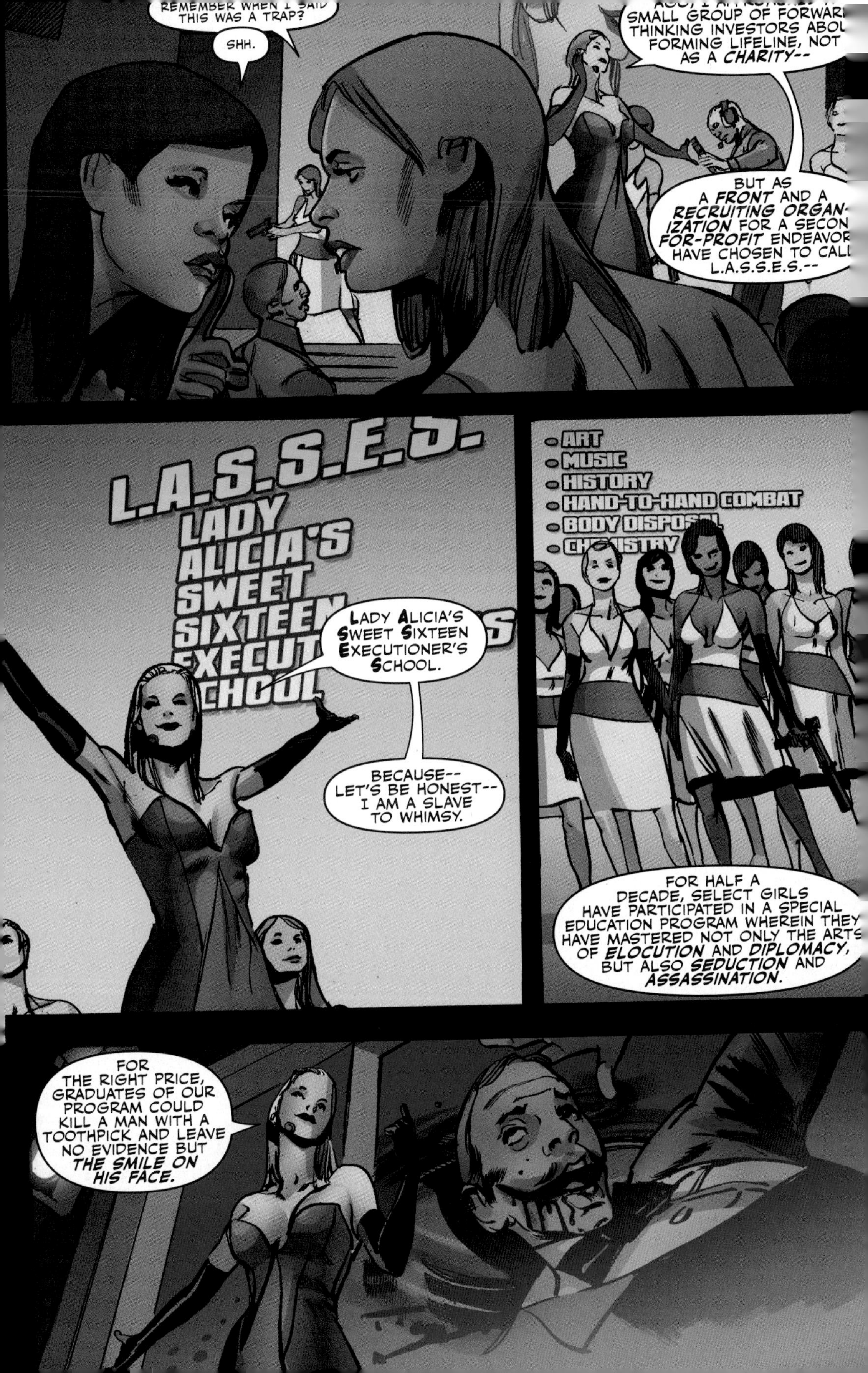
REMEMBER WHEN I SAID THIS WAS A TRAP?
SHH.
SMALL GROUP OF FORWAR THINKING INVESTORS ABOU FORMING LIFELINE, NOT AS A CHARITY--
BUT AS A FRONT AND A RECRUITING ORGAN-IZATION FOR A SECON FOR-PROFIT ENDEAVOR HAVE CHOSEN TO CALL L.A.S.S.E.S.--
L.A.S.S.E.S.
LADY ALICIA'S SWEET SIXTEEN
LADY ALICIA'S SWEET SIXTEEN EXECUTIONER'S SCHOOL.
BECAUSE-- LET'S BE HONEST-- I AM A SLAVE TO WHIMSY.
ART
MUSIC
HISTORY
HAND-TO-HAND COMBAT
FOR HALF A DECADE, SELECT GIRLS HAVE PARTICIPATED IN A SPECIAL EDUCATION PROGRAM WHEREIN THEY HAVE MASTERED NOT ONLY THE ARTS OF ELOCUTION AND DIPLOMACY, BUT ALSO SEDUCTION AND ASSASSINATION.
FOR THE RIGHT PRICE, GRADUATES OF OUR PROGRAM COULD KILL A MAN WITH A TOOTHPICK AND LEAVE NO EVIDENCE BUT THE SMILE ON HIS FACE.

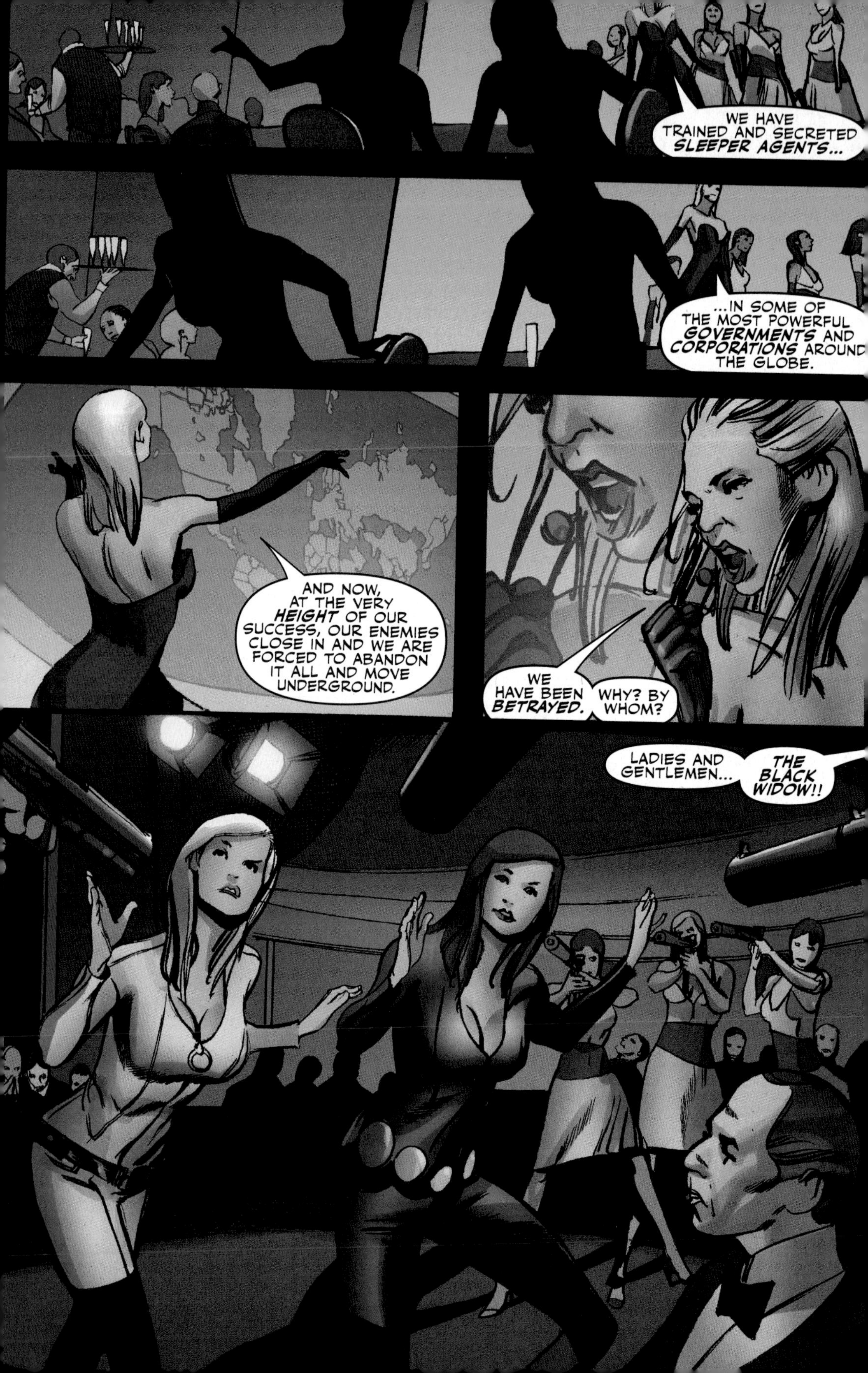
WE HAVE TRAINED AND SECRETED SLEEPER AGENTS...
...IN SOME OF THE MOST POWERFUL GOVERNMENTS AND CORPORATIONS AROUND THE GLOBE.
AND NOW, AT THE VERY HEIGHT OF OUR SUCCESS, OUR ENEMIES CLOSE IN AND WE ARE FORCED TO ABANDON IT ALL AND MOVE UNDERGROUND.
WE HAVE BEEN BETRAYED.
WHY? BY WHOM?
LADIES AND GENTLEMEN...
THE BLACK WIDOW!!

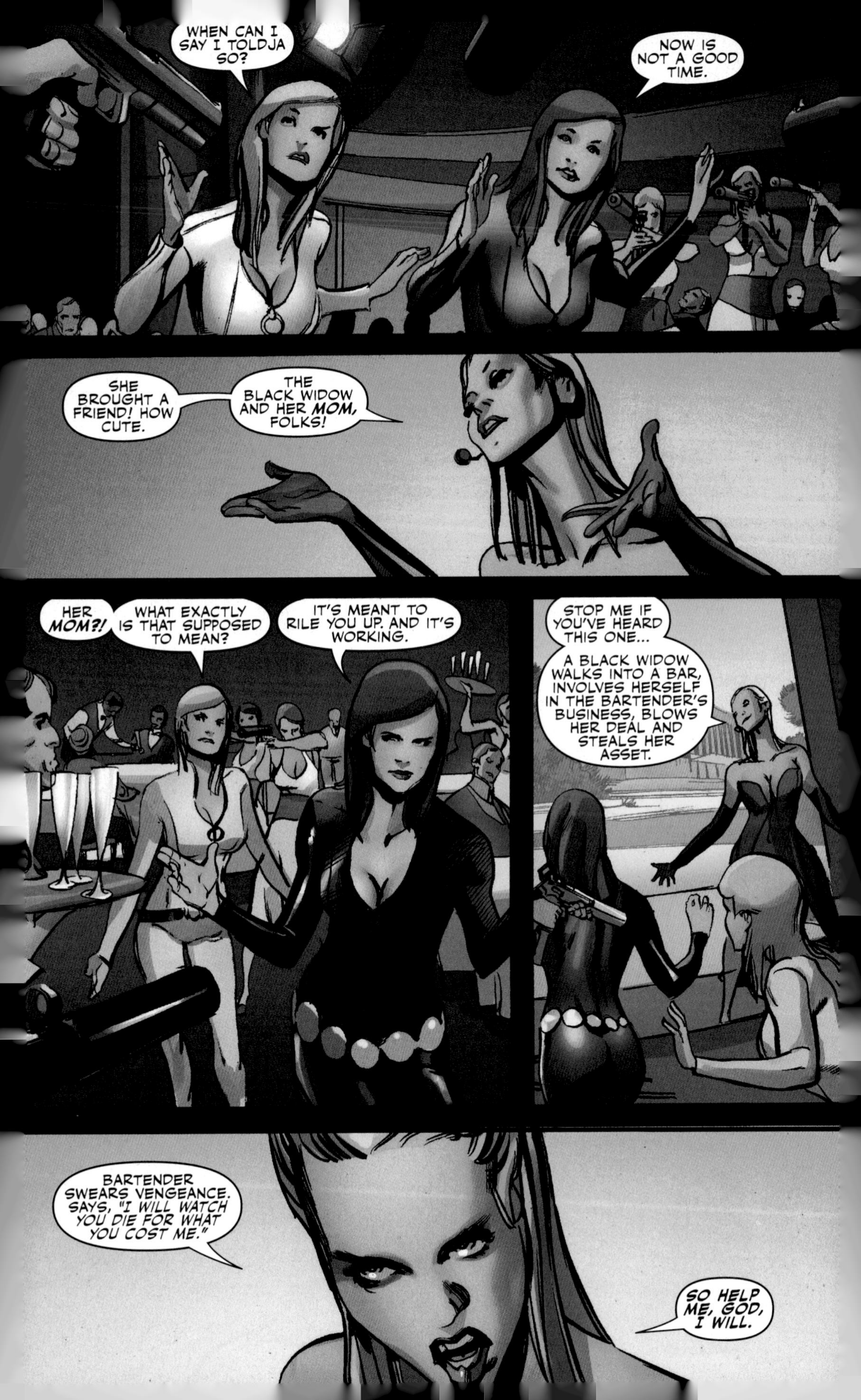
WHEN CAN I SAY I TOLDJA SO?
NOW IS NOT A GOOD TIME.
SHE BROUGHT A FRIEND! HOW CUTE.
THE BLACK WIDOW AND HER *MOM,* FOLKS!
HER *MOM?!*
WHAT EXACTLY IS THAT SUPPOSED TO MEAN?
IT'S MEANT TO RILE YOU UP. AND IT'S WORKING.
STOP ME IF YOU'VE HEARD THIS ONE...
A BLACK WIDOW WALKS INTO A BAR, INVOLVES HERSELF IN THE BARTENDER'S BUSINESS, BLOWS HER DEAL AND STEALS HER ASSET.
BARTENDER SWEARS VENGEANCE. SAYS, *"I WILL WATCH YOU DIE FOR WHAT YOU COST ME."*
SO HELP ME, GOD, I WILL.

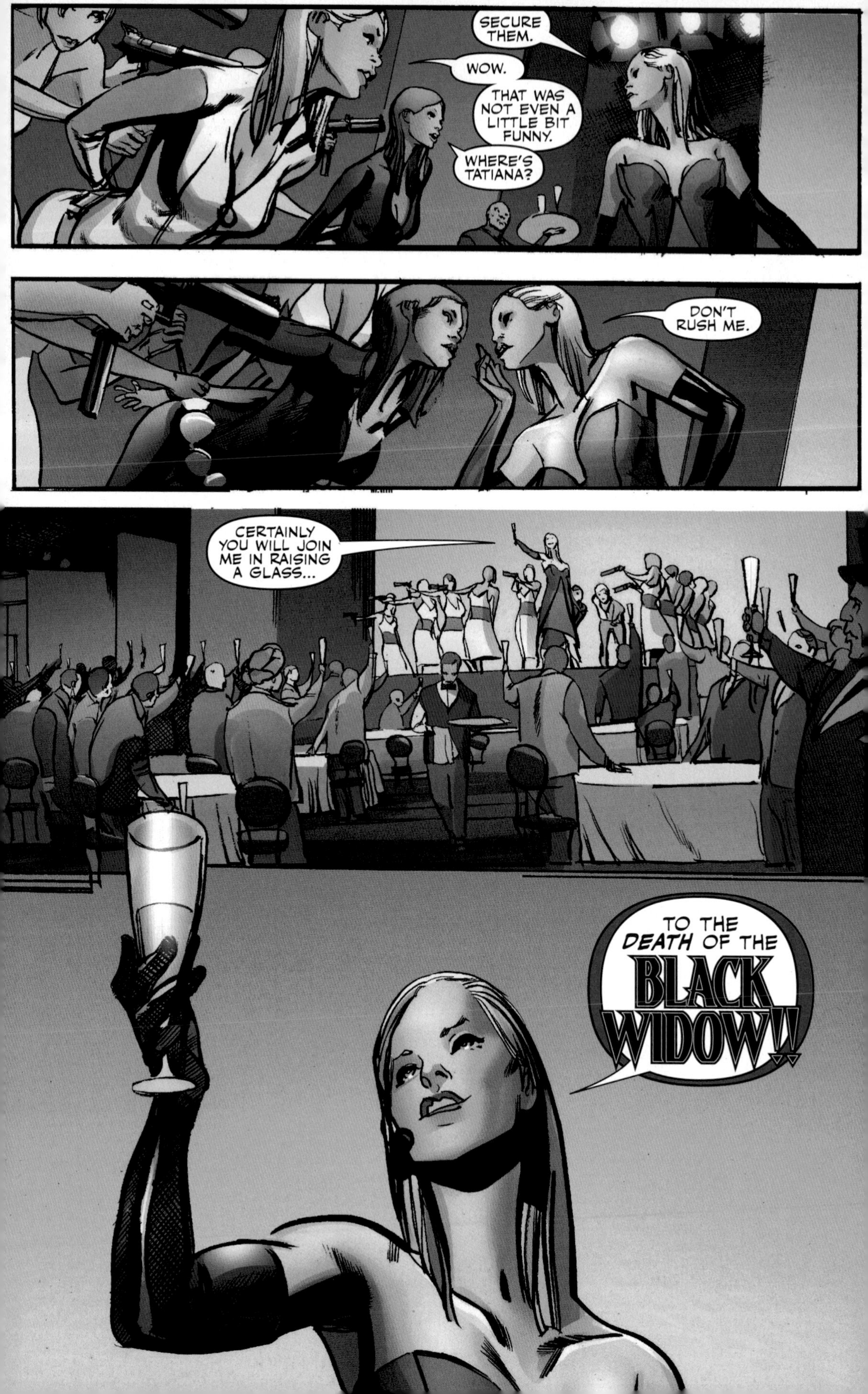
SECURE THEM.
WOW.
THAT WAS NOT EVEN A LITTLE BIT FUNNY.
WHERE'S TATIANA?
DON'T RUSH ME.
CERTAINLY YOU WILL JOIN ME IN RAISING A GLASS...
TO THE *DEATH* OF THE BLACK WIDOW!!

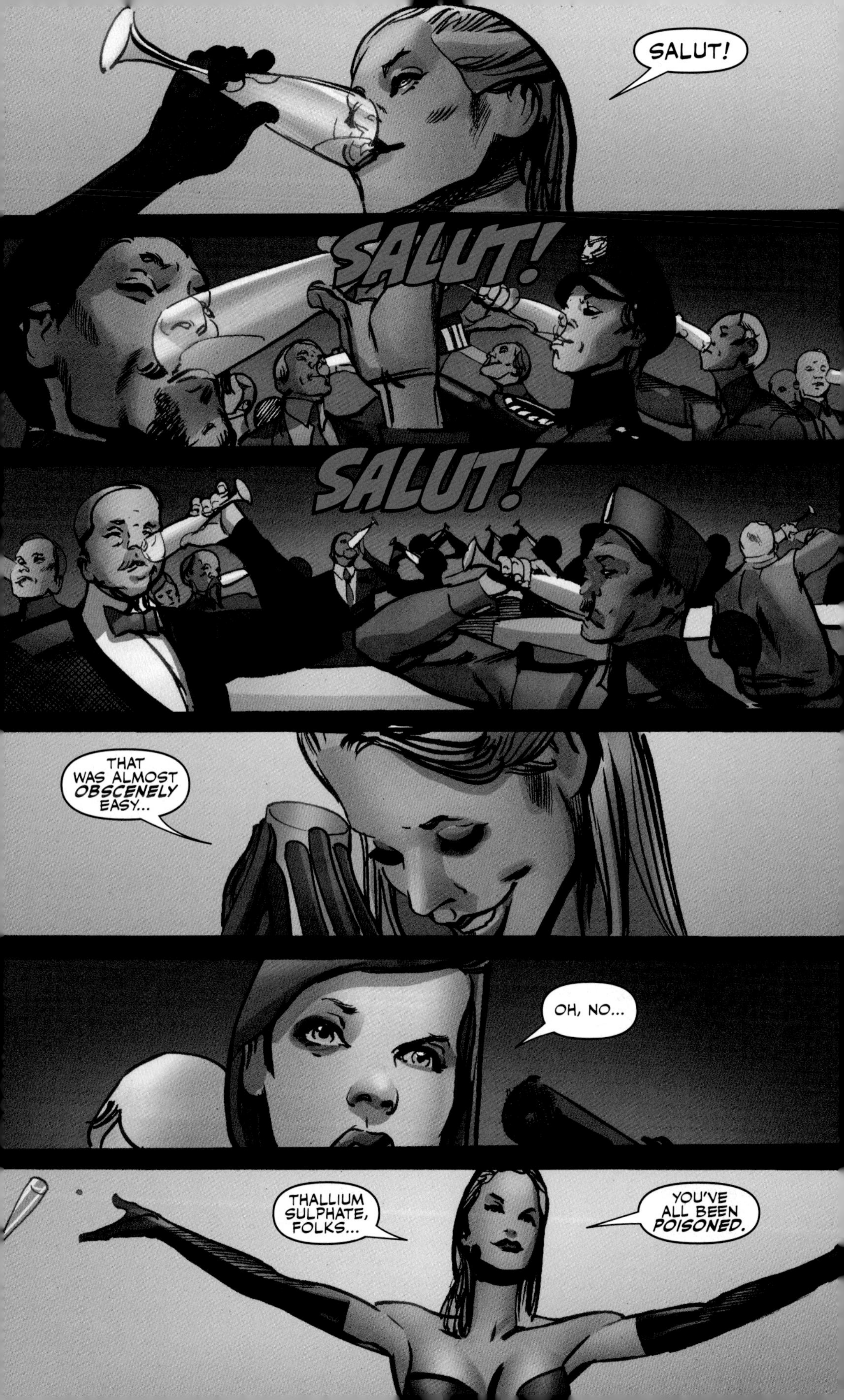
SALUT!
SALUT!
SALUT!
THAT WAS ALMOST OBSCENELY EASY...
OH, NO...
THALLIUM SULPHATE, FOLKS...
YOU'VE ALL BEEN POISONED.

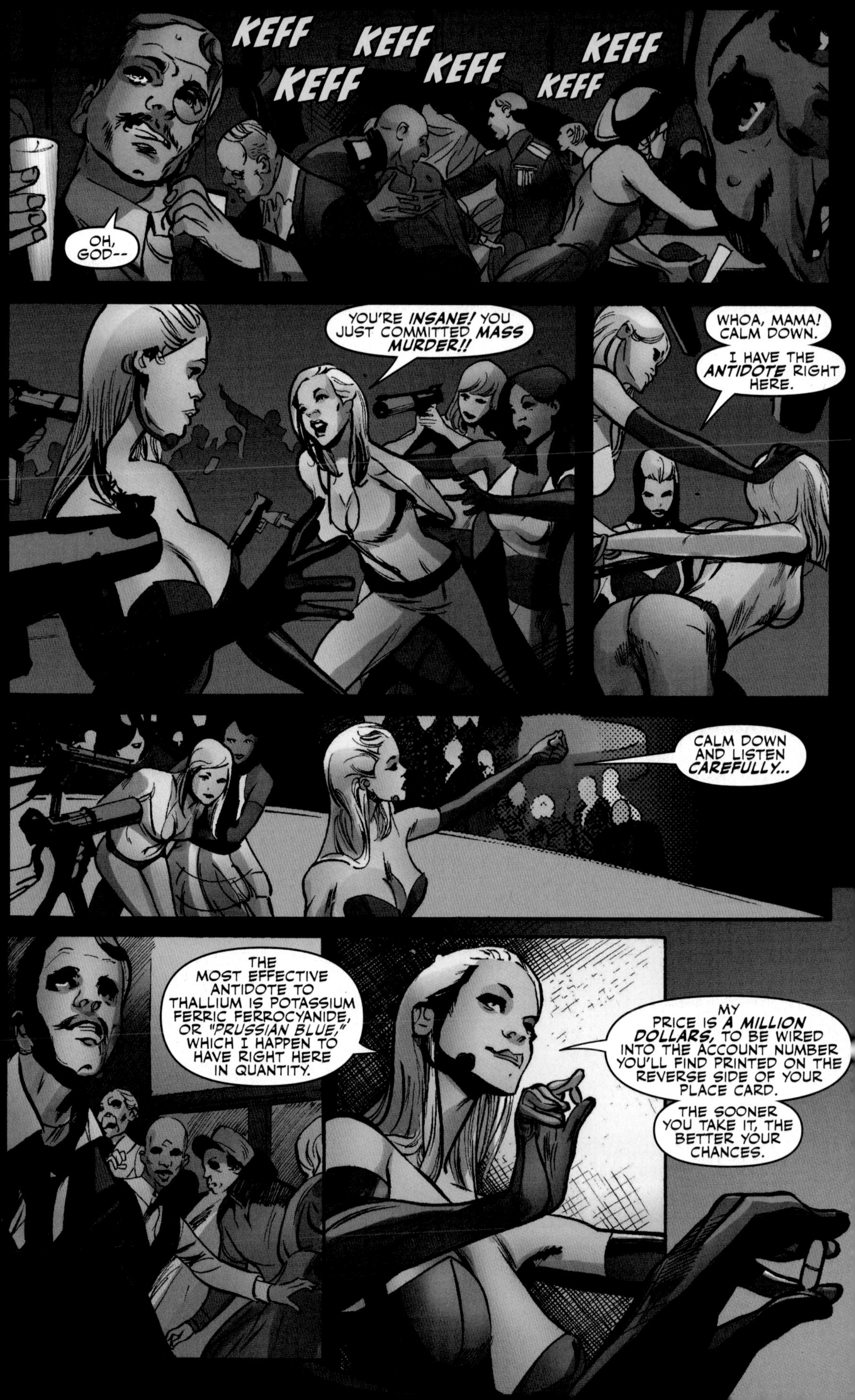
KEFF KEFF KEFF KEFF KEFF KEFF
OH, GOD--
YOU'RE *INSANE!* YOU JUST COMMITTED *MASS MURDER!!*
WHOA, MAMA! CALM DOWN.
I HAVE THE *ANTIDOTE* RIGHT HERE.
CALM DOWN AND LISTEN *CAREFULLY...*
THE MOST EFFECTIVE ANTIDOTE TO THALLIUM IS POTASSIUM FERRIC FERROCYANIDE, OR *"PRUSSIAN BLUE,"* WHICH I HAPPEN TO HAVE RIGHT HERE IN QUANTITY.
MY PRICE IS *A MILLION DOLLARS,* TO BE WIRED INTO THE ACCOUNT NUMBER YOU'LL FIND PRINTED ON THE REVERSE SIDE OF YOUR PLACE CARD.
THE SOONER YOU TAKE IT, THE BETTER YOUR CHANCES.

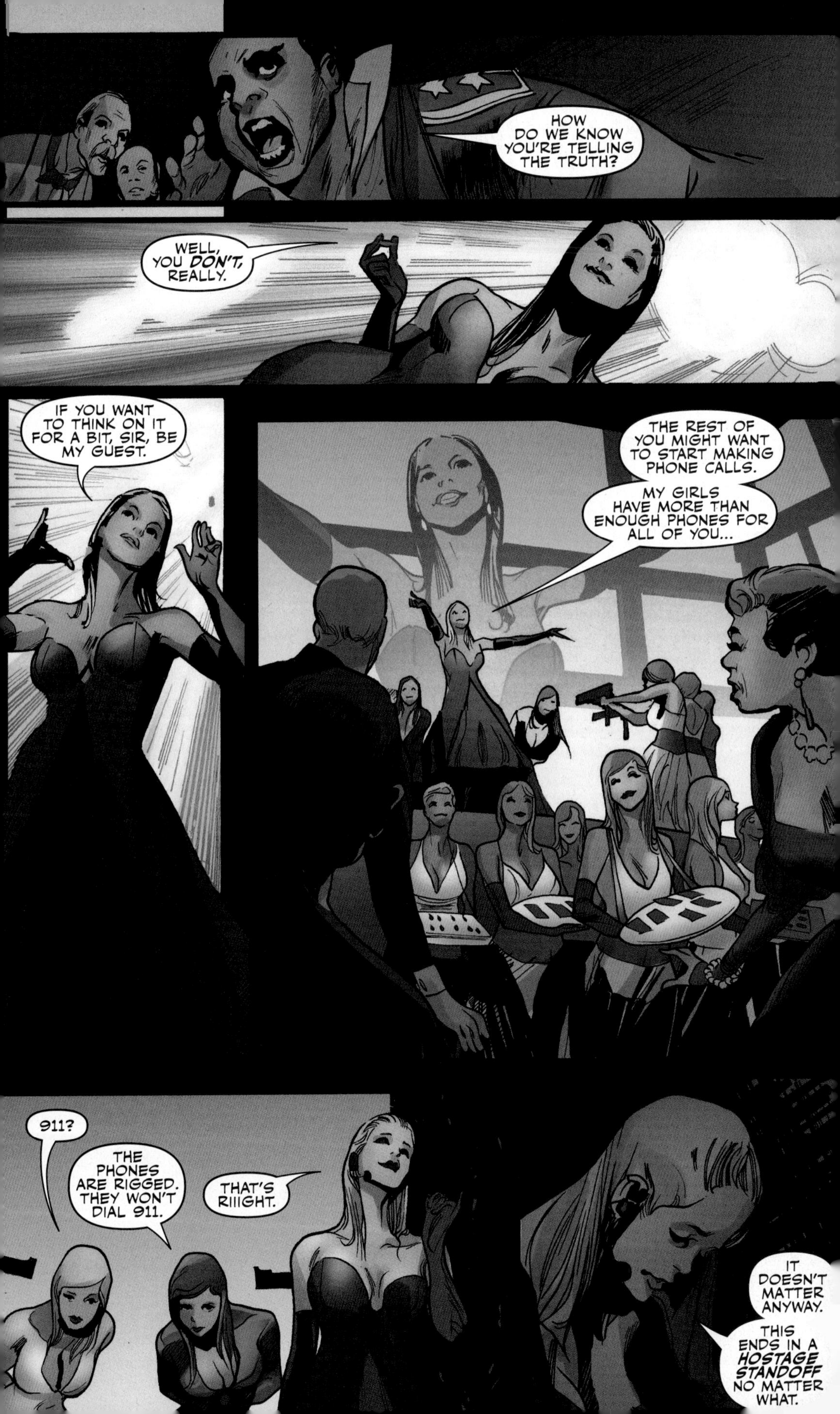
HOW DO WE KNOW YOU'RE TELLING THE TRUTH?
WELL, YOU DON'T, REALLY.
IF YOU WANT TO THINK ON IT FOR A BIT, SIR, BE MY GUEST.
THE REST OF YOU MIGHT WANT TO START MAKING PHONE CALLS.
MY GIRLS HAVE MORE THAN ENOUGH PHONES FOR ALL OF YOU...
911?
THE PHONES ARE RIGGED. THEY WON'T DIAL 911.
THAT'S RIIIGHT.
IT DOESN'T MATTER ANYWAY.
THIS ENDS IN A HOSTAGE STANDOFF NO MATTER WHAT.

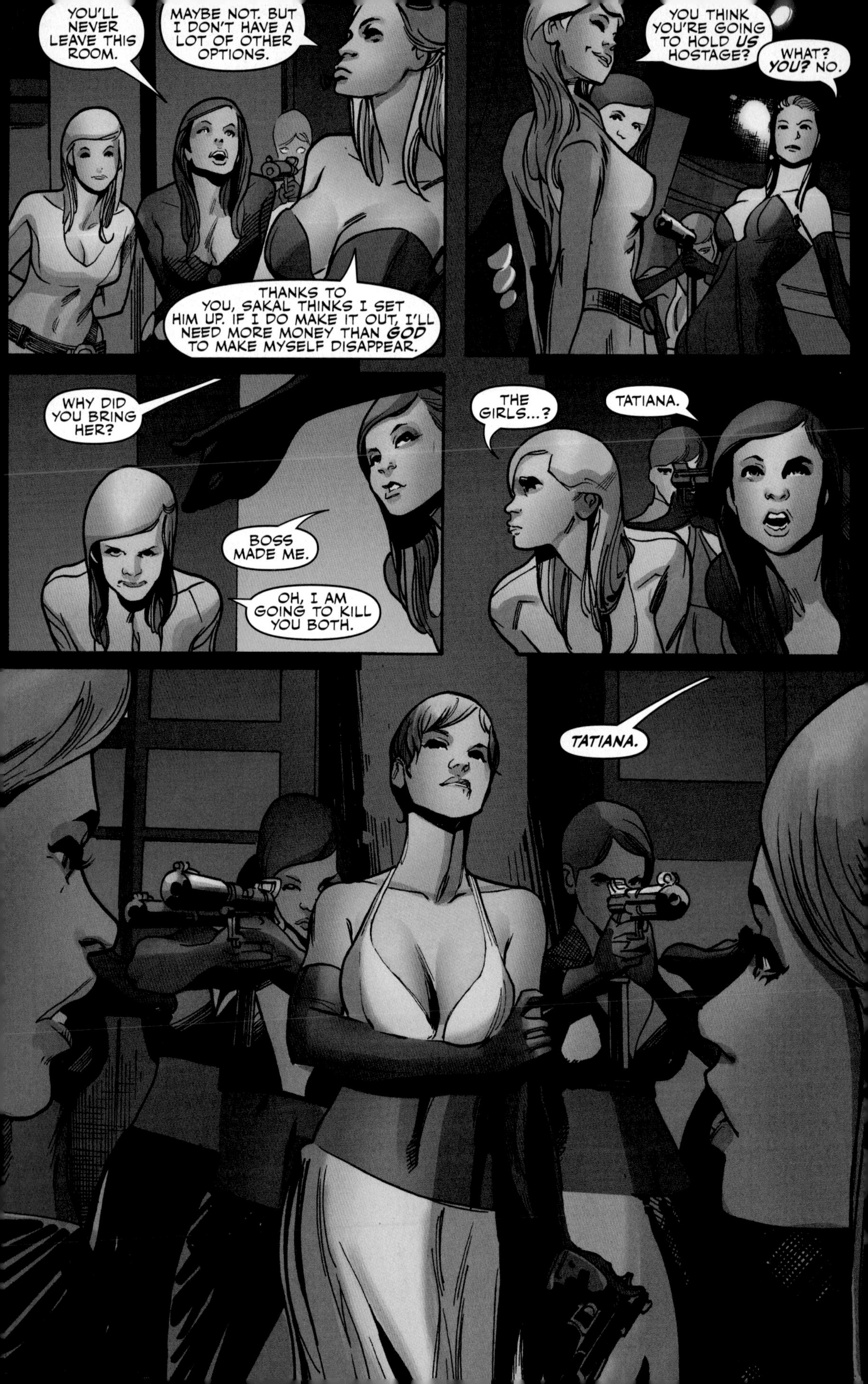

YOU'LL NEVER LEAVE THIS ROOM.
MAYBE NOT. BUT I DON'T HAVE A LOT OF OTHER OPTIONS.
THANKS TO YOU, SAKAL THINKS I SET HIM UP. IF I DO MAKE IT OUT, I'LL NEED MORE MONEY THAN GOD TO MAKE MYSELF DISAPPEAR.
YOU THINK YOU'RE GOING TO HOLD US HOSTAGE?
WHAT? YOU? NO.
WHY DID YOU BRING HER?
BOSS MADE ME.
OH, I AM GOING TO KILL YOU BOTH.
THE GIRLS...?
TATIANA.
TATIANA.

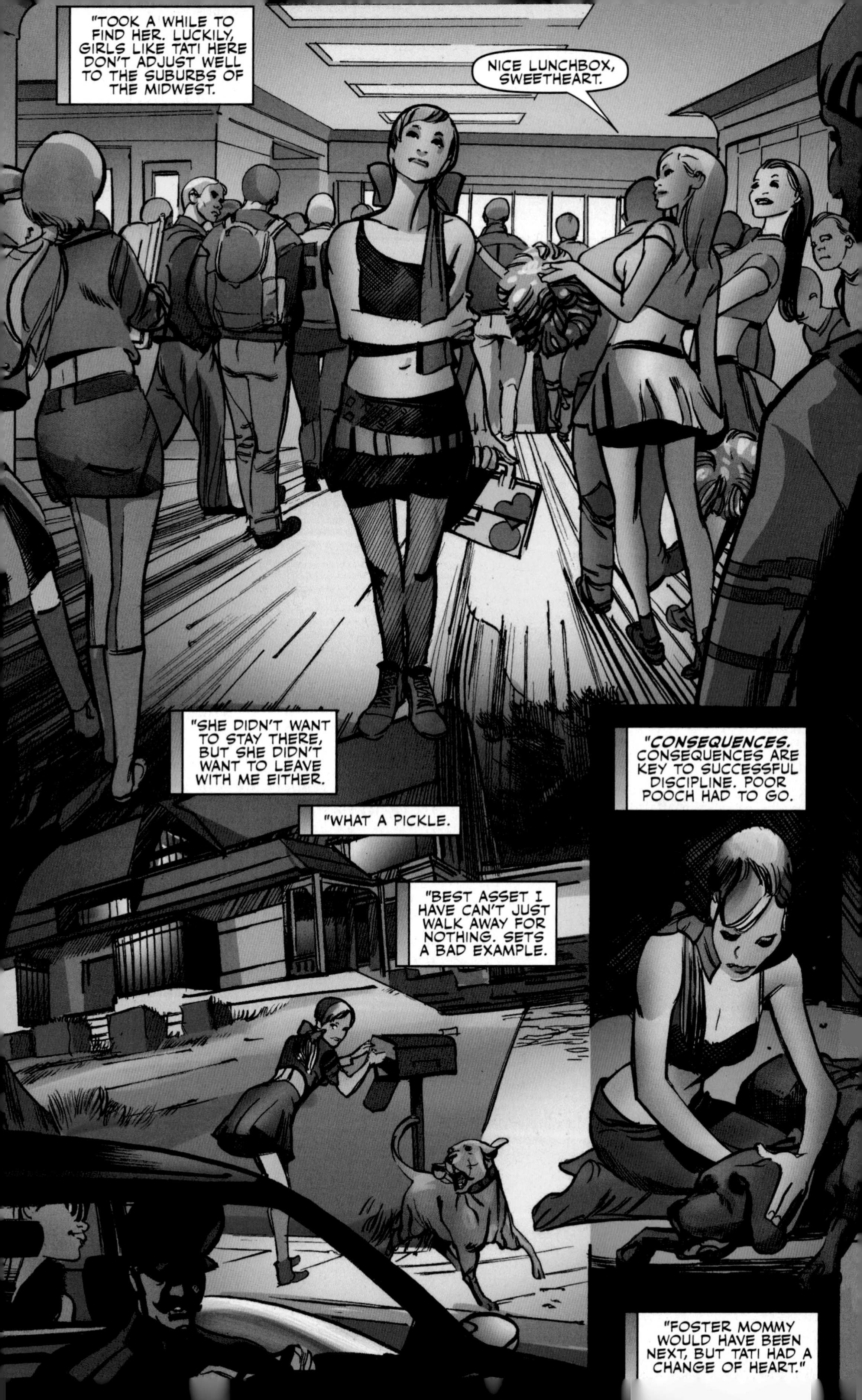
"TOOK A WHILE TO FIND HER. LUCKILY, GIRLS LIKE TATI HERE DON'T ADJUST WELL TO THE SUBURBS OF THE MIDWEST.
NICE LUNCHBOX, SWEETHEART.
"SHE DIDN'T WANT TO STAY THERE, BUT SHE DIDN'T WANT TO LEAVE WITH ME EITHER.
"WHAT A PICKLE.
"BEST ASSET I HAVE CAN'T JUST WALK AWAY FOR NOTHING. SETS A BAD EXAMPLE.
"CONSEQUENCES. CONSEQUENCES ARE KEY TO SUCCESSFUL DISCIPLINE. POOR POOCH HAD TO GO.
"FOSTER MOMMY WOULD HAVE BEEN NEXT, BUT TATI HAD A CHANGE OF HEART."

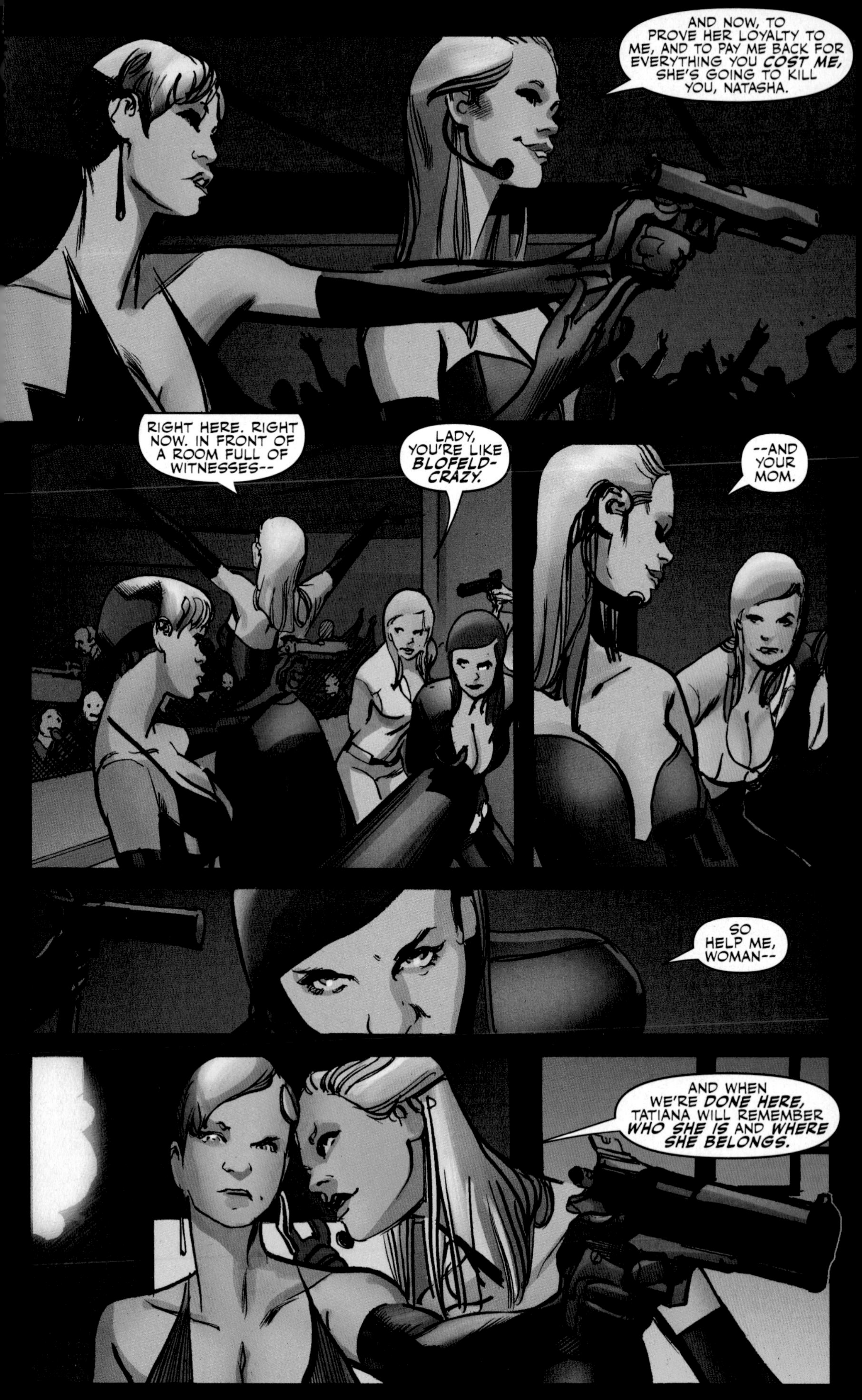
AND NOW, TO PROVE HER LOYALTY TO ME, AND TO PAY ME BACK FOR EVERYTHING YOU *COST ME,* SHE'S GOING TO KILL YOU, NATASHA.
RIGHT HERE. RIGHT NOW. IN FRONT OF A ROOM FULL OF WITNESSES--
LADY, YOU'RE LIKE *BLOFELD-CRAZY.*
--AND YOUR MOM.
SO HELP ME, WOMAN--
AND WHEN WE'RE *DONE HERE,* TATIANA WILL REMEMBER *WHO SHE IS* AND *WHERE SHE BELONGS.*

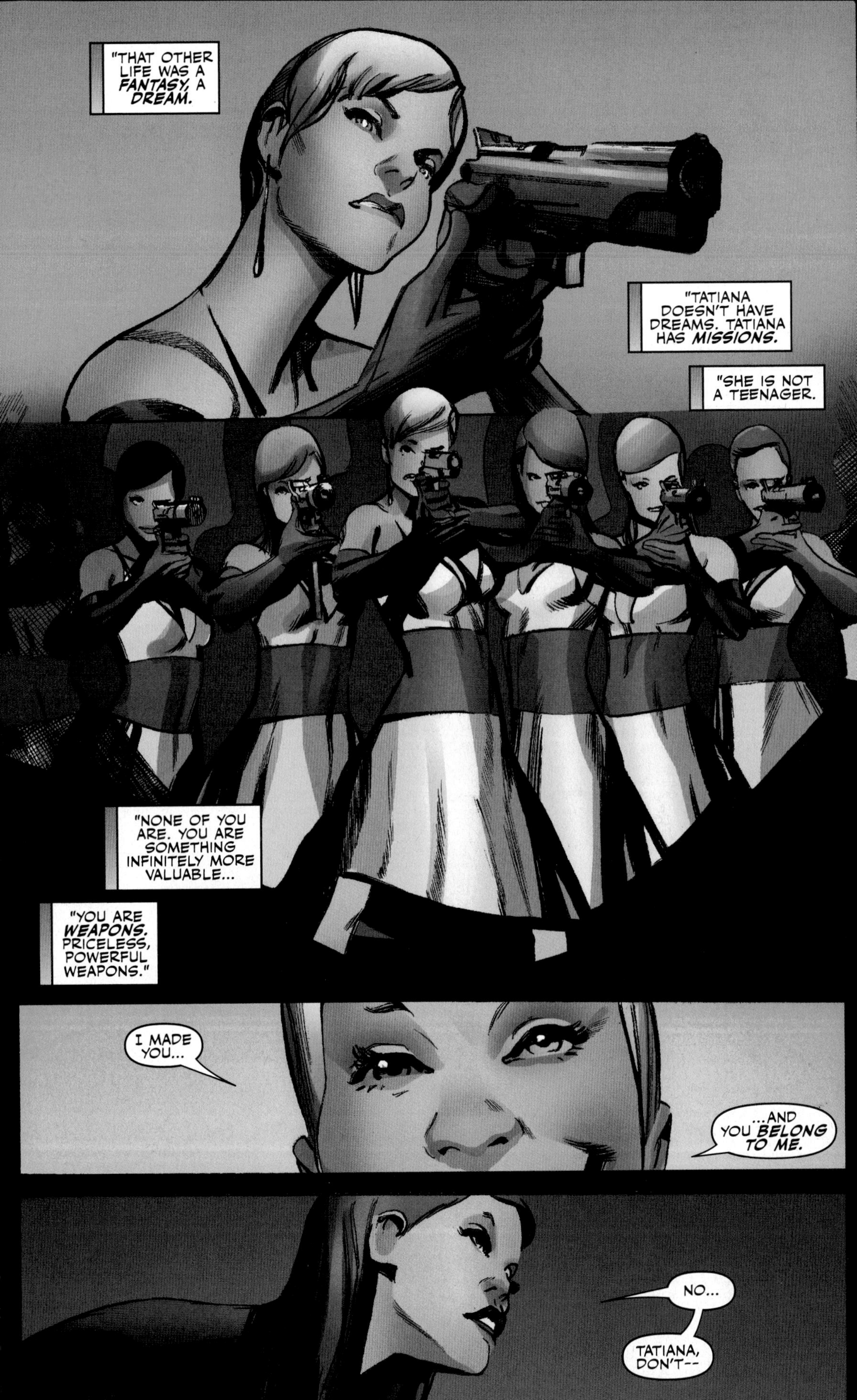
"THAT OTHER LIFE WAS A *FANTASY,* A *DREAM.*
"TATIANA DOESN'T HAVE DREAMS. TATIANA HAS *MISSIONS.*
"SHE IS NOT A TEENAGER.
"NONE OF YOU ARE. YOU ARE SOMETHING INFINITELY MORE VALUABLE...
"YOU ARE ***WEAPONS.*** PRICELESS, POWERFUL WEAPONS."
I MADE YOU...
...AND YOU *BELONG TO ME.*
NO...
TATIANA, DON'T--

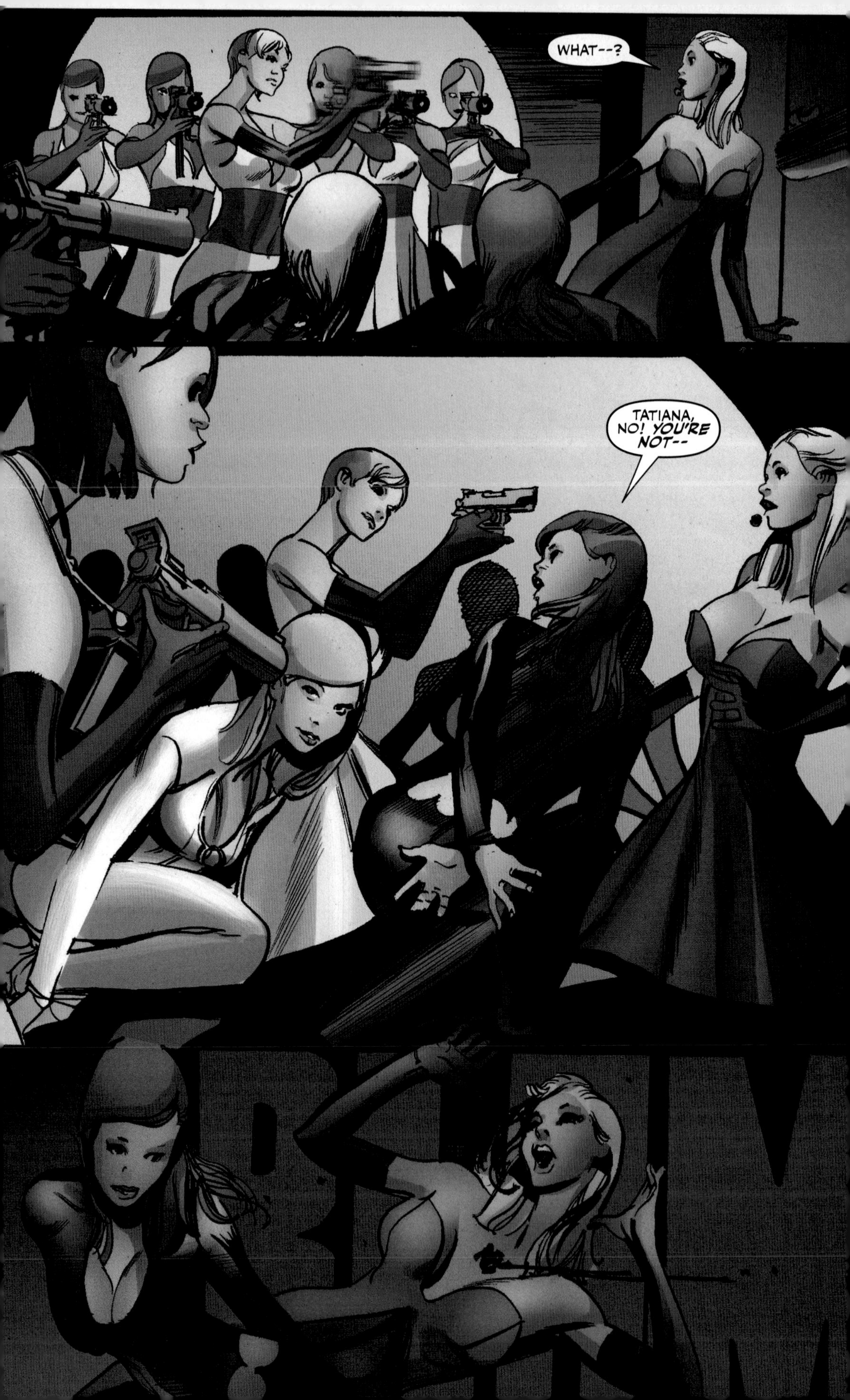

WHAT--?
TATIANA, NO! *YOU'RE NOT--*

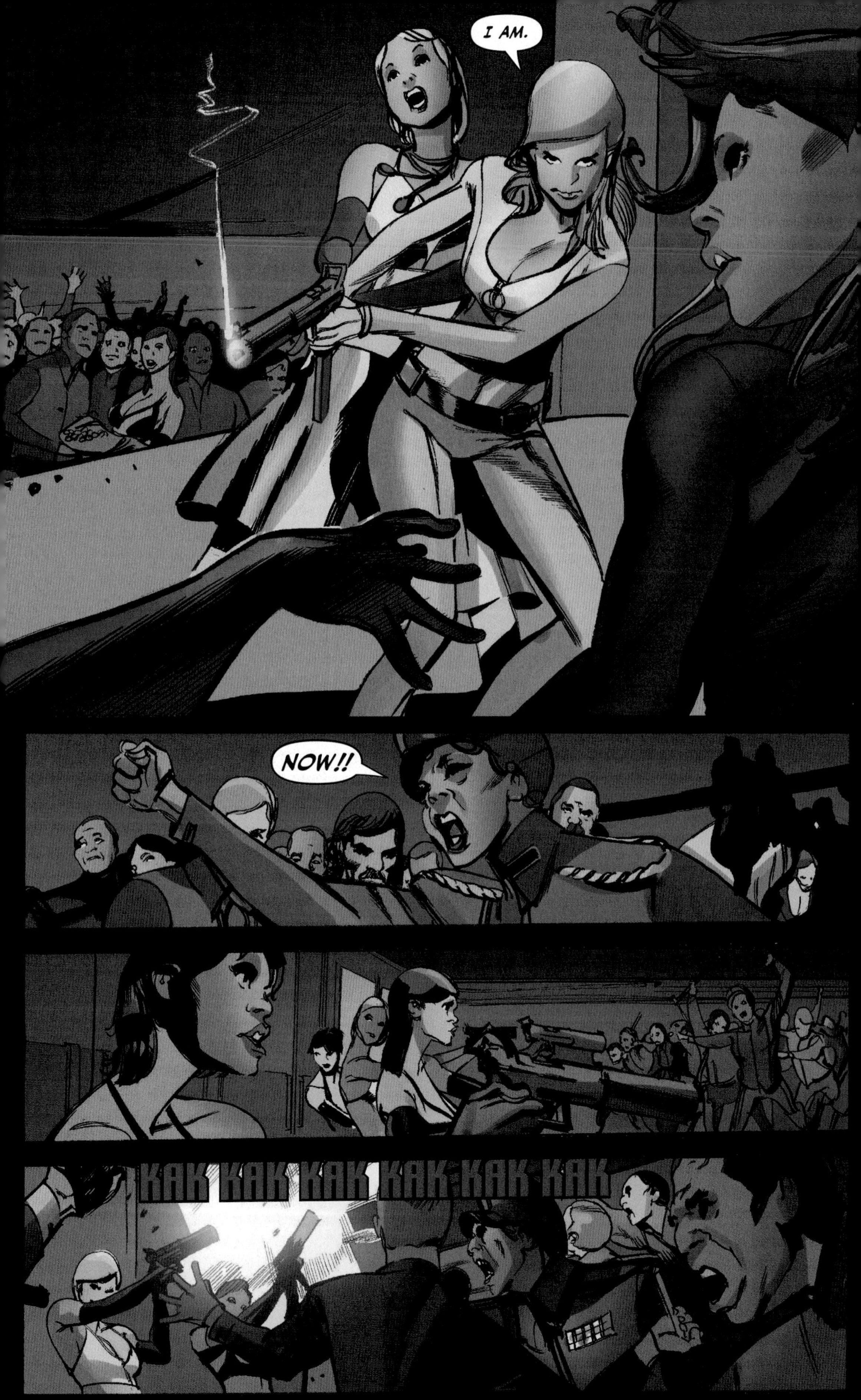
I AM.
NOW!!
KAK KAK KAK KAK KAK KAK

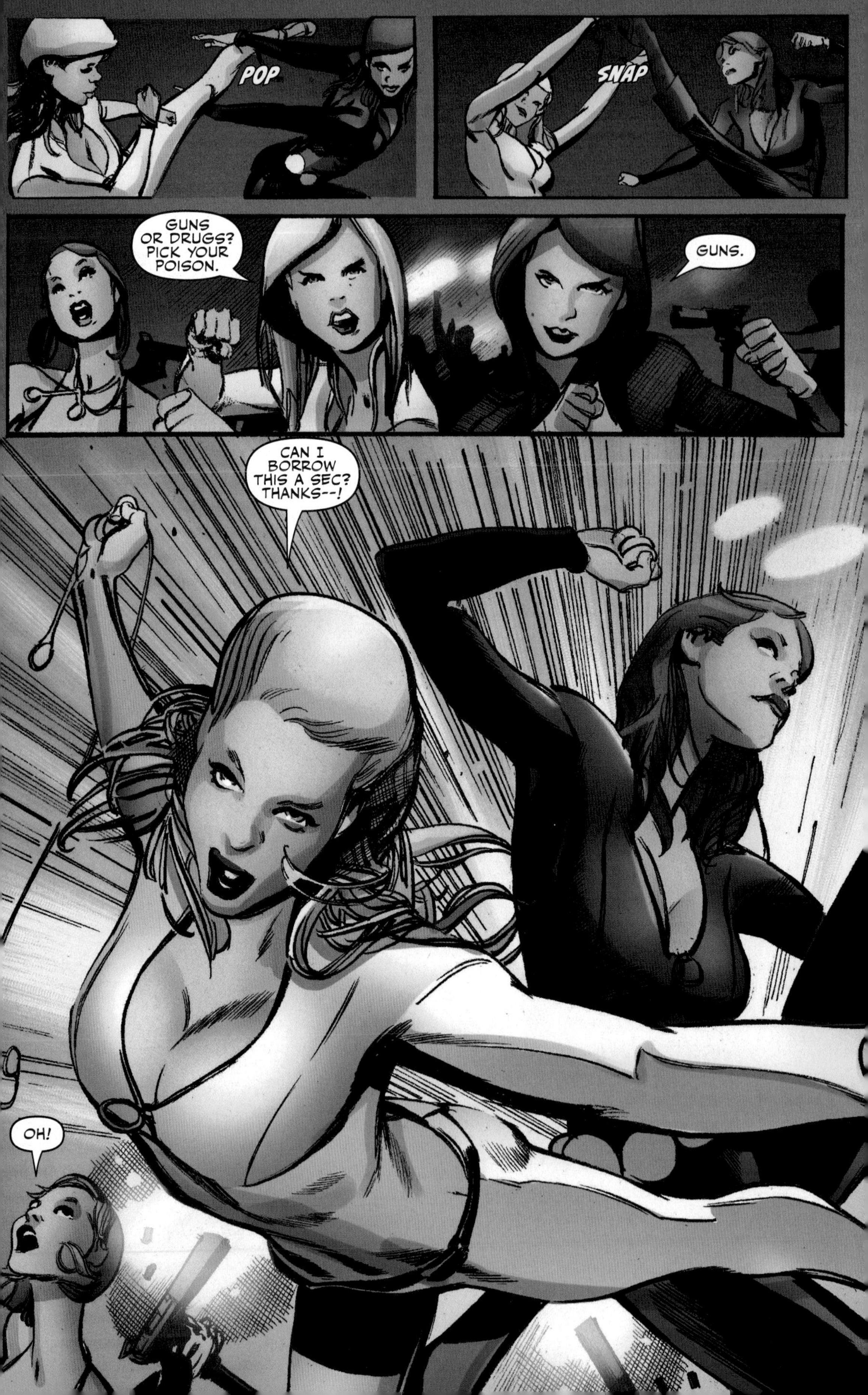
POP
SNAP
GUNS OR DRUGS? PICK YOUR POISON.
GUNS.
CAN I BORROW THIS A SEC? THANKS--!
OH!

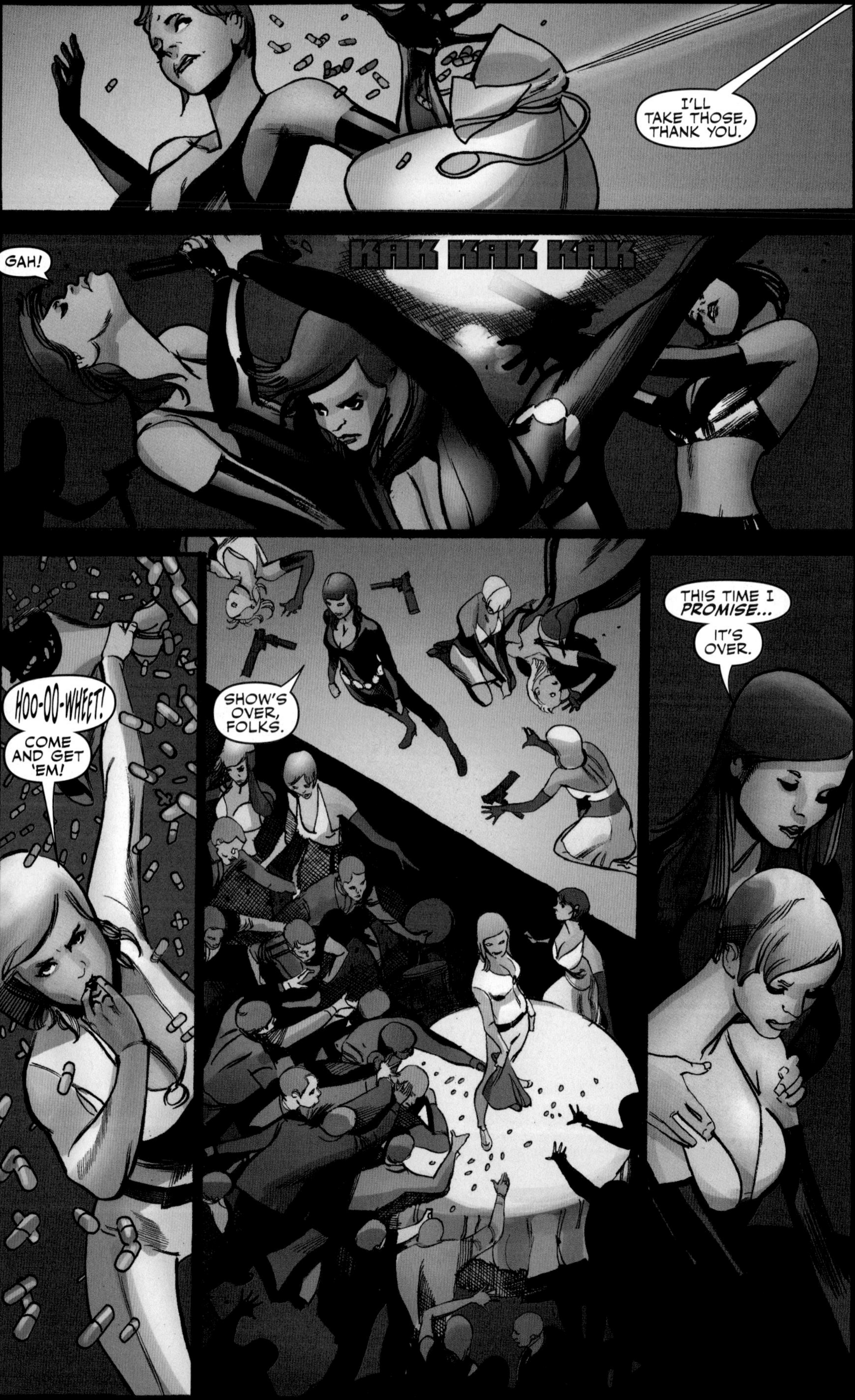
I'LL TAKE THOSE, THANK YOU.
KAK KAK KAK
GAH!
HOO-OO-WHEET!
COME AND GET 'EM!
SHOW'S OVER, FOLKS.
THIS TIME I PROMISE...
IT'S OVER.

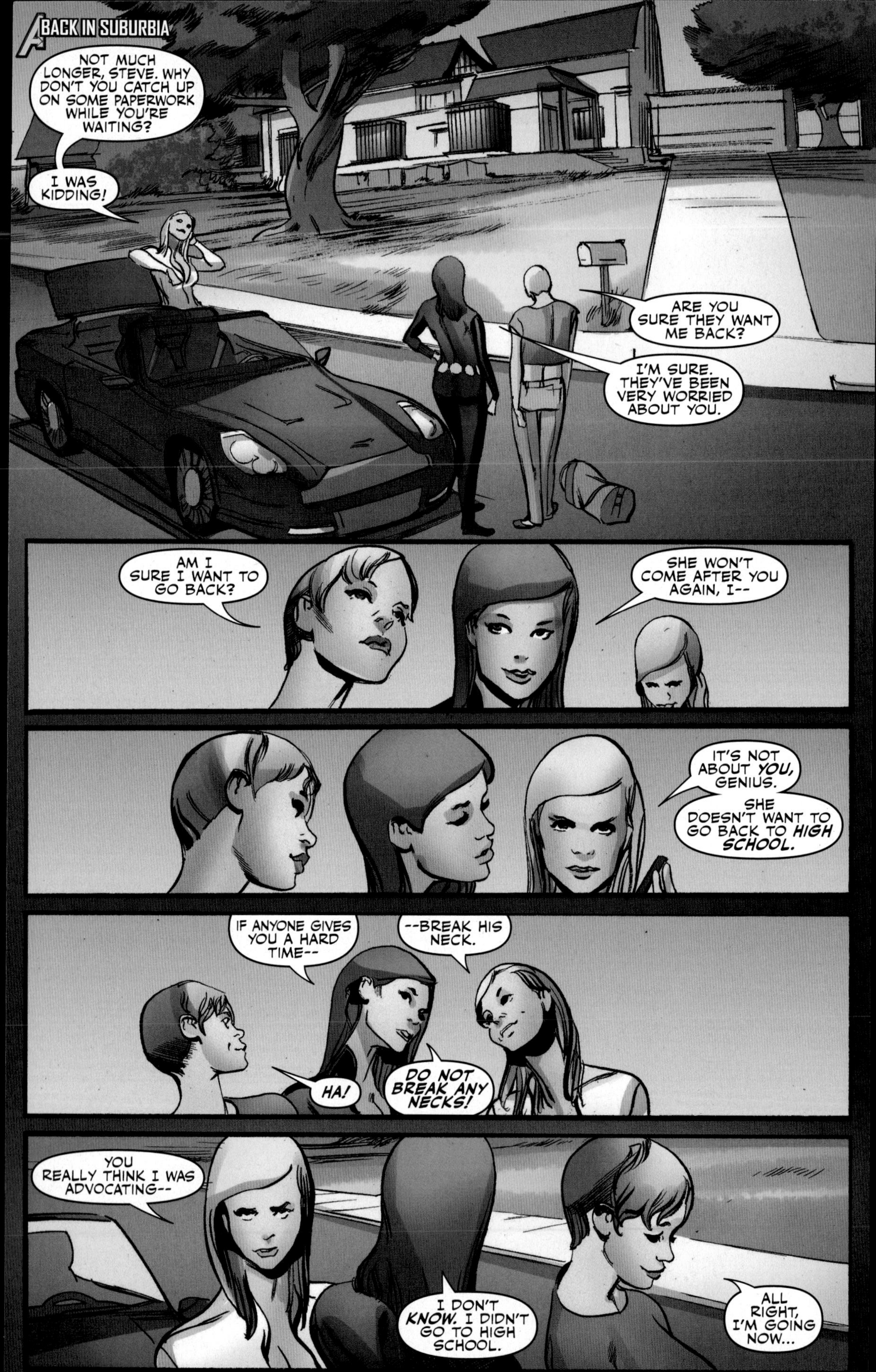
BACK IN SUBURBIA
NOT MUCH LONGER, STEVE. WHY DON'T YOU CATCH UP ON SOME PAPERWORK WHILE YOU'RE WAITING?
I WAS KIDDING!
ARE YOU SURE THEY WANT ME BACK?
I'M SURE. THEY'VE BEEN VERY WORRIED ABOUT YOU.
AM I SURE I WANT TO GO BACK?
SHE WON'T COME AFTER YOU AGAIN, I--
IT'S NOT ABOUT *YOU,* GENIUS.
SHE DOESN'T WANT TO GO BACK TO ***HIGH SCHOOL.***
IF ANYONE GIVES YOU A HARD TIME--
--BREAK HIS NECK.
HA!
DO NOT BREAK ANY NECKS!
YOU REALLY THINK I WAS ADVOCATING--
I DON'T ***KNOW.*** I DIDN'T GO TO HIGH SCHOOL.
ALL RIGHT, I'M GOING NOW...

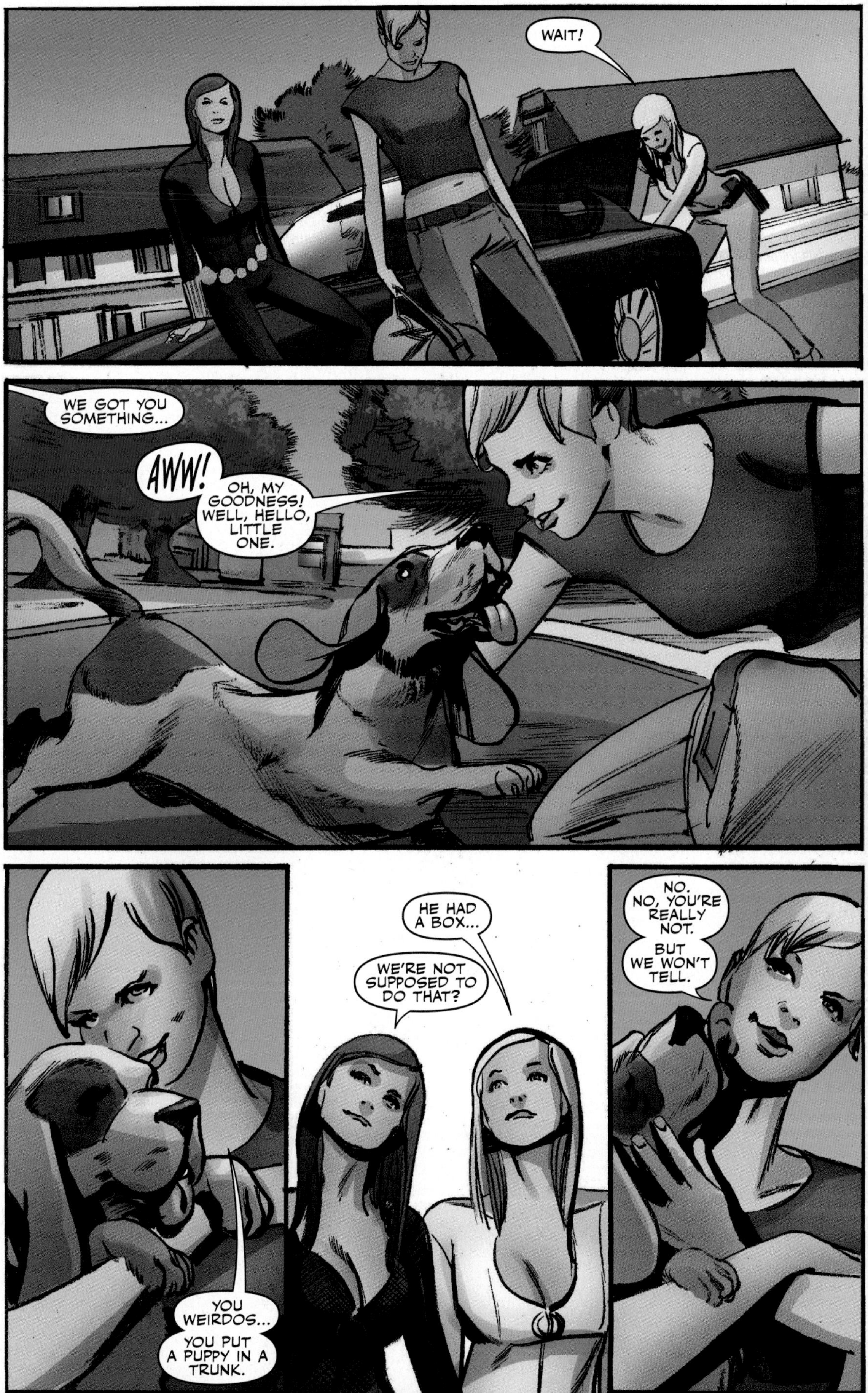
WAIT!
WE GOT YOU SOMETHING...
AWW!
OH, MY GOODNESS! WELL, HELLO, LITTLE ONE.
YOU WEIRDOS...
YOU PUT A PUPPY IN A TRUNK.
WE'RE NOT SUPPOSED TO DO THAT?
HE HAD A BOX...
NO. NO, YOU'RE REALLY NOT.
BUT WE WON'T TELL.

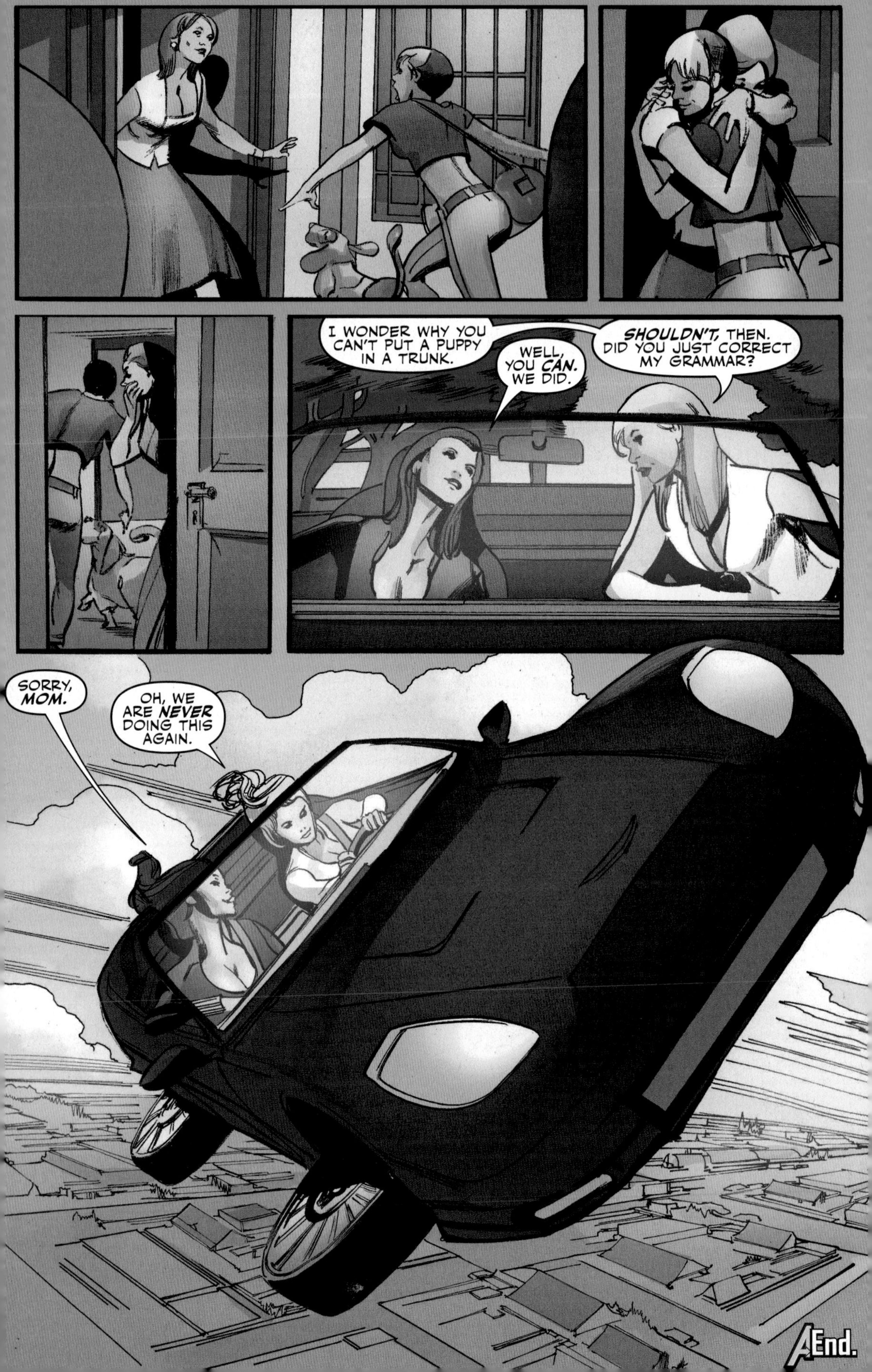
I WONDER WHY YOU CAN'T PUT A PUPPY IN A TRUNK.
WELL, YOU CAN. WE DID.
SHOULDN'T, THEN. DID YOU JUST CORRECT MY GRAMMAR?
SORRY, MOM.
OH, WE ARE NEVER DOING THIS AGAIN.
End.

HISTORY: Born into a wealthy Virginia family, Sharon Carter grew up hearing stories of Captain America (Steve Rogers) from her aunt Peggy, who, as the French Resistance fighter Mademoiselle, had fought alongside and romanced the Super-Soldier. Inspired by her aunt's adventures with Cap, the idealistic Sharon joined the recently formed international espionage agency SHIELD. During an early mission against Hydra, Sharon, delivering the powerful explosive Inferno 42, was attacked by the mercenary Batroc, who absconded with the explosive; Captain America, again active after surviving in suspended animation, aided Sharon in preventing the explosive's misuse. Initially knowing her only as Agent 13 and haunted by her strong resemblance to Peggy, Cap worked alongside Sharon on several subsequent missions, such as infiltrating AIM to learn about its new leader MODOK, preventing the Red Skull (Johann Shmidt) from destroying the SHIELD Helicarrier, and others. As romantic feelings developed between the two, Cap proposed marriage, but Sharon declined, citing her responsibilities to SHIELD. A rift developed between the two, but after Sharon, while impersonating German spy Irma Kruhl, rescued Cap during a clash with would-be conqueror Franz Gruber (then impersonating Baron (Heinrich) Zemo), she and Cap reconciled and continued their romance. Following their defeat of the Red Skull's Fourth Sleeper, Sharon told Cap her real name, although she did not reveal her familial relationship to Peggy Carter.

Concerned for Sharon's safety, Cap convinced her to transfer from SHIELD field operations to support staff, but when Cap was endangered by the AIM operative called Cyborg, she quickly returned to action to save him. Her unwillingness to stay out of combat troubled Cap for a time, but the couple reconciled following Cap's battle with Dr. Gorbo, aka the Monster Ape. While heading SHIELD's specially outfitted Femme Force, Sharon assisted Cap and his crime-fighting partner Falcon in undermining Hydra's Las Vegas activities, which proved to be a front by the Red Skull to lure them into the gigantic Fifth Sleeper's range of attack. Cap defeated both Skull and Sleeper, but when he subsequently quarreled with SHIELD Director Nick Fury, Fury forbade all SHIELD agents, particularly Sharon, from associating with Cap. Although Fury soon recanted his orders, Sharon, perhaps thinking that life as Captain America's girlfriend provided enough adventure on its own, resigned from SHIELD and accompanied Cap on a vacation, one that was interrupted by a battle with the two madmen who had used the identities of Captain America and Bucky in the 1950s.

Following a clash with the Cowled Commander's Crime Wave, Sharon's new life at Cap's side was quickly interrupted when word reached her of a decline in Peggy Carter's condition. Departing New York without explanation, she traveled to the Carter family home and was captured by criminal psychiatrist Dr. Faustus, who was manipulating her family to lure Cap and Falcon into a trap to drive them mad. Sharon and her friends resisted Faustus' mind-control efforts and freed Peggy, who emerged from her decades-long illness upon her reunion with Cap. Initially, Peggy had little concept of how much time had passed, and she sought to again join Cap in action, but he and Sharon dissuaded her, and Peggy instead joined SHIELD, her position now oddly reversed with Sharon's.

Weeks later, after Sharon and Cap accompanied the Thing (Ben Grimm) to the future era of Earth-691 and assisted the Guardians of the Galaxy against the invading Badoon, Cap, deeply troubled by a recent encounter with the Secret Empire, again gave up his costumed identity, its associations with corrupt government officials more than he could bear. While many of his friends were angered by his decision, the supportive Sharon remained by his side, but his Avengers teammate Hawkeye convinced him to take a new costumed identity. Disappointed, Sharon returned to the Carter home and remained in relative isolation during Cap's brief career as Nomad. When the Red Skull murdered Cap's would-be replacement Roscoe, Cap resumed his traditional identity and avenged his imitator.

REAL NAME: Sharon Carter
ALIASES: Agent 13, Fraulein Rogers, Irma Kruhl ("the Most Dangerous Spy in the World"), others
IDENTITY: No dual identity
OCCUPATION: Secret Avengers, SHIELD
CITIZENSHIP: USA
PLACE OF BIRTH: Richmond, Virginia
KNOWN RELATIVES: Harrison (father), Amanda (mother), Margaret ("Peggy," aunt)
GROUP AFFILIATION: SHIELD (both incarnations); formerly Femme Force; brainwashed into National Force; infiltrated Kubekult, AIM, others
EDUCATION: Unrevealed
FIRST APPEARANCE: Tales of Suspense #75 (1966)

"IRMA KRUHL"

Art by Steve Epting with Jack Kirby (inset)

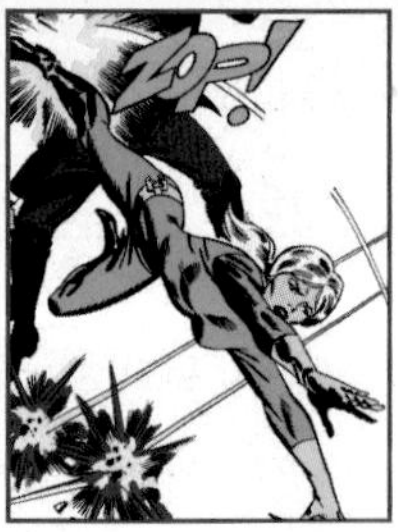
ZOP!

Art by John Romita

Despite quarrels over Cap's growing reluctance to live any sort of civilian life, Cap and Sharon continued their relationship, but matters were further complicated when Sharon rejoined SHIELD at the request of Regional Director Kurt B. Jacobson. Her investigations uncovered the Red Skull's role in the upsurge of worldwide monster activity, orchestrated by Arnim Zola. Although Sharon helped Cap escape his enemies, her renewed field agent status resurrected their earlier differences and strained their relationship further.

Eventually, Sharon was assigned as SHIELD liaison to the NYC Police Department while both agencies were investigating the racist and terroristic National Force, secretly led by her enemies Dr. Faustus and the 1950s Captain America, now the Force's Grand Director. Supposedly affected by mind-influencing gas when a Central Park rally turned violent, Sharon infiltrated the National Force, participating in attacks on New York citizenry and putting Harlem to the torch under the Grand Director's orders. When confronted by the National Guard, she and her Force cohorts apparently incinerated themselves via the self-destruct device in their uniforms. Himself brainwashed by the National Force for a time, Cap overcame Faustus' control and ended the Force's activities, only to learn about Sharon's apparent death days after the fact. Cap mourned his lover's death for years but ultimately moved on with his life, dating Bernadette "Bernie" Rosenthal and Diamondback (Rachel Leighton).

Neither Cap nor any of Sharon's other super-hero allies suspected that her death was a ruse by SHIELD, which, having faked her incineration, sent her on a top-secret mission, its details unrevealed to this day. Following the mission's completion, Sharon failed to rendezvous with SHIELD at her predetermined extraction point, and her fellow agents, including Nick Fury, believed her killed in the line of duty, but this too was a misapprehension, for Sharon remained alive, though imprisoned. Abandoned in enemy territory, Sharon spent months being held under inhumane conditions in the dictatorship of Tap-Kwai. Finally escaping and incorrectly believing SHIELD had simply abandoned her, she spent the next few years as a mercenary, her assignments often forcing her into violent or degrading activity; operating outside the law, she cooperated with various criminal figures, including the Punisher's right-hand man Microchip and the misanthropic robot Ultron. These years weighed heavily upon Sharon, robbing her of the idealism that had drawn her to SHIELD and later to Cap, and she grew hardened and embittered.

Eventually infiltrating an organization known as the Kubekult, Sharon learned of its plans to resurrect the cloned persona of Adolf Hitler, aka the Hate-Monger, via the Cosmic Cube, and she became the unlikely ally of the Red Skull, who opposed the cult's efforts to conquer the world before he could. To aid their mission, the Skull revived the temporarily comatose Cap, who was stunned to learn of Sharon's survival. After defeating both Kubekult and the Skull, Sharon, still scarred by her experiences, attempted to keep her former lover at a distance, but when Cap was exiled from the US due to machinations by Machinesmith, Sharon followed, ultimately preventing Machinesmith from crashing SHIELD's current Helicarrier. She soon rejoined SHIELD and sought information on Nick Fury, supposedly slain by the Punisher; learning Fury had faked his death, she rescued him from imprisonment in a pocket dimension, which his subconscious had remade into a World War II battlefield where he trod alongside his former unit, the Howling Commandos. Fury remained off duty for a time, during which Sharon served as SHIELD director, working alongside Cap against such opponents as Nightmare and the Red Skull, briefly wielding the Cosmic Cube.

Despite Sharon's cynicism, her continued association with Cap, alongside whom she fought Count Nefaria and Protocide, awoke the idealism that had led her to first join SHIELD. Following the defeat of the latest partnership between the Red Skull and the Hate-Monger, the two men who had ultimately reunited Sharon and Cap to begin with, the couple renewed their romance. Unfortunately, their relationship again became strained when Cap learned of her reluctant involvement with SHIELD's anti-mutant Contingency, and the couple again parted ways. For a time, Sharon dated another SHIELD agent, Neal Tapper, but he was soon killed by a bomb set by the Winter Solder, formerly Cap's wartime partner Bucky who was a brainwashed agent of Aleksander Lukin.

When the Winter Soldier regained his memories, Sharon accompanied Cap in searching for him, she and Cap rekindling their romance in the process. Tragically, Sharon was brainwashed by Dr. Faustus under the Red Skull's orders, and following the so-called "Civil War" of super heroes, she covertly shot Cap at point-blank range, supposedly killing him but unknowingly sending his consciousness back in time, and somehow temporally linking him to her. After Sharon discovered she was pregnant, her brainwashing reactivated. She joined Faustus' forces, but after the Red Skull captured Winter Soldier, Sharon freed him, supposedly to distract heroes pursuing Faustus' forces. After Sharon miscarried during battle, Faustus inexplicably removed her memories of being pregnant and helped her escape. The Skull later used Sharon's temporal link to retrieve Cap, whose body he intended to possess, but Cap overcame the Skull's influence and fully recovered. After ceding the Captain America identity to Winter Soldier, Steve Rogers asked Sharon to join a secret faction of the Avengers.

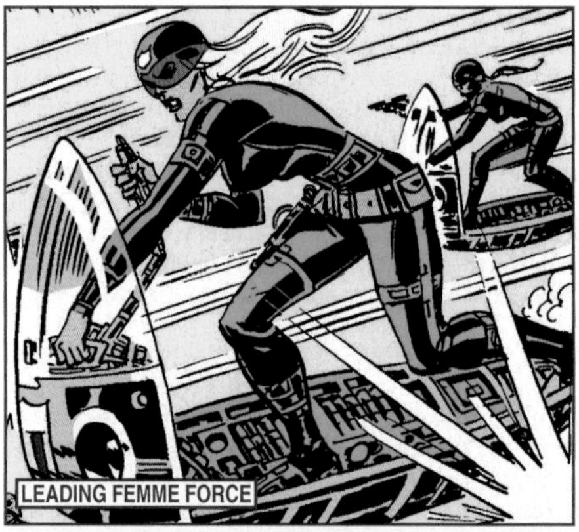

LEADING FEMME FORCE

Art by John Romita

HEIGHT: 5'8" EYES: Blue
WEIGHT: 135 lbs. HAIR: Blonde

ABILITIES/ACCESSORIES: Sharon Carter is an excellent hand-to-hand combatant, martial artist, athlete, and markswoman, as well as a highly trained espionage agent, fluent in several languages, and an expert with weapons and computers. As a SHIELD agent, she has access to a wide array of advanced technology.

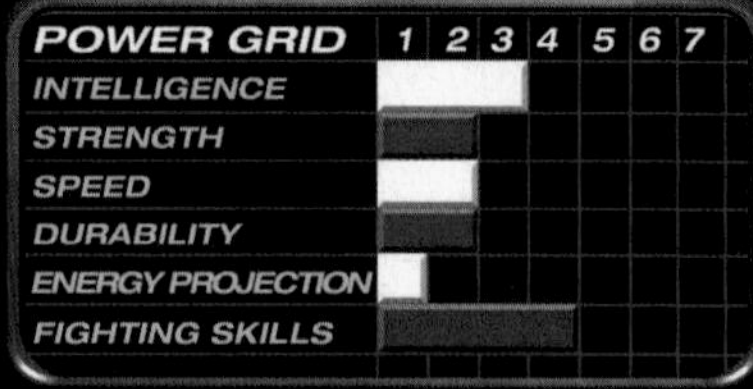
POWER GRID
1 2 3 4 5 6 7
INTELLIGENCE
STRENGTH
SPEED
DURABILITY
ENERGY PROJECTION
FIGHTING SKILLS

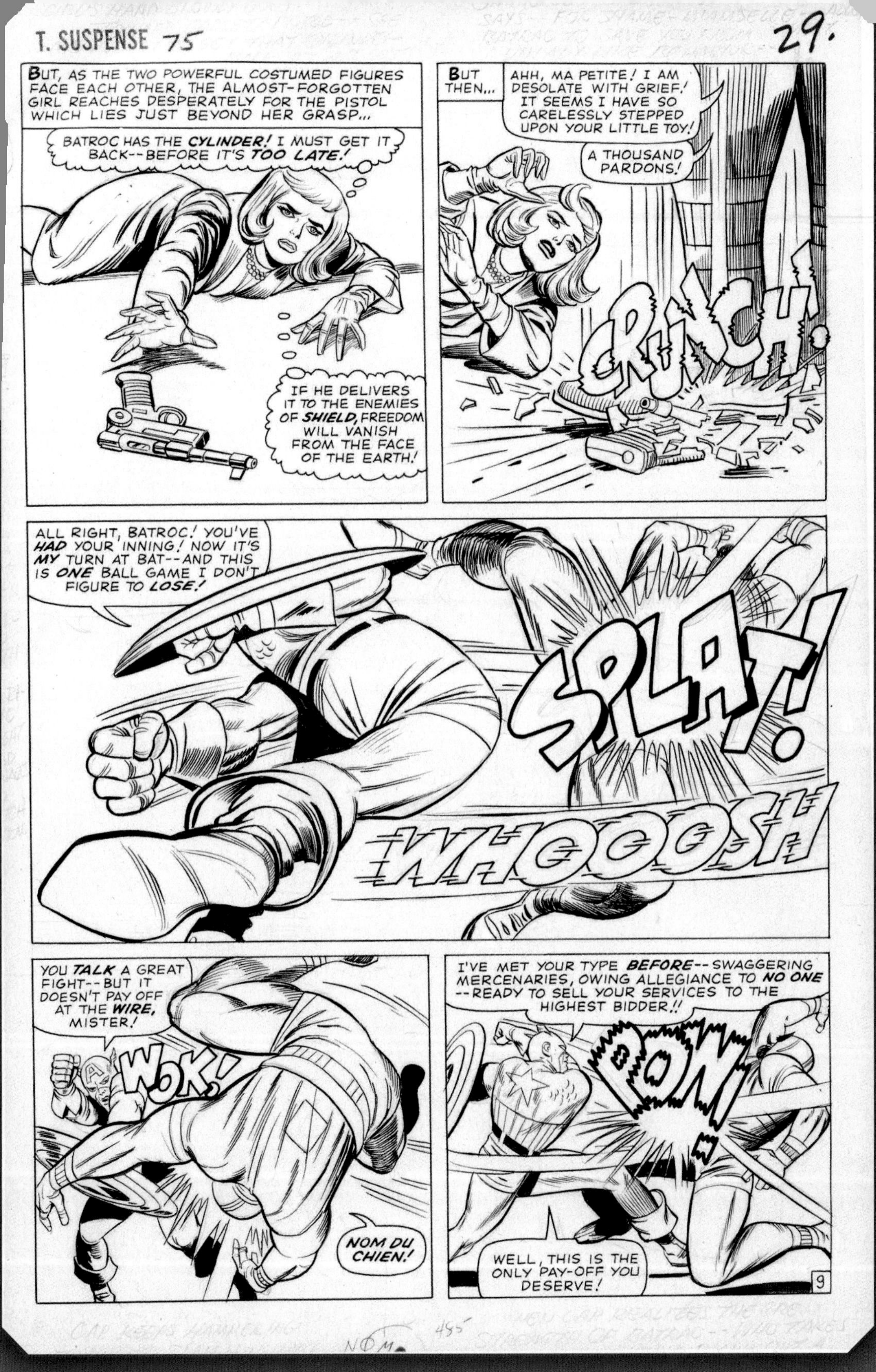
T. SUSPENSE 75
29.
BUT, AS THE TWO POWERFUL COSTUMED FIGURES FACE EACH OTHER, THE ALMOST-FORGOTTEN GIRL REACHES DESPERATELY FOR THE PISTOL WHICH LIES JUST BEYOND HER GRASP...
BATROC HAS THE CYLINDER! I MUST GET IT BACK--BEFORE IT'S TOO LATE!
IF HE DELIVERS IT TO THE ENEMIES OF SHIELD, FREEDOM WILL VANISH FROM THE FACE OF THE EARTH!
BUT THEN...
AHH, MA PETITE! I AM DESOLATE WITH GRIEF! IT SEEMS I HAVE SO CARELESSLY STEPPED UPON YOUR LITTLE TOY!
A THOUSAND PARDONS!
CRUNCH!
ALL RIGHT, BATROC! YOU'VE HAD YOUR INNING! NOW IT'S MY TURN AT BAT--AND THIS IS ONE BALL GAME I DON'T FIGURE TO LOSE!
SPLAT!
WHOOOSH
YOU TALK A GREAT FIGHT--BUT IT DOESN'T PAY OFF AT THE WIRE, MISTER!
WOK!
NOM DU CHIEN!
I'VE MET YOUR TYPE BEFORE--SWAGGERING MERCENARIES, OWING ALLEGIANCE TO NO ONE--READY TO SELL YOUR SERVICES TO THE HIGHEST BIDDER!!
POW!
WELL, THIS IS THE ONLY PAY-OFF YOU DESERVE!
9

TALES OF SUSPENSE #75, PAGE 9 ART BY JACK KIRBY, DICK AYERS & JOHN TARTAGLIONE

COURTESY OF HERITAGEAUCTIONS.COM

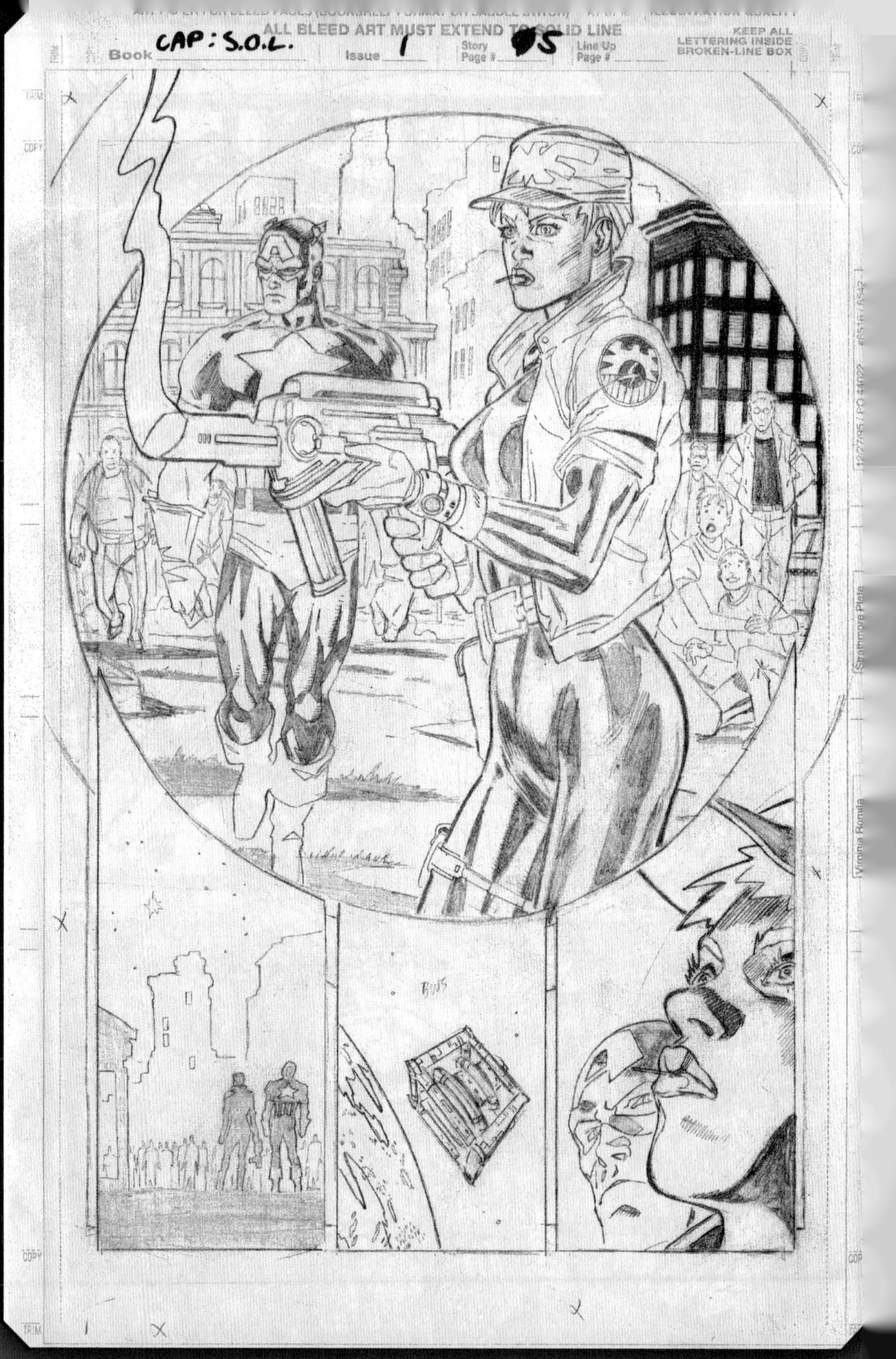
ALL BLEED ART MUST EXTEND TO SOLID LINE
Book CAP: S.O.L.
Issue 1
Story Page # 5
Line Up Page #
KEEP ALL LETTERING INSIDE BROKEN-LINE BOX
Strathmore Plate
Virginia Romita

CAPTAIN AMERICA: SENTINEL OF LIBERTY #1, PAGE 5 PENCILS BY RON GARNEY

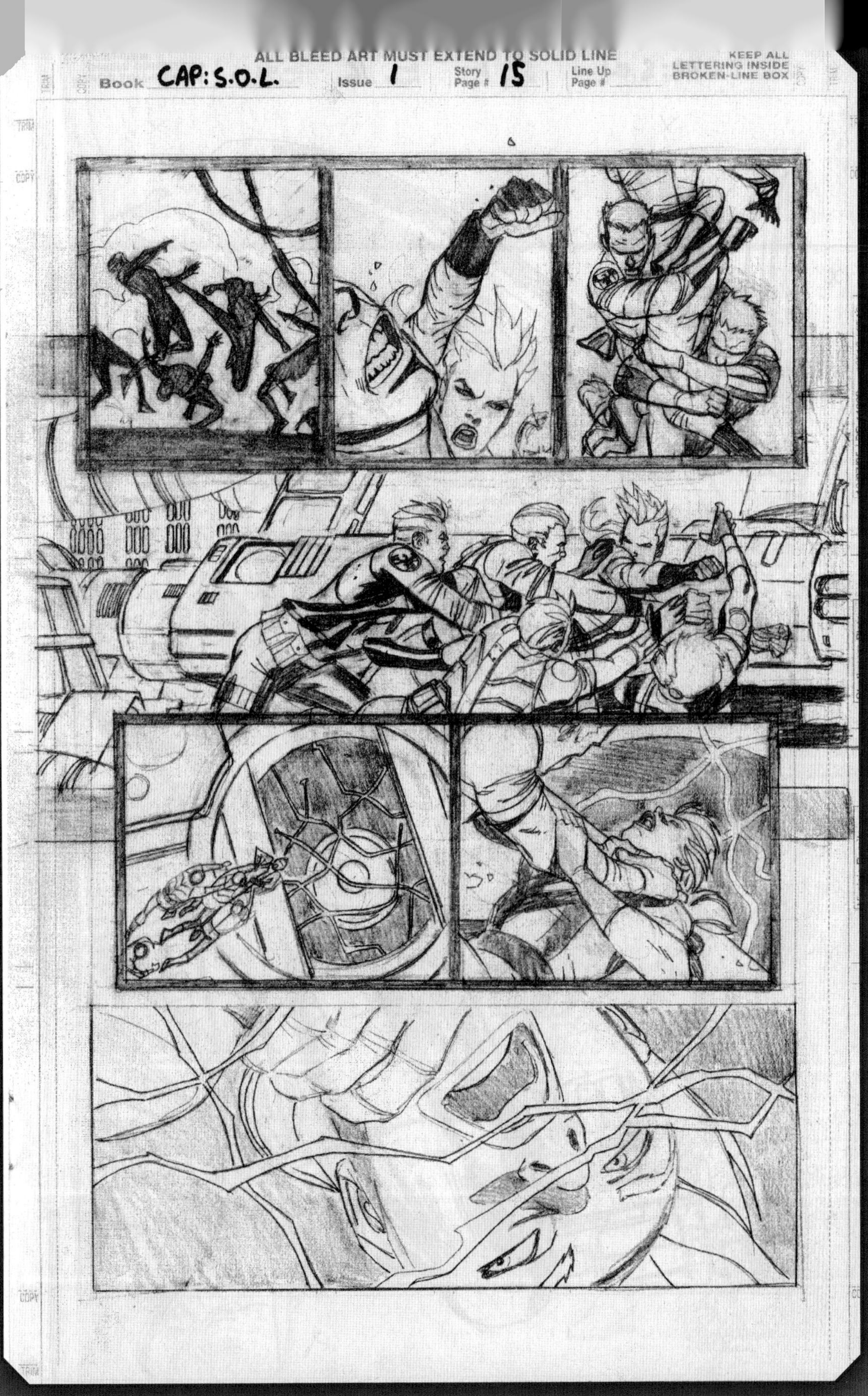
ALL BLEED ART MUST EXTEND TO SOLID LINE
KEEP ALL LETTERING INSIDE BROKEN-LINE BOX
Book CAP: S.O.L.
Issue 1
Story Page # 15
Line Up Page #

CAPTAIN AMERICA: SENTINEL OF LIBERTY #1, PAGE 15 PENCILS BY RON GARNEY

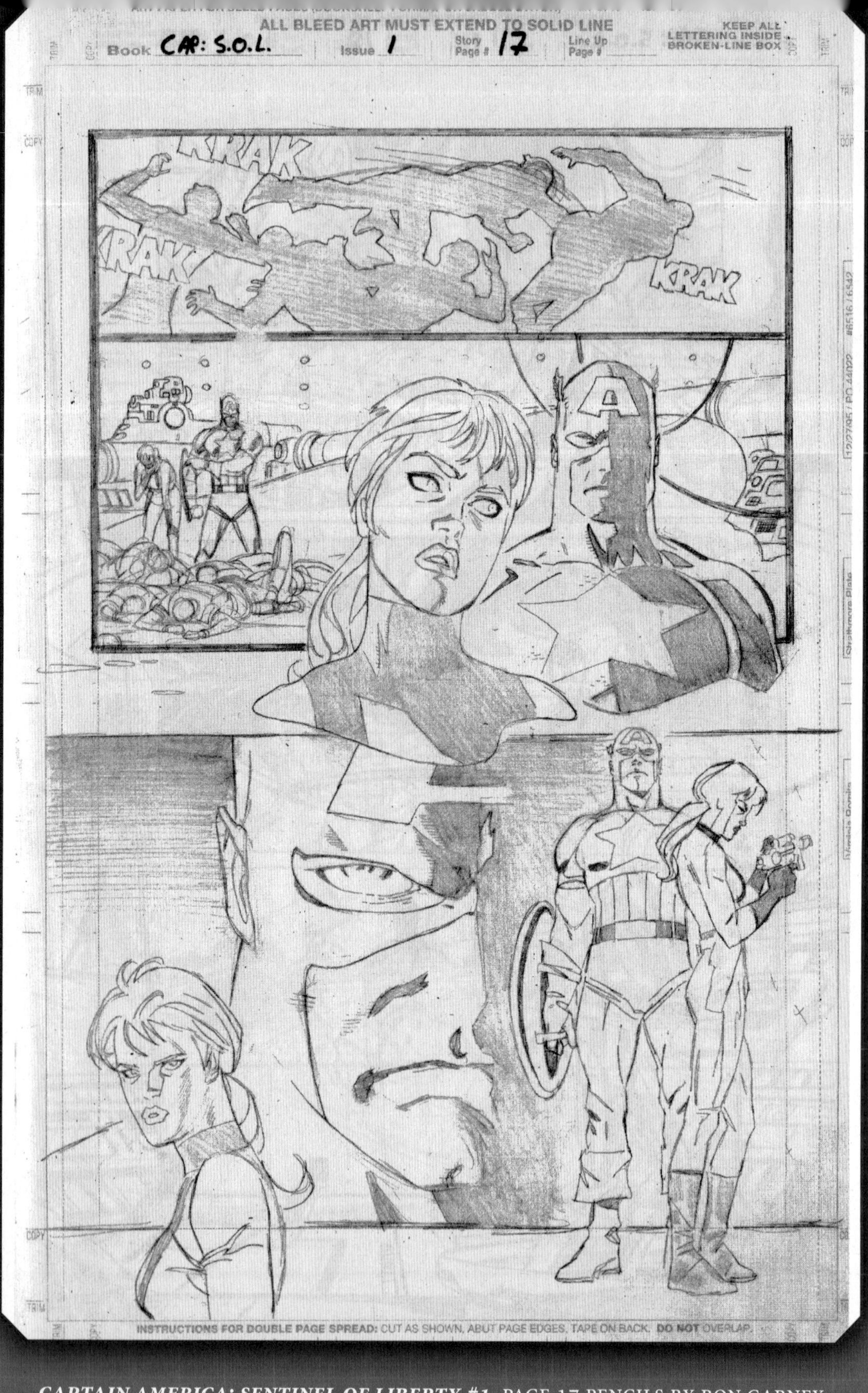
ALL BLEED ART MUST EXTEND TO SOLID LINE
Book CAP: S.O.L.
Issue 1
Story Page # 17
Line Up Page #
KEEP ALL LETTERING INSIDE BROKEN-LINE BOX
KRAK
KRAK
KRAK
INSTRUCTIONS FOR DOUBLE PAGE SPREAD: CUT AS SHOWN, ABUT PAGE EDGES, TAPE ON BACK. DO NOT OVERLAP.

CAPTAIN AMERICA: SENTINEL OF LIBERTY #1, PAGE 17 PENCILS BY RON GARNEY

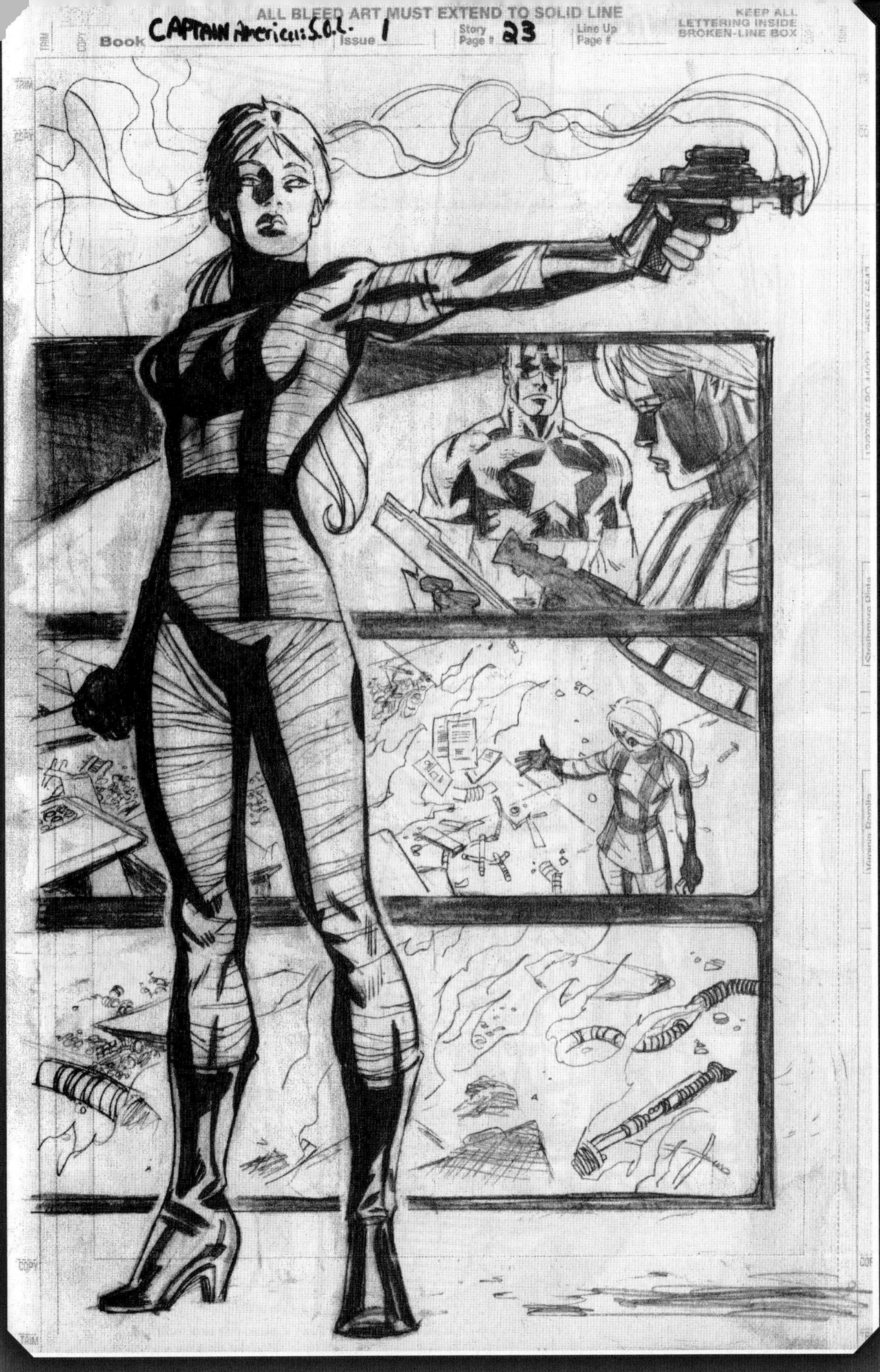
ALL BLEED ART MUST EXTEND TO SOLID LINE
Book CAPTAIN America: S.O.L.
Issue 1
Story Page # 23
Line Up Page #
KEEP ALL LETTERING INSIDE BROKEN-LINE BOX

CAPTAIN AMERICA: SENTINEL OF LIBERTY #1, PAGE 23 PENCILS BY RON GARNEY

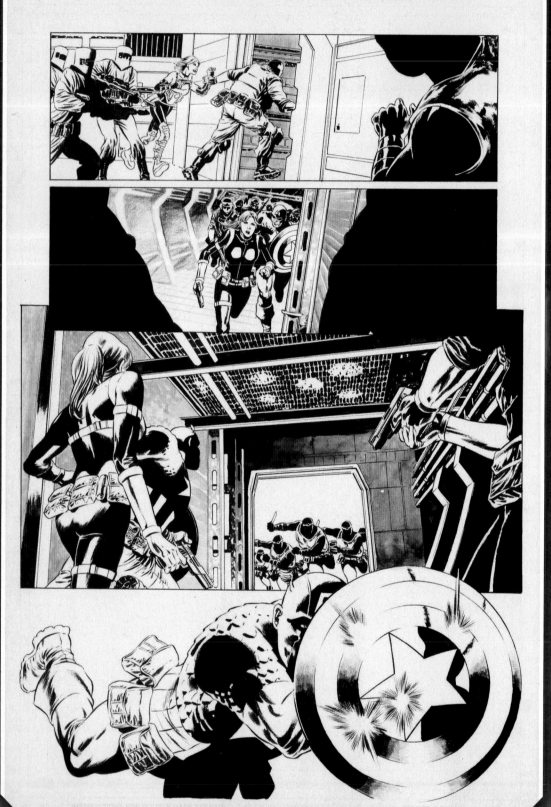

CAPTAIN AMERICA
17
12
MIKE PERKINS

CAPTAIN AMERICA #17, PAGE 12 ART BY MIKE PERKINS

COURTESY OF HERITAGEAUCTIONS.COM